Lost Lad London

❷

SHIMA SHINYA

Contents

7 ——————————— 3

8 ——————————— 33

9 ——————————— 65

10 ——————————— 95

11 ——————————— 127

12 ——————————— 157

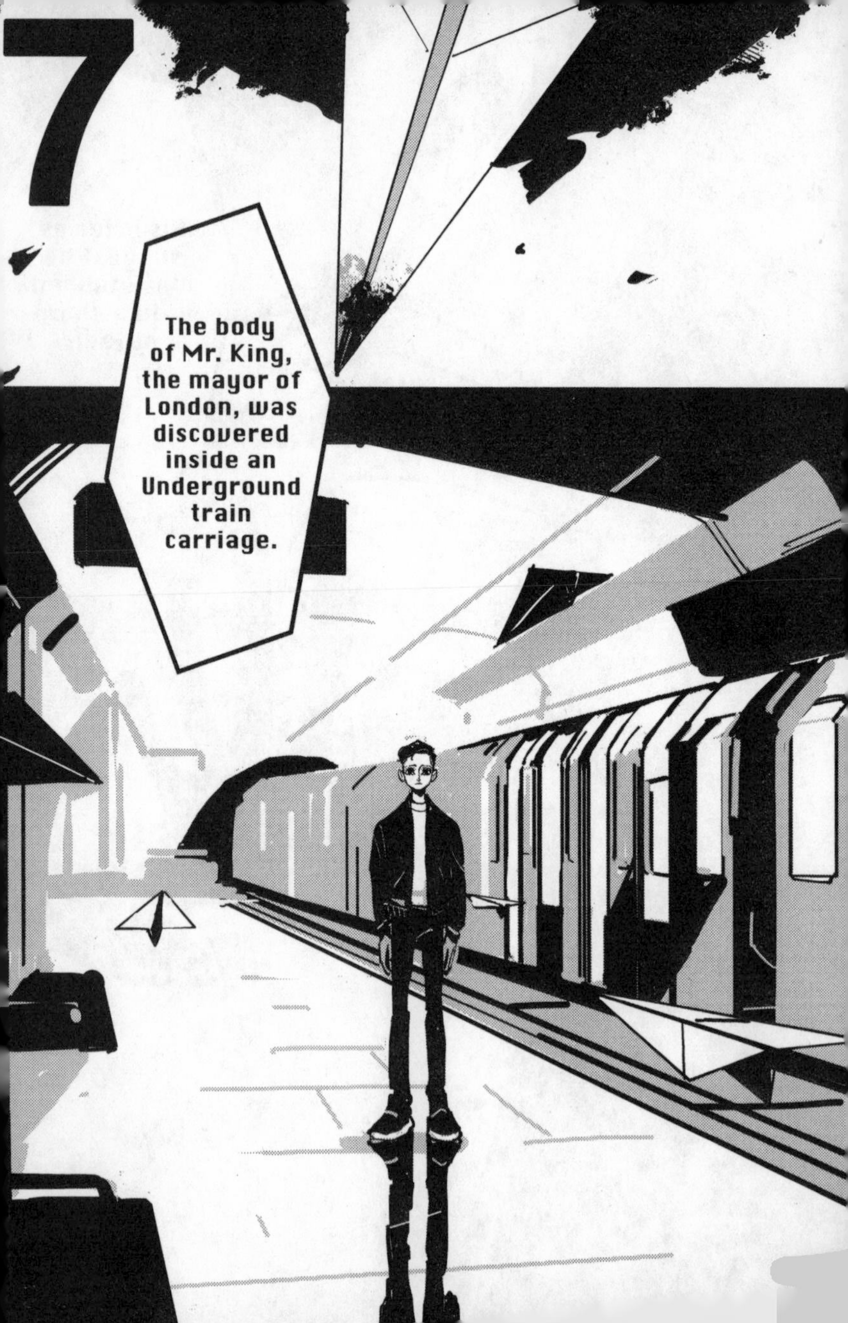
7
The body of Mr. King, the mayor of London, was discovered inside an Underground train carriage.

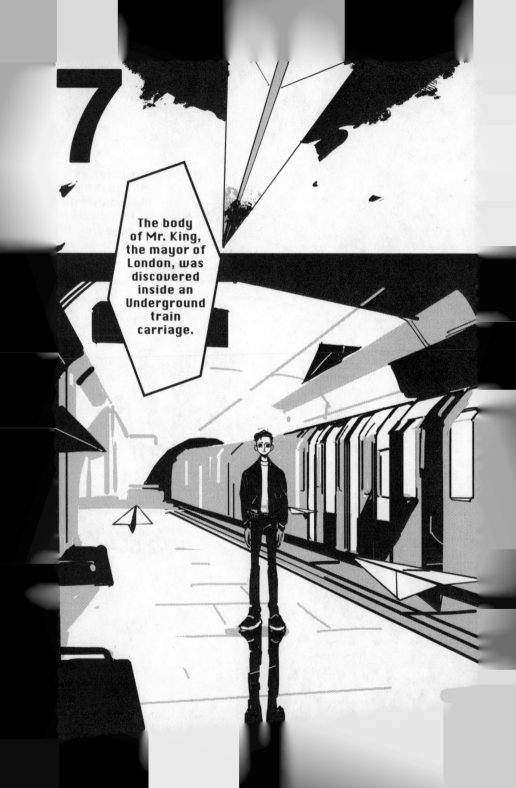

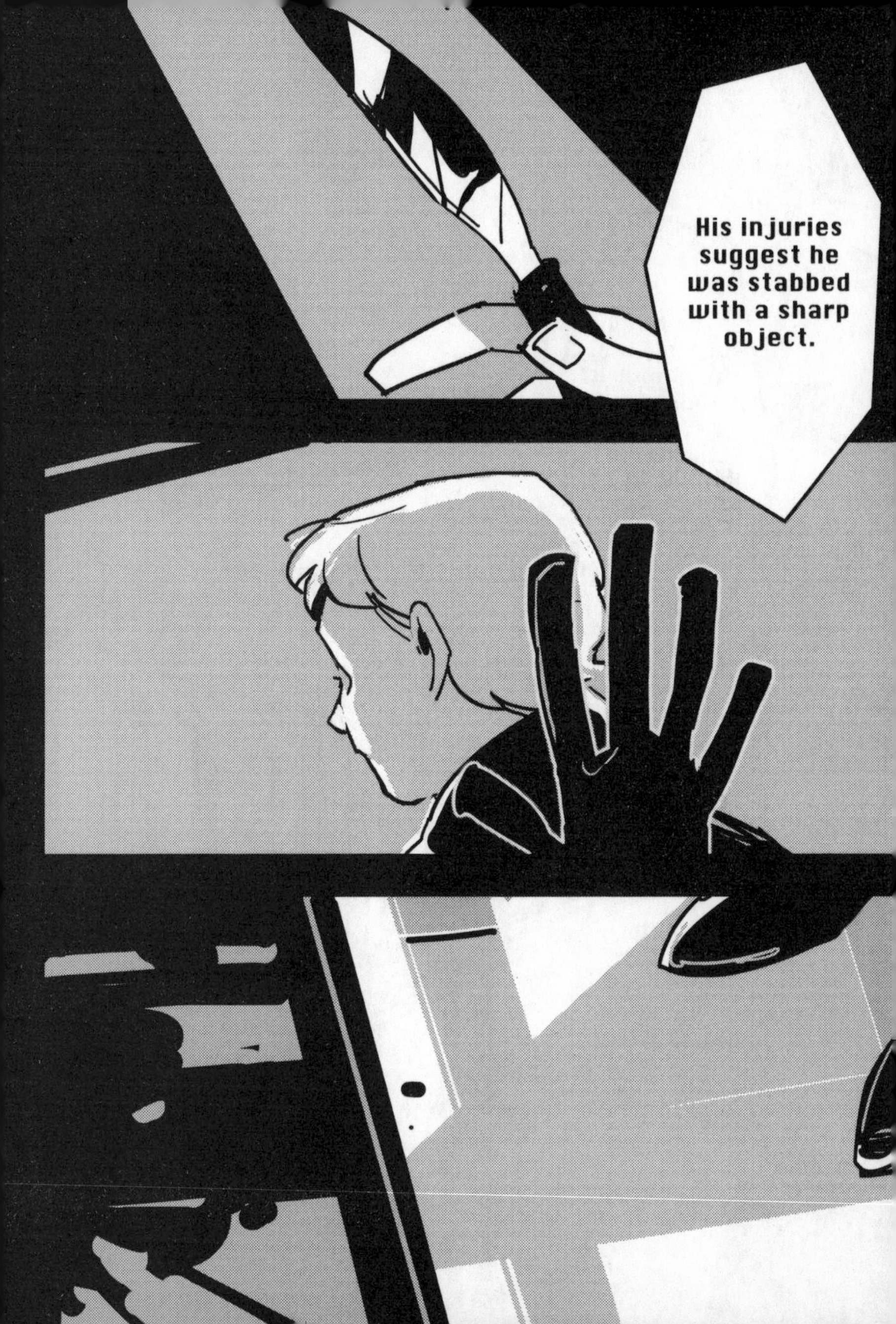
His injuries suggest he was stabbed with a sharp object.

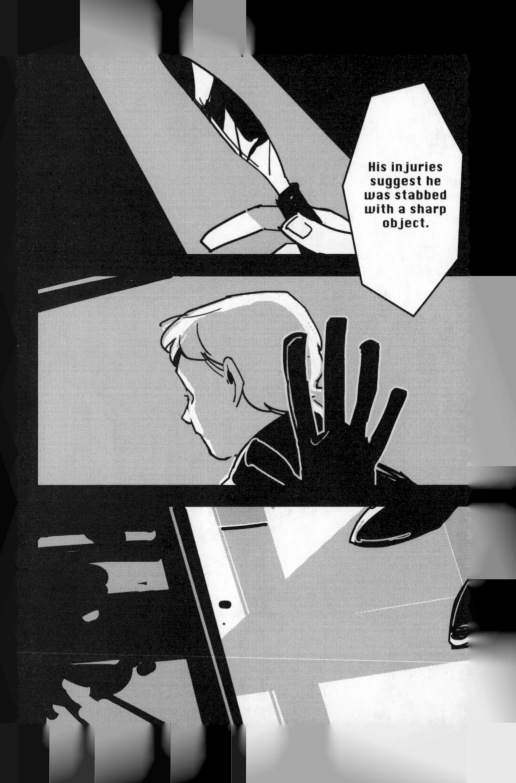

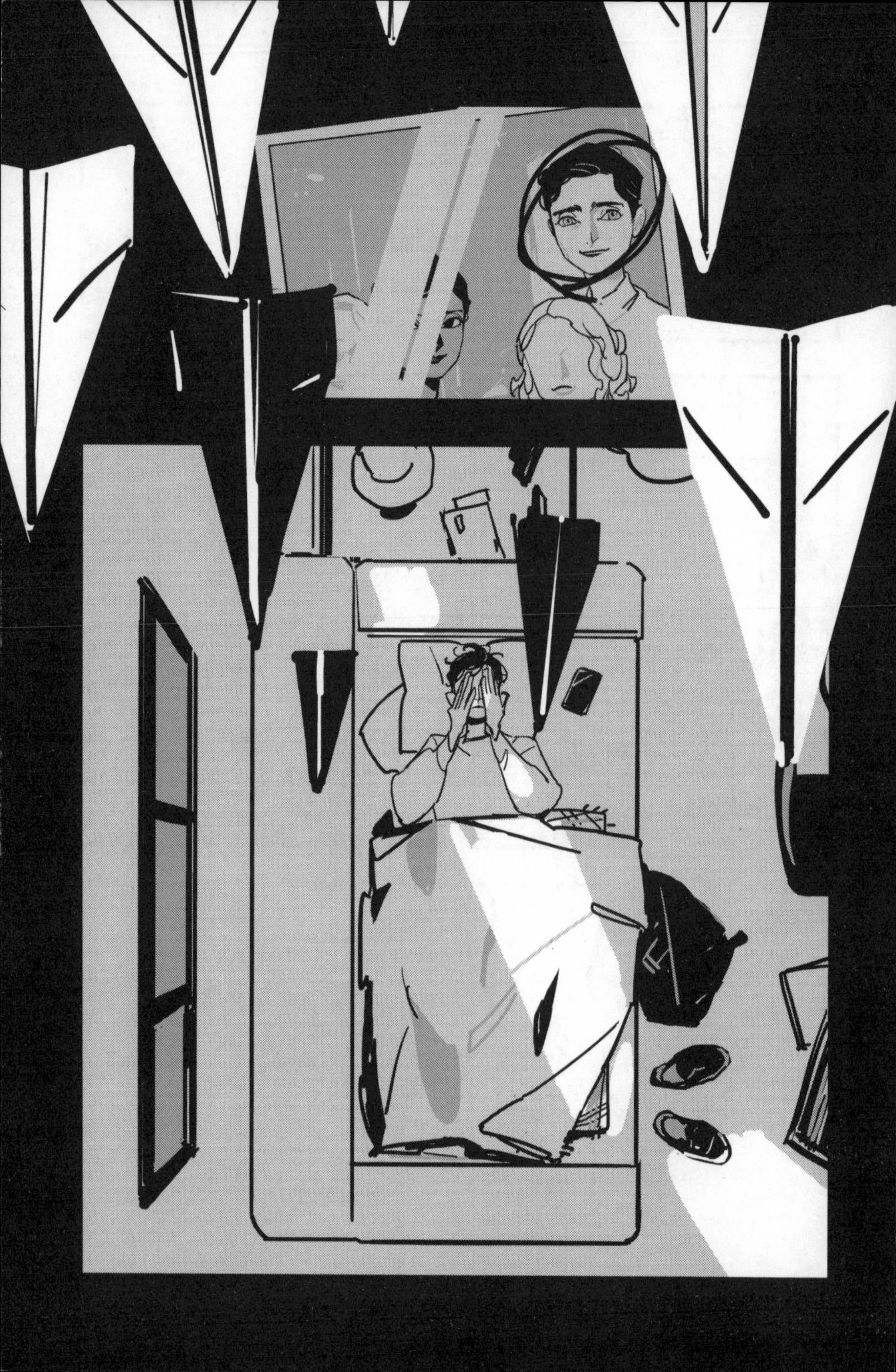

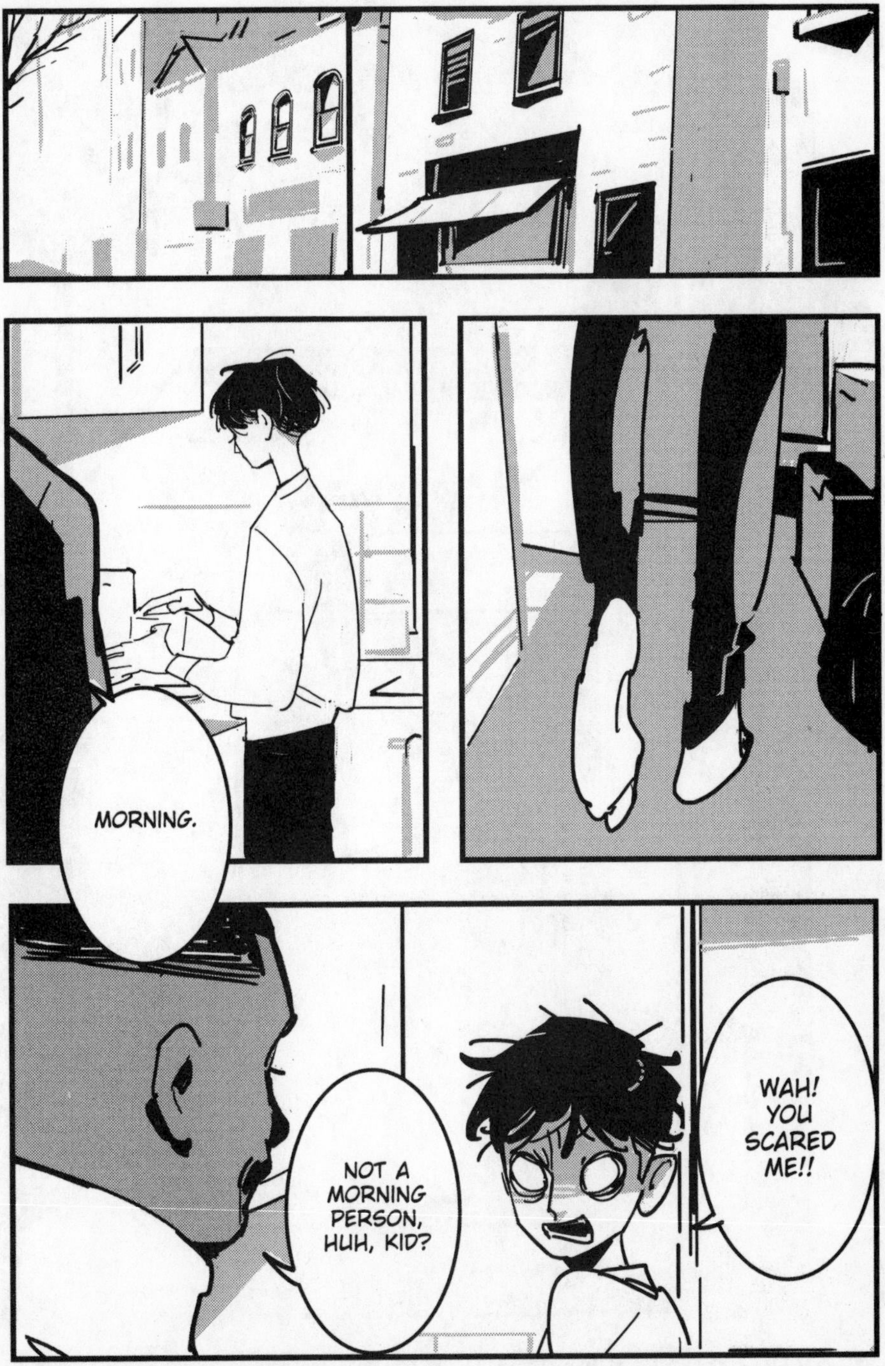
MORNING.
WAH! YOU SCARED ME!!
NOT A MORNING PERSON, HUH, KID?

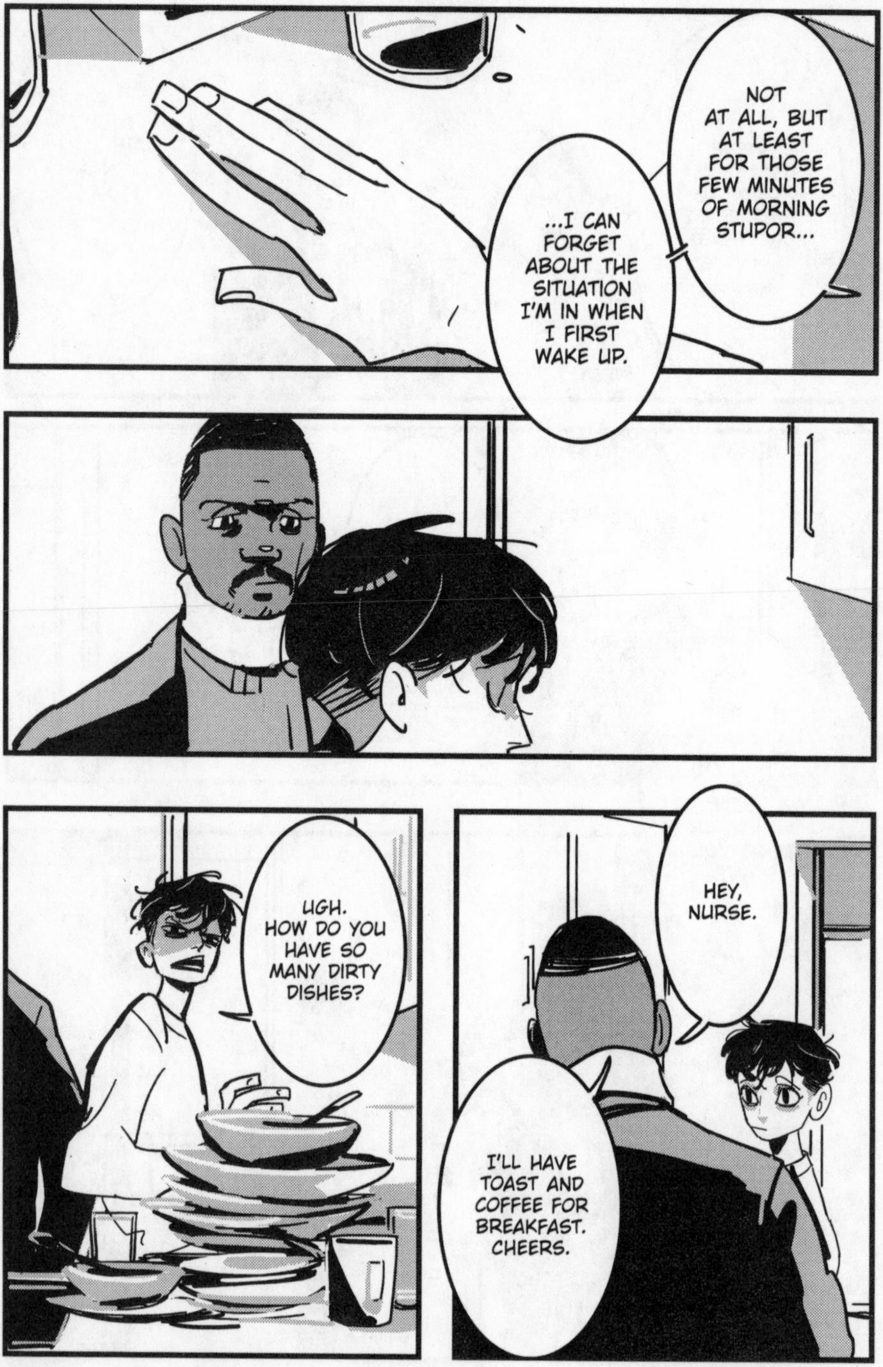
NOT AT ALL, BUT AT LEAST FOR THOSE FEW MINUTES OF MORNING STUPOR...
...I CAN FORGET ABOUT THE SITUATION I'M IN WHEN I FIRST WAKE UP.
HEY, NURSE.
I'LL HAVE TOAST AND COFFEE FOR BREAKFAST. CHEERS.
UGH. HOW DO YOU HAVE SO MANY DIRTY DISHES?

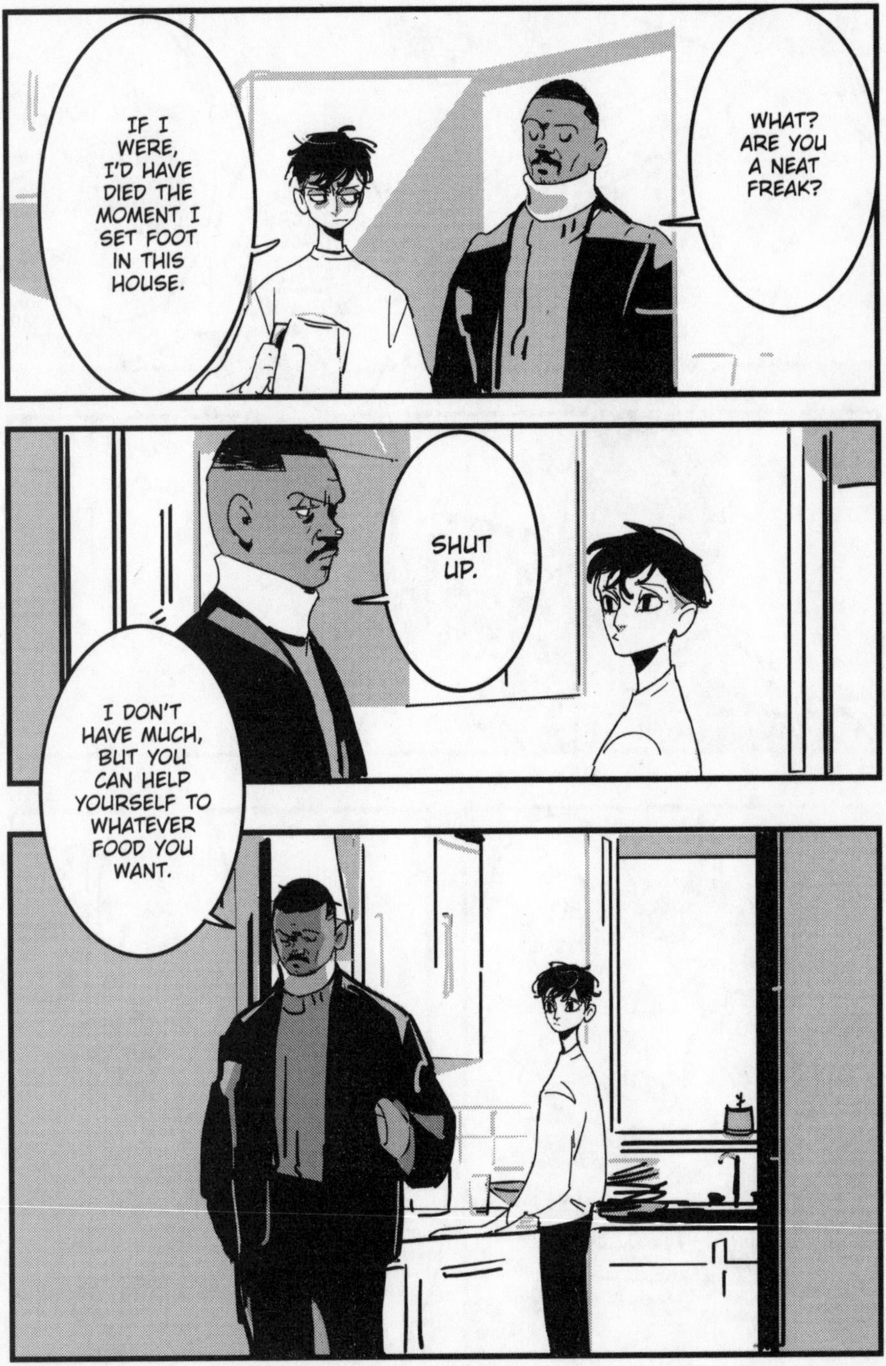
WHAT? ARE YOU A NEAT FREAK?
IF I WERE, I'D HAVE DIED THE MOMENT I SET FOOT IN THIS HOUSE.
SHUT UP.
I DON'T HAVE MUCH, BUT YOU CAN HELP YOURSELF TO WHATEVER FOOD YOU WANT.

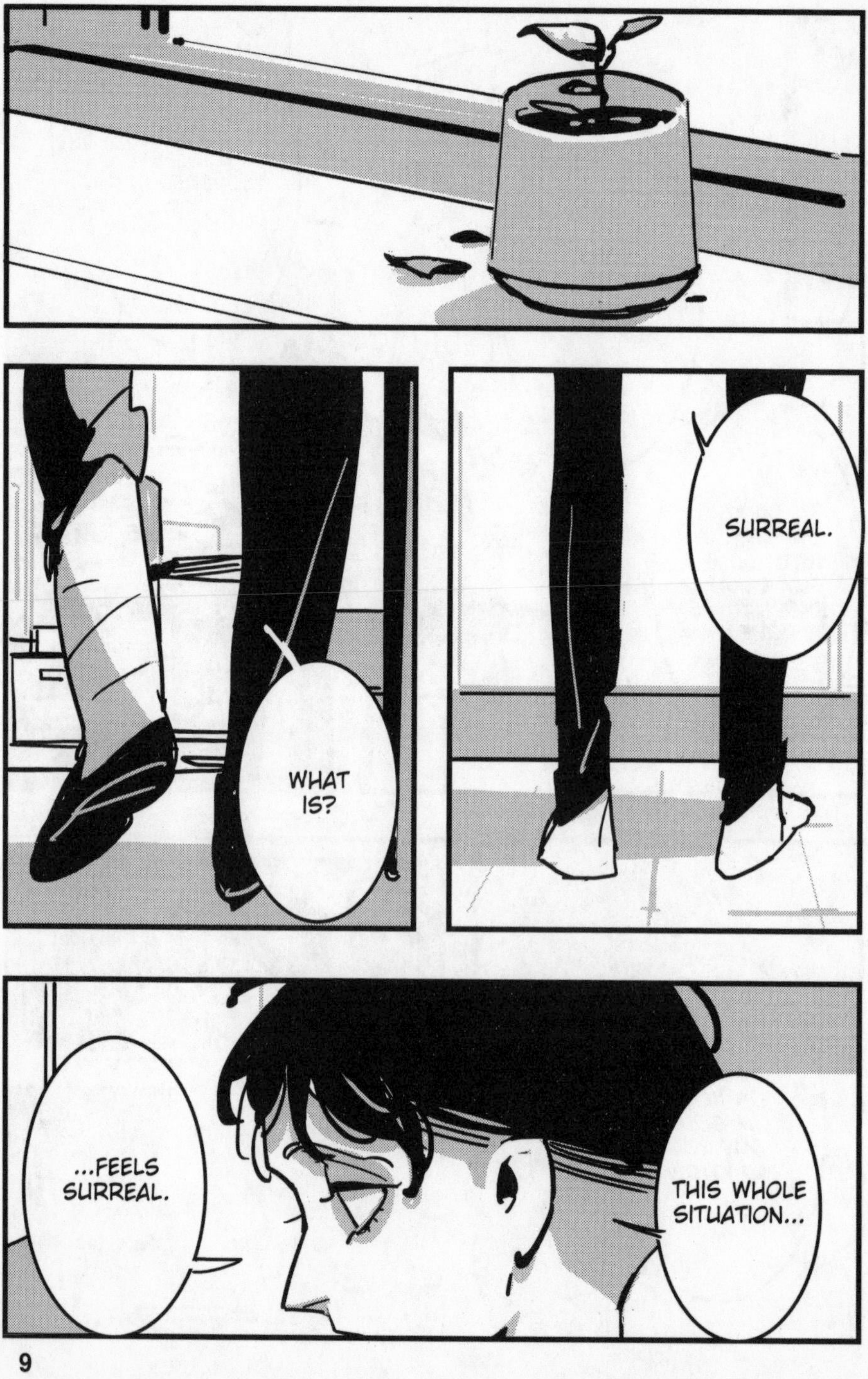
SURREAL.
WHAT IS?
THIS WHOLE SITUATION...
...FEELS SURREAL.

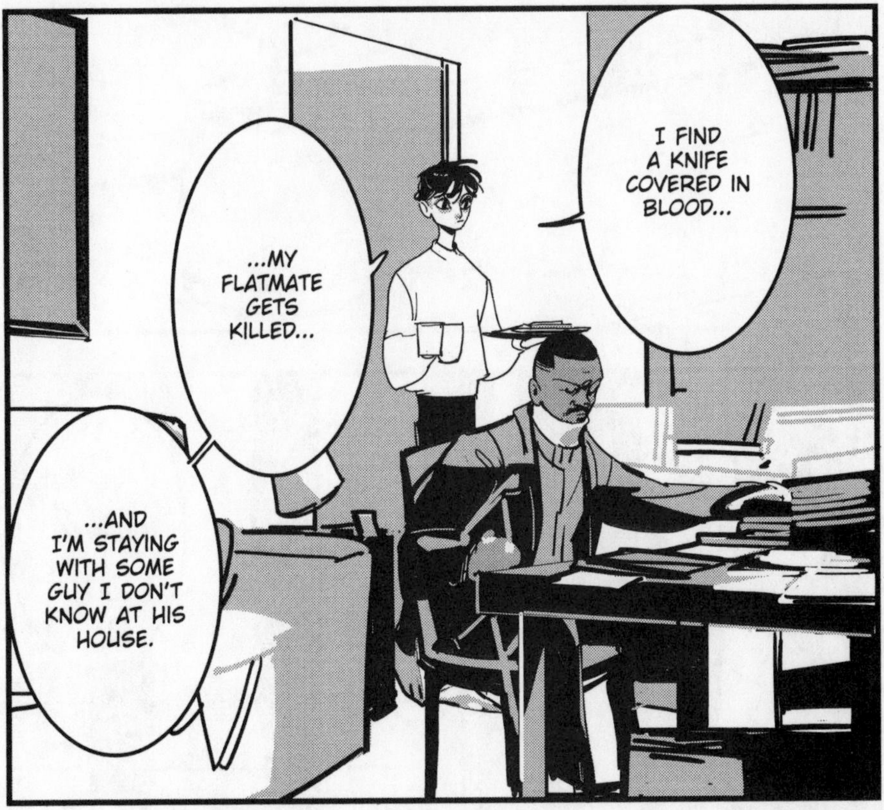
I FIND A KNIFE COVERED IN BLOOD...
...MY FLATMATE GETS KILLED...
...AND I'M STAYING WITH SOME GUY I DON'T KNOW AT HIS HOUSE.

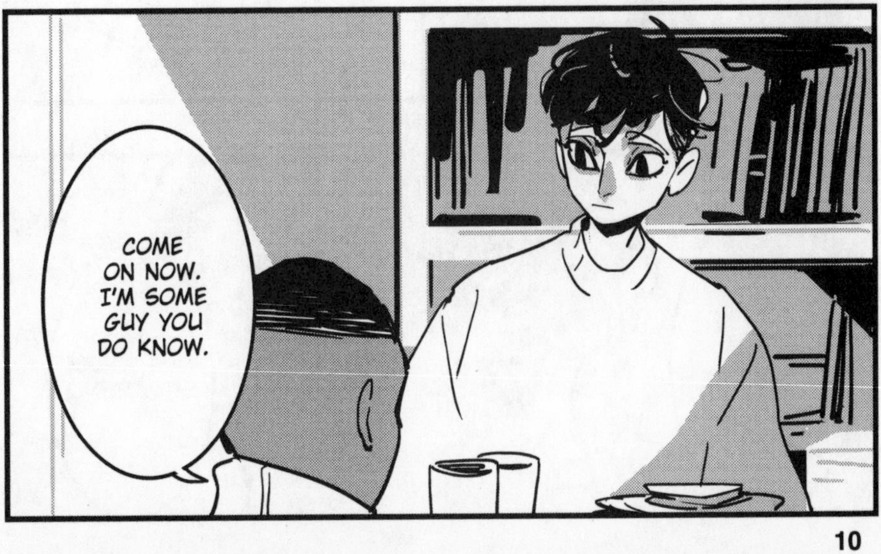
COME ON NOW. I'M SOME GUY YOU DO KNOW.

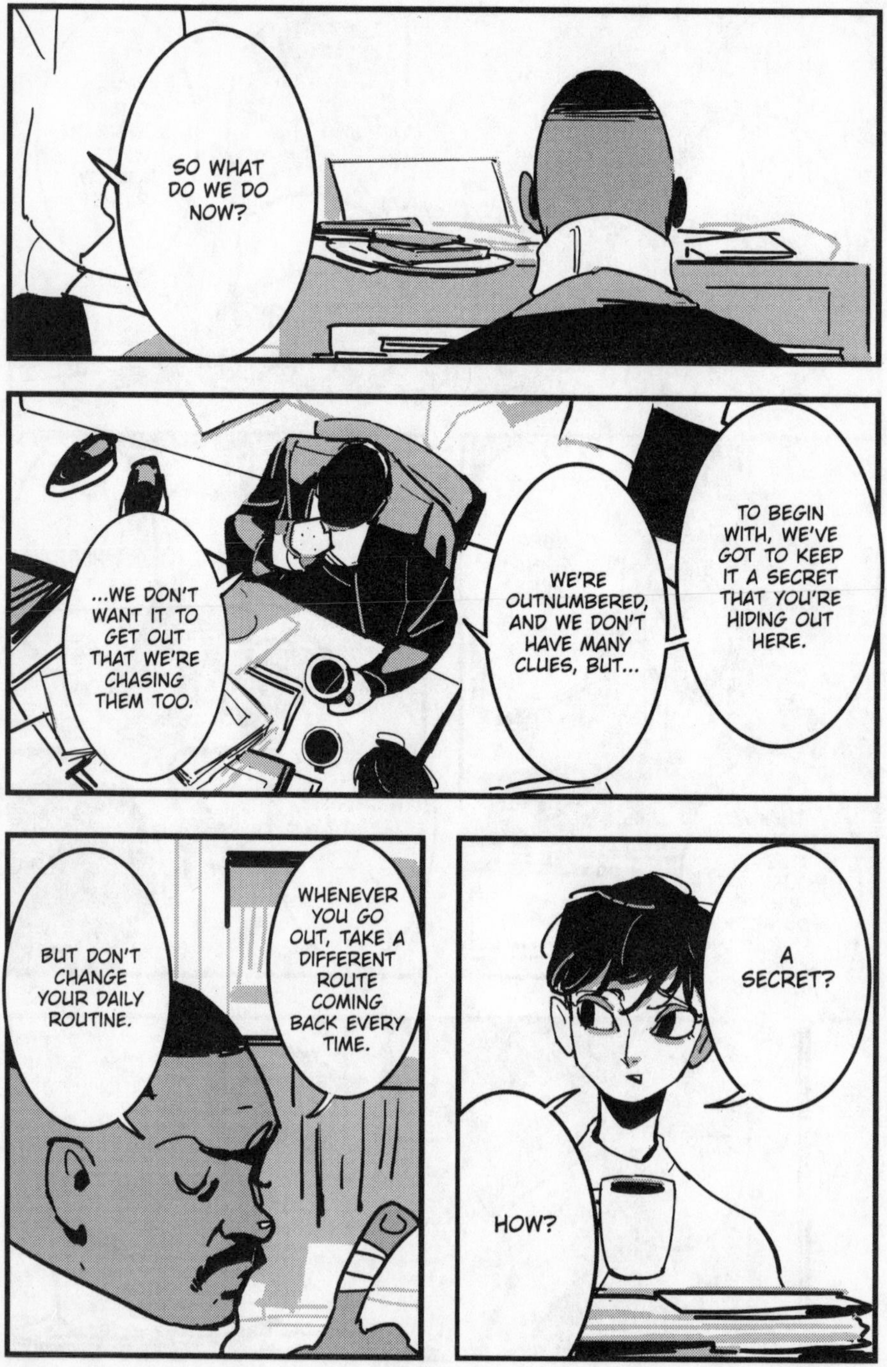
SO WHAT DO WE DO NOW?
TO BEGIN WITH, WE'VE GOT TO KEEP IT A SECRET THAT YOU'RE HIDING OUT HERE.
WE'RE OUTNUMBERED, AND WE DON'T HAVE MANY CLUES, BUT...
...WE DON'T WANT IT TO GET OUT THAT WE'RE CHASING THEM TOO.
A SECRET?
HOW?
WHENEVER YOU GO OUT, TAKE A DIFFERENT ROUTE COMING BACK EVERY TIME.
BUT DON'T CHANGE YOUR DAILY ROUTINE.

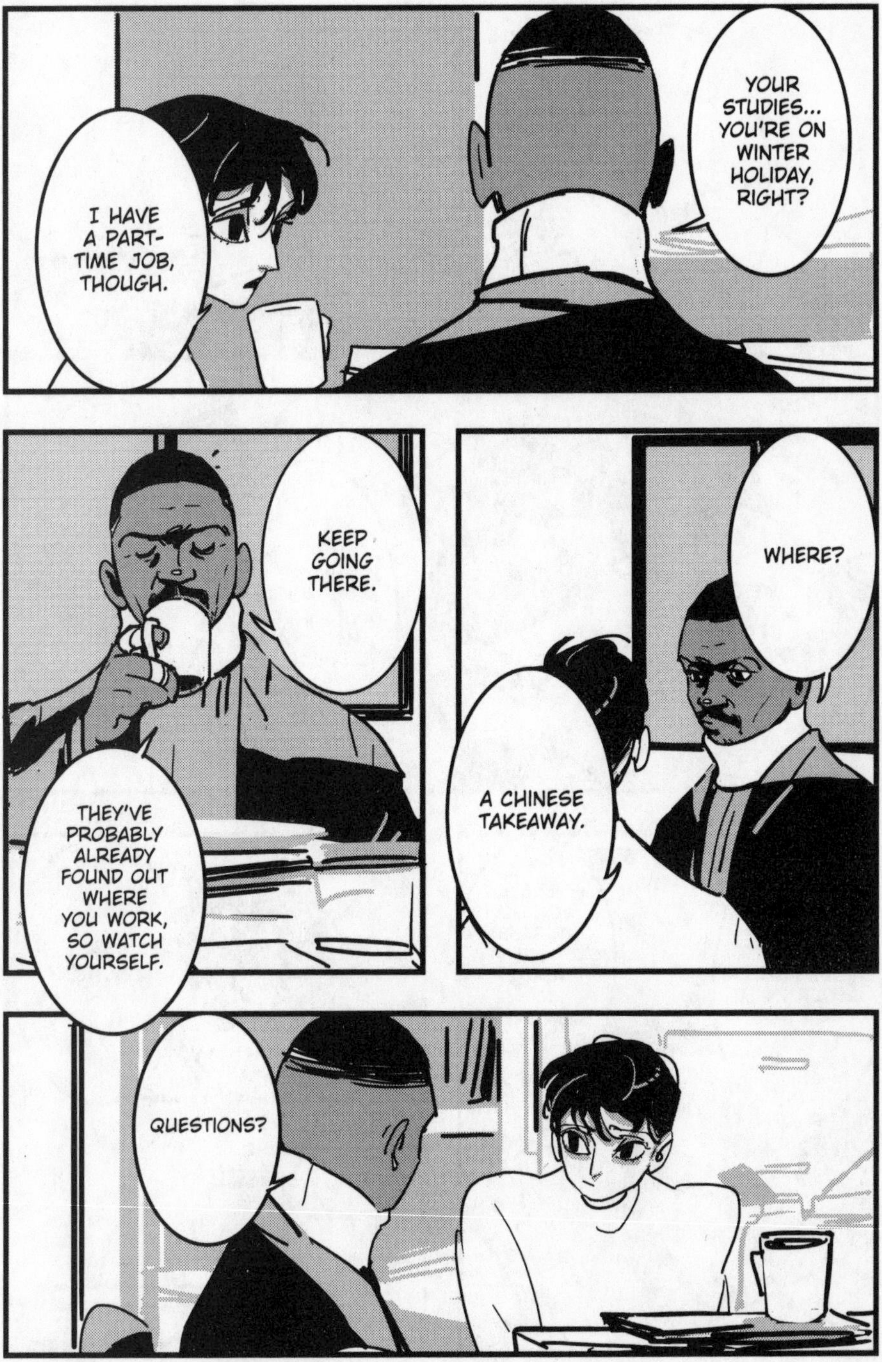
YOUR STUDIES... YOU'RE ON WINTER HOLIDAY, RIGHT?
I HAVE A PART-TIME JOB, THOUGH.
WHERE?
A CHINESE TAKEAWAY.
KEEP GOING THERE.
THEY'VE PROBABLY ALREADY FOUND OUT WHERE YOU WORK, SO WATCH YOURSELF.
QUESTIONS?

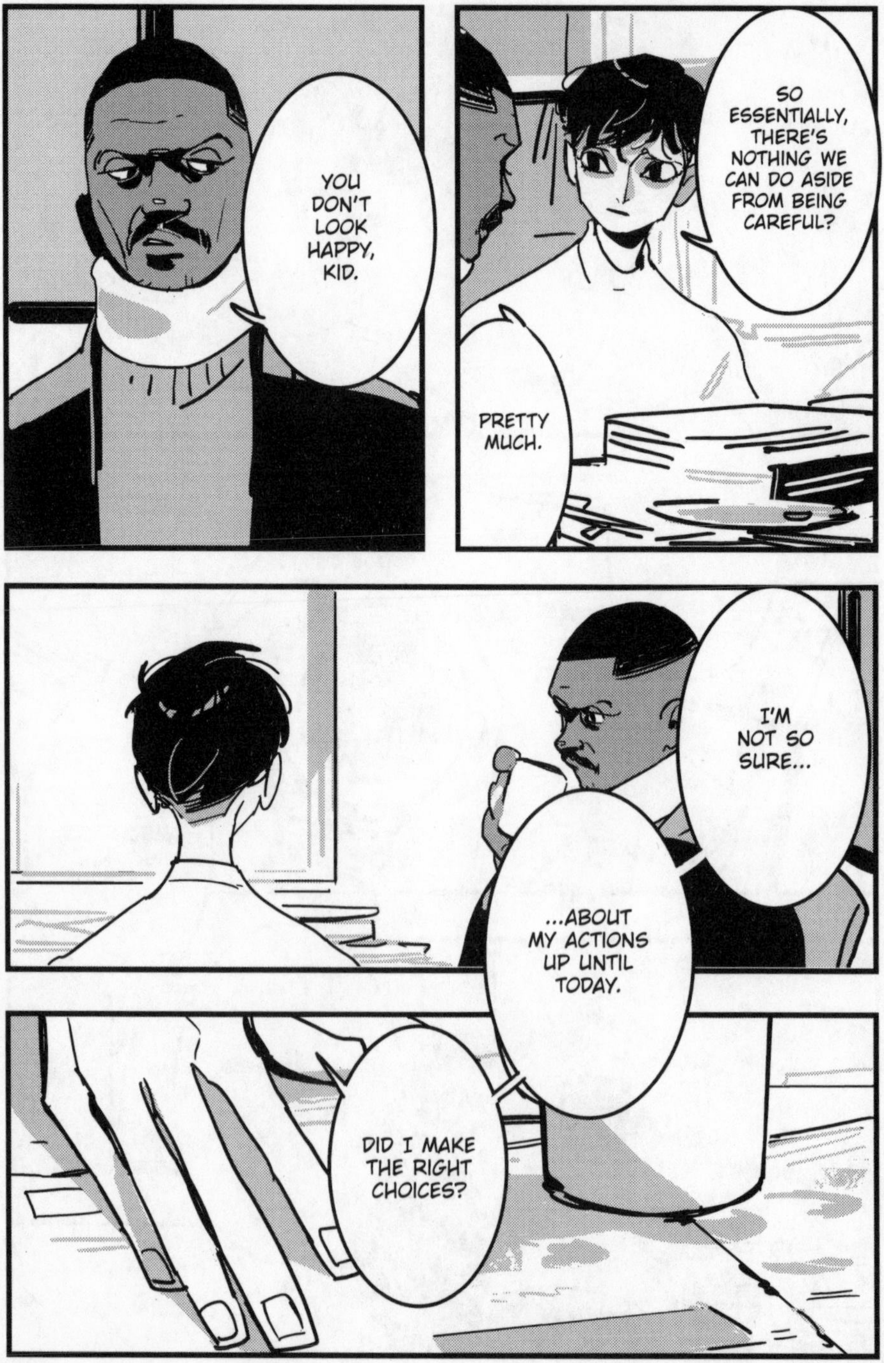
SO ESSENTIALLY, THERE'S NOTHING WE CAN DO ASIDE FROM BEING CAREFUL?
PRETTY MUCH.
YOU DON'T LOOK HAPPY, KID.
I'M NOT SO SURE...
...ABOUT MY ACTIONS UP UNTIL TODAY.
DID I MAKE THE RIGHT CHOICES?

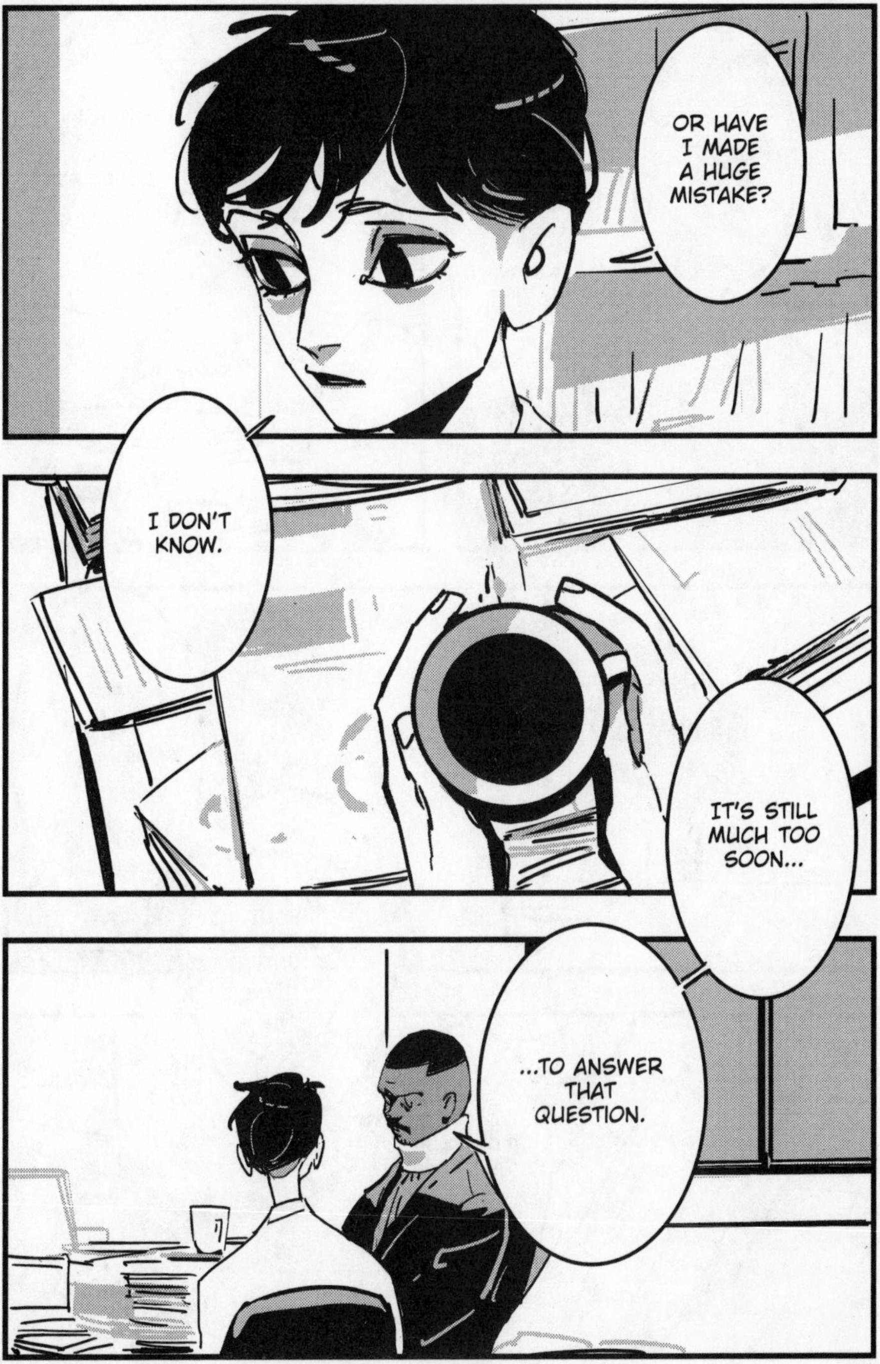
OR HAVE I MADE A HUGE MISTAKE?
I DON'T KNOW.
IT'S STILL MUCH TOO SOON...
...TO ANSWER THAT QUESTION.

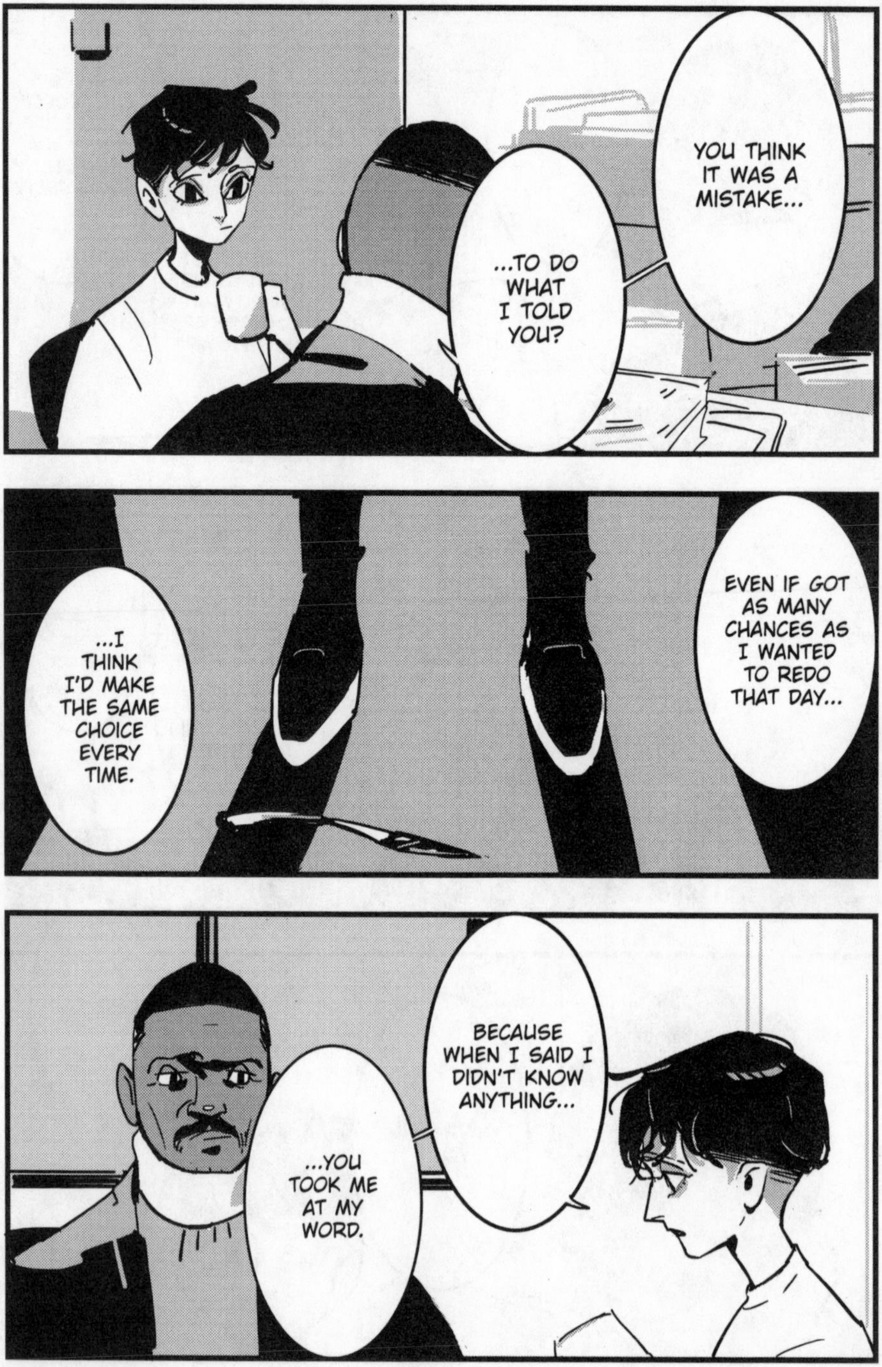
YOU THINK IT WAS A MISTAKE...
...TO DO WHAT I TOLD YOU?
EVEN IF GOT AS MANY CHANCES AS I WANTED TO REDO THAT DAY...
...I THINK I'D MAKE THE SAME CHOICE EVERY TIME.
BECAUSE WHEN I SAID I DIDN'T KNOW ANYTHING...
...YOU TOOK ME AT MY WORD.

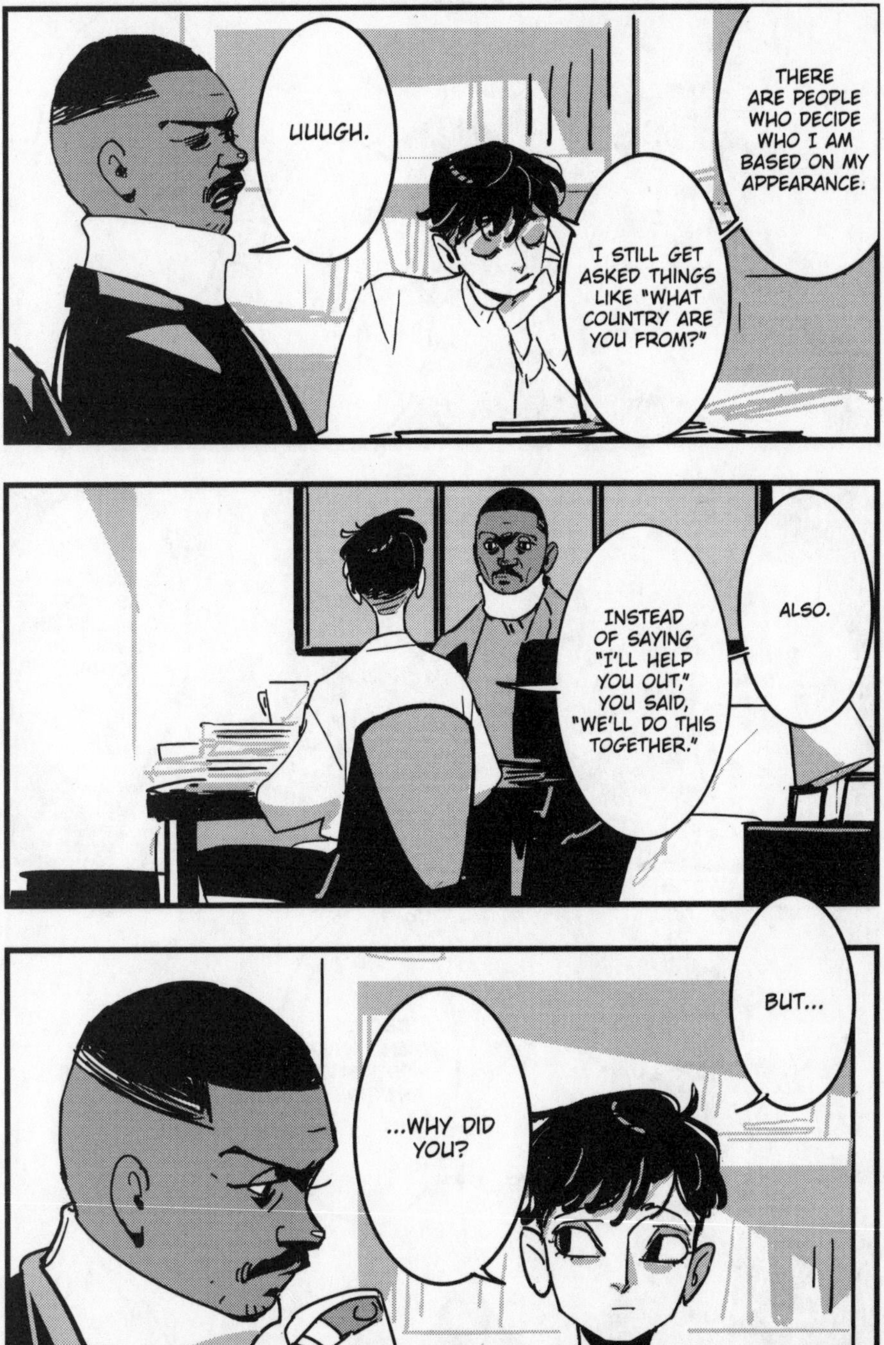
THERE ARE PEOPLE WHO DECIDE WHO I AM BASED ON MY APPEARANCE.
I STILL GET ASKED THINGS LIKE "WHAT COUNTRY ARE YOU FROM?"
UUUGH.
ALSO.
INSTEAD OF SAYING "I'LL HELP YOU OUT," YOU SAID, "WE'LL DO THIS TOGETHER."
BUT...
...WHY DID YOU?

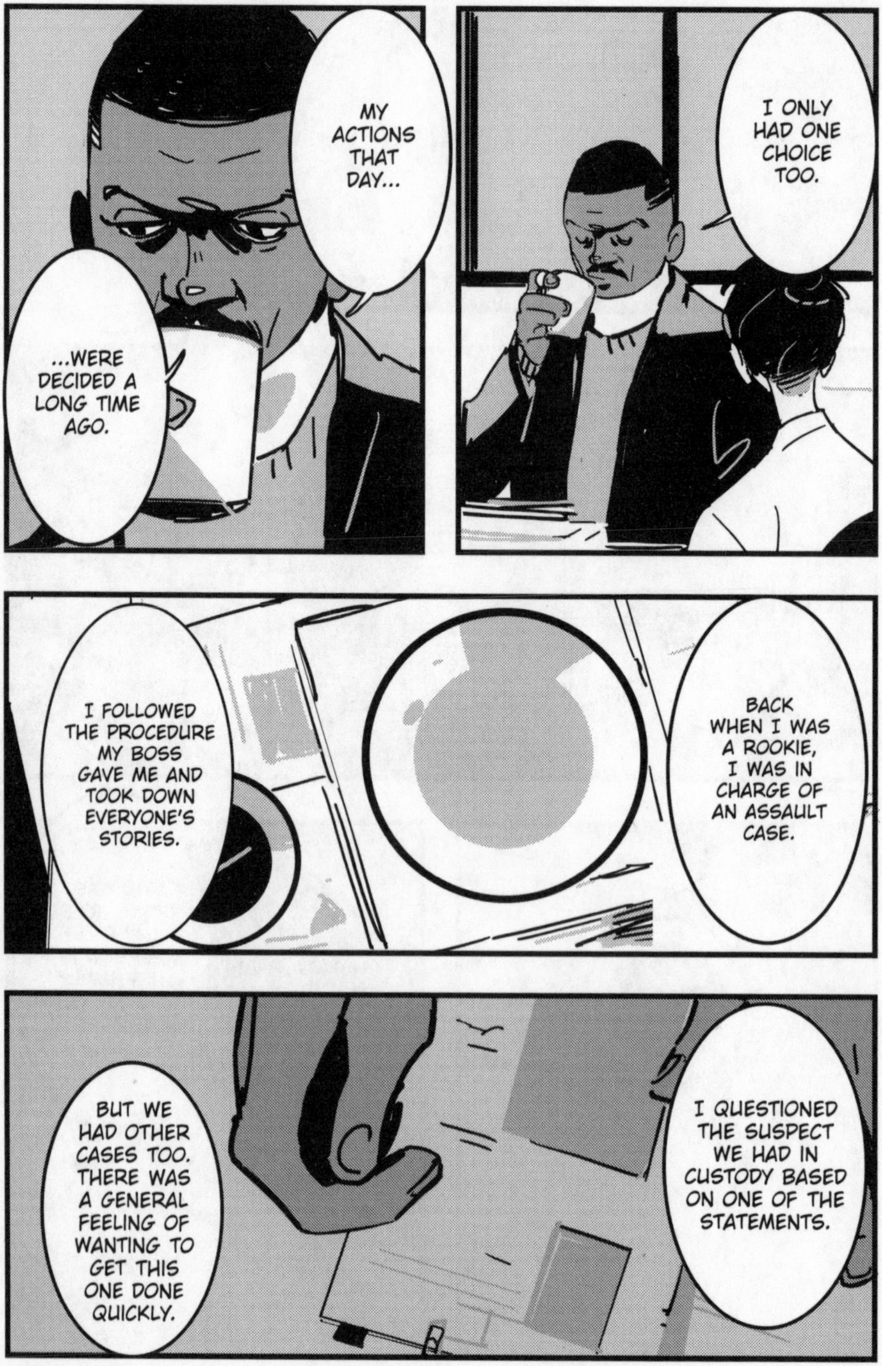
I ONLY HAD ONE CHOICE TOO.
MY ACTIONS THAT DAY...
...WERE DECIDED A LONG TIME AGO.
BACK WHEN I WAS A ROOKIE, I WAS IN CHARGE OF AN ASSAULT CASE.
I FOLLOWED THE PROCEDURE MY BOSS GAVE ME AND TOOK DOWN EVERYONE'S STORIES.
I QUESTIONED THE SUSPECT WE HAD IN CUSTODY BASED ON ONE OF THE STATEMENTS.
BUT WE HAD OTHER CASES TOO. THERE WAS A GENERAL FEELING OF WANTING TO GET THIS ONE DONE QUICKLY.

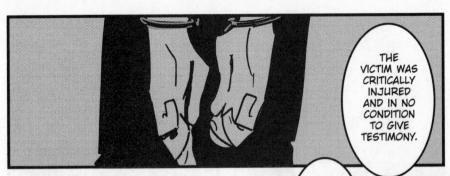

THE VICTIM WAS CRITICALLY INJURED AND IN NO CONDITION TO GIVE TESTIMONY.

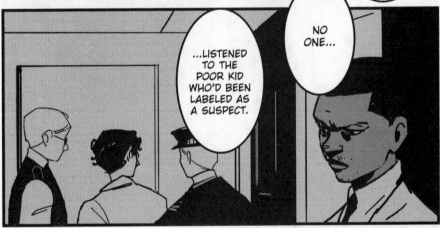

NO ONE...

...LISTENED TO THE POOR KID WHO'D BEEN LABELED AS A SUSPECT.

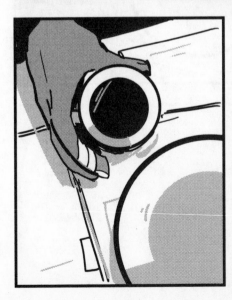

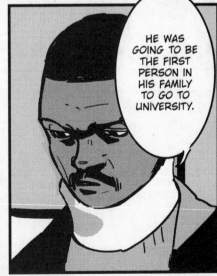

HE WAS GOING TO BE THE FIRST PERSON IN HIS FAMILY TO GO TO UNIVERSITY.

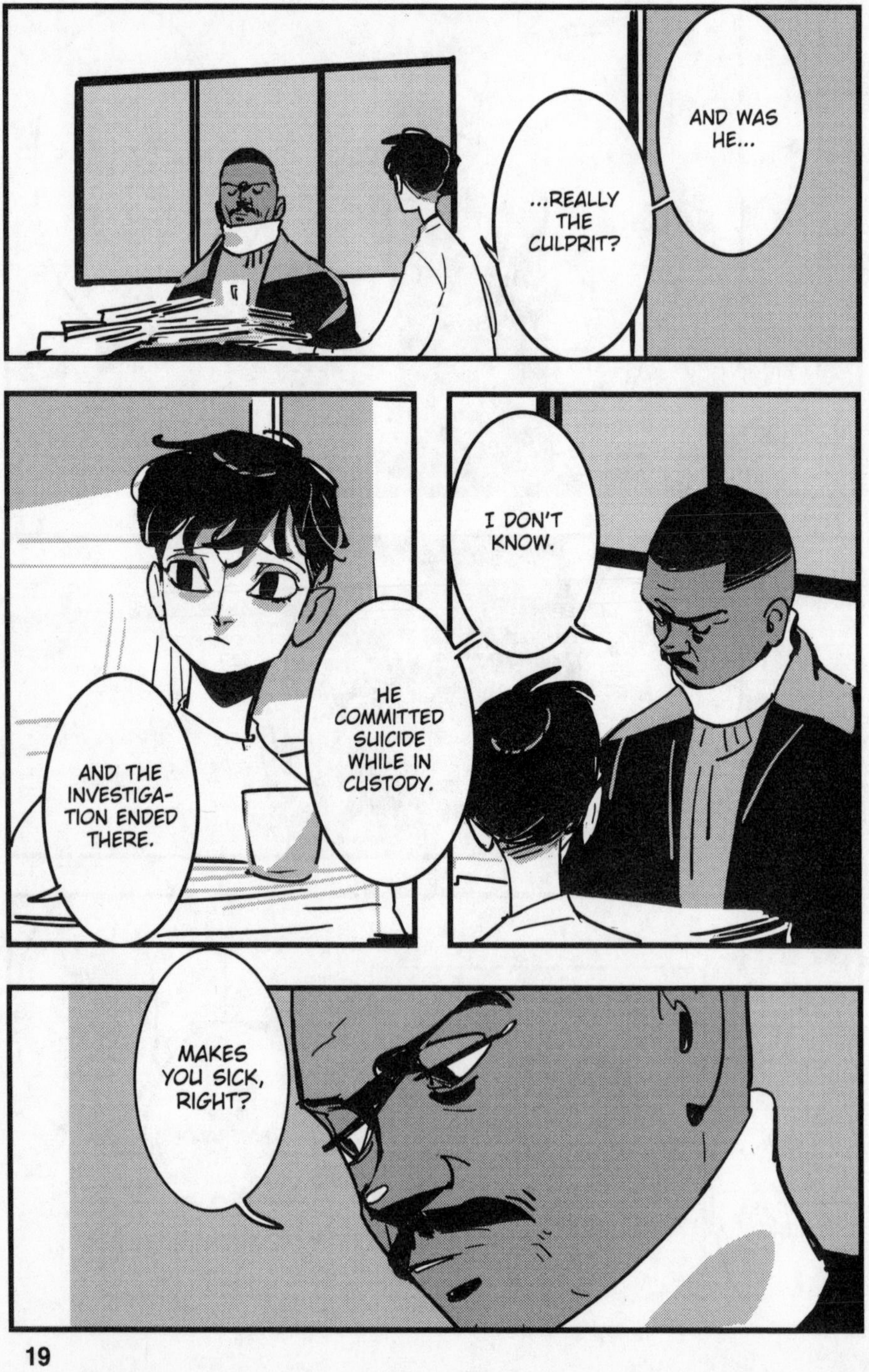
AND WAS HE...
...REALLY THE CULPRIT?
I DON'T KNOW.
HE COMMITTED SUICIDE WHILE IN CUSTODY.
AND THE INVESTIGA-TION ENDED THERE.
MAKES YOU SICK, RIGHT?

I DON'T INTEND TO HAVE A REPEAT OF THAT SICKENING STORY...
...EVEN IF IT COSTS ME MY JOB. EVEN IF I WIND UP FACING CRIMINAL CHARGES.
I GUESS ULTIMATELY I'M DOING THIS FOR MYSELF.
ALL RIGHT. THIS GUY YOU DON'T KNOW IS OFF TO WORK.
I DON'T GENERALLY GET VISITORS, SO IF ANYONE COMES, DON'T OPEN THE DOOR.
YOU SURE HOLD A GRUDGE, HUH?

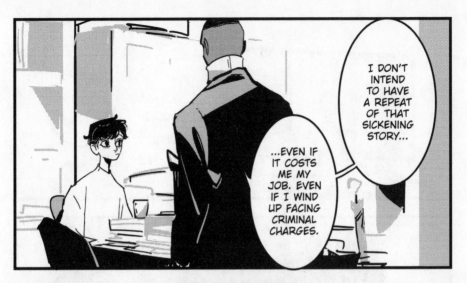

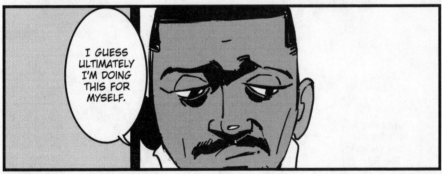

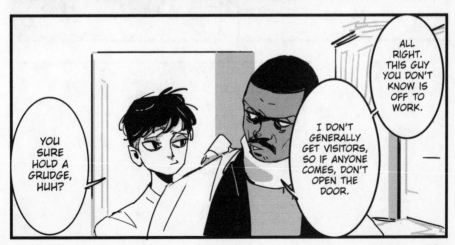

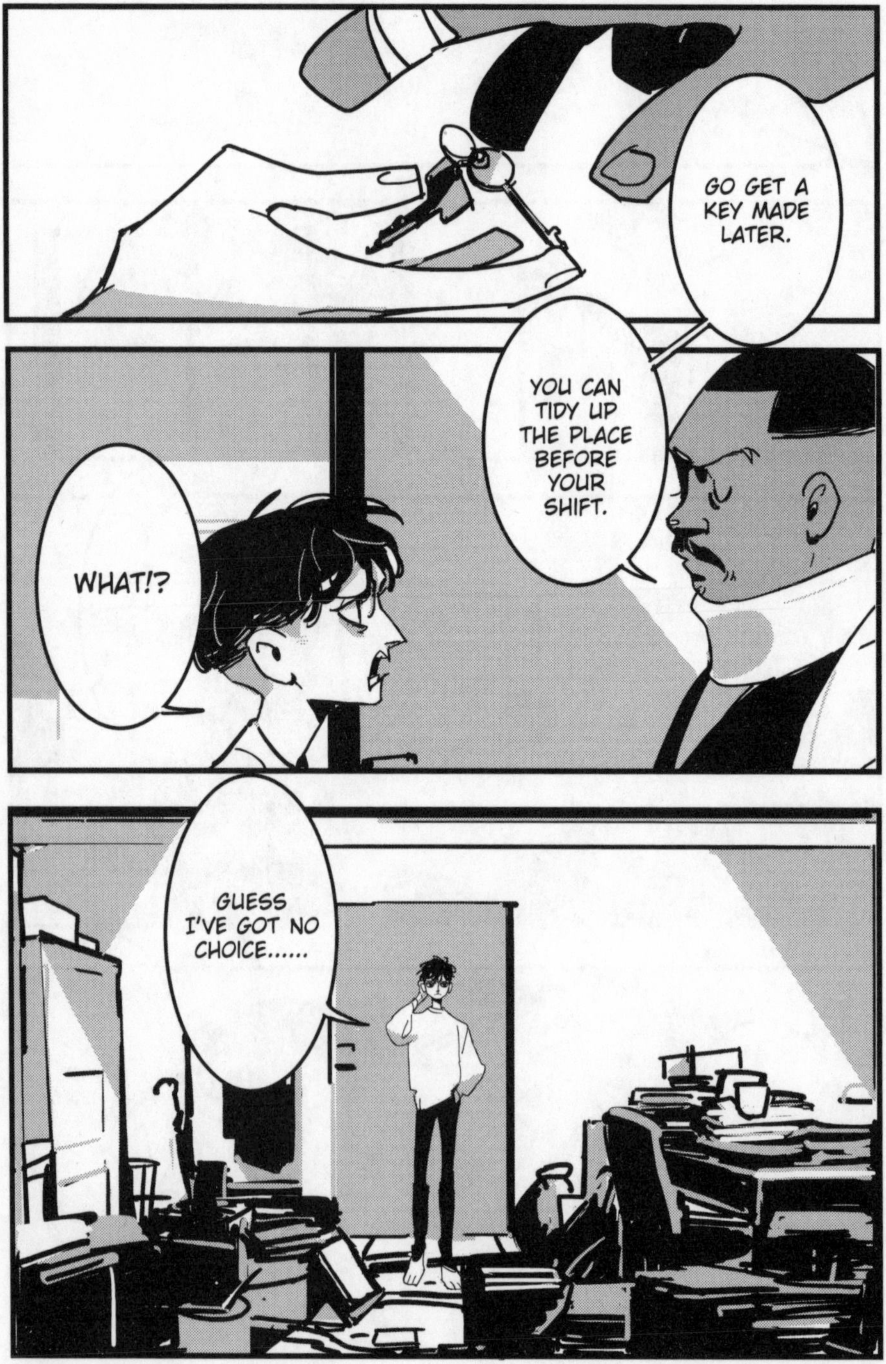
GO GET A KEY MADE LATER.
YOU CAN TIDY UP THE PLACE BEFORE YOUR SHIFT.
WHAT!?
GUESS I'VE GOT NO CHOICE......

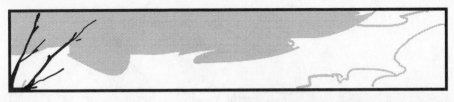

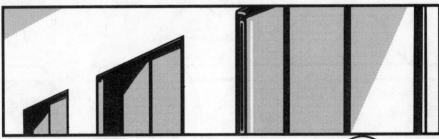

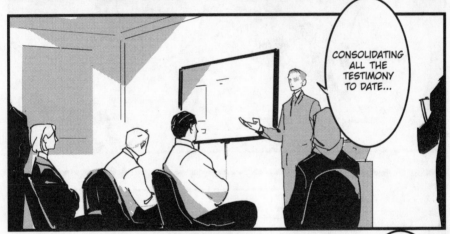

CONSOLIDATING ALL THE TESTIMONY TO DATE...

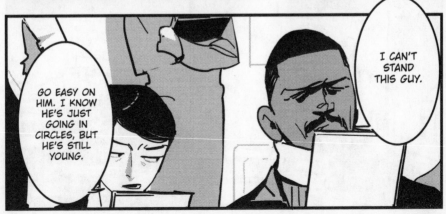

I CAN'T STAND THIS GUY.

GO EASY ON HIM. I KNOW HE'S JUST GOING IN CIRCLES, BUT HE'S STILL YOUNG.

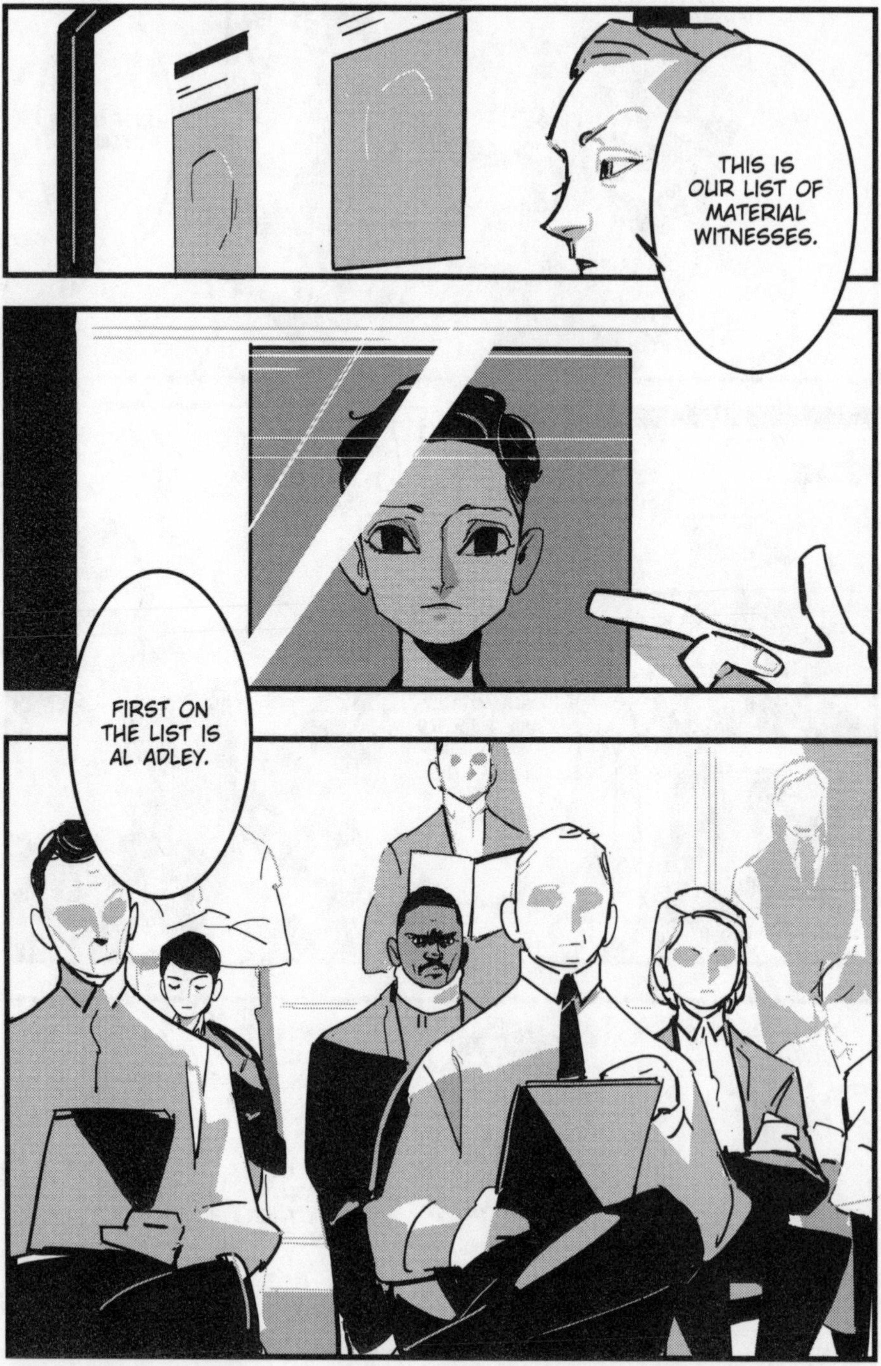
THIS IS OUR LIST OF MATERIAL WITNESSES.
FIRST ON THE LIST IS AL ADLEY.

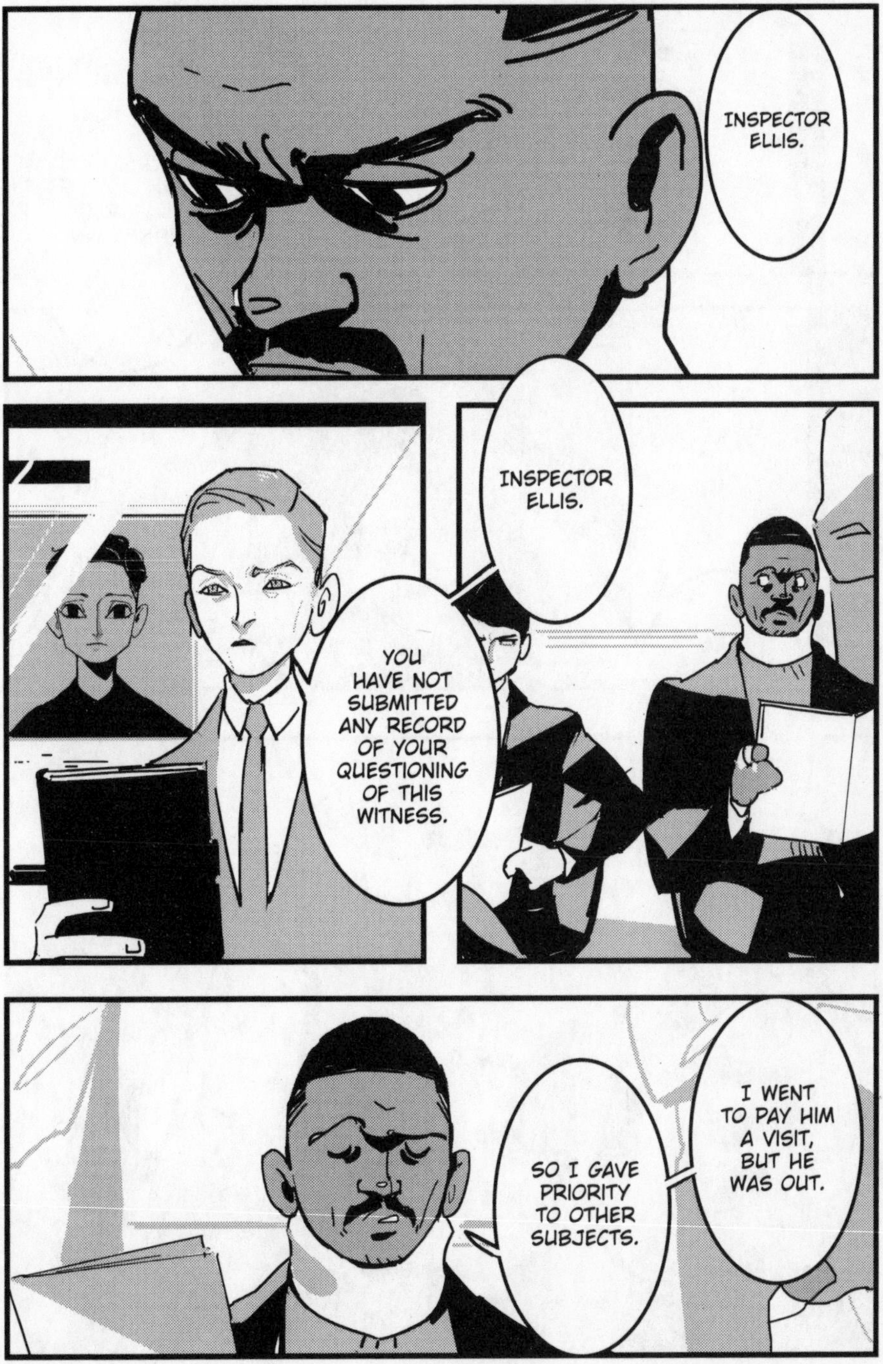
INSPECTOR ELLIS.
INSPECTOR ELLIS.
YOU HAVE NOT SUBMITTED ANY RECORD OF YOUR QUESTIONING OF THIS WITNESS.
I WENT TO PAY HIM A VISIT, BUT HE WAS OUT.
SO I GAVE PRIORITY TO OTHER SUBJECTS.

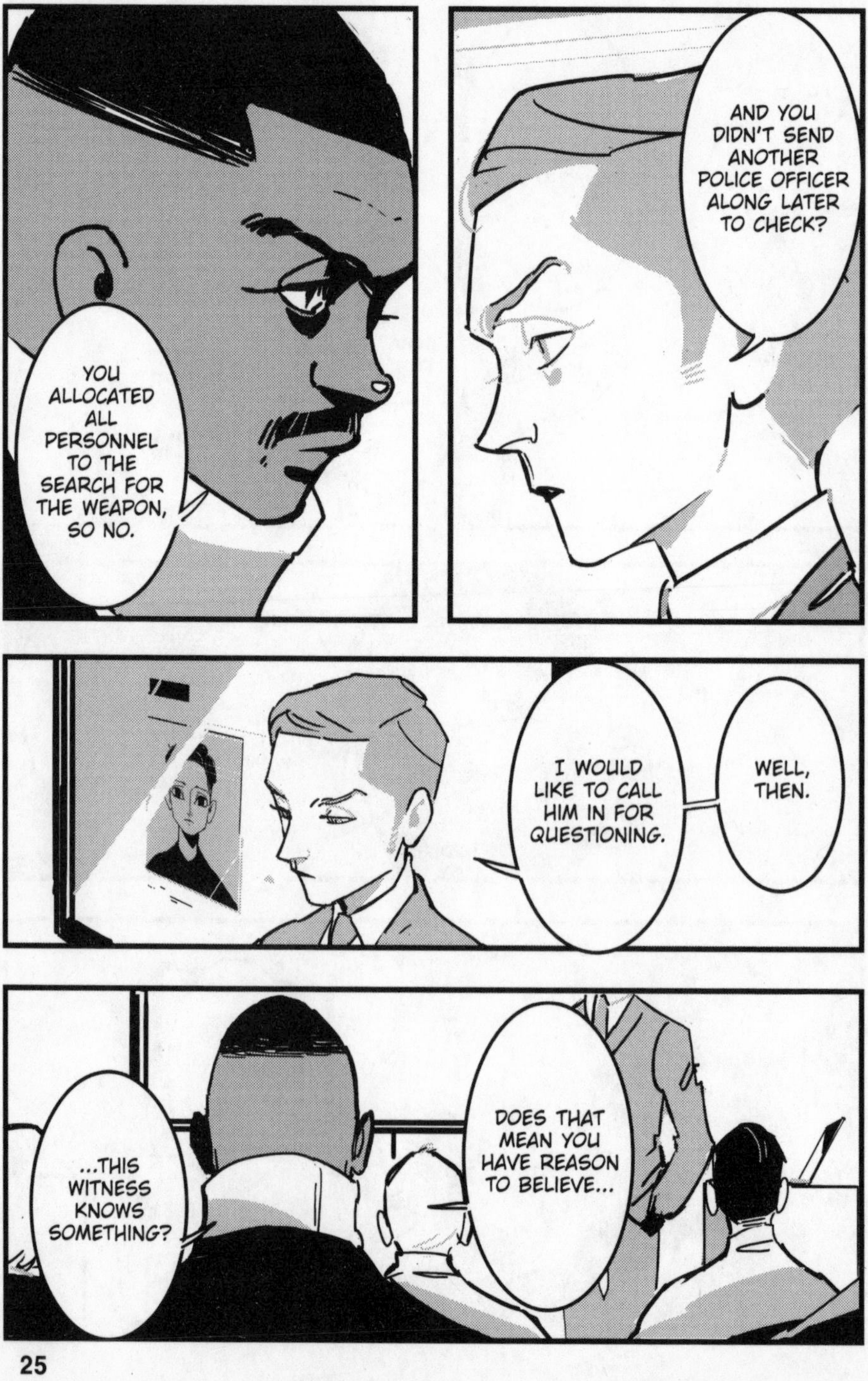
AND YOU DIDN'T SEND ANOTHER POLICE OFFICER ALONG LATER TO CHECK?
YOU ALLOCATED ALL PERSONNEL TO THE SEARCH FOR THE WEAPON, SO NO.
WELL, THEN.
I WOULD LIKE TO CALL HIM IN FOR QUESTIONING.
DOES THAT MEAN YOU HAVE REASON TO BELIEVE...
...THIS WITNESS KNOWS SOMETHING?

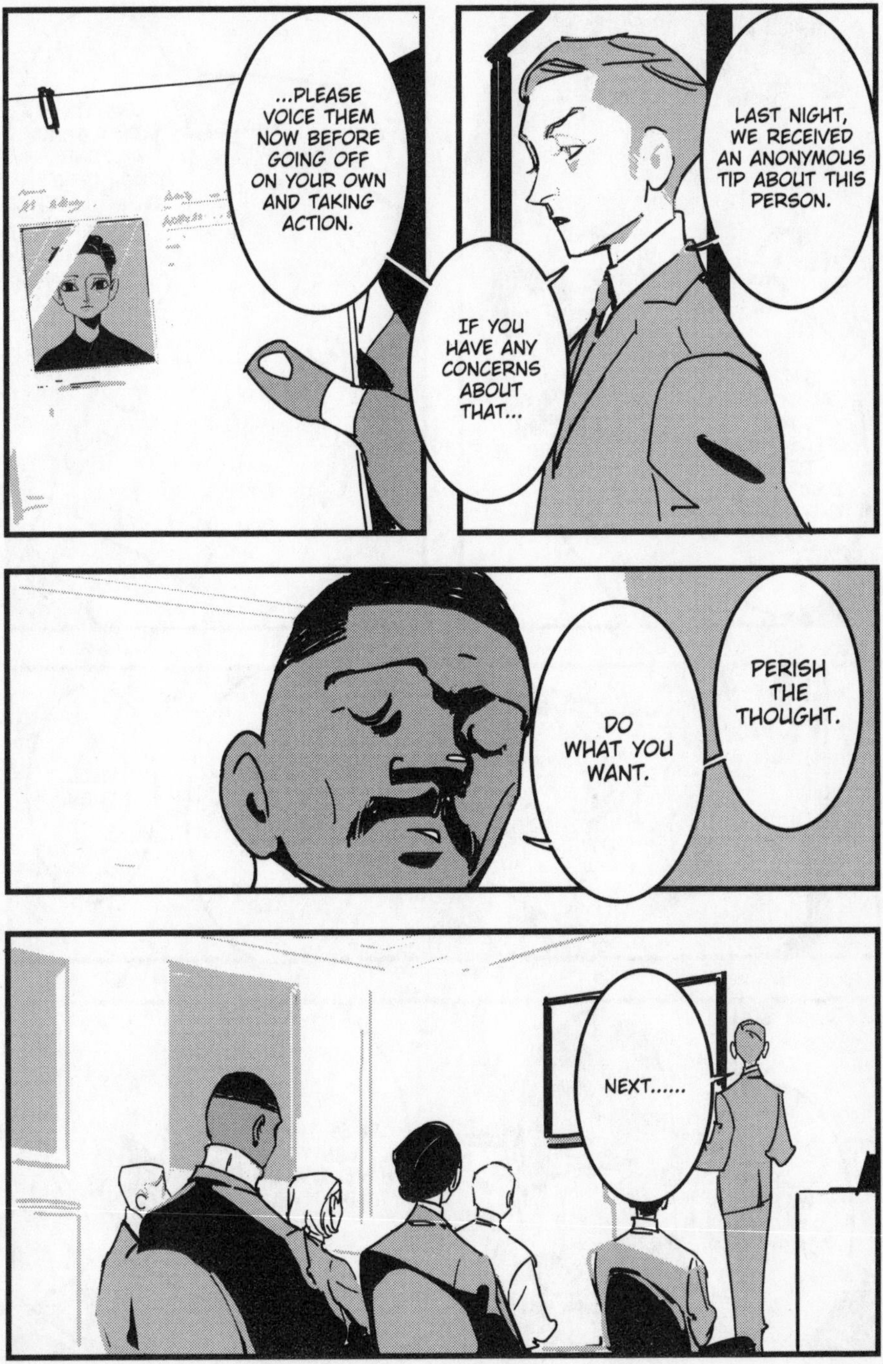
LAST NIGHT, WE RECEIVED AN ANONYMOUS TIP ABOUT THIS PERSON.
IF YOU HAVE ANY CONCERNS ABOUT THAT...
...PLEASE VOICE THEM NOW BEFORE GOING OFF ON YOUR OWN AND TAKING ACTION.
PERISH THE THOUGHT.
DO WHAT YOU WANT.
NEXT......

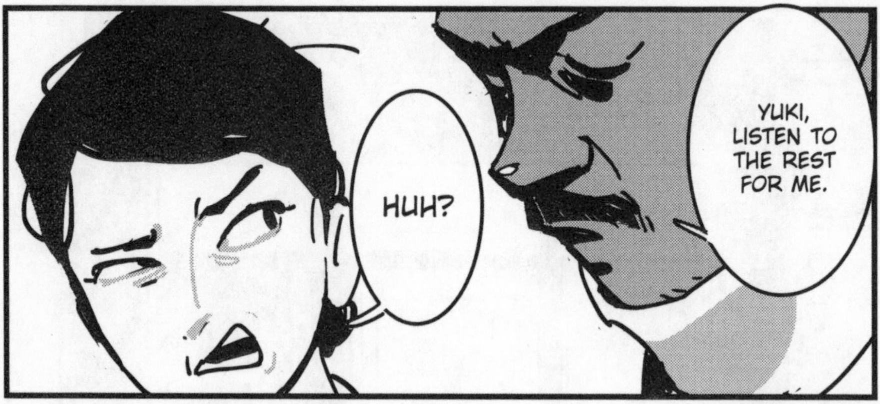
YUKI, LISTEN TO THE REST FOR ME.
HUH?

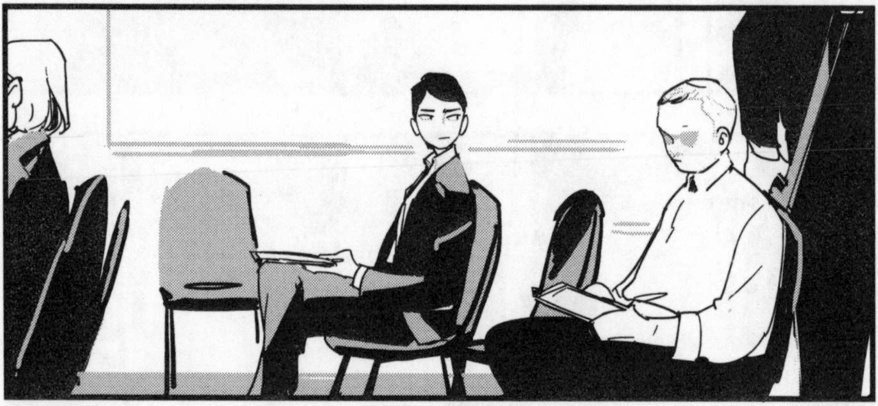

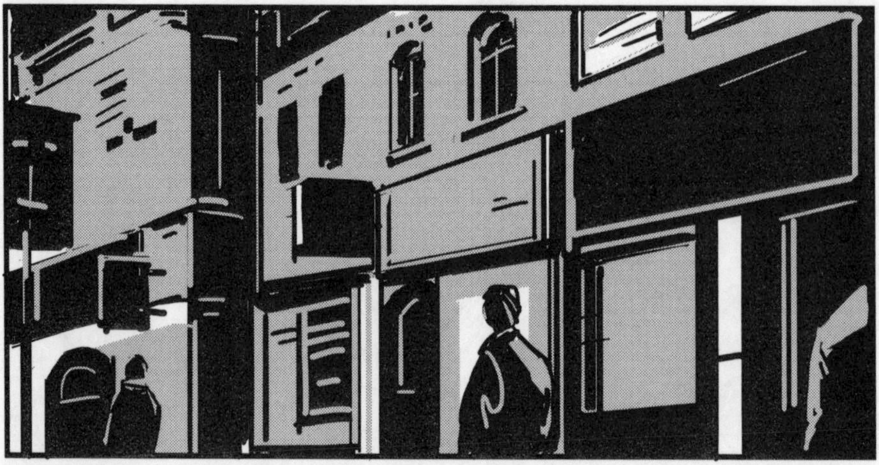

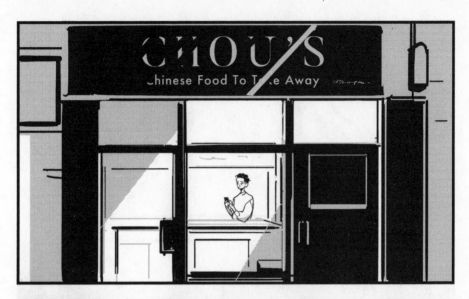

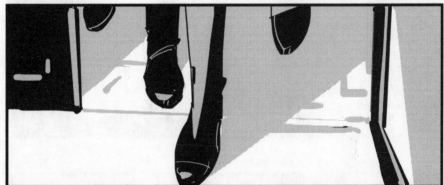

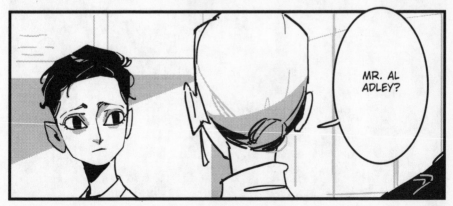

MR. AL ADLEY?

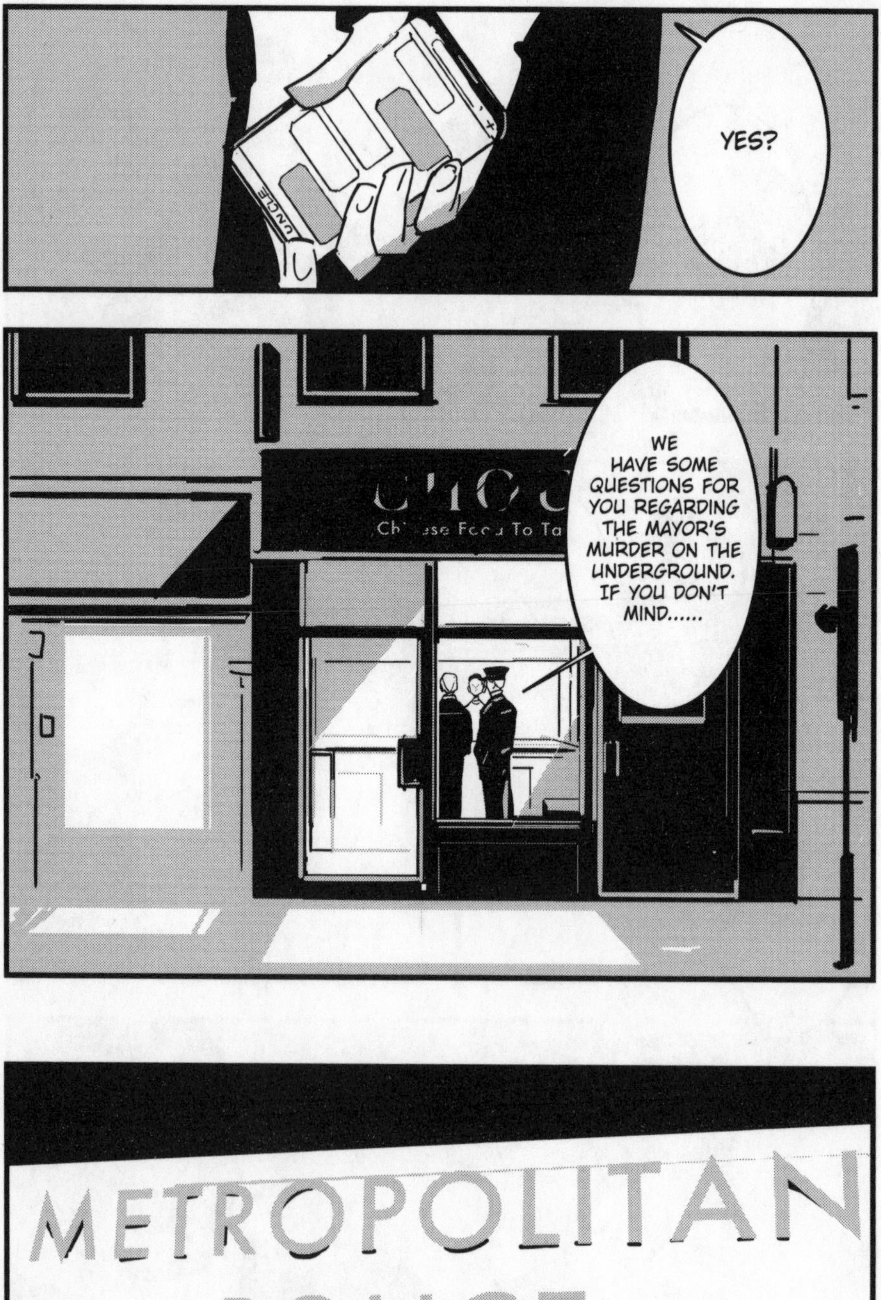
YES?
WE HAVE SOME QUESTIONS FOR YOU REGARDING THE MAYOR'S MURDER ON THE UNDERGROUND. IF YOU DON'T MIND......
METROPOLITAN
POLICE

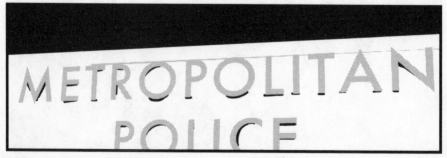

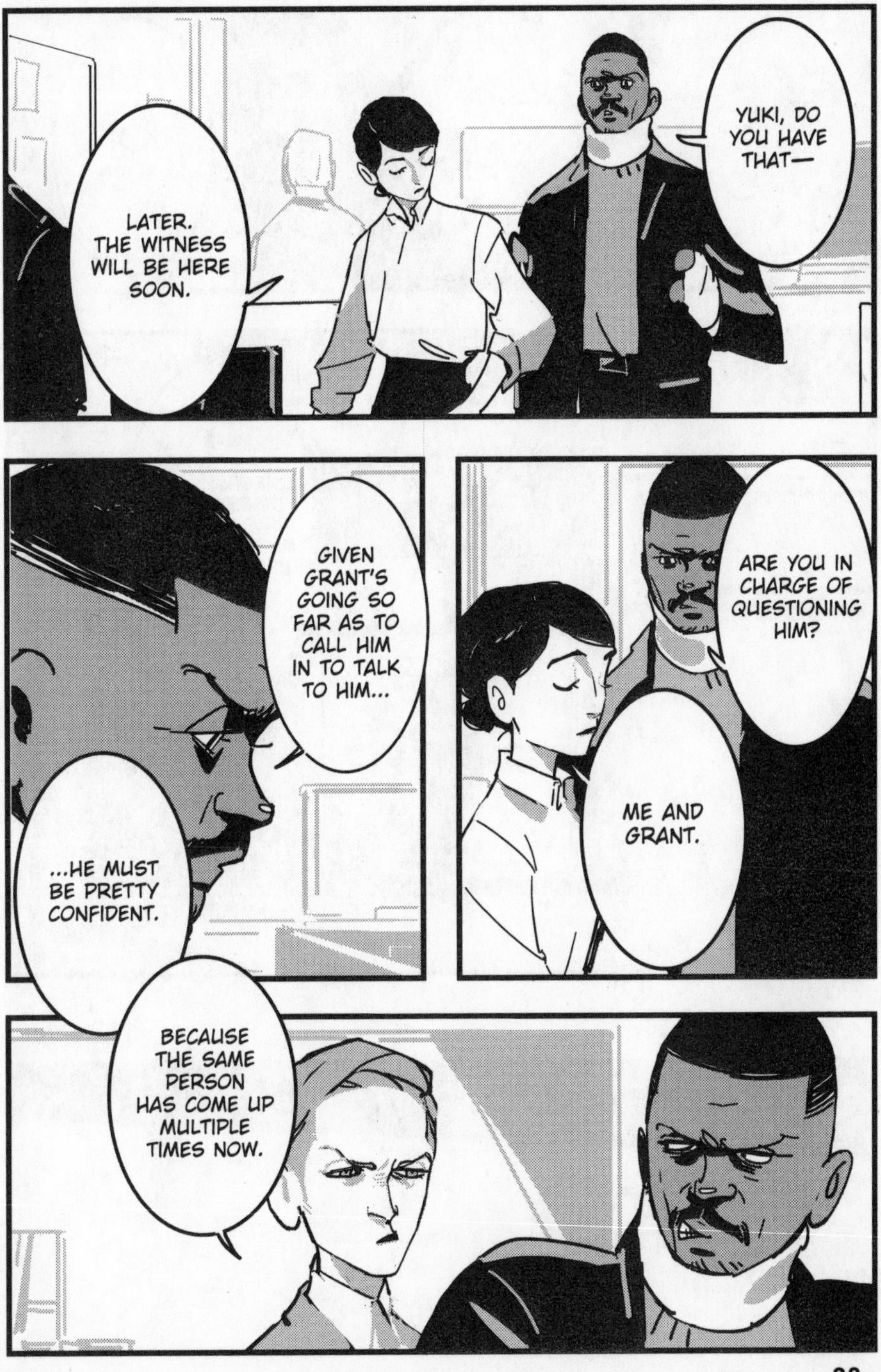
YUKI, DO YOU HAVE THAT—
LATER. THE WITNESS WILL BE HERE SOON.
ARE YOU IN CHARGE OF QUESTIONING HIM?
ME AND GRANT.
GIVEN GRANT'S GOING SO FAR AS TO CALL HIM IN TO TALK TO HIM...
...HE MUST BE PRETTY CONFIDENT.
BECAUSE THE SAME PERSON HAS COME UP MULTIPLE TIMES NOW.

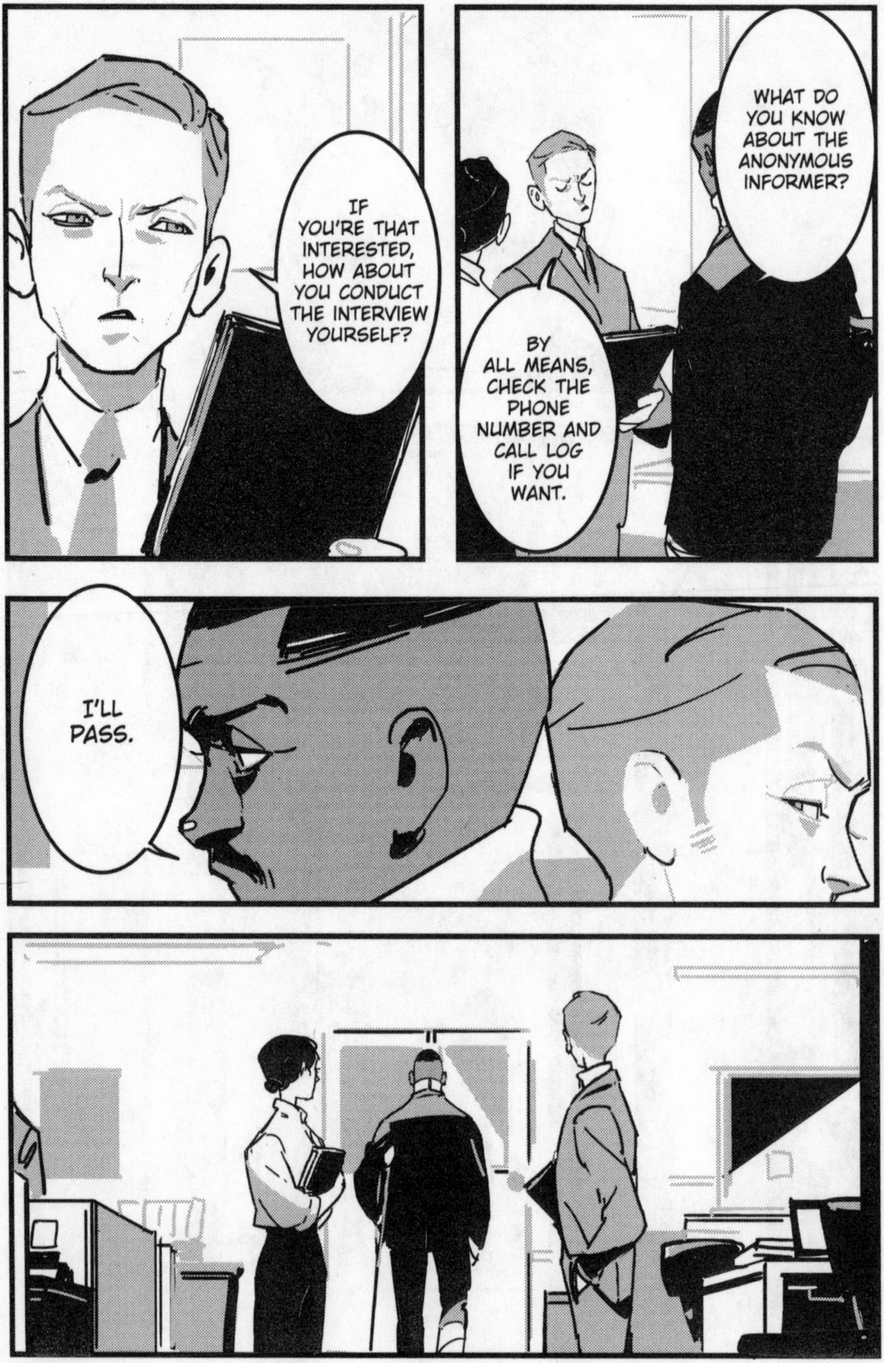
WHAT DO YOU KNOW ABOUT THE ANONYMOUS INFORMER?
BY ALL MEANS, CHECK THE PHONE NUMBER AND CALL LOG IF YOU WANT.
IF YOU'RE THAT INTERESTED, HOW ABOUT YOU CONDUCT THE INTERVIEW YOURSELF?
I'LL PASS.

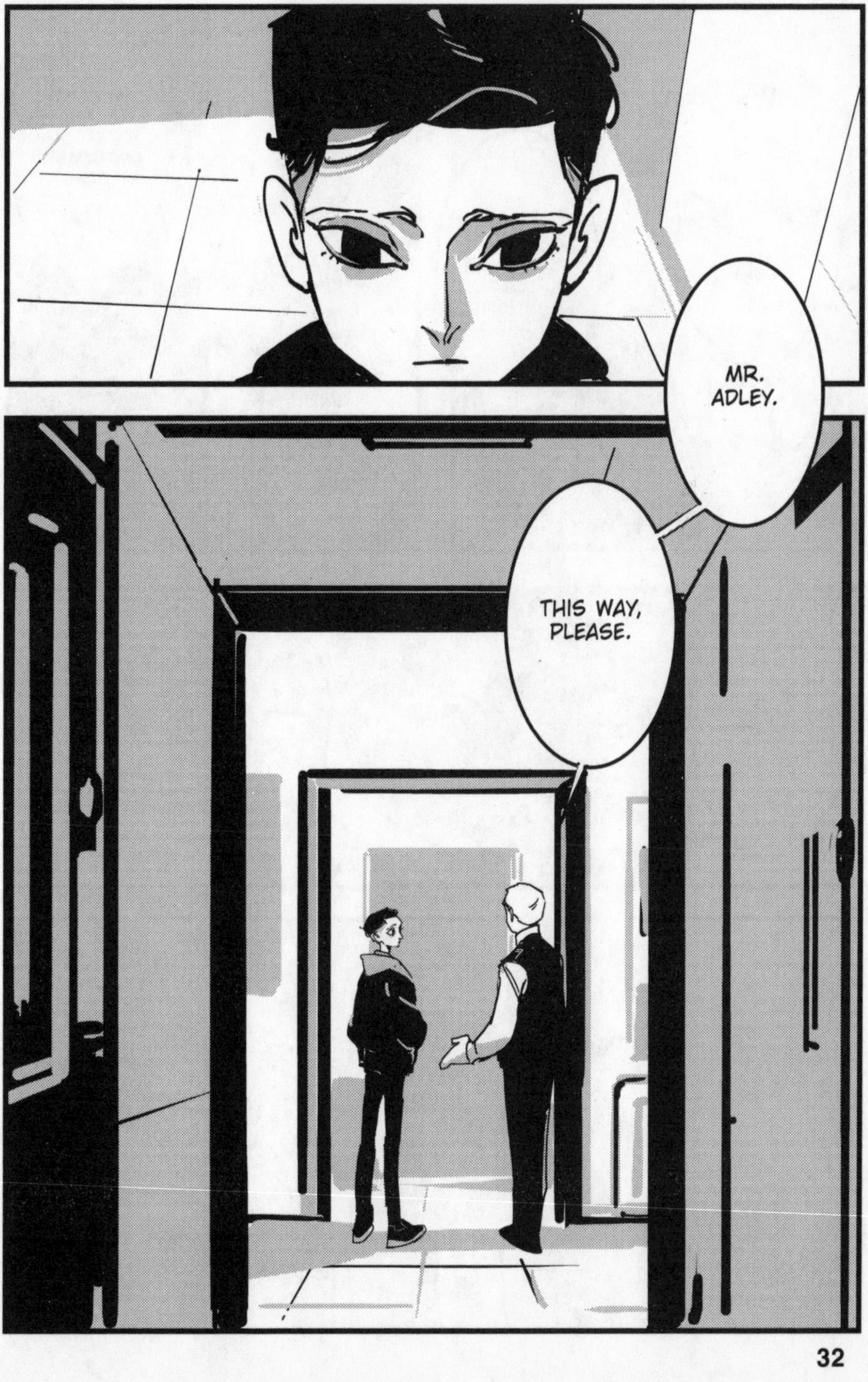
MR. ADLEY.
THIS WAY, PLEASE.

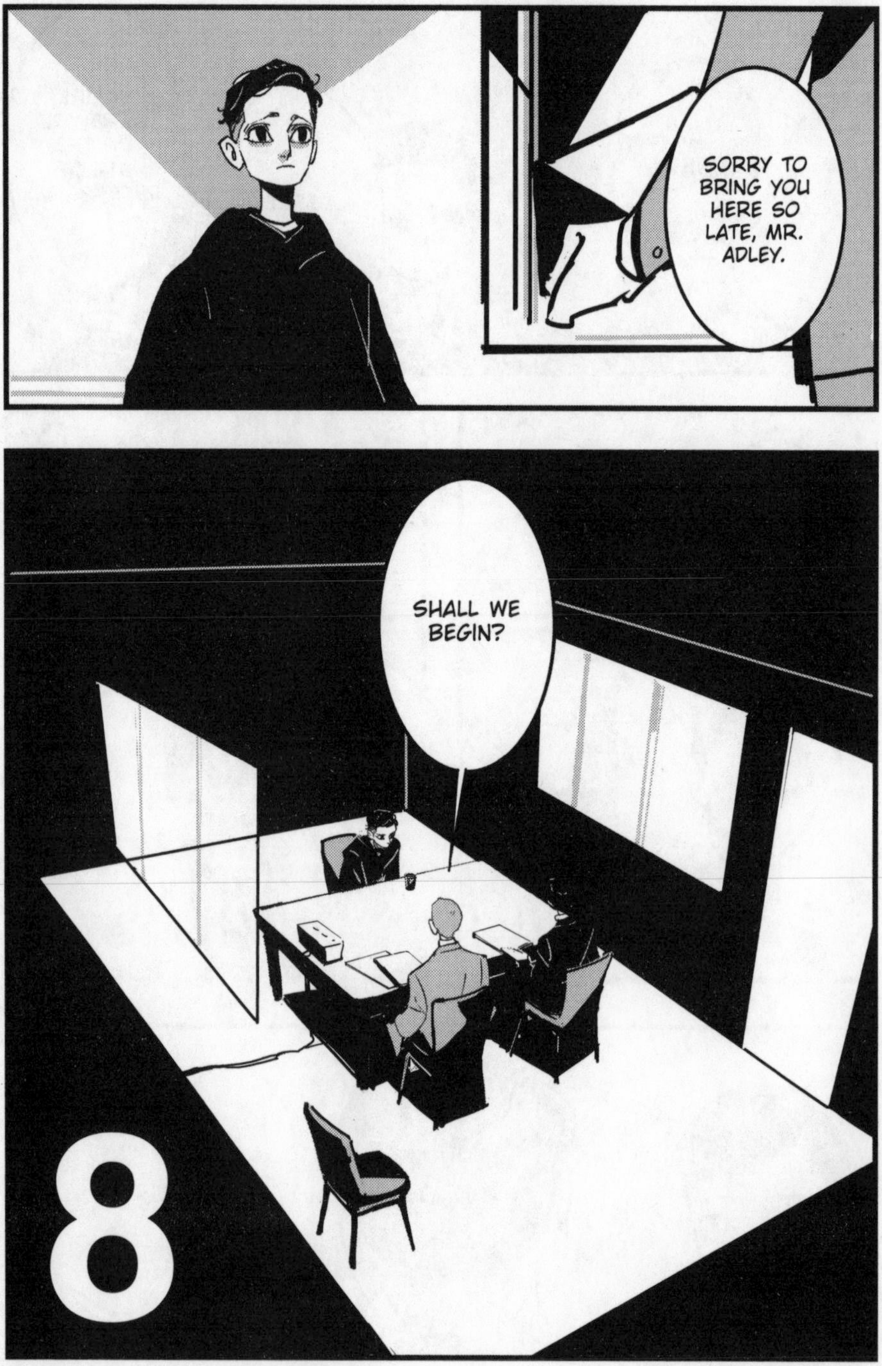
SORRY TO BRING YOU HERE SO LATE, MR. ADLEY.
SHALL WE BEGIN?
8

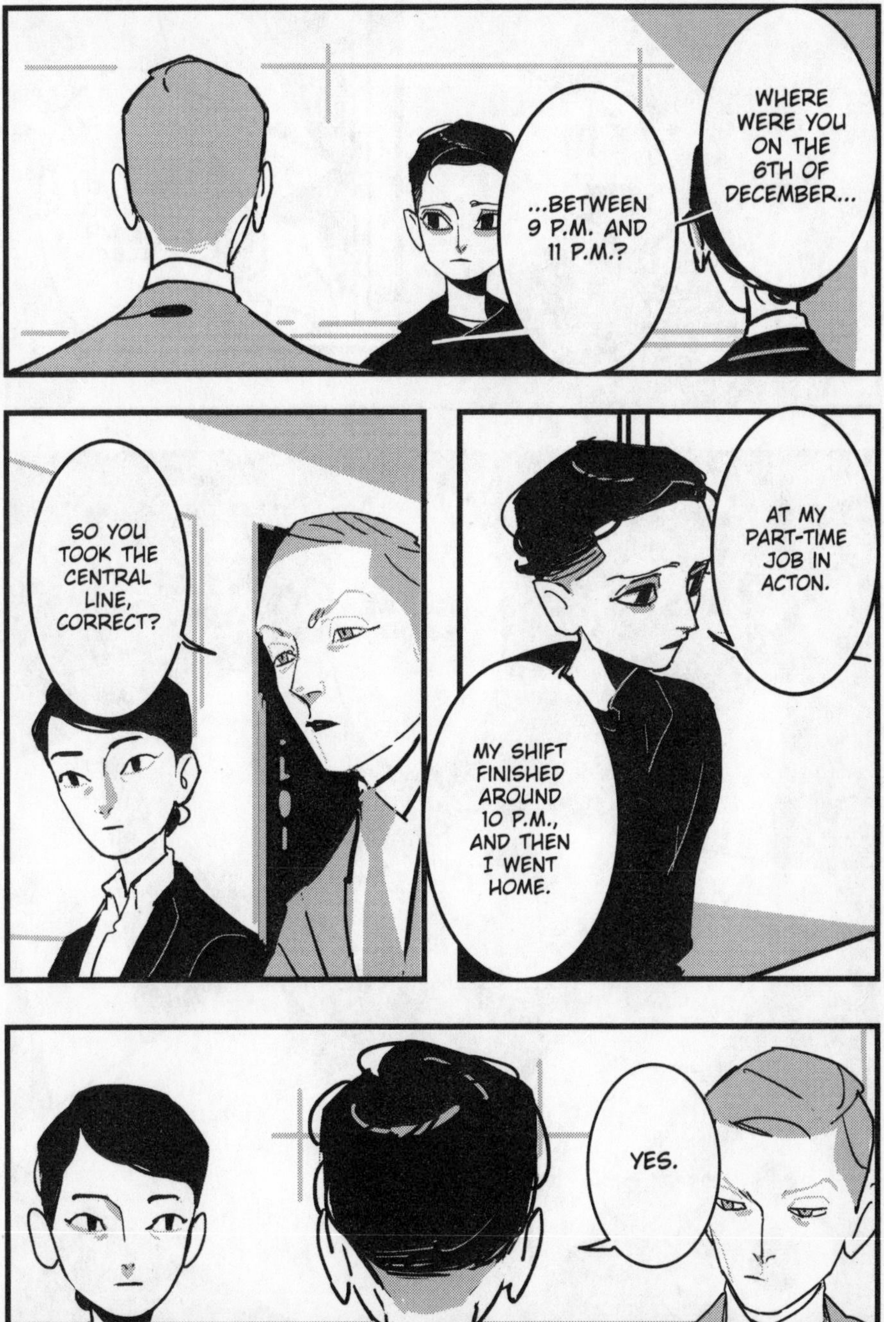
WHERE WERE YOU ON THE 6TH OF DECEMBER...
...BETWEEN 9 P.M. AND 11 P.M.?
AT MY PART-TIME JOB IN ACTON.
MY SHIFT FINISHED AROUND 10 P.M., AND THEN I WENT HOME.
SO YOU TOOK THE CENTRAL LINE, CORRECT?
YES.

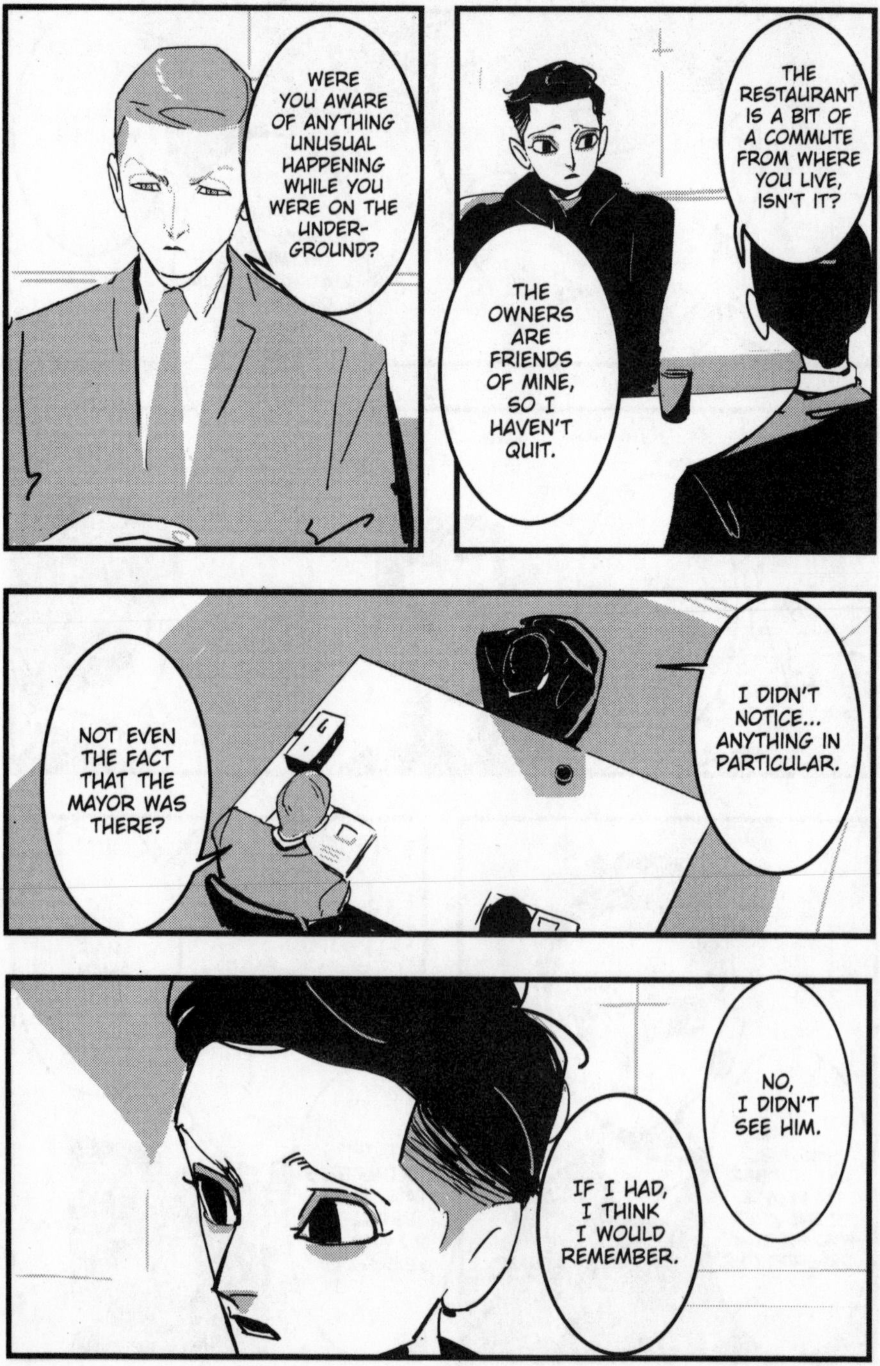
THE RESTAURANT IS A BIT OF A COMMUTE FROM WHERE YOU LIVE, ISN'T IT?
THE OWNERS ARE FRIENDS OF MINE, SO I HAVEN'T QUIT.
WERE YOU AWARE OF ANYTHING UNUSUAL HAPPENING WHILE YOU WERE ON THE UNDER-GROUND?
I DIDN'T NOTICE... ANYTHING IN PARTICULAR.
NOT EVEN THE FACT THAT THE MAYOR WAS THERE?
NO, I DIDN'T SEE HIM.
IF I HAD, I THINK I WOULD REMEMBER.

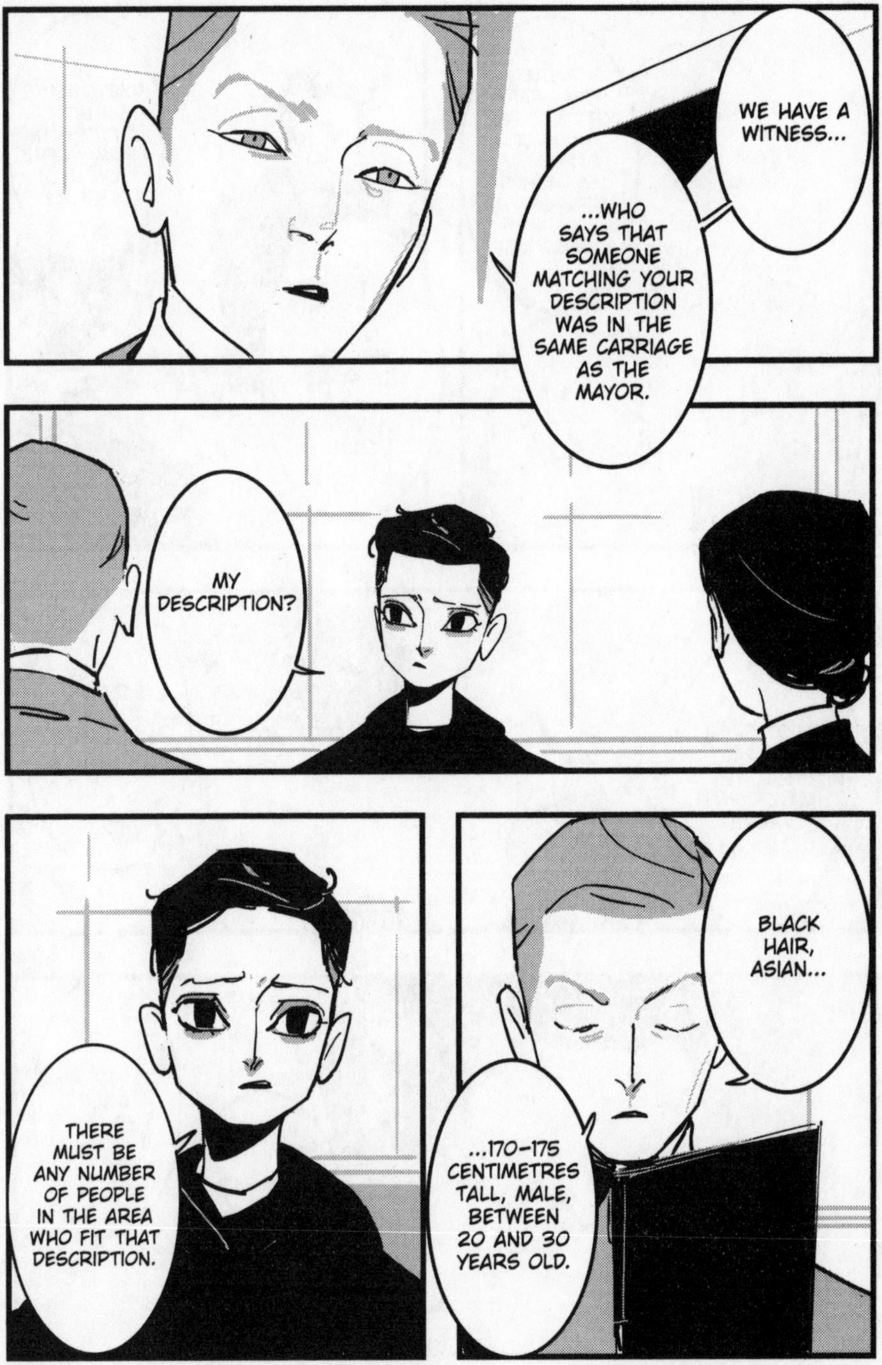
WE HAVE A WITNESS...
...WHO SAYS THAT SOMEONE MATCHING YOUR DESCRIPTION WAS IN THE SAME CARRIAGE AS THE MAYOR.
MY DESCRIPTION?
BLACK HAIR, ASIAN...
...170–175 CENTIMETRES TALL, MALE, BETWEEN 20 AND 30 YEARS OLD.
THERE MUST BE ANY NUMBER OF PEOPLE IN THE AREA WHO FIT THAT DESCRIPTION.

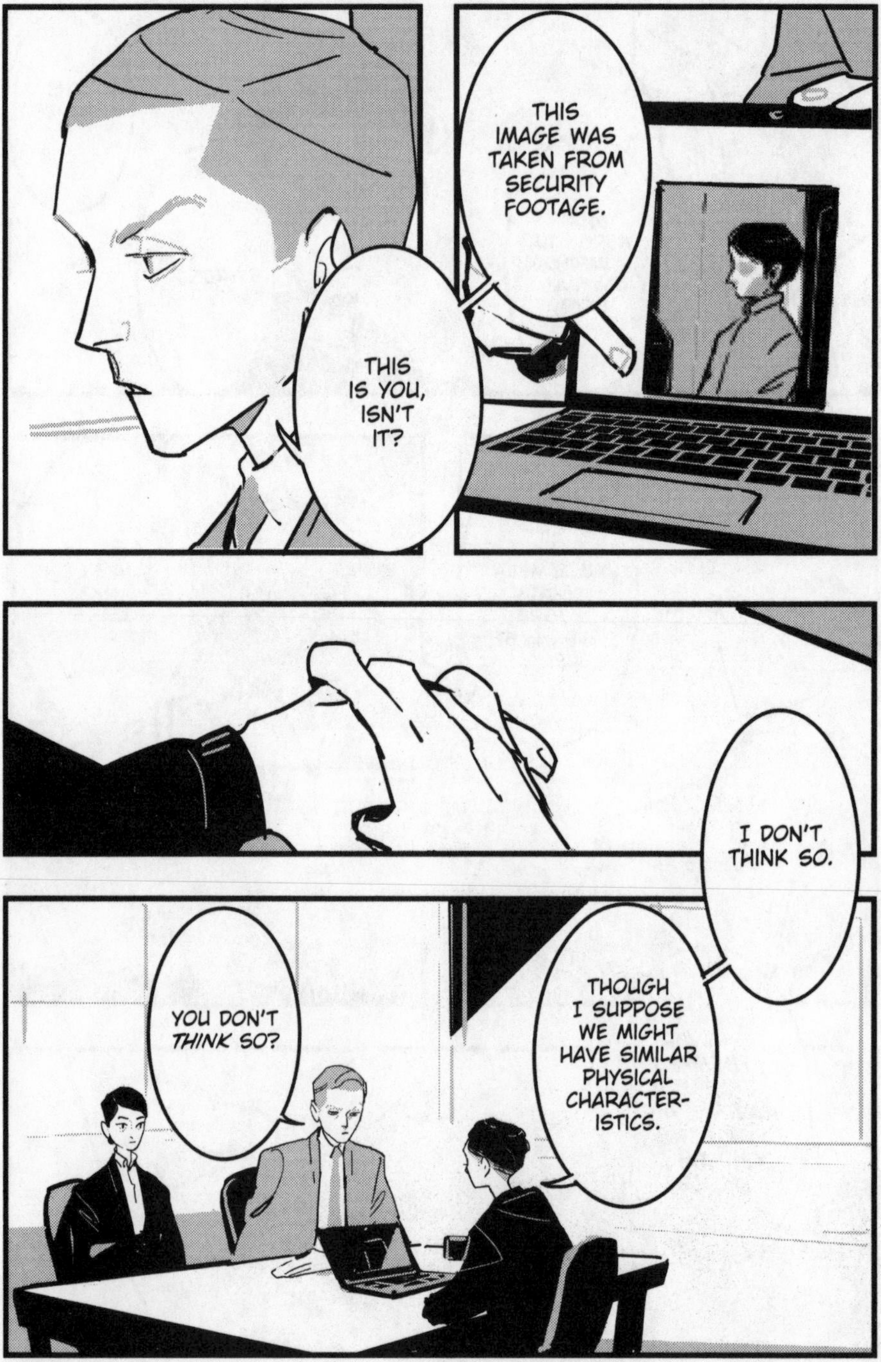
THIS IMAGE WAS TAKEN FROM SECURITY FOOTAGE.
THIS IS YOU, ISN'T IT?
I DON'T THINK SO.
THOUGH I SUPPOSE WE MIGHT HAVE SIMILAR PHYSICAL CHARACTER-ISTICS.
YOU DON'T *THINK* SO?

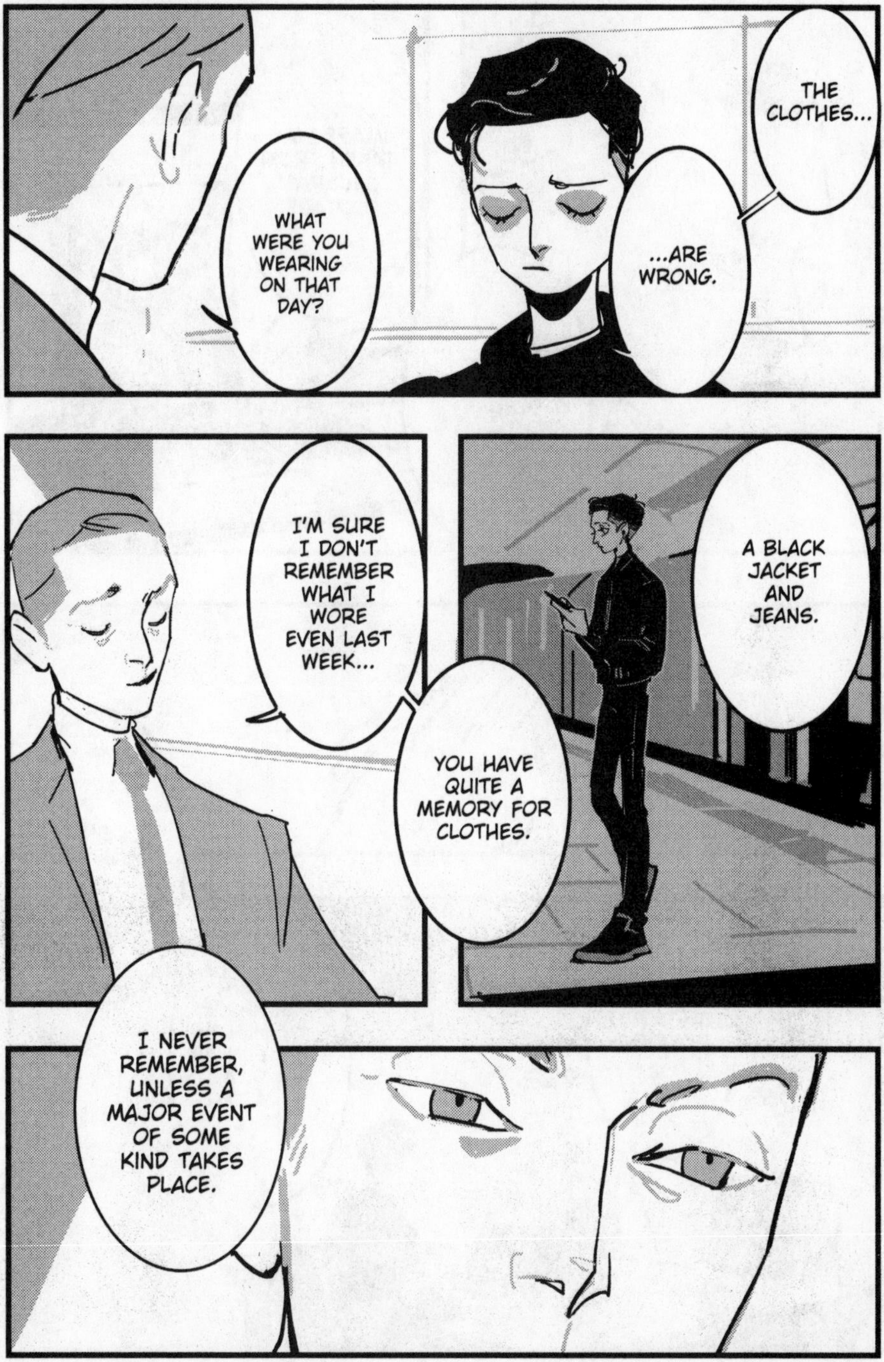
THE CLOTHES...
...ARE WRONG.
WHAT WERE YOU WEARING ON THAT DAY?
A BLACK JACKET AND JEANS.
YOU HAVE QUITE A MEMORY FOR CLOTHES.
I'M SURE I DON'T REMEMBER WHAT I WORE EVEN LAST WEEK...
I NEVER REMEMBER, UNLESS A MAJOR EVENT OF SOME KIND TAKES PLACE.

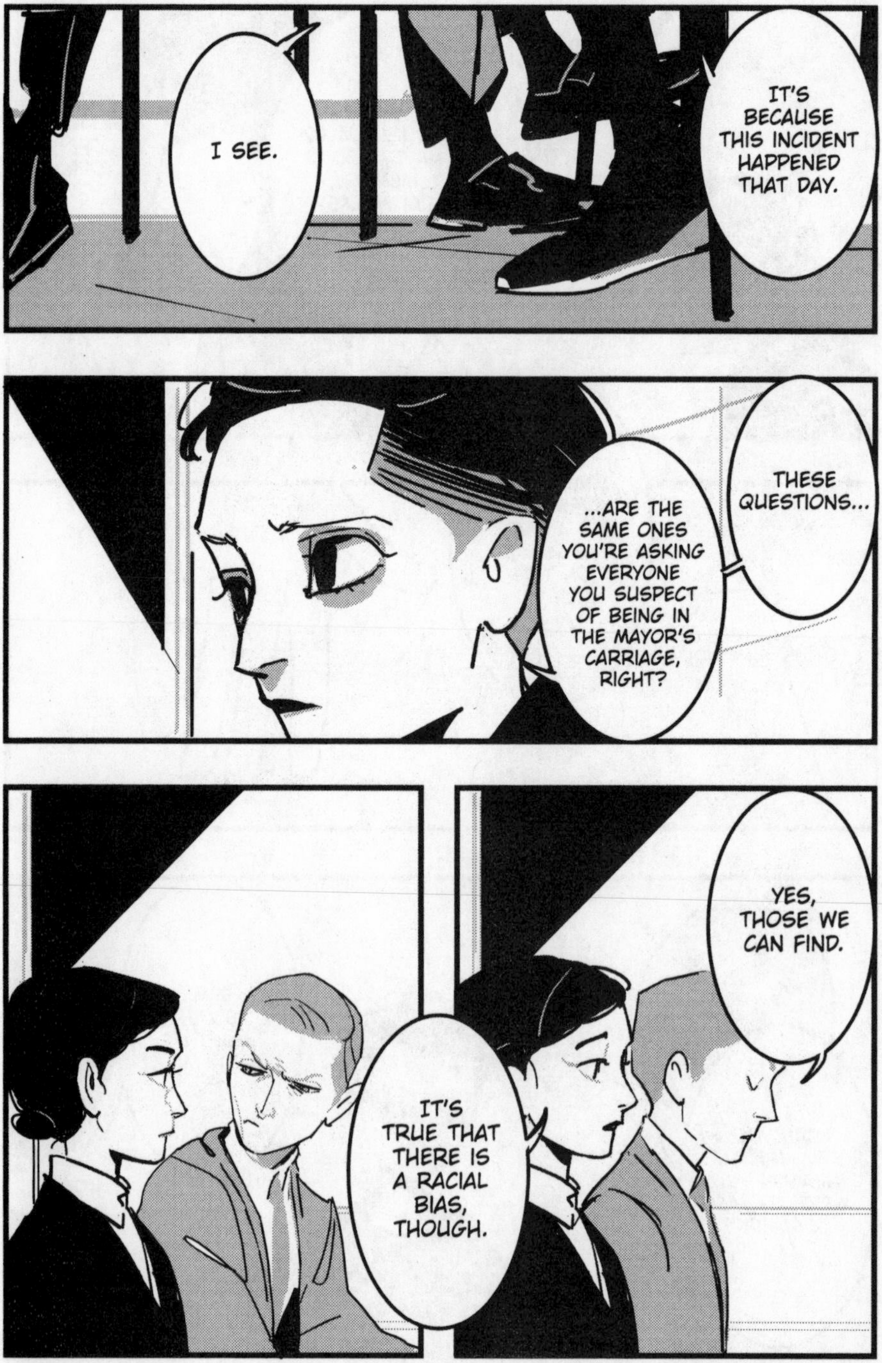
IT'S BECAUSE THIS INCIDENT HAPPENED THAT DAY.
I SEE.
THESE QUESTIONS...
...ARE THE SAME ONES YOU'RE ASKING EVERYONE YOU SUSPECT OF BEING IN THE MAYOR'S CARRIAGE, RIGHT?
YES, THOSE WE CAN FIND.
IT'S TRUE THAT THERE IS A RACIAL BIAS, THOUGH.

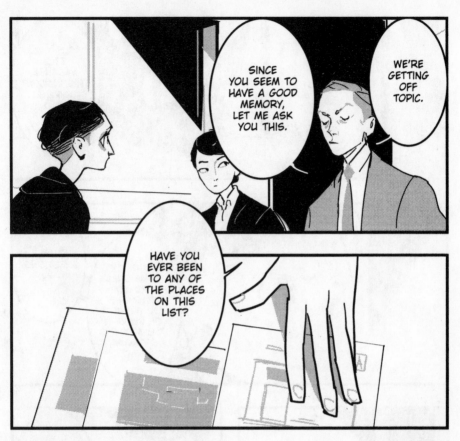

WE'RE GETTING OFF TOPIC.
SINCE YOU SEEM TO HAVE A GOOD MEMORY, LET ME ASK YOU THIS.
HAVE YOU EVER BEEN TO ANY OF THE PLACES ON THIS LIST?
HMM... I RECOGNISE MOST OF THEM.
CAN YOU TELL ME THE REASON YOU WENT TO EACH LOCATION?

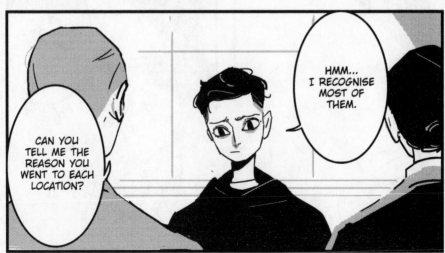

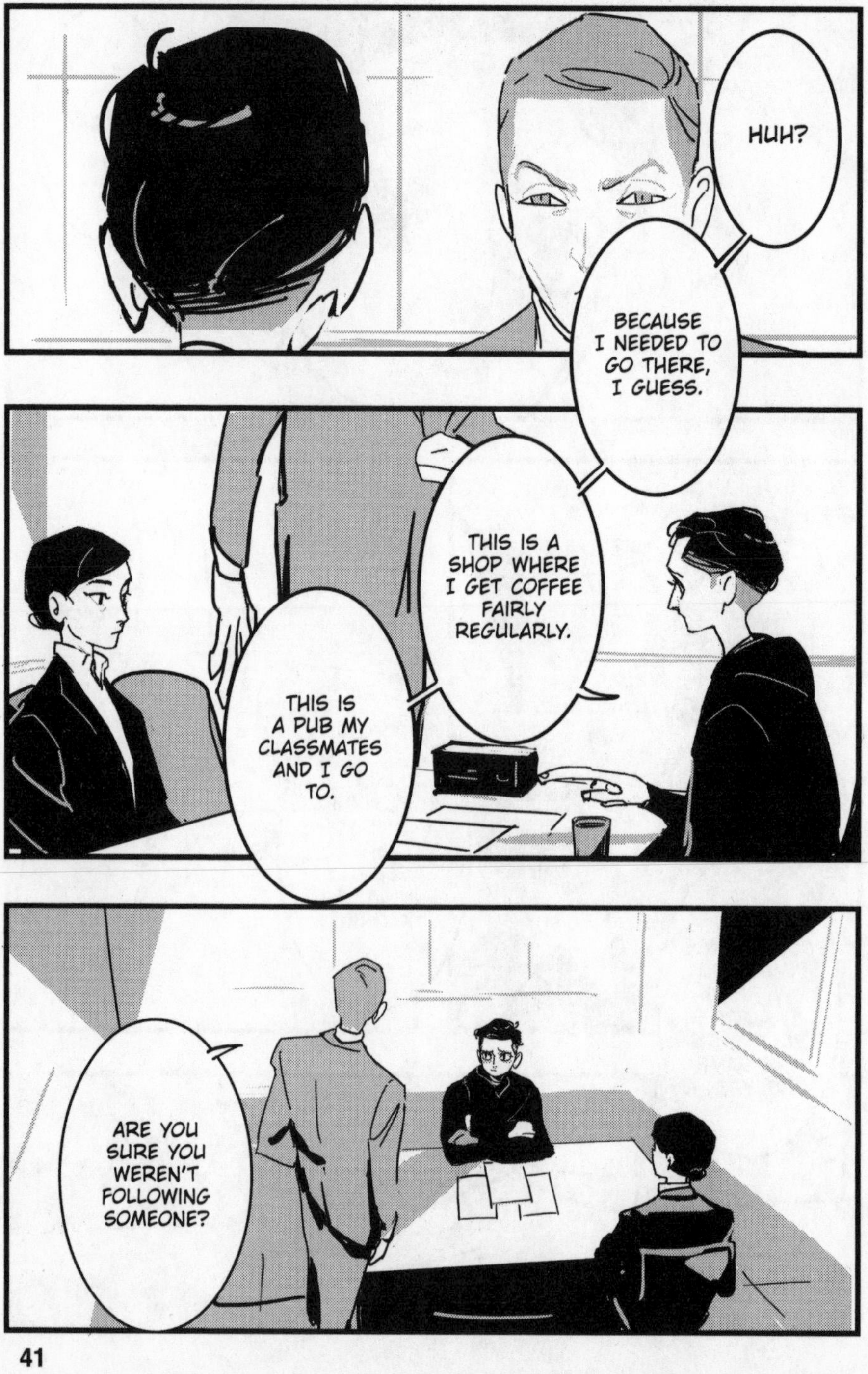
HUH?
BECAUSE I NEEDED TO GO THERE, I GUESS.
THIS IS A SHOP WHERE I GET COFFEE FAIRLY REGULARLY.
THIS IS A PUB MY CLASSMATES AND I GO TO.
ARE YOU SURE YOU WEREN'T FOLLOWING SOMEONE?

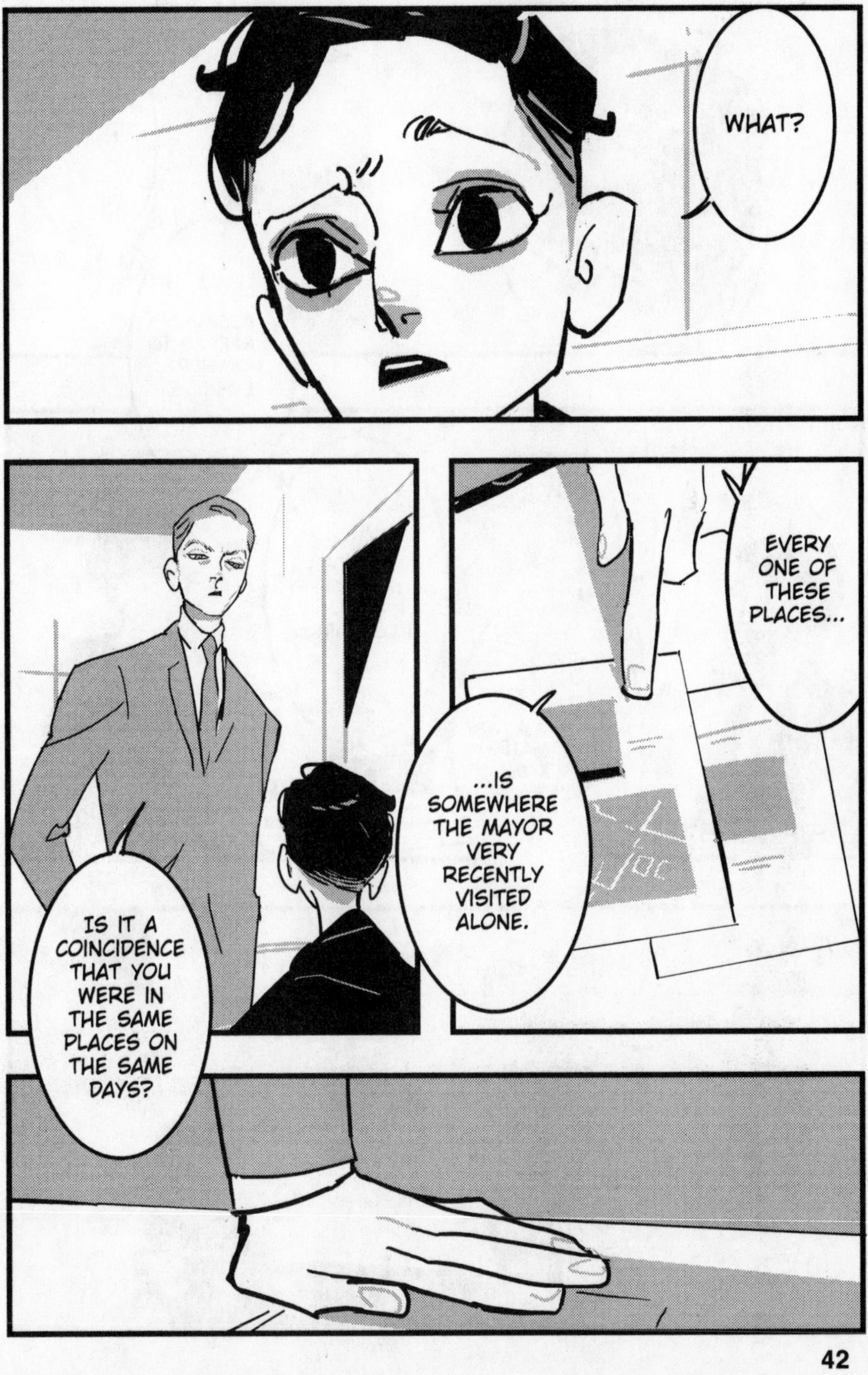
WHAT?
EVERY ONE OF THESE PLACES...
...IS SOMEWHERE THE MAYOR VERY RECENTLY VISITED ALONE.
IS IT A COINCIDENCE THAT YOU WERE IN THE SAME PLACES ON THE SAME DAYS?

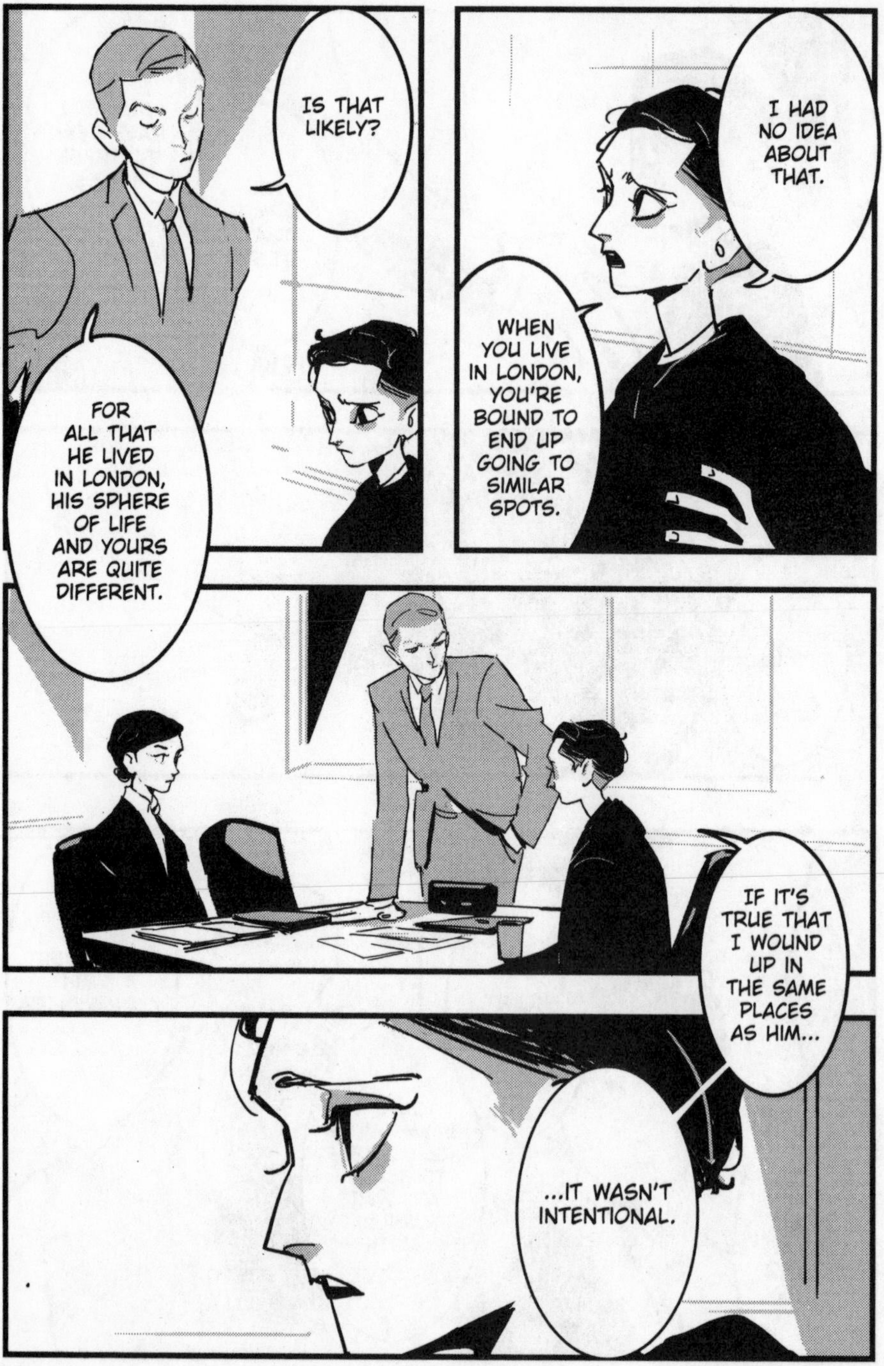
I HAD NO IDEA ABOUT THAT.
WHEN YOU LIVE IN LONDON, YOU'RE BOUND TO END UP GOING TO SIMILAR SPOTS.
IS THAT LIKELY?
FOR ALL THAT HE LIVED IN LONDON, HIS SPHERE OF LIFE AND YOURS ARE QUITE DIFFERENT.
IF IT'S TRUE THAT I WOUND UP IN THE SAME PLACES AS HIM...
...IT WASN'T INTENTIONAL.

BUT YOU HAVE BEEN TO THESE PLACES.
YOU ADMIT THAT, YES?
YES.
WAS IT REALLY JUST A SIMPLE COINCIDENCE?
TO ME, IT SEEMS MORE REASONABLE TO BELIEVE YOU WERE PLANNING SOMETH—
GRANT.
WHY DON'T YOU SIT DOWN?

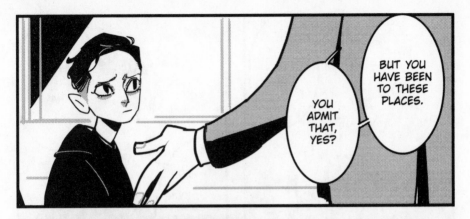

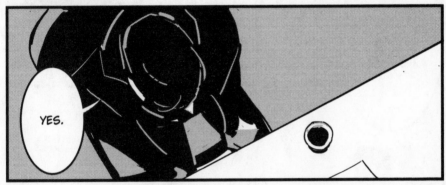

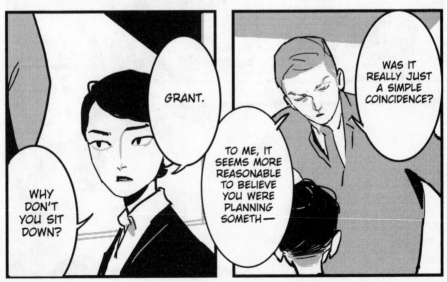

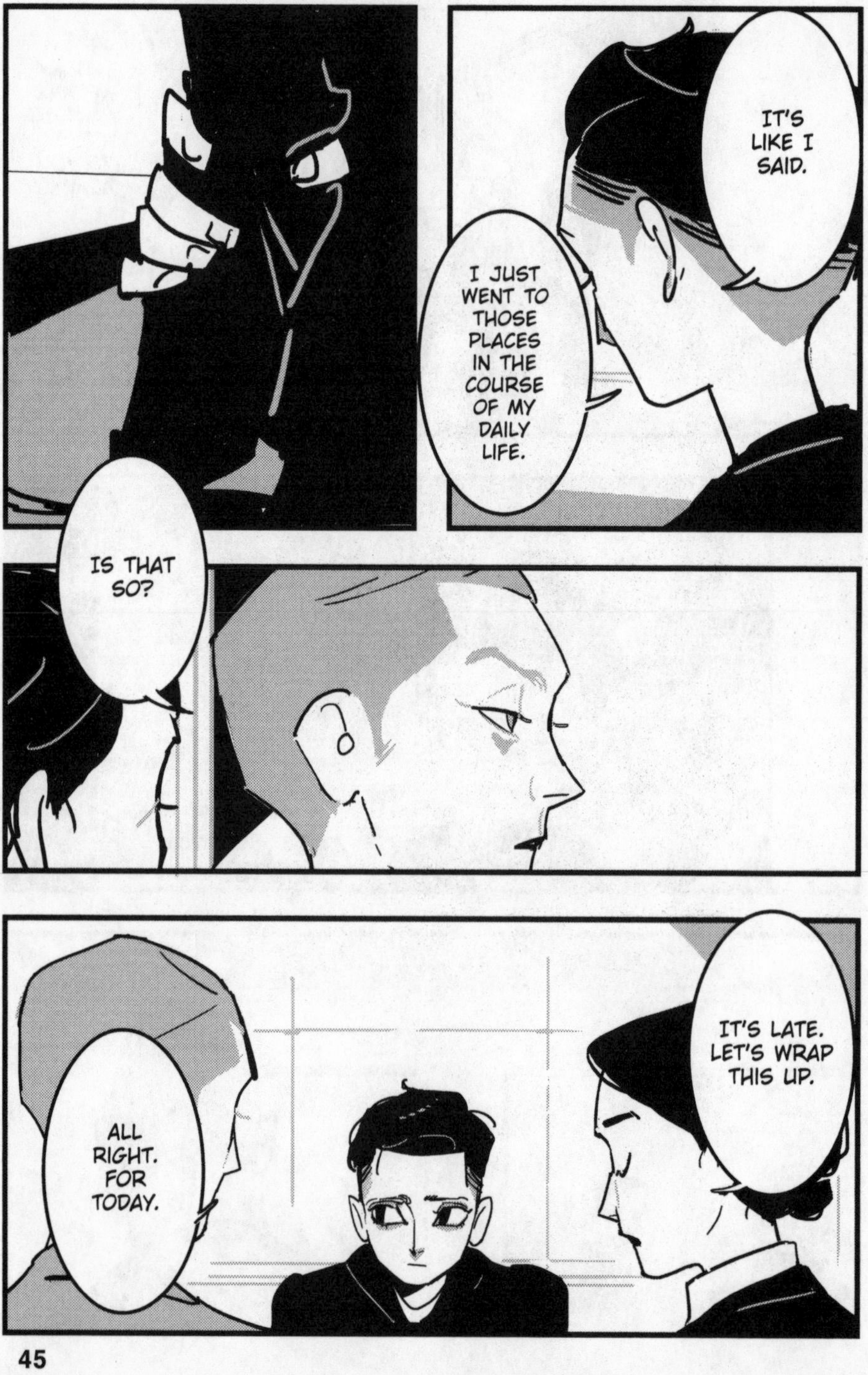
IT'S LIKE I SAID.
I JUST WENT TO THOSE PLACES IN THE COURSE OF MY DAILY LIFE.
IS THAT SO?
IT'S LATE. LET'S WRAP THIS UP.
ALL RIGHT. FOR TODAY.

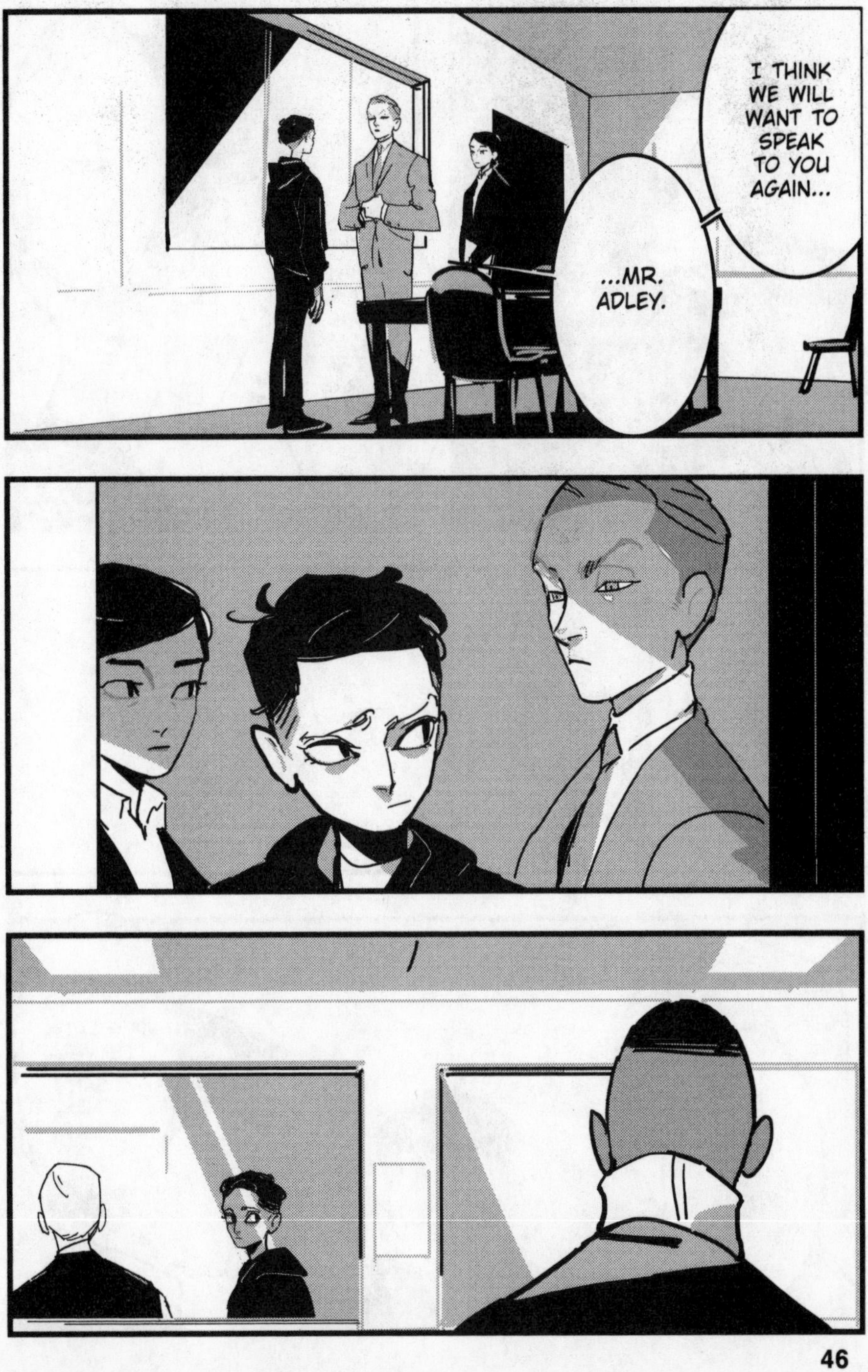
I THINK WE WILL WANT TO SPEAK TO YOU AGAIN...
...MR. ADLEY.

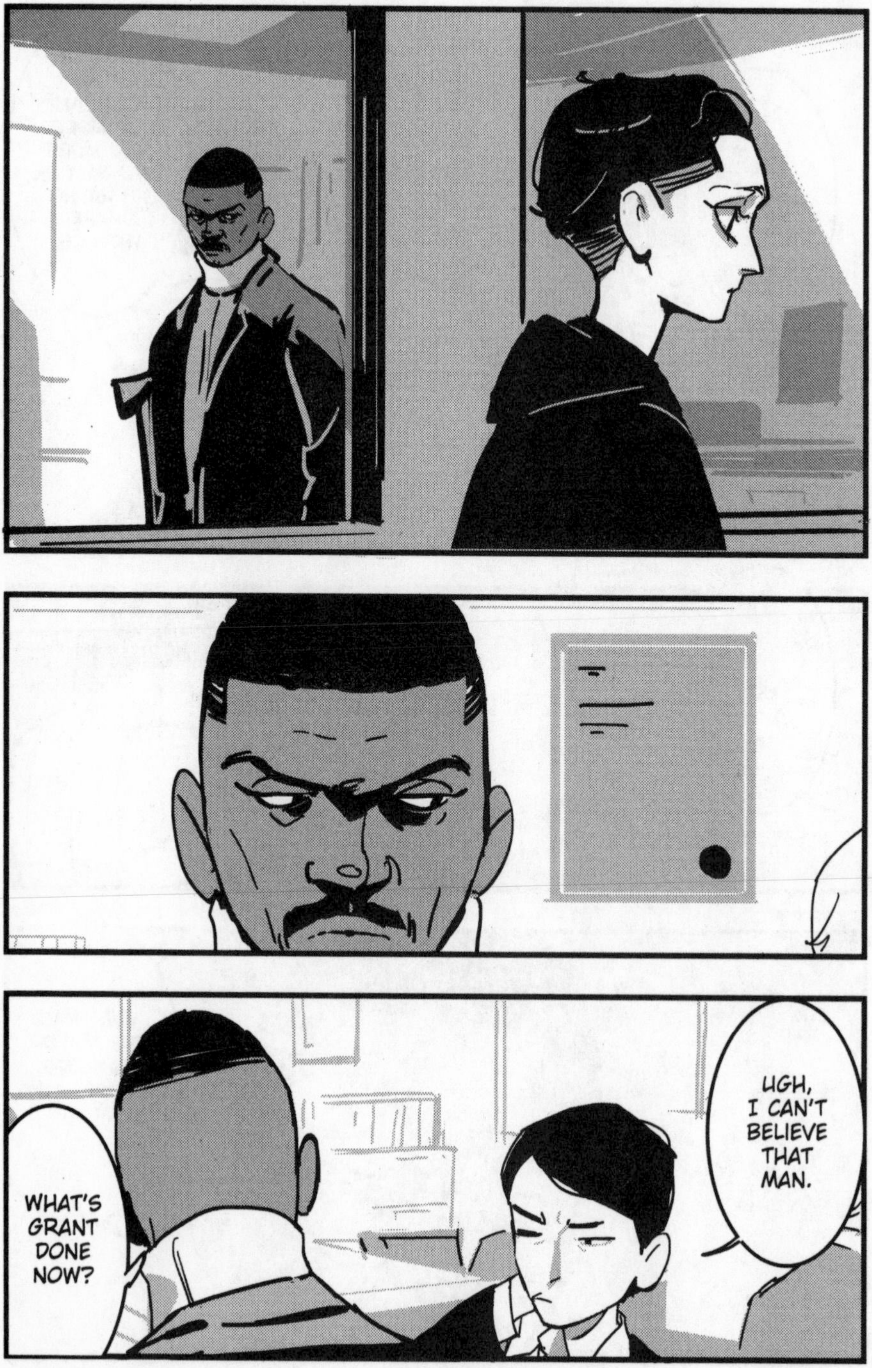
UGH, I CAN'T BELIEVE THAT MAN.
WHAT'S GRANT DONE NOW?

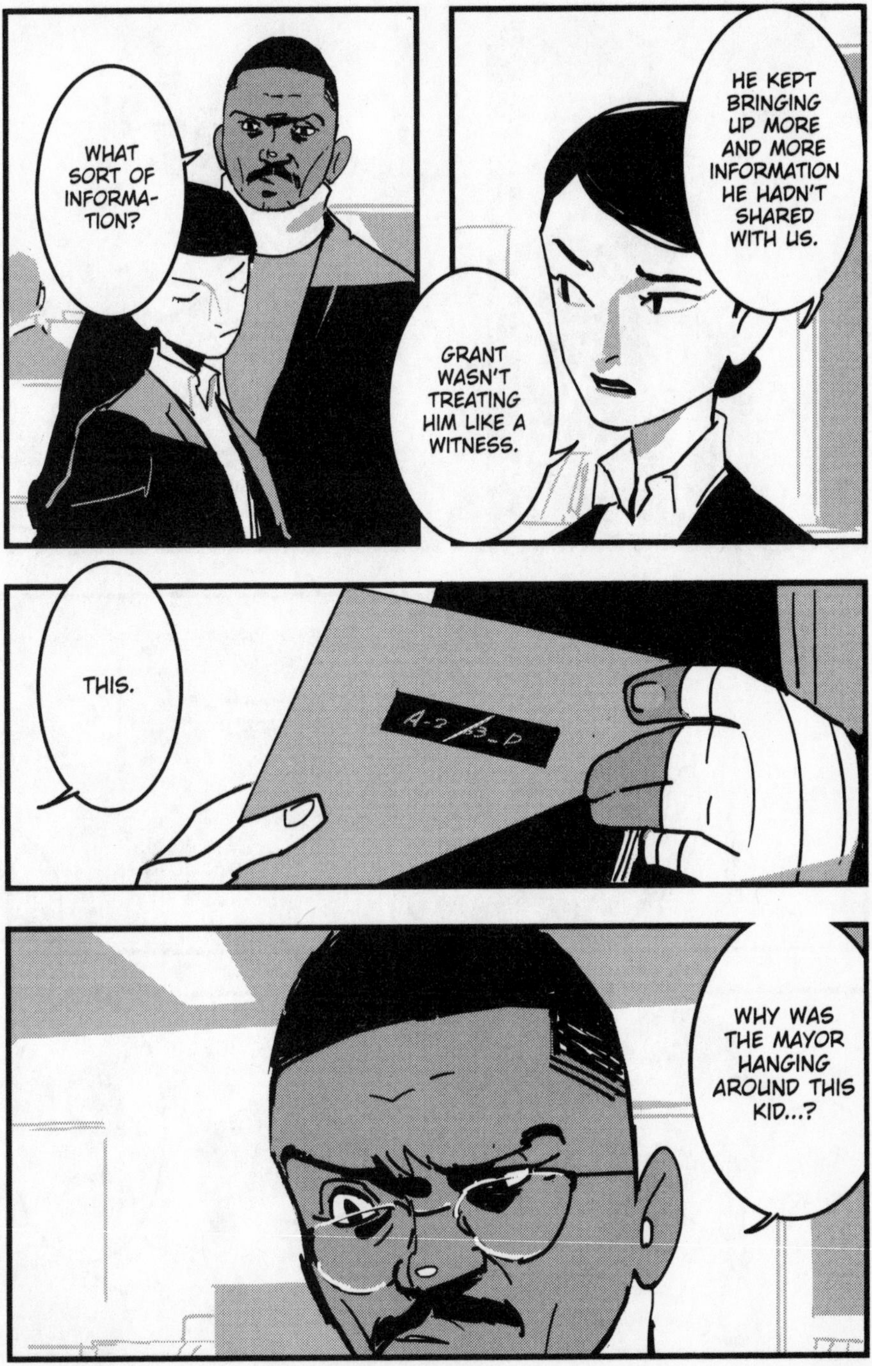
HE KEPT BRINGING UP MORE AND MORE INFORMATION HE HADN'T SHARED WITH US.
GRANT WASN'T TREATING HIM LIKE A WITNESS.
WHAT SORT OF INFORMA-TION?
THIS.
WHY WAS THE MAYOR HANGING AROUND THIS KID...?

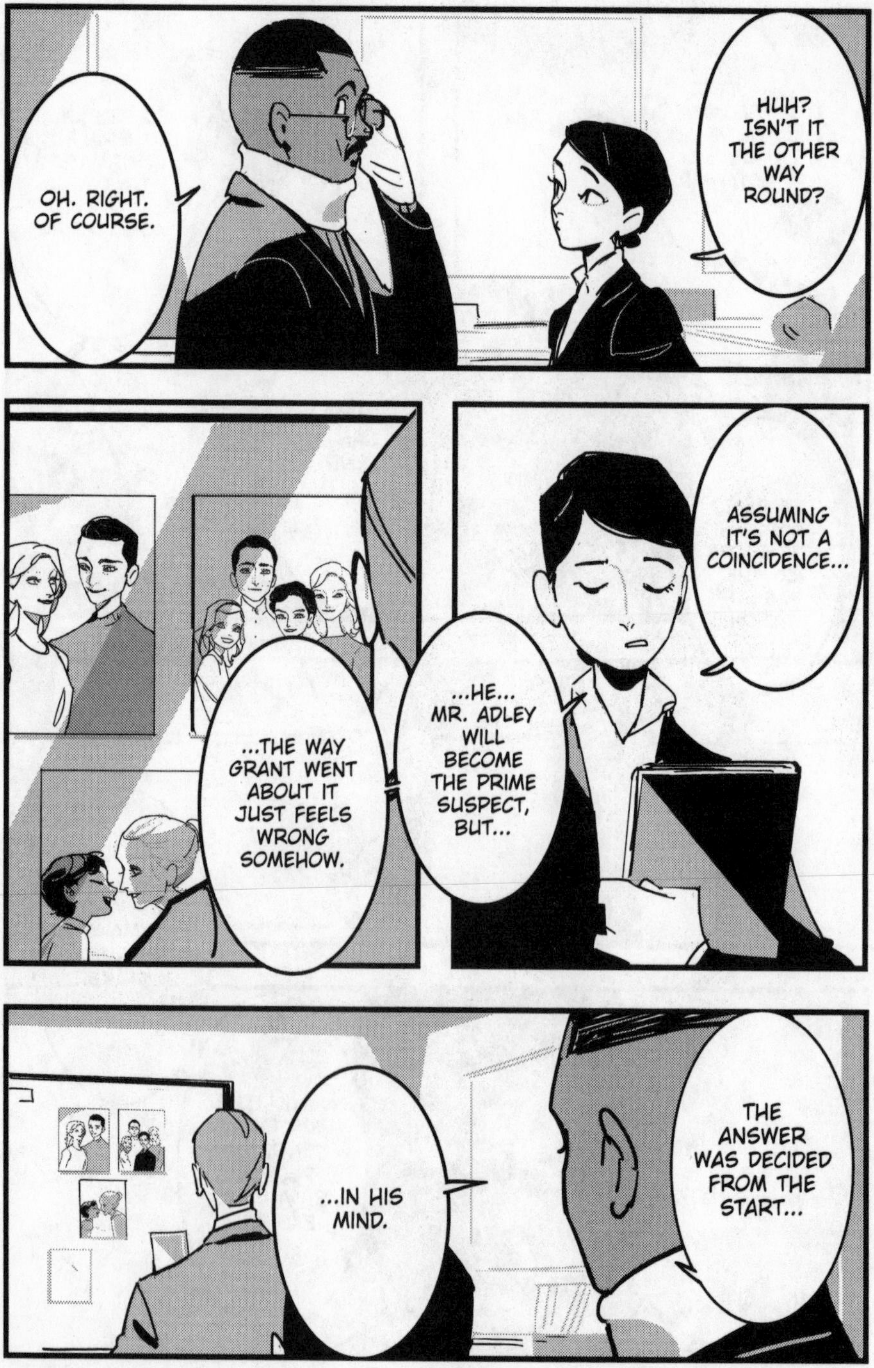
HUH? ISN'T IT THE OTHER WAY ROUND?
OH. RIGHT. OF COURSE.
ASSUMING IT'S NOT A COINCIDENCE...
...HE... MR. ADLEY WILL BECOME THE PRIME SUSPECT, BUT...
...THE WAY GRANT WENT ABOUT IT JUST FEELS WRONG SOMEHOW.
THE ANSWER WAS DECIDED FROM THE START...
...IN HIS MIND.

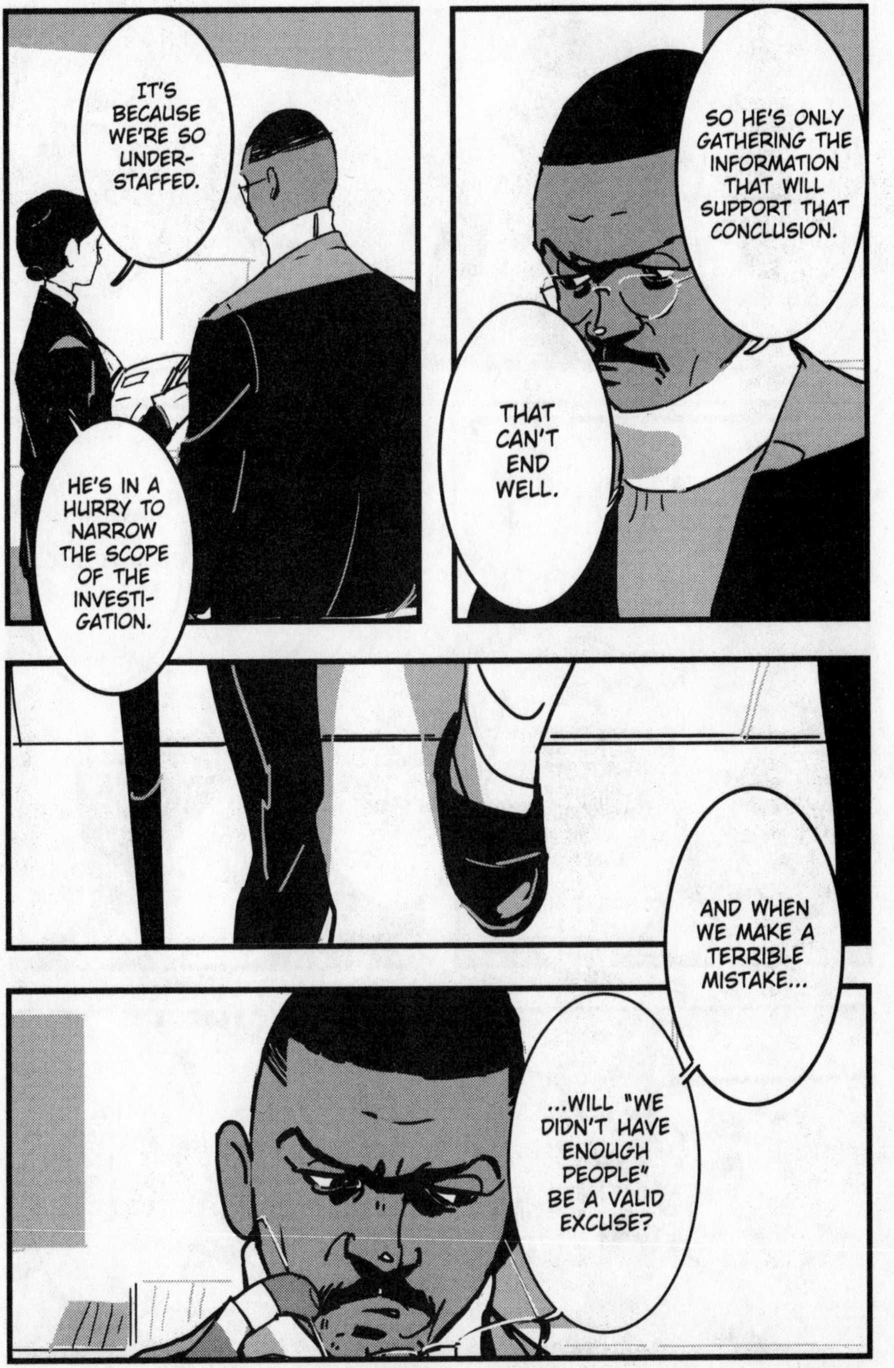
SO HE'S ONLY GATHERING THE INFORMATION THAT WILL SUPPORT THAT CONCLUSION.
THAT CAN'T END WELL.
IT'S BECAUSE WE'RE SO UNDER-STAFFED.
HE'S IN A HURRY TO NARROW THE SCOPE OF THE INVESTI-GATION.
AND WHEN WE MAKE A TERRIBLE MISTAKE...
...WILL "WE DIDN'T HAVE ENOUGH PEOPLE" BE A VALID EXCUSE?

FAIR POINT.
IT'S DANGEROUS TO SEE ONLY THE THINGS YOU WANT TO SEE.
OUR JOB...
...CAN EASILY DESTROY OTHER PEOPLE'S LIVES.

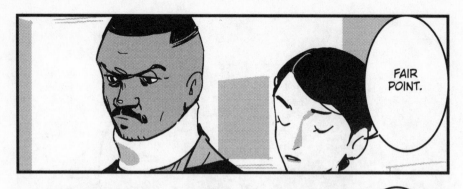

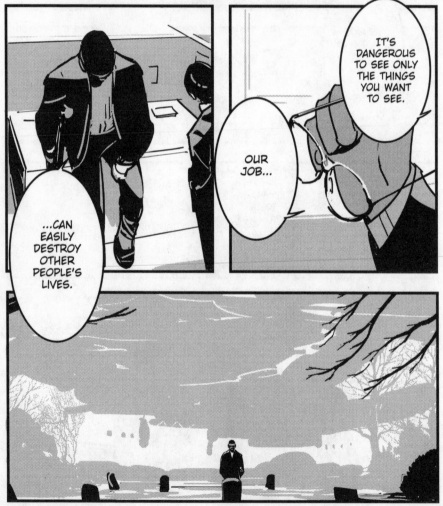

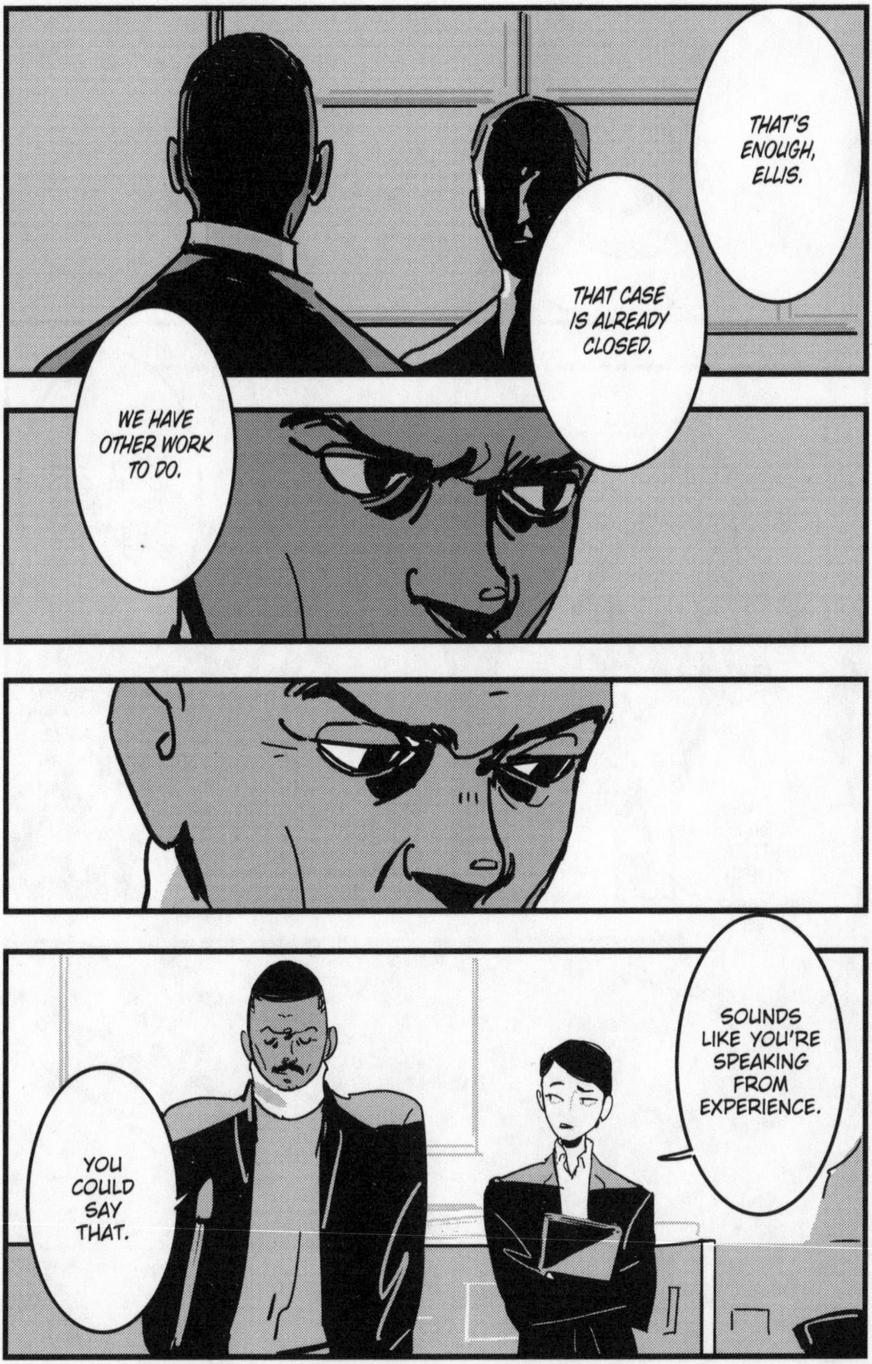
THAT'S ENOUGH, ELLIS.
THAT CASE IS ALREADY CLOSED.
WE HAVE OTHER WORK TO DO.
SOUNDS LIKE YOU'RE SPEAKING FROM EXPERIENCE.
YOU COULD SAY THAT.

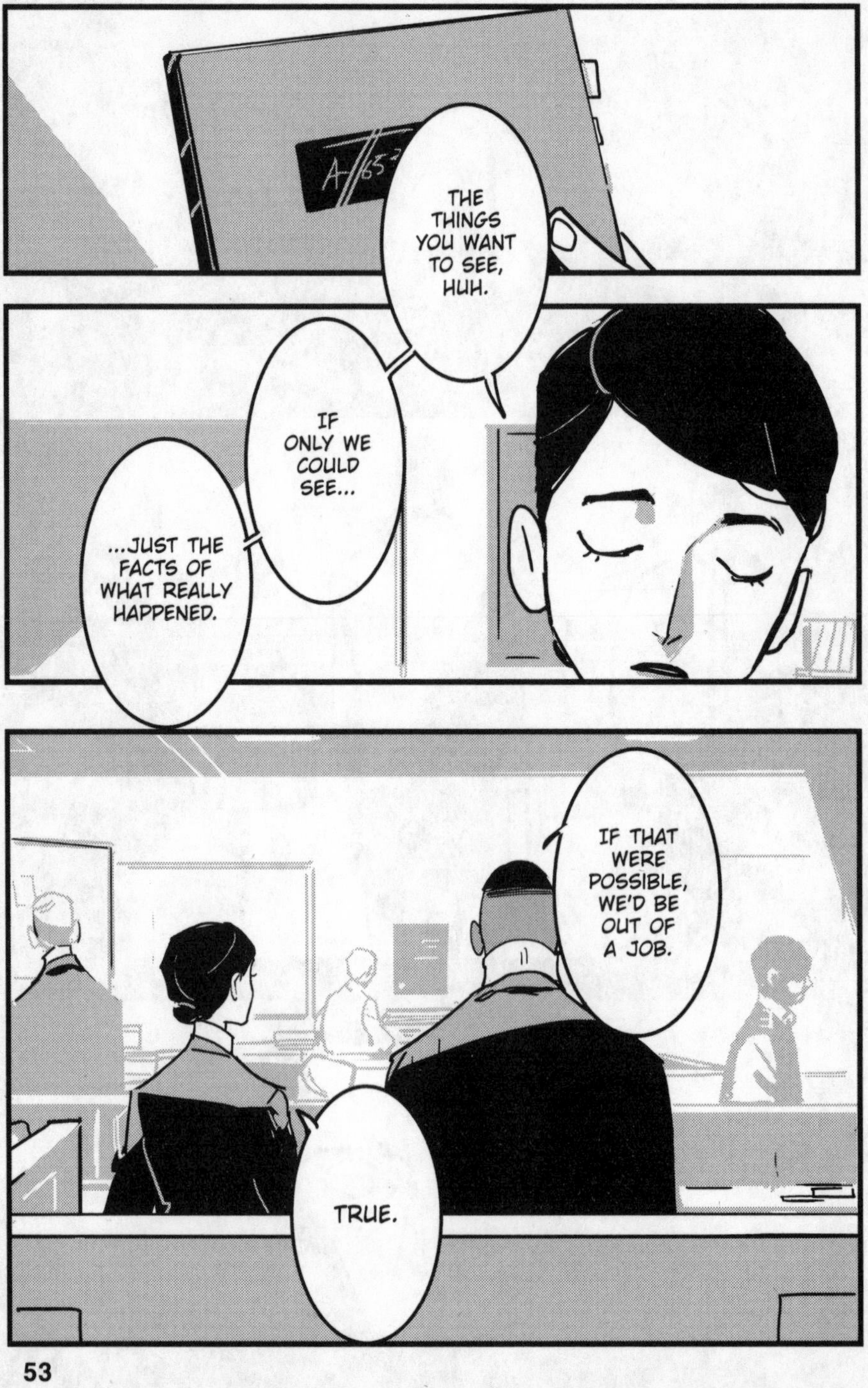
THE THINGS YOU WANT TO SEE, HUH.
IF ONLY WE COULD SEE...
...JUST THE FACTS OF WHAT REALLY HAPPENED.
IF THAT WERE POSSIBLE, WE'D BE OUT OF A JOB.
TRUE.

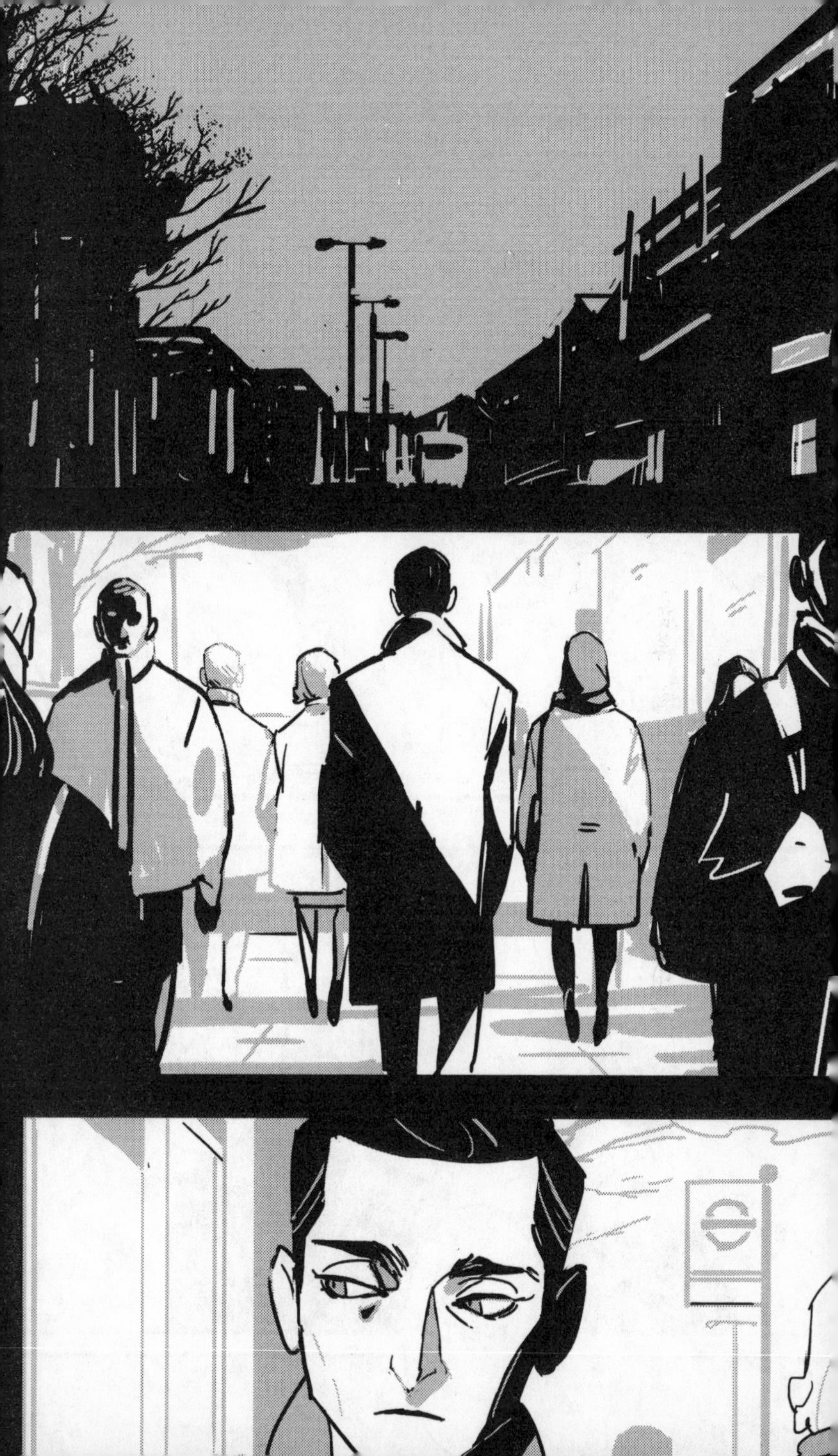

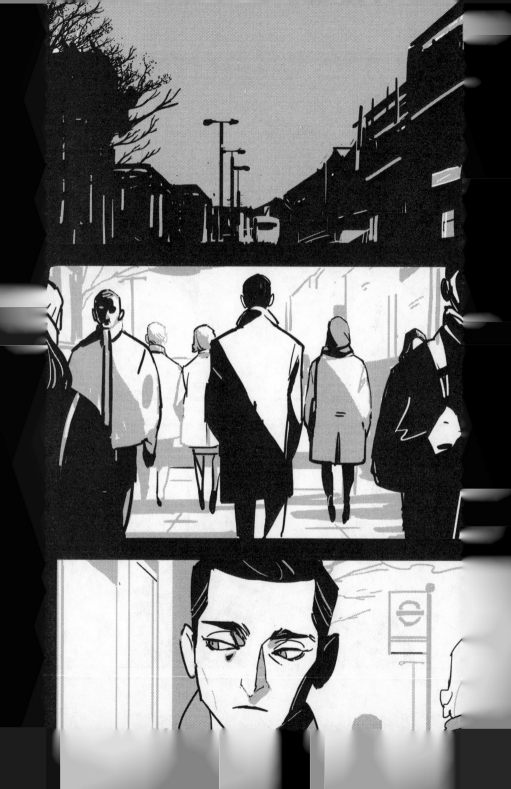

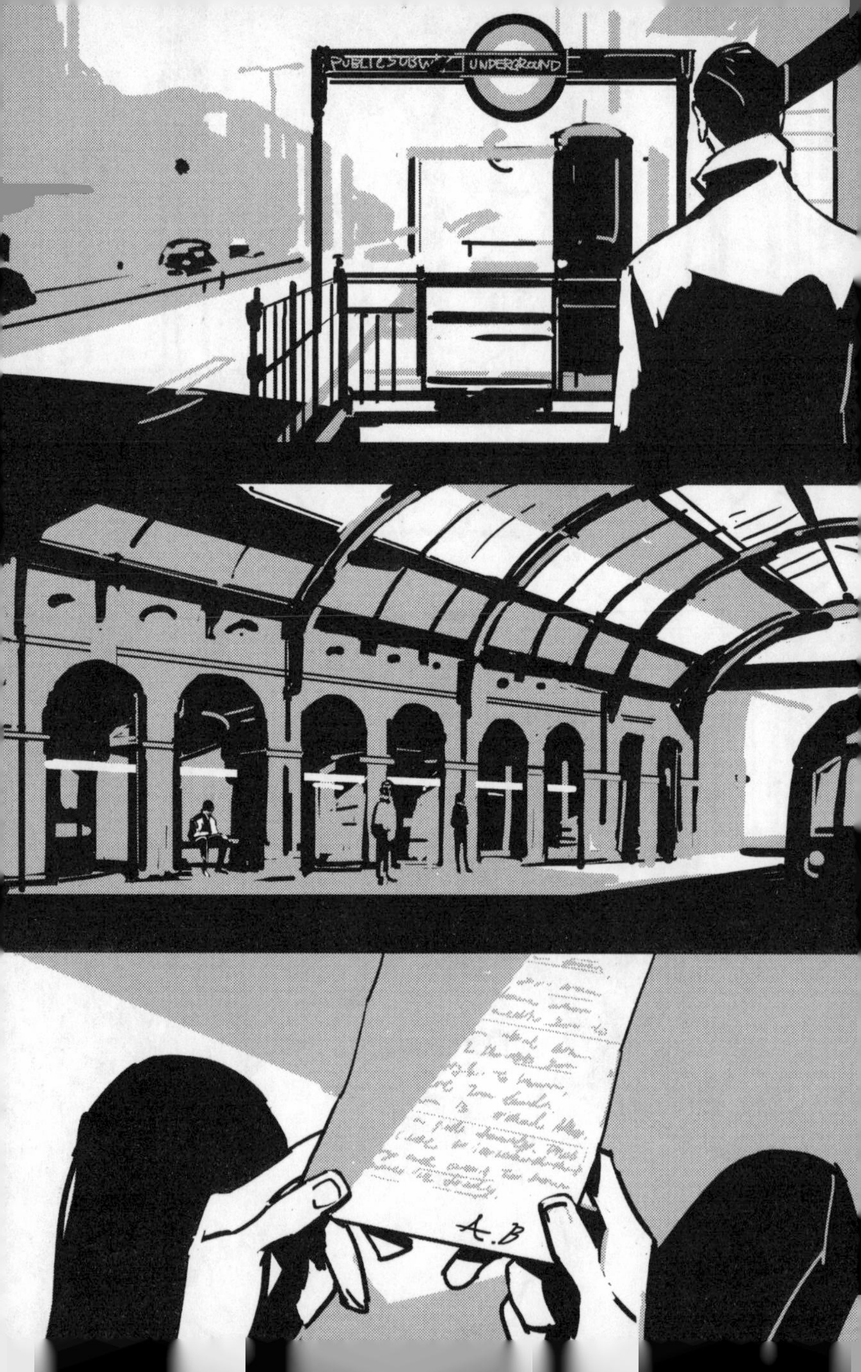
UNDERGROUND
A.B

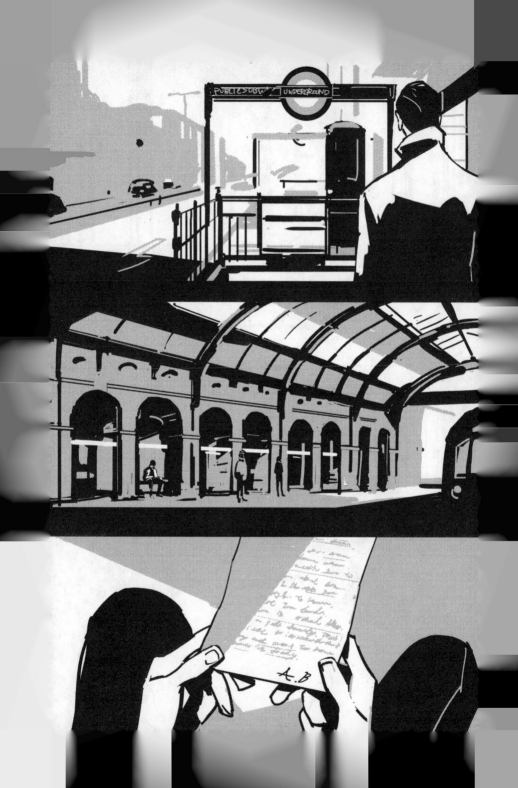

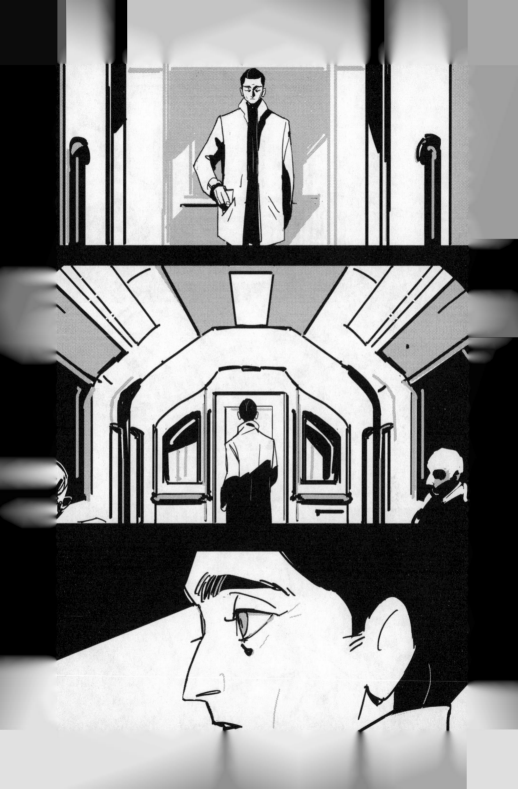

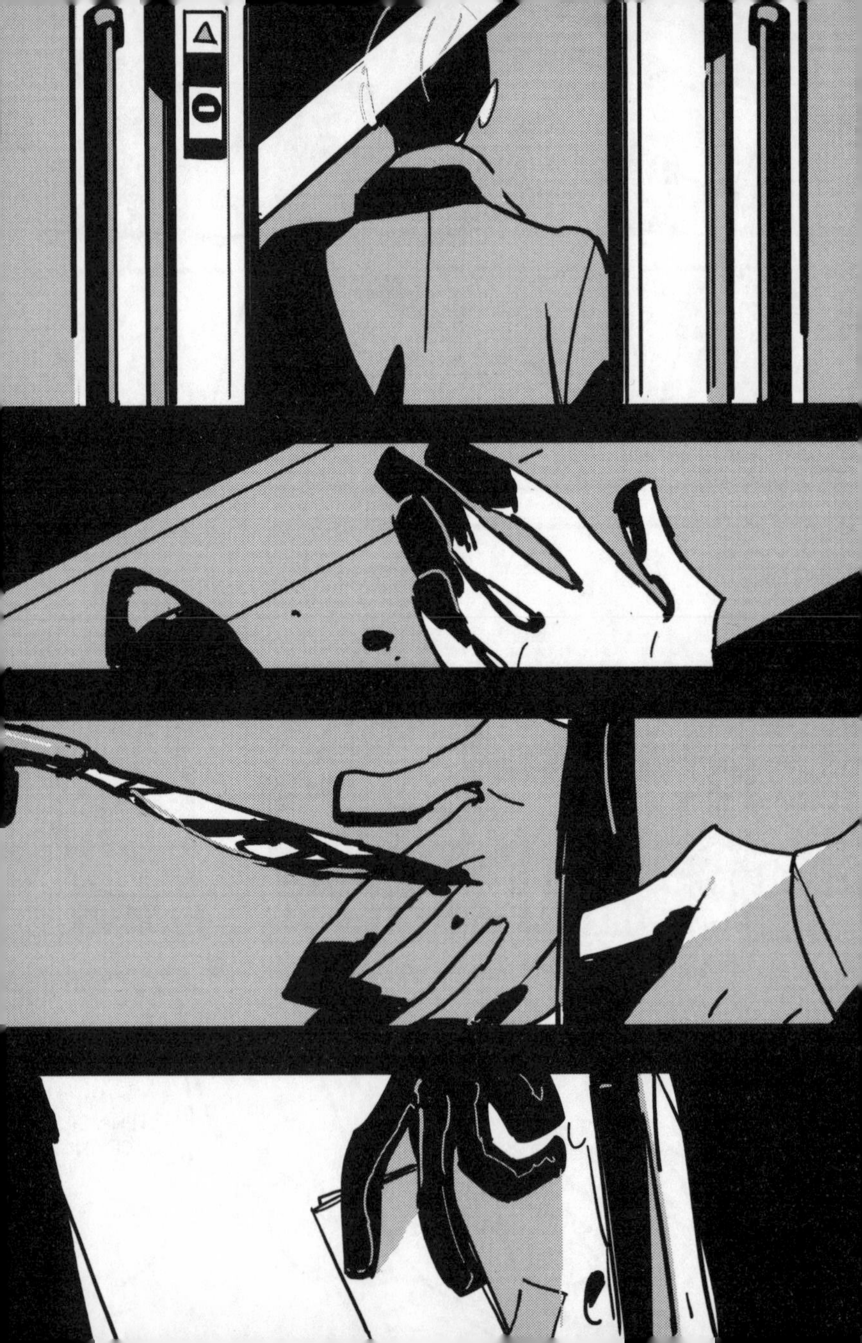

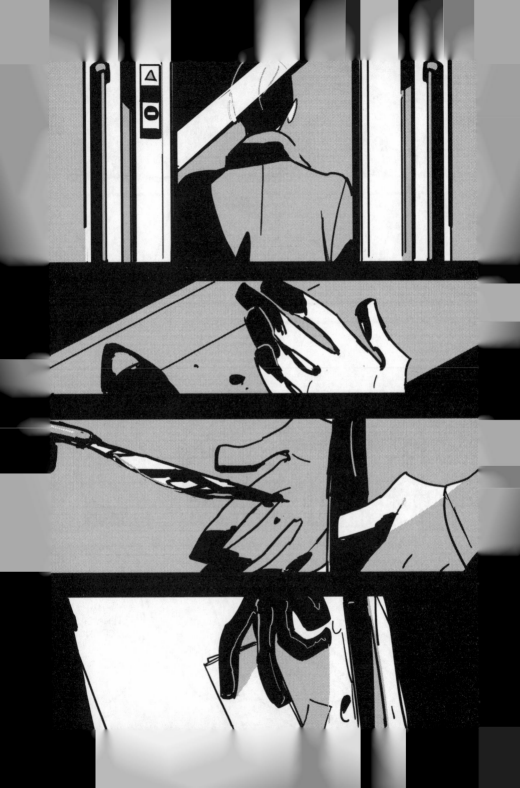

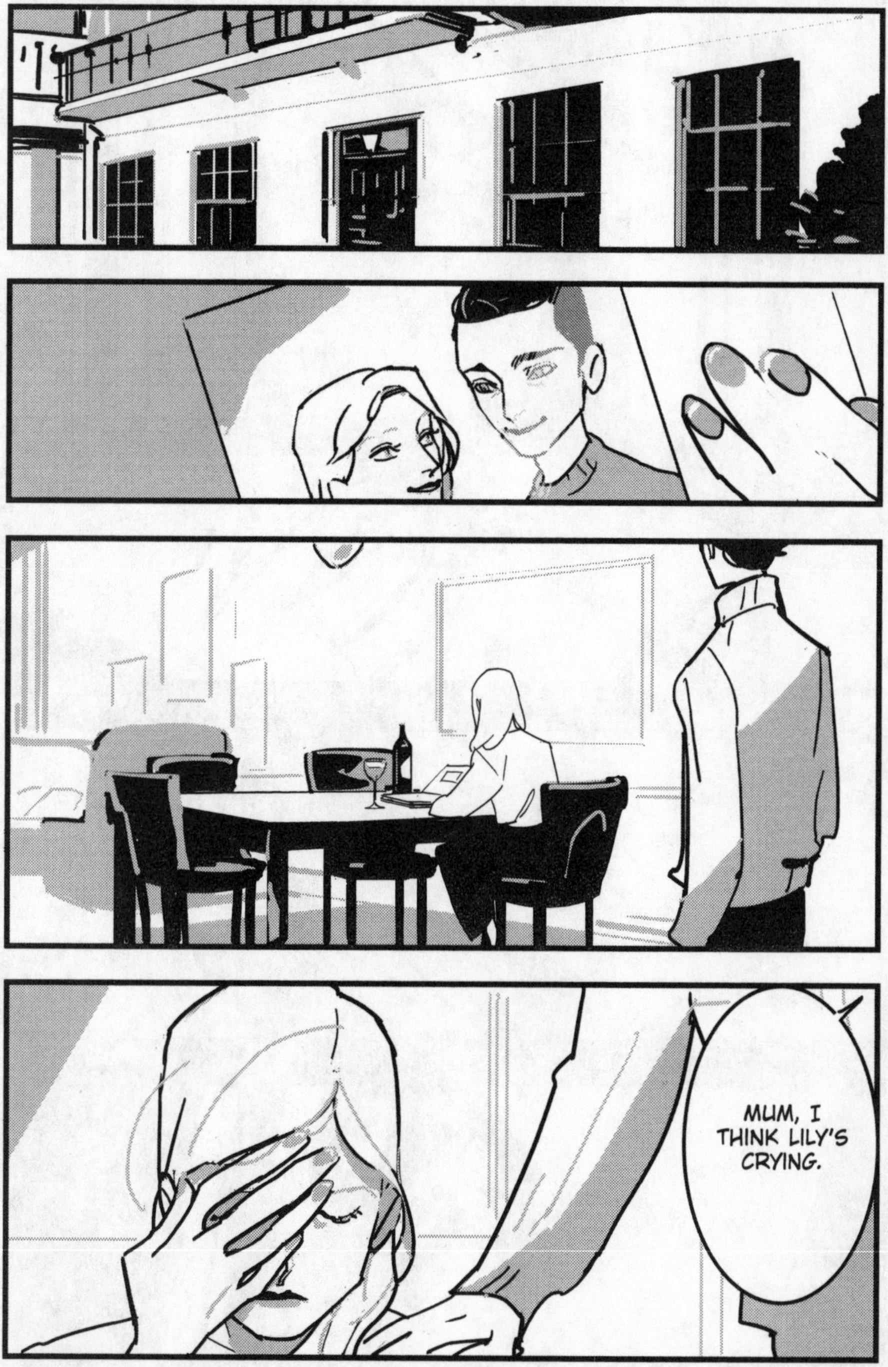
MUM, I THINK LILY'S CRYING.

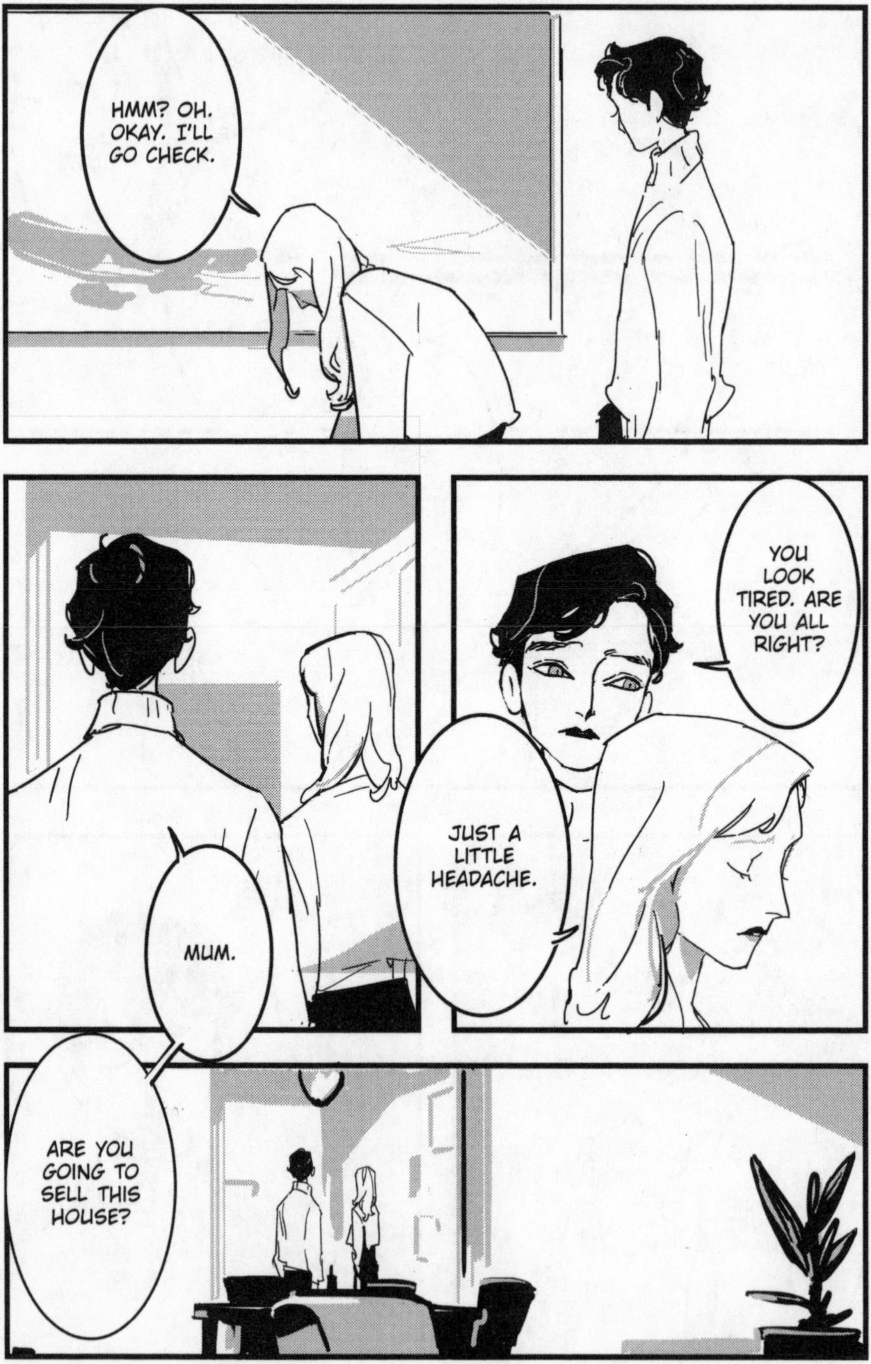
HMM? OH. OKAY. I'LL GO CHECK.
YOU LOOK TIRED. ARE YOU ALL RIGHT?
JUST A LITTLE HEADACHE.
MUM.
ARE YOU GOING TO SELL THIS HOUSE?

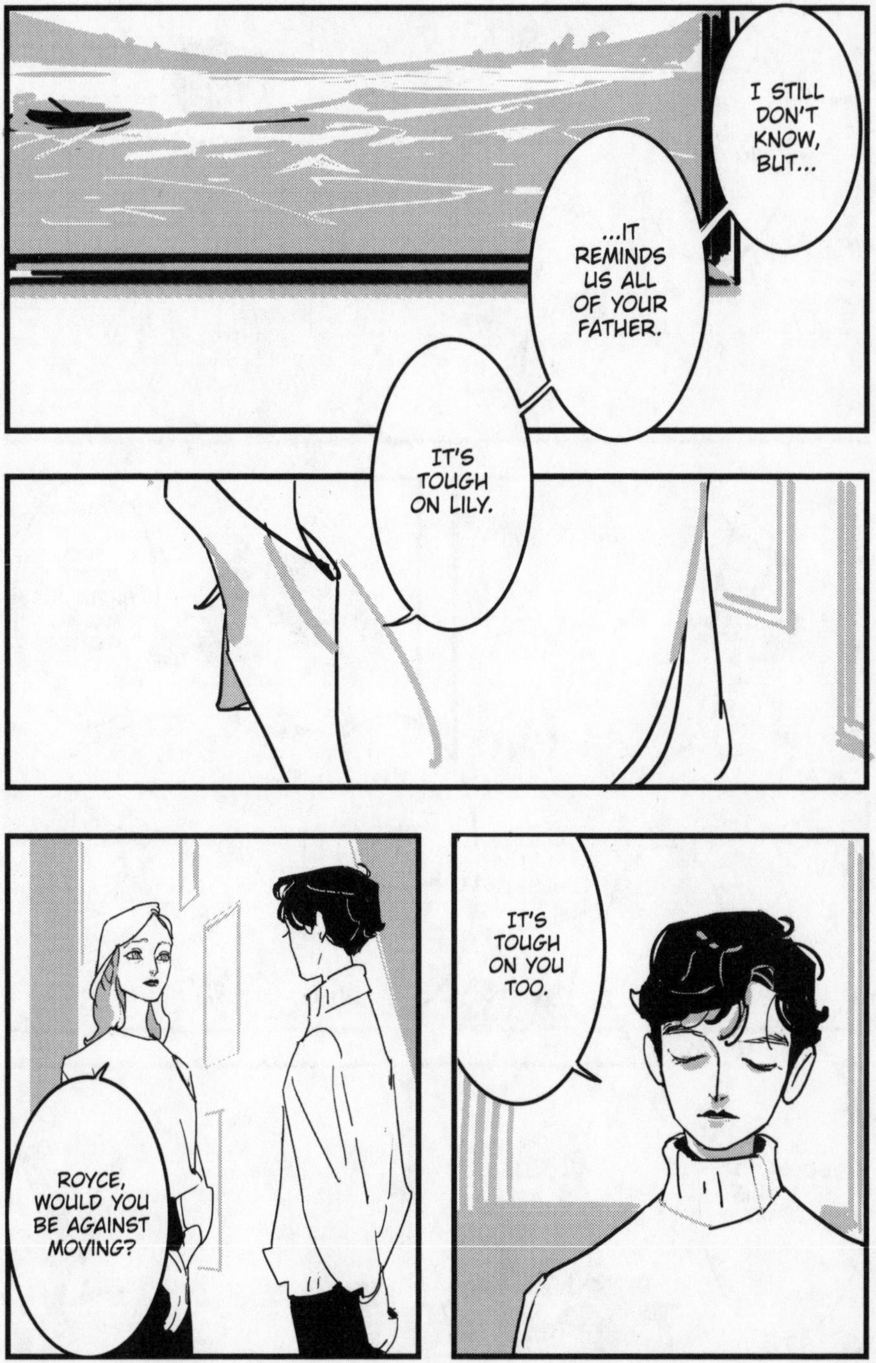
I STILL DON'T KNOW, BUT...
...IT REMINDS US ALL OF YOUR FATHER.
IT'S TOUGH ON LILY.
IT'S TOUGH ON YOU TOO.
ROYCE, WOULD YOU BE AGAINST MOVING?

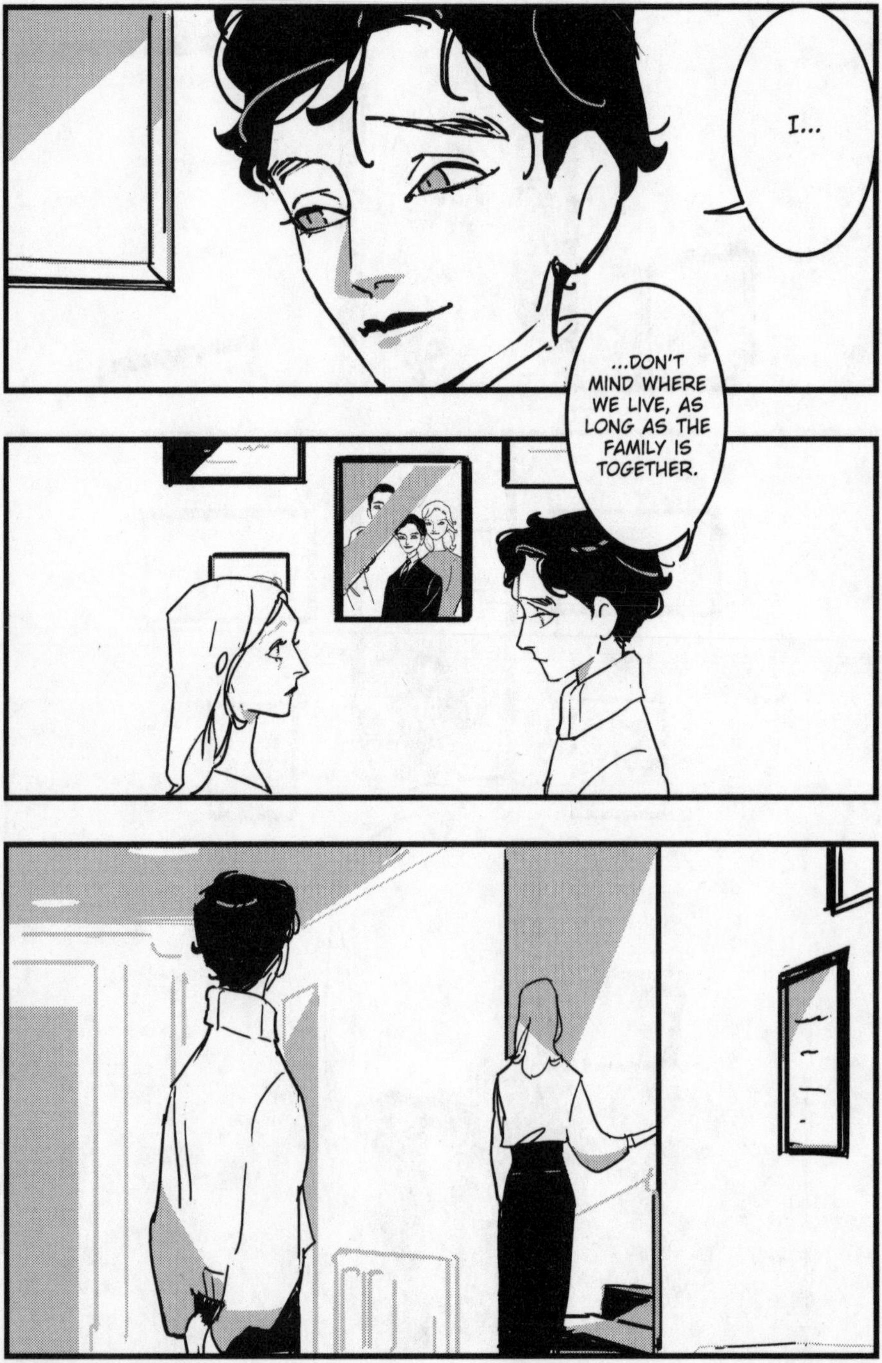
I...
...DON'T MIND WHERE WE LIVE, AS LONG AS THE FAMILY IS TOGETHER.

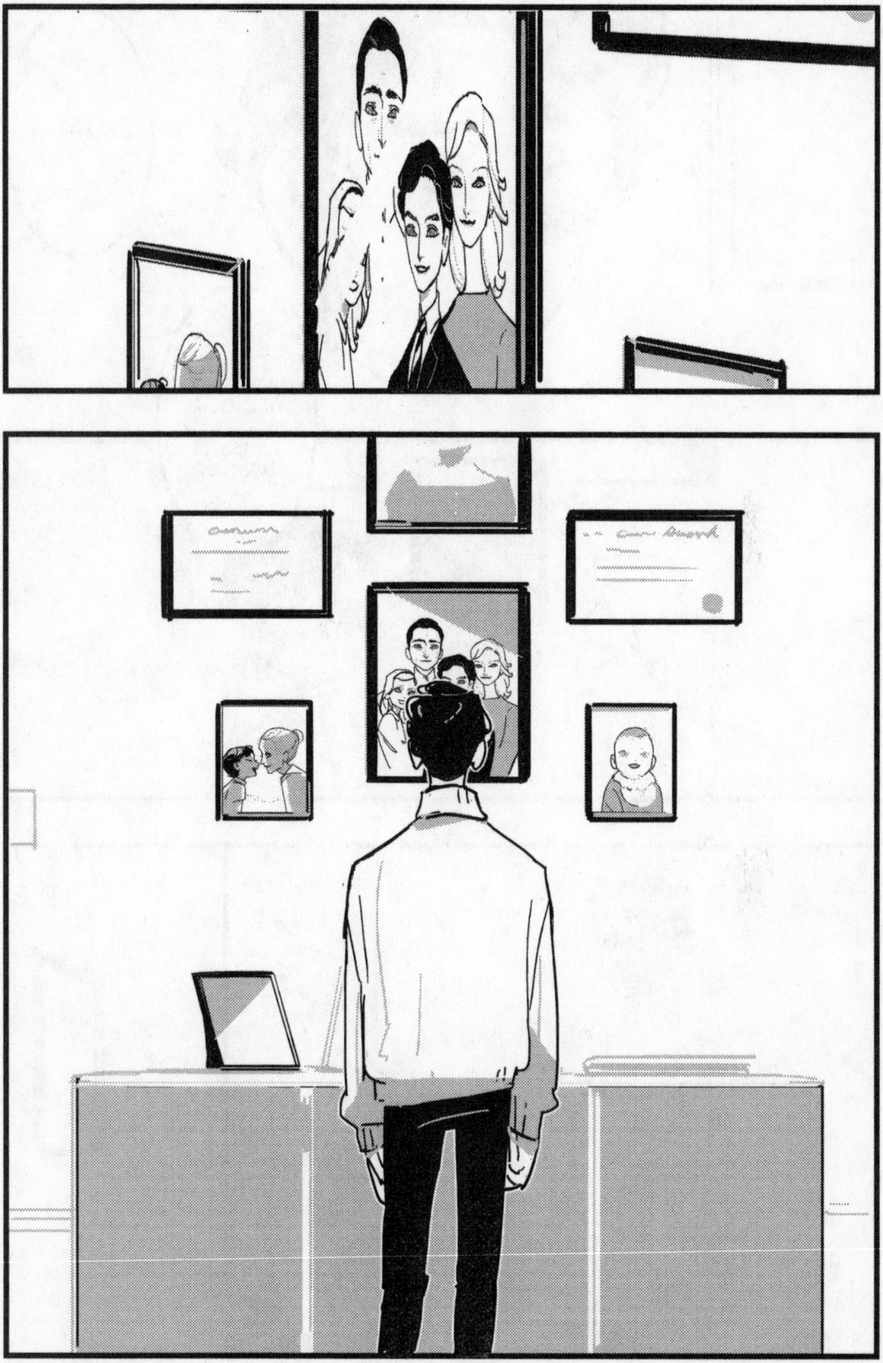

**Lost
Lad
London**

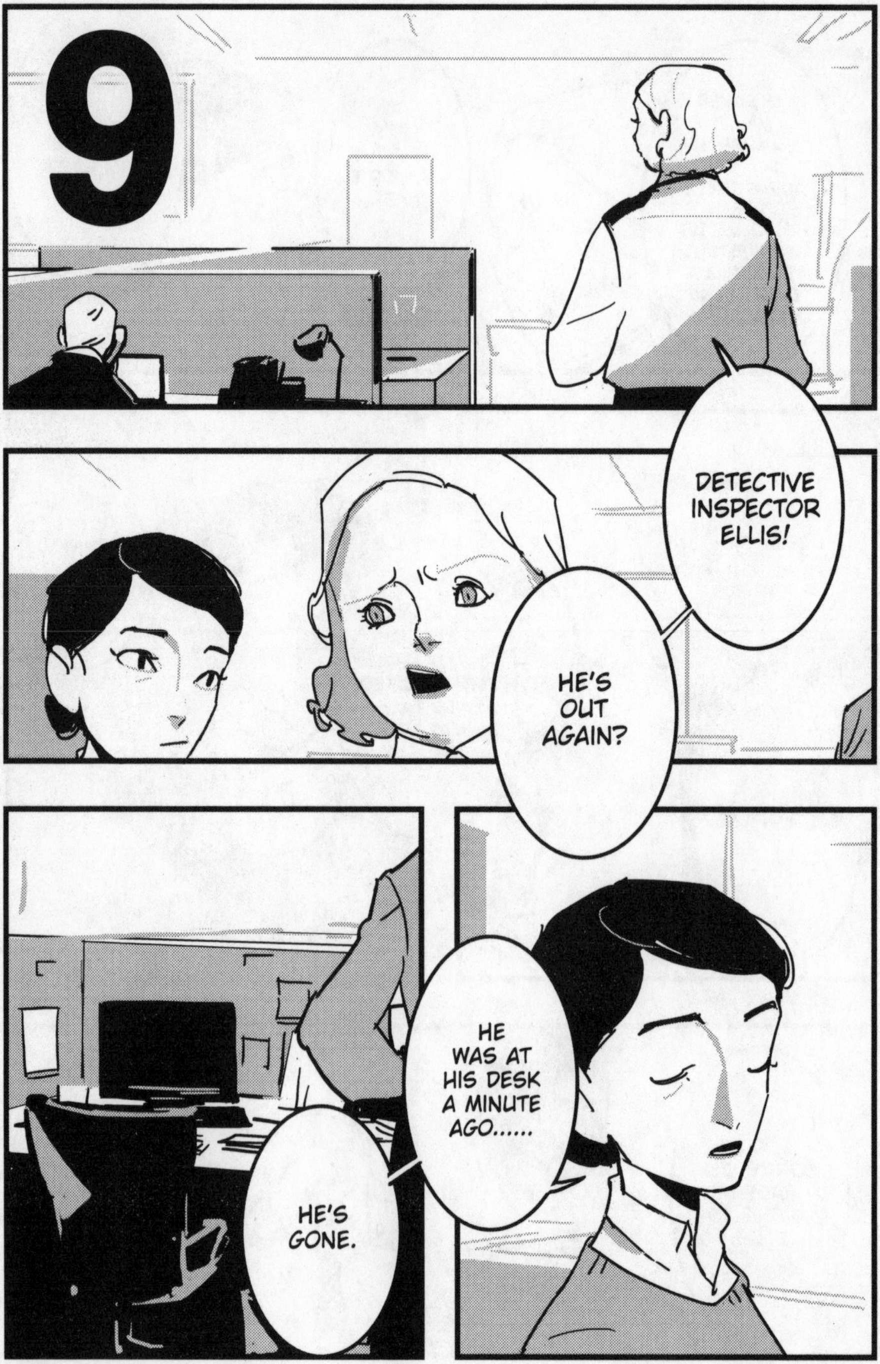
9
DETECTIVE INSPECTOR ELLIS!
HE'S OUT AGAIN?
HE WAS AT HIS DESK A MINUTE AGO......
HE'S GONE.

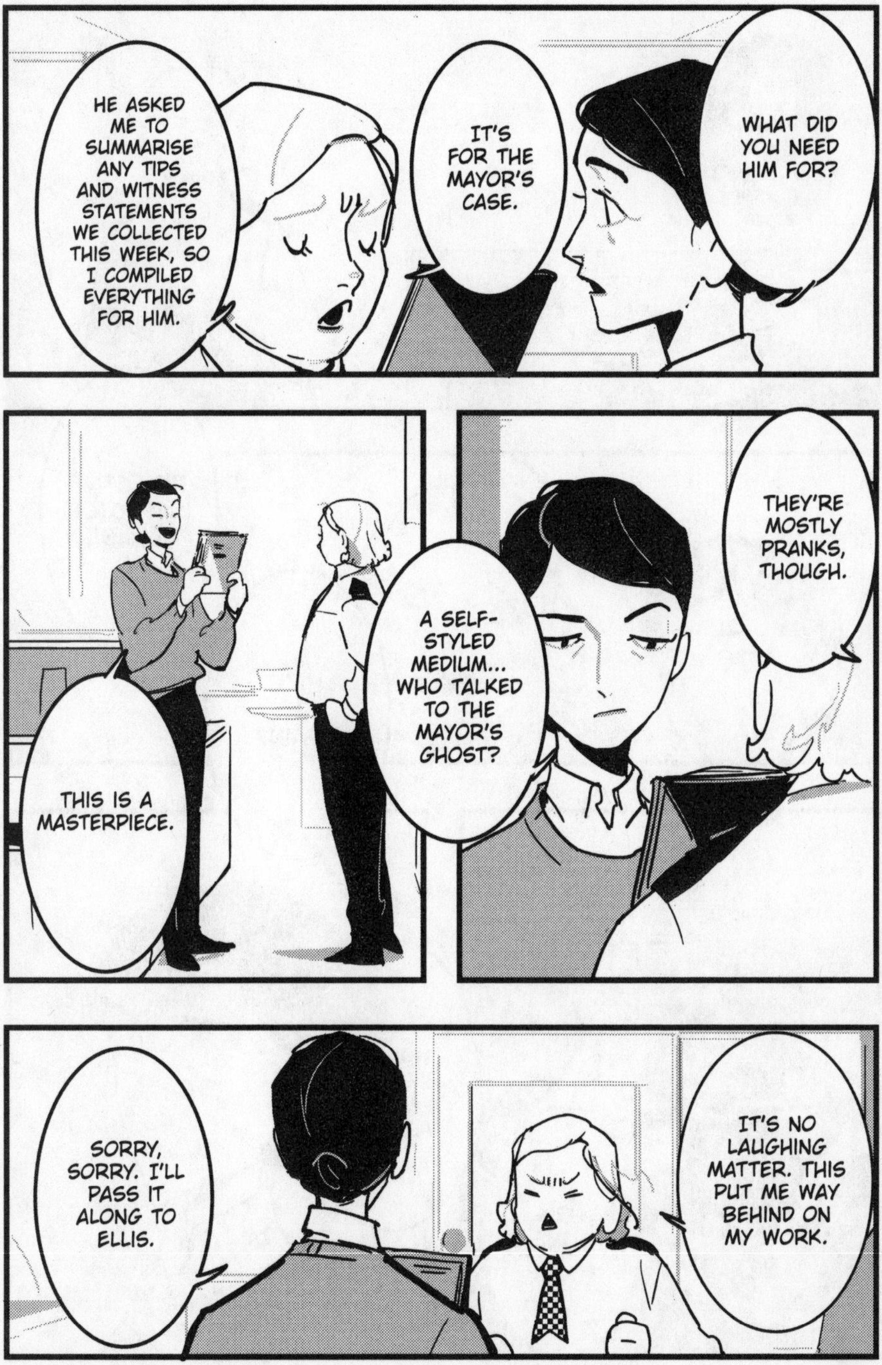
WHAT DID YOU NEED HIM FOR?
IT'S FOR THE MAYOR'S CASE.
HE ASKED ME TO SUMMARISE ANY TIPS AND WITNESS STATEMENTS WE COLLECTED THIS WEEK, SO I COMPILED EVERYTHING FOR HIM.
THEY'RE MOSTLY PRANKS, THOUGH.
A SELF-STYLED MEDIUM... WHO TALKED TO THE MAYOR'S GHOST?
THIS IS A MASTERPIECE.
IT'S NO LAUGHING MATTER. THIS PUT ME WAY BEHIND ON MY WORK.
SORRY, SORRY. I'LL PASS IT ALONG TO ELLIS.

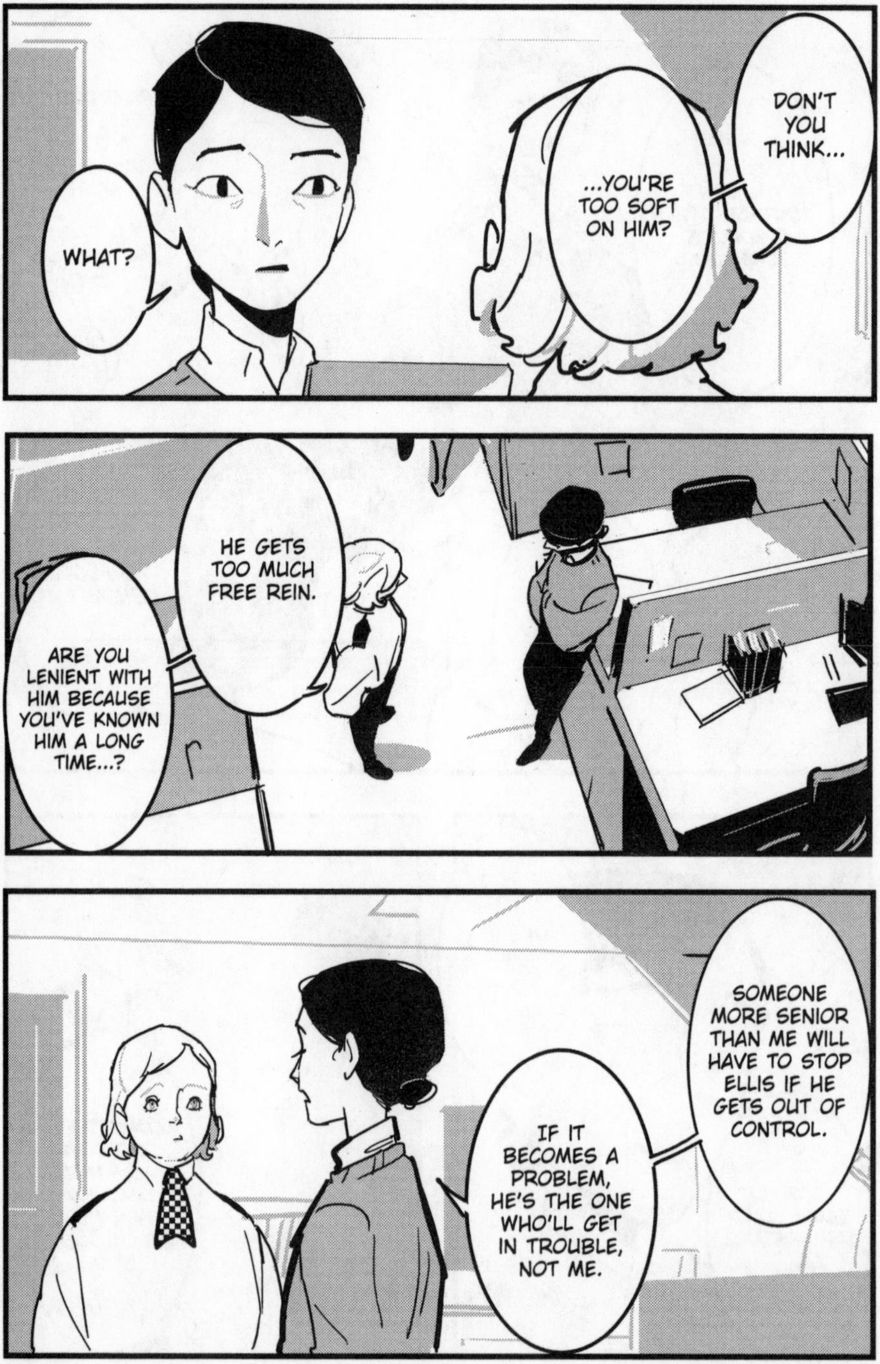
DON'T YOU THINK...
...YOU'RE TOO SOFT ON HIM?
WHAT?
HE GETS TOO MUCH FREE REIN.
ARE YOU LENIENT WITH HIM BECAUSE YOU'VE KNOWN HIM A LONG TIME...?
SOMEONE MORE SENIOR THAN ME WILL HAVE TO STOP ELLIS IF HE GETS OUT OF CONTROL.
IF IT BECOMES A PROBLEM, HE'S THE ONE WHO'LL GET IN TROUBLE, NOT ME.

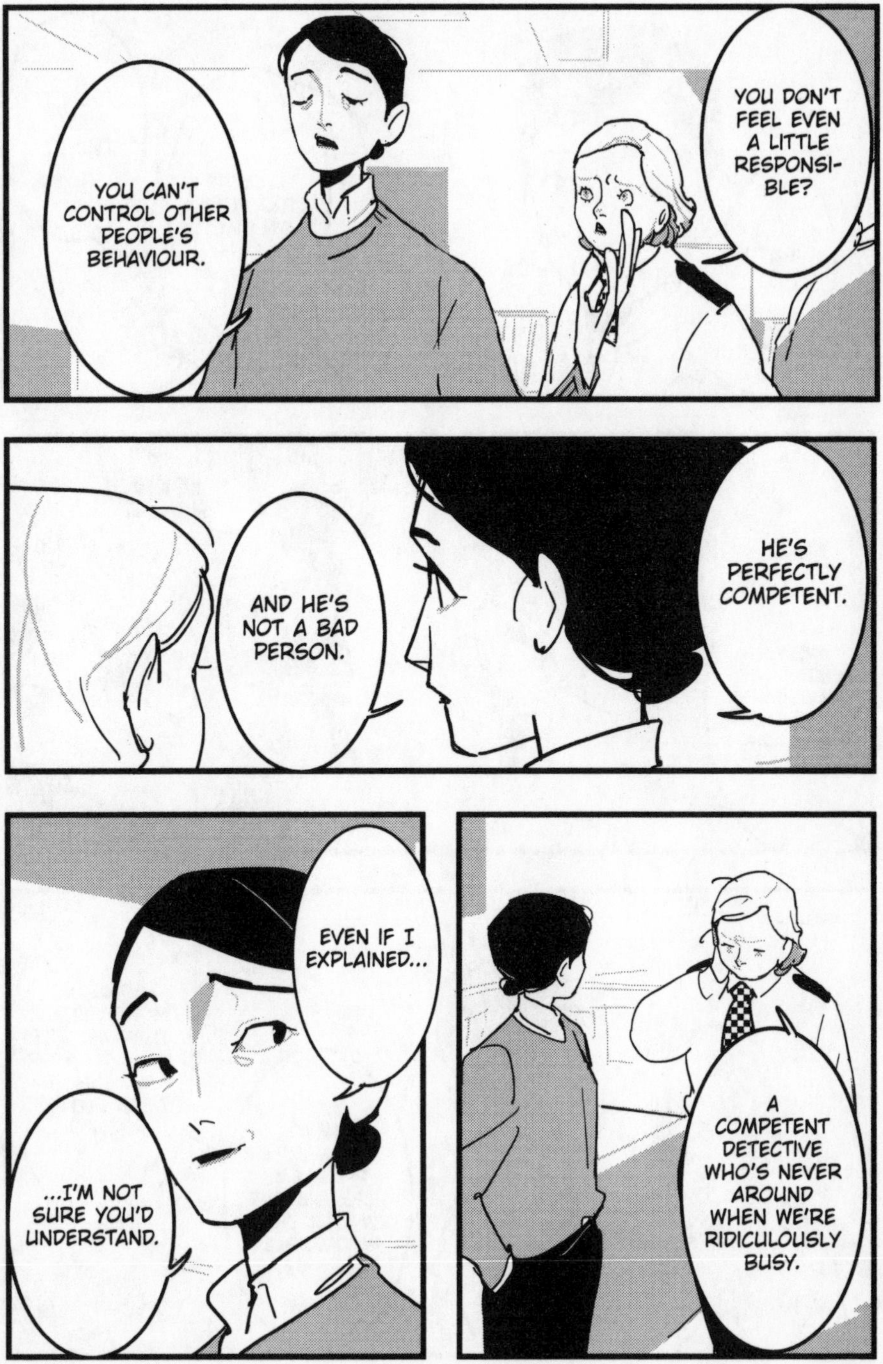
YOU DON'T FEEL EVEN A LITTLE RESPONSI- BLE?
YOU CAN'T CONTROL OTHER PEOPLE'S BEHAVIOUR.
HE'S PERFECTLY COMPETENT.
AND HE'S NOT A BAD PERSON.
A COMPETENT DETECTIVE WHO'S NEVER AROUND WHEN WE'RE RIDICULOUSLY BUSY.
EVEN IF I EXPLAINED...
...I'M NOT SURE YOU'D UNDERSTAND.

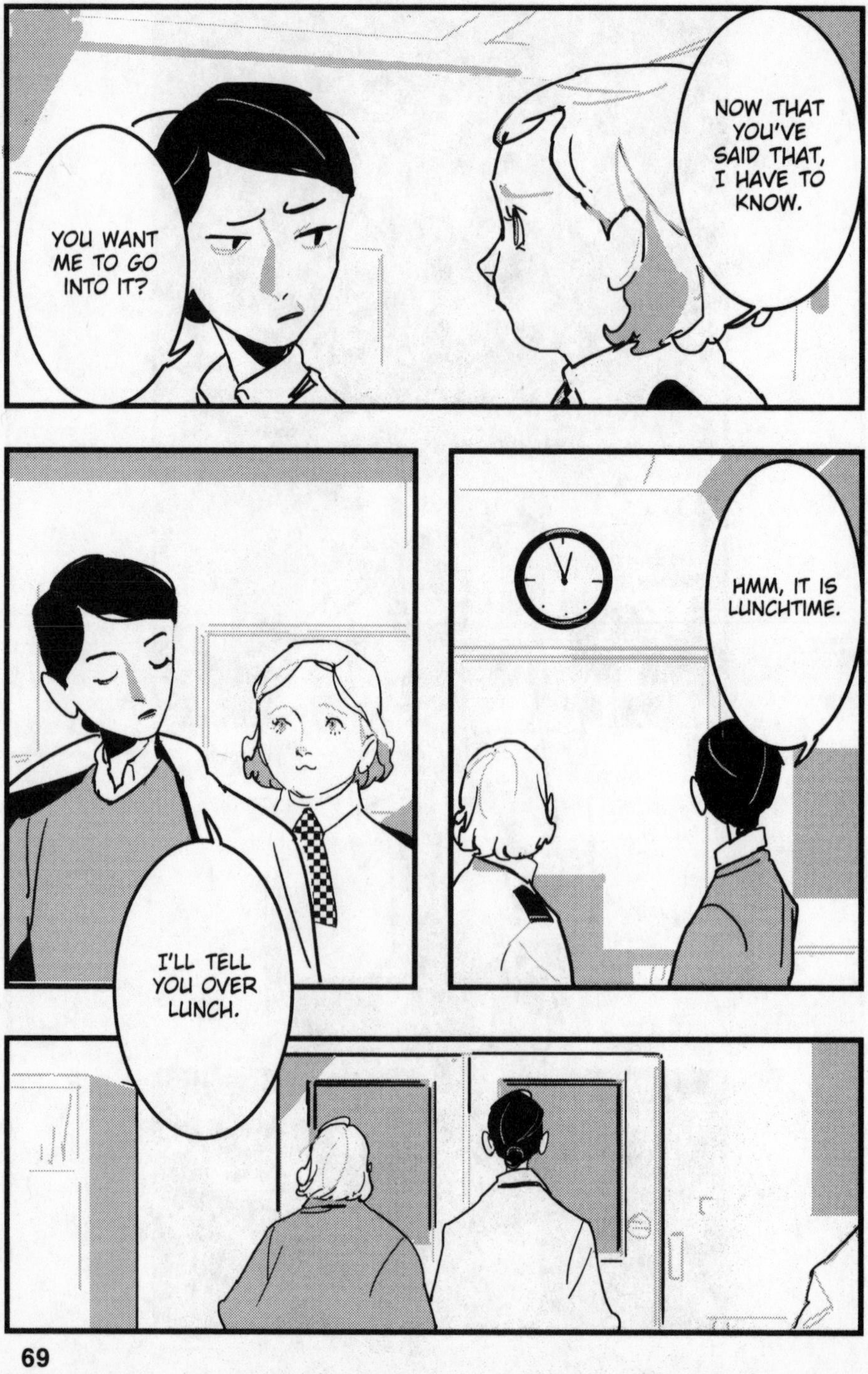
NOW THAT YOU'VE SAID THAT, I HAVE TO KNOW.
YOU WANT ME TO GO INTO IT?
HMM, IT IS LUNCHTIME.
I'LL TELL YOU OVER LUNCH.

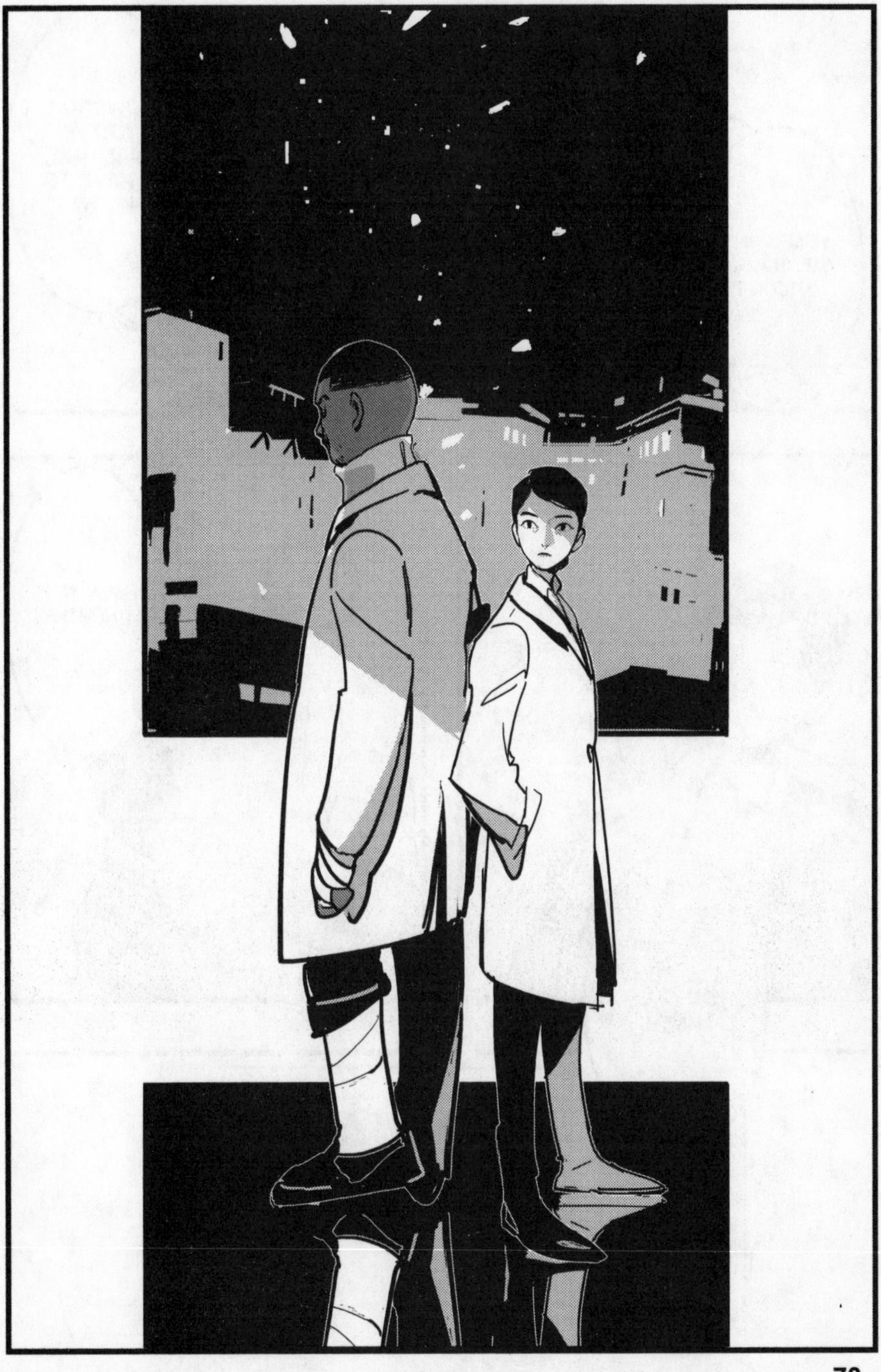

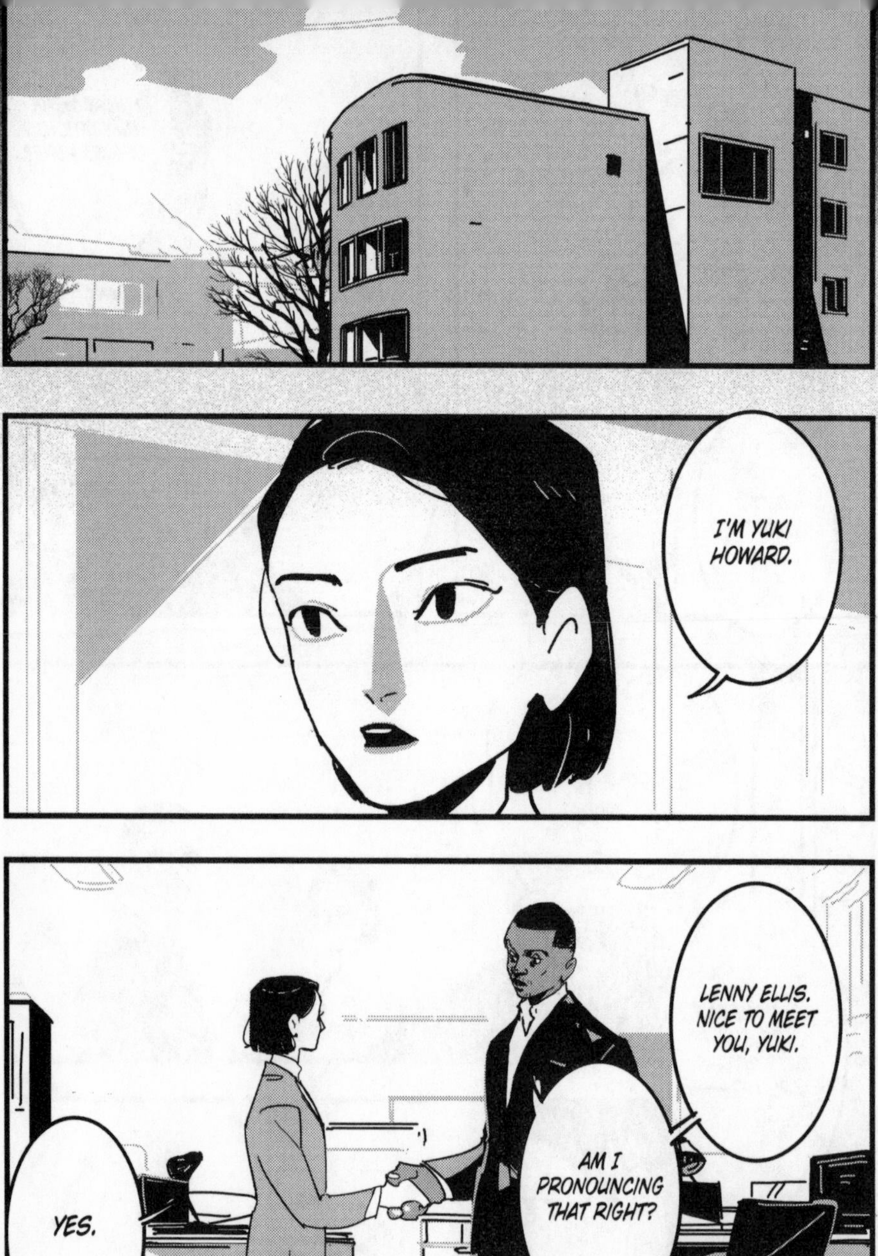
I'M YUKI HOWARD.
LENNY ELLIS. NICE TO MEET YOU, YUKI.
AM I PRONOUNCING THAT RIGHT?
YES.

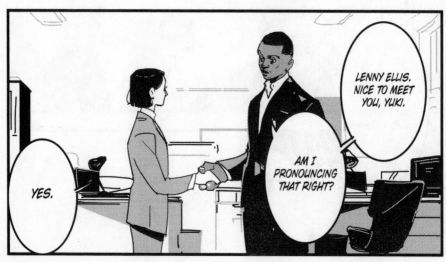

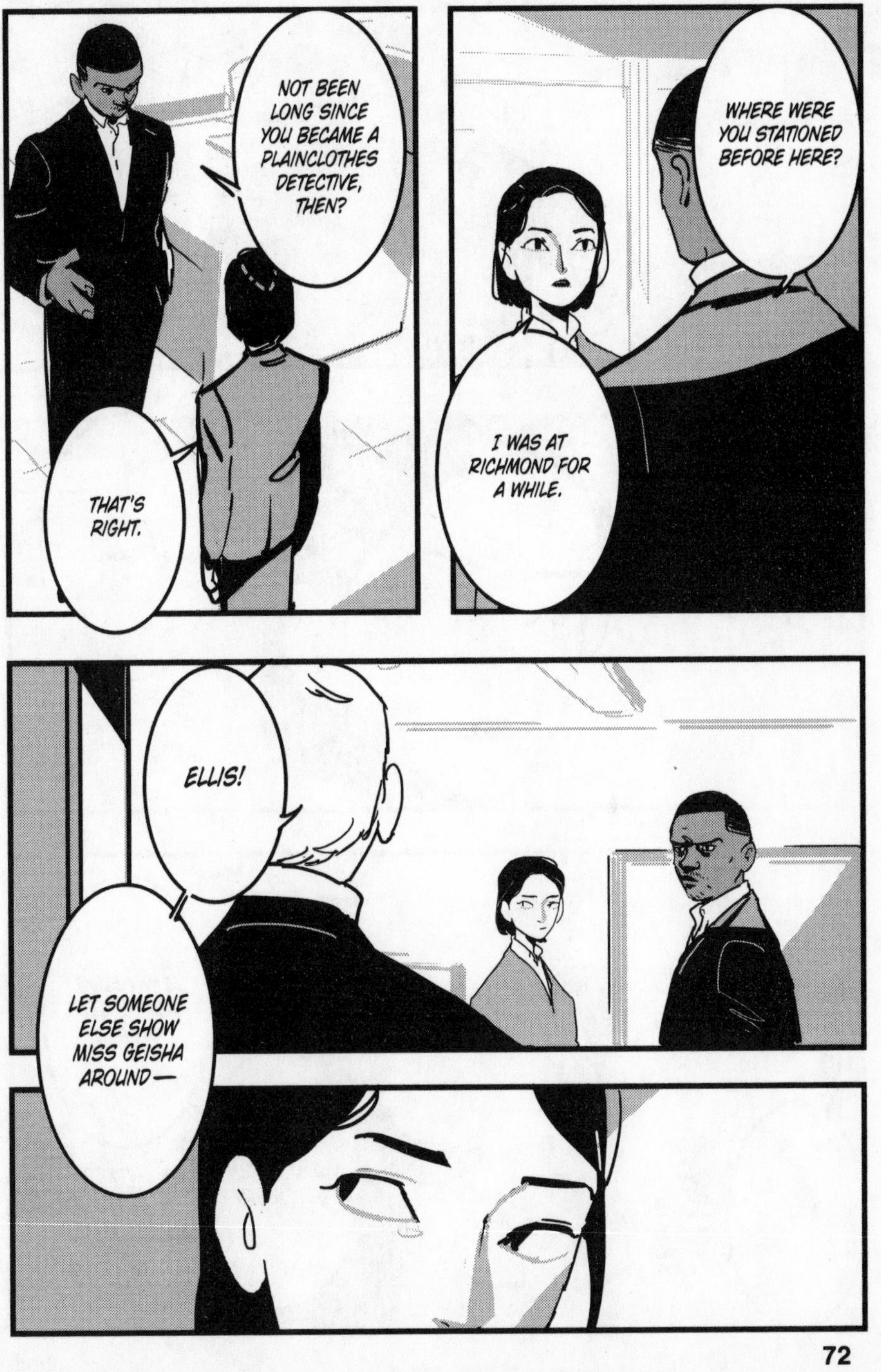
WHERE WERE YOU STATIONED BEFORE HERE?
I WAS AT RICHMOND FOR A WHILE.
NOT BEEN LONG SINCE YOU BECAME A PLAINCLOTHES DETECTIVE, THEN?
THAT'S RIGHT.
ELLIS!
LET SOMEONE ELSE SHOW MISS GEISHA AROUND—

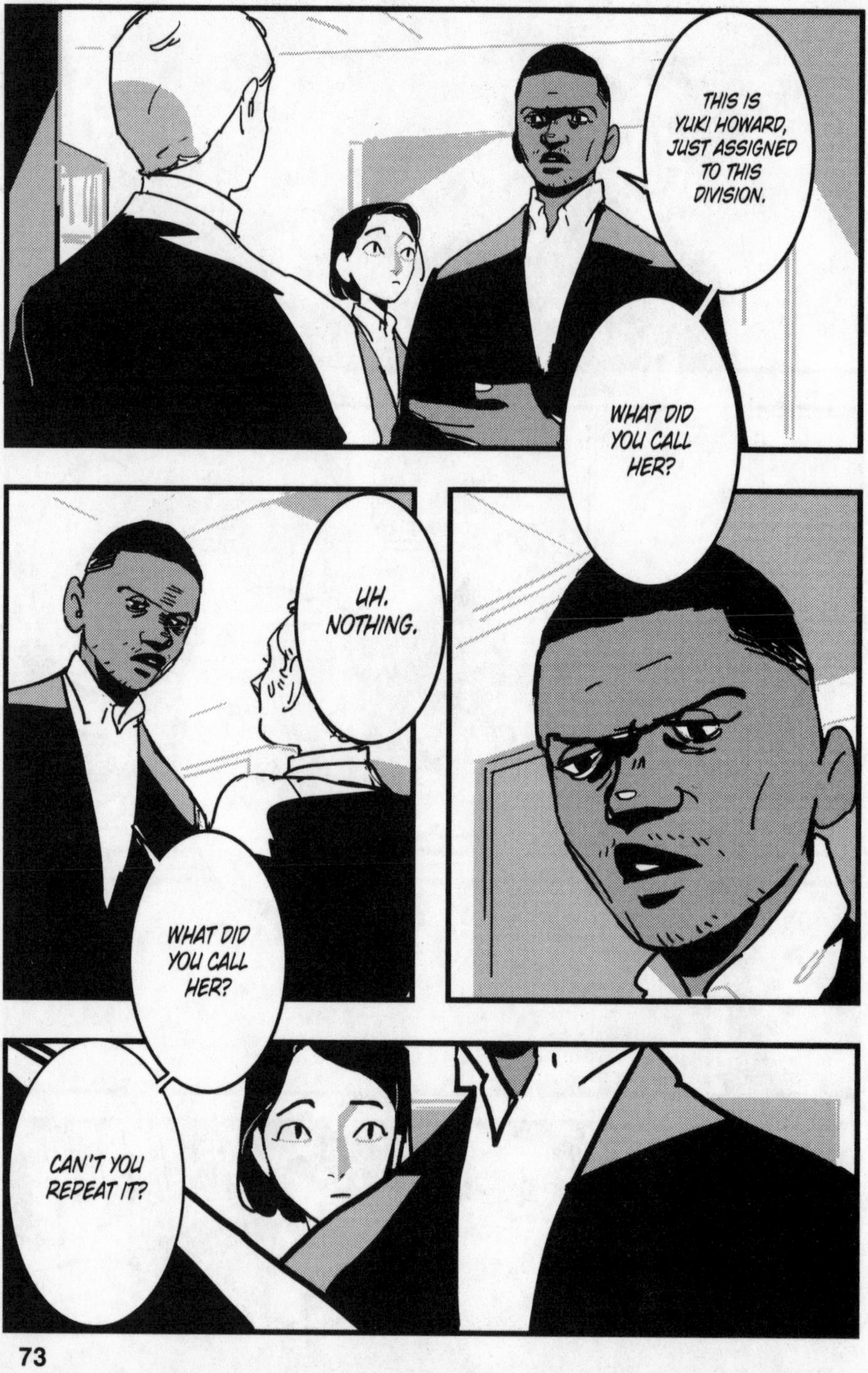
THIS IS YUKI HOWARD, JUST ASSIGNED TO THIS DIVISION.
WHAT DID YOU CALL HER?
UH. NOTHING.
WHAT DID YOU CALL HER?
CAN'T YOU REPEAT IT?

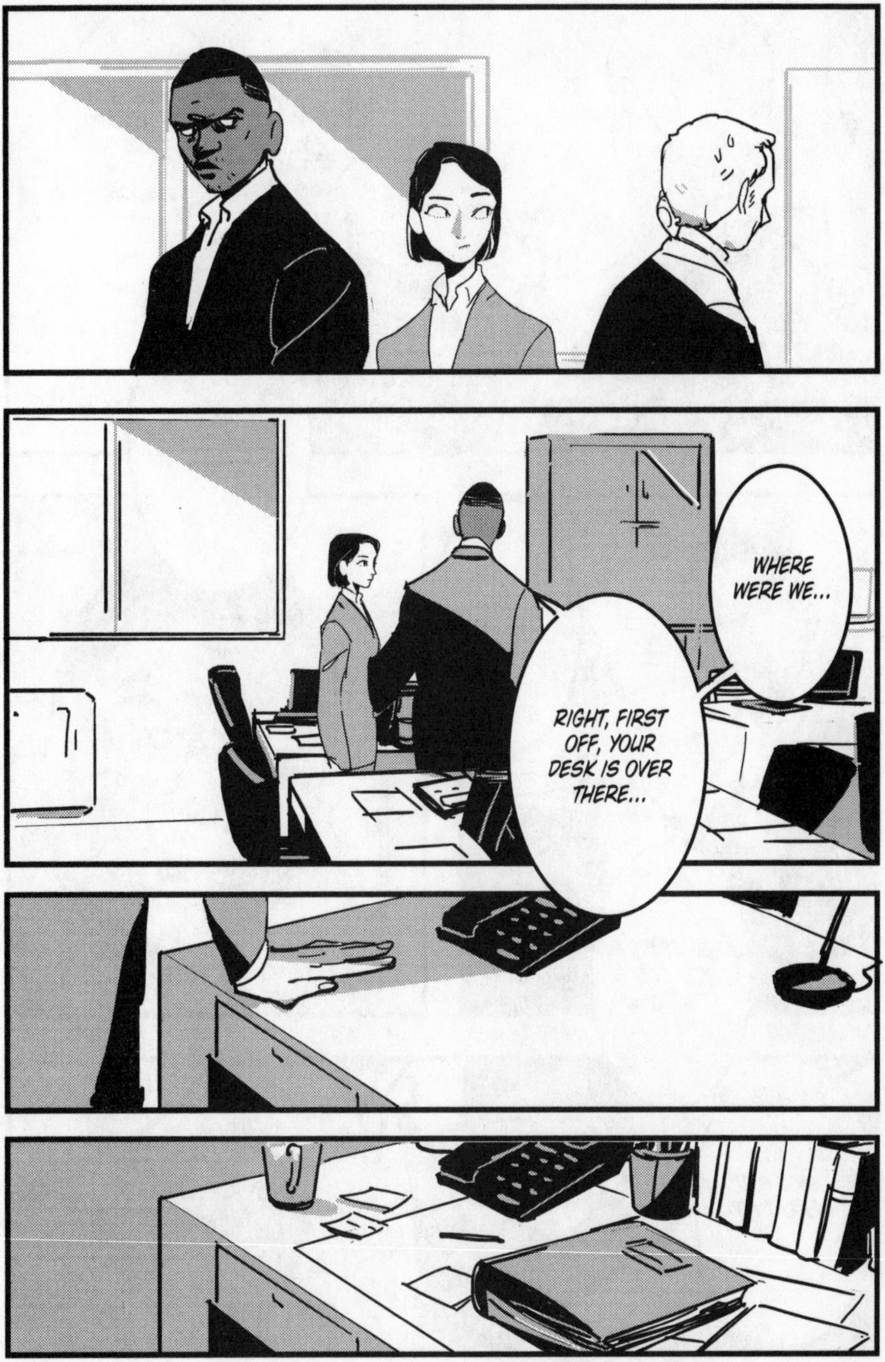
WHERE WERE WE...
RIGHT, FIRST OFF, YOUR DESK IS OVER THERE...

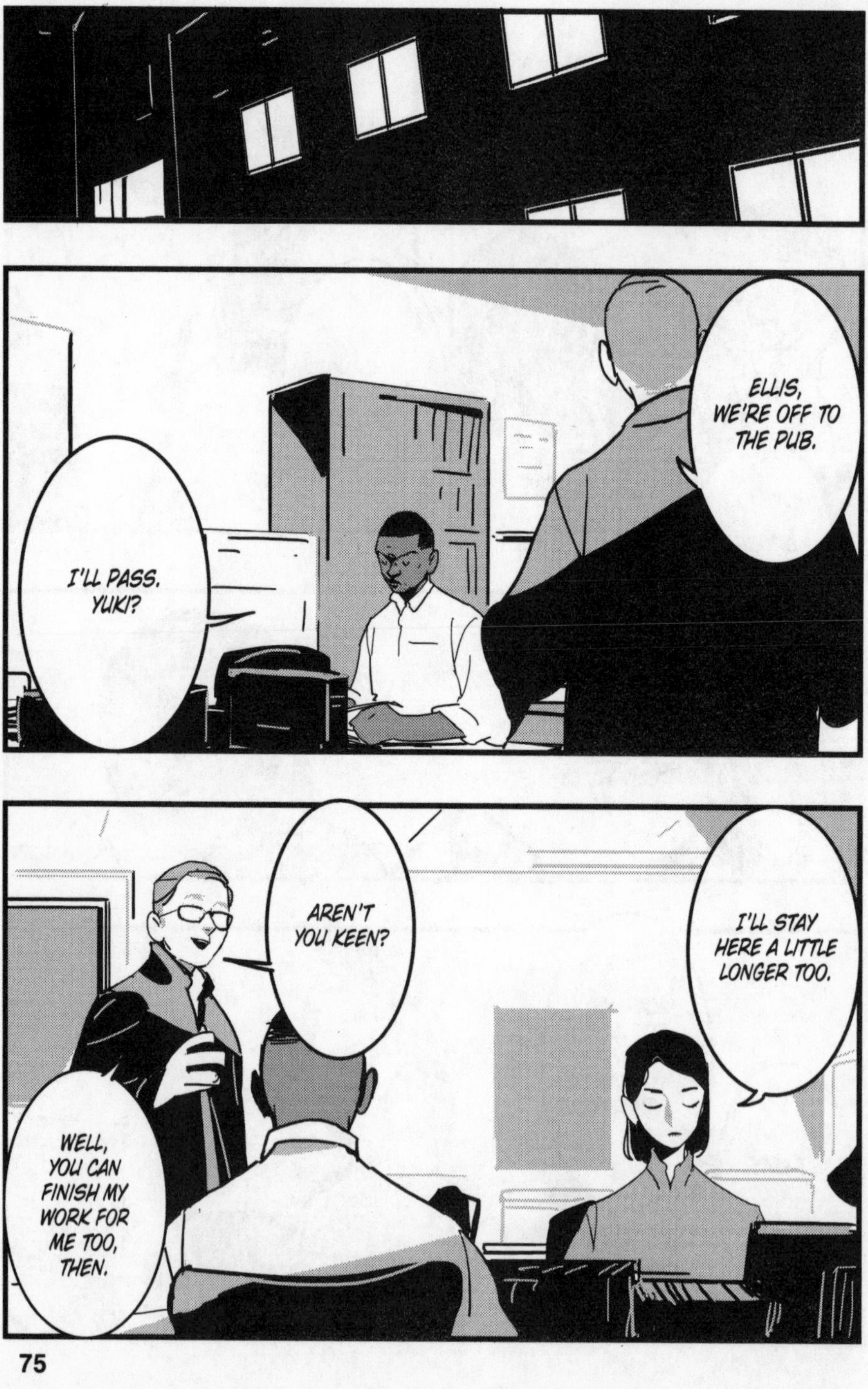
ELLIS, WE'RE OFF TO THE PUB.
I'LL PASS. YUKI?
I'LL STAY HERE A LITTLE LONGER TOO.
AREN'T YOU KEEN?
WELL, YOU CAN FINISH MY WORK FOR ME TOO, THEN.

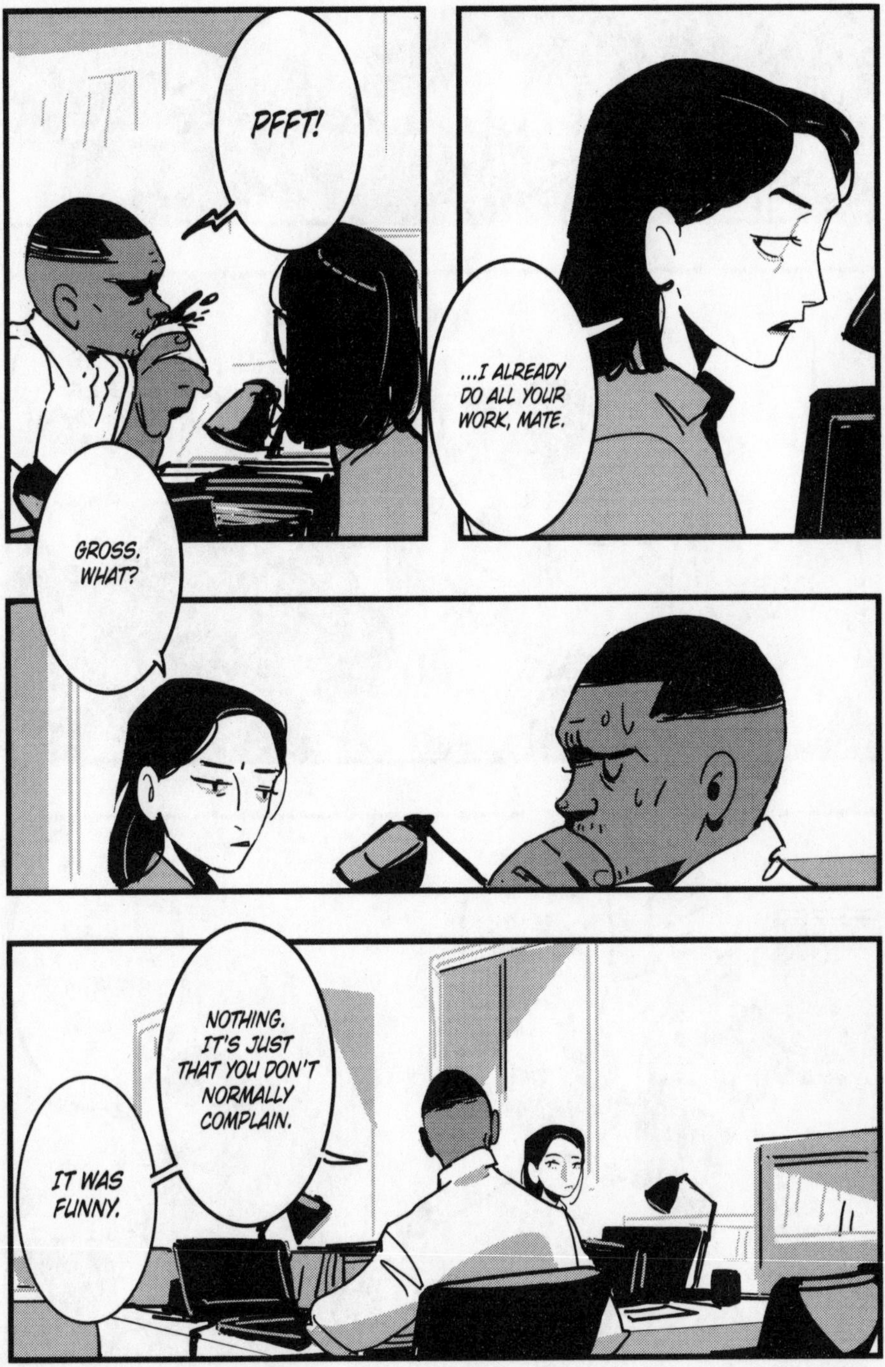
...I ALREADY DO ALL YOUR WORK, MATE.
PFFT!
GROSS. WHAT?
NOTHING. IT'S JUST THAT YOU DON'T NORMALLY COMPLAIN.
IT WAS FUNNY.

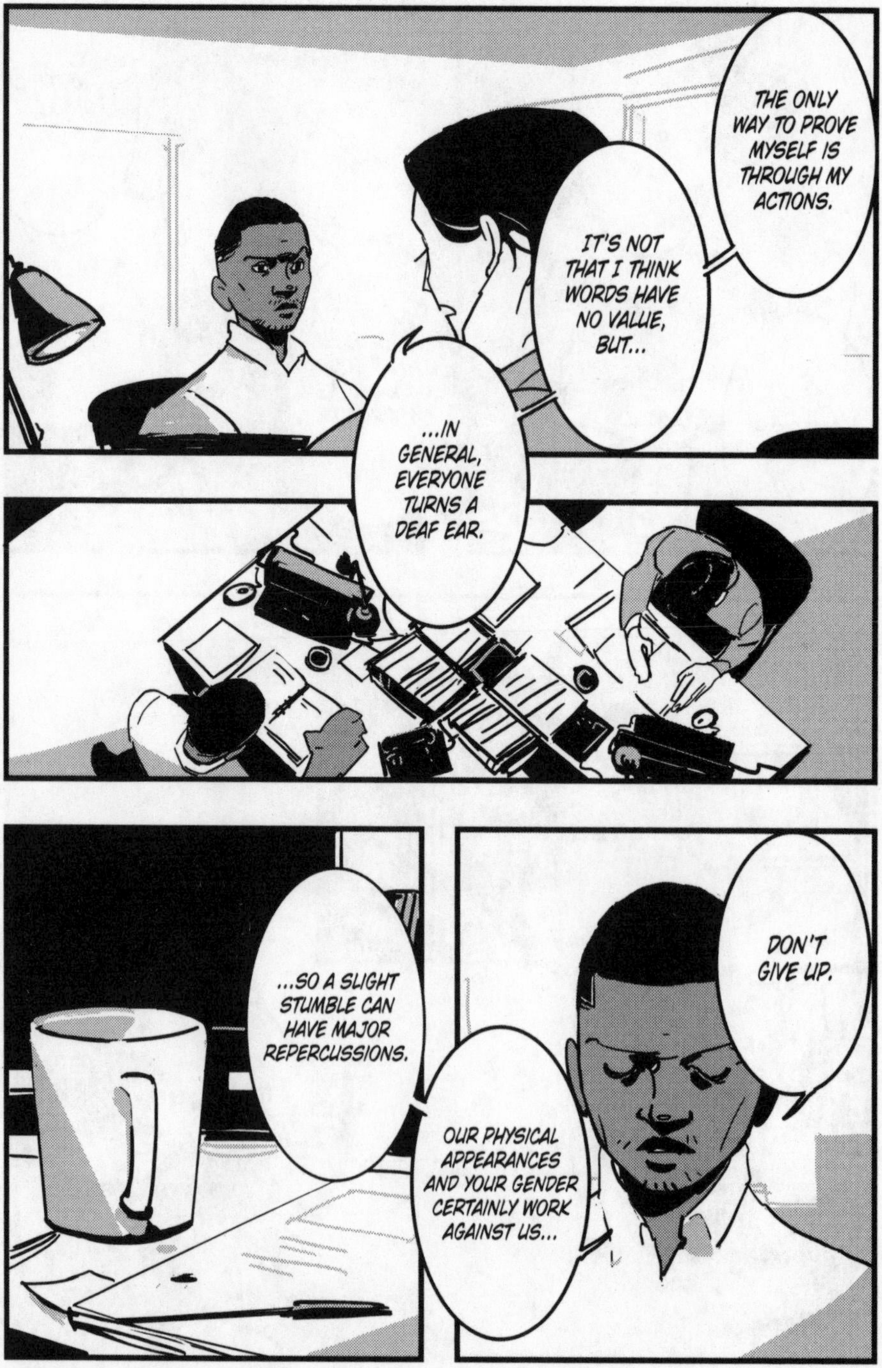
THE ONLY WAY TO PROVE MYSELF IS THROUGH MY ACTIONS.
IT'S NOT THAT I THINK WORDS HAVE NO VALUE, BUT...
...IN GENERAL, EVERYONE TURNS A DEAF EAR.
DON'T GIVE UP.
OUR PHYSICAL APPEARANCES AND YOUR GENDER CERTAINLY WORK AGAINST US...
...SO A SLIGHT STUMBLE CAN HAVE MAJOR REPERCUSSIONS.

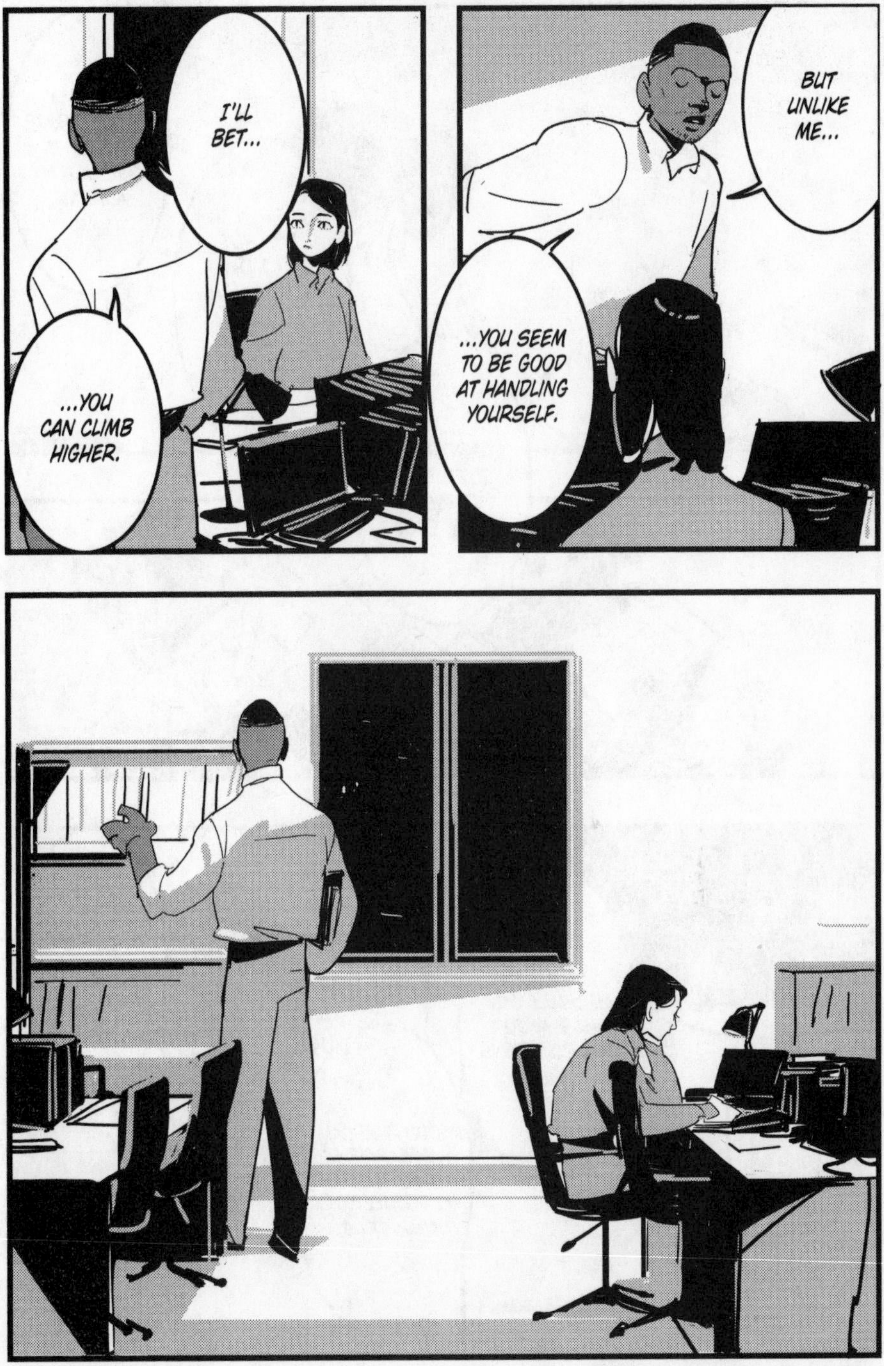
BUT UNLIKE ME...
...YOU SEEM TO BE GOOD AT HANDLING YOURSELF.
I'LL BET...
...YOU CAN CLIMB HIGHER.

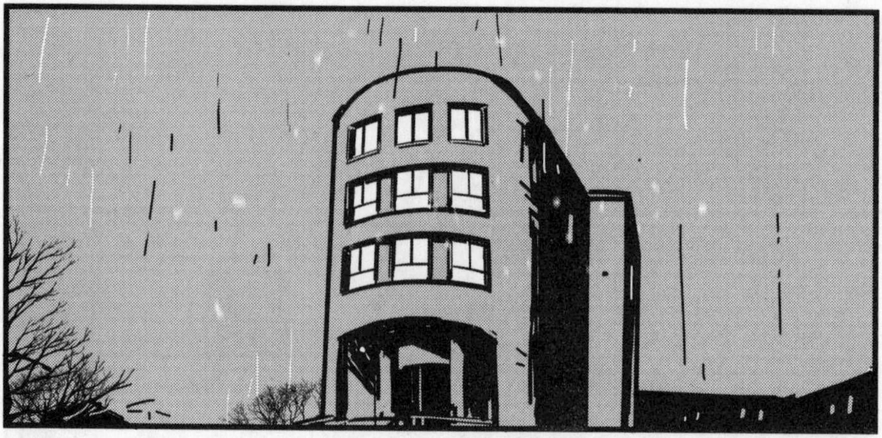
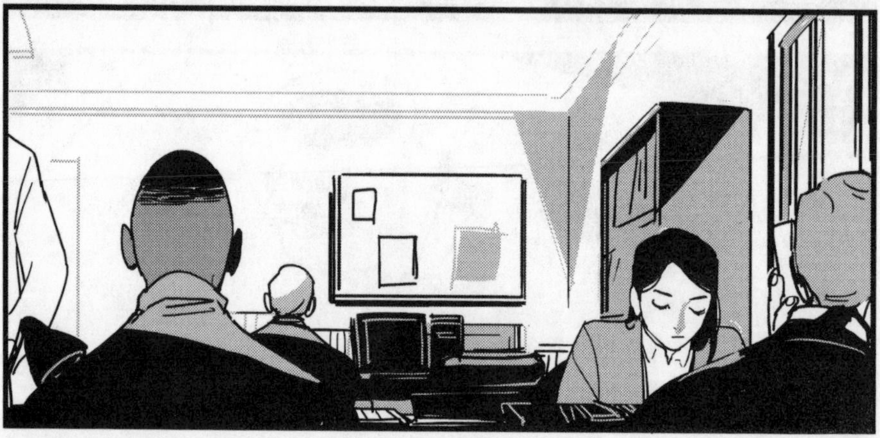
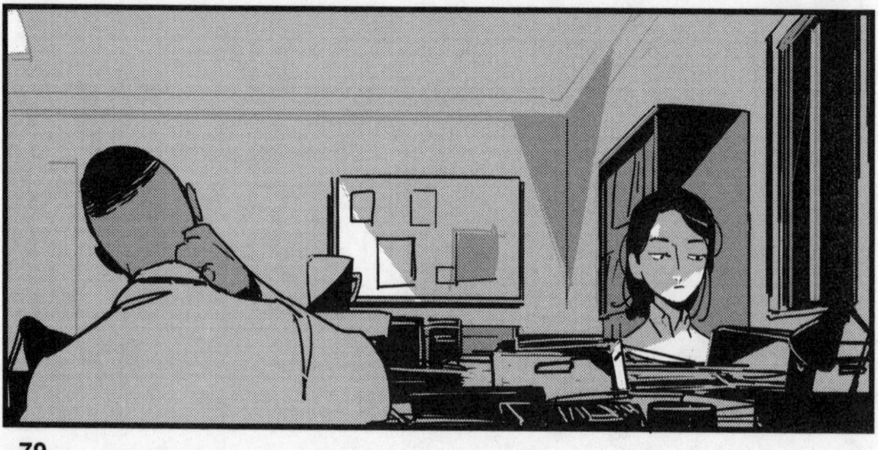

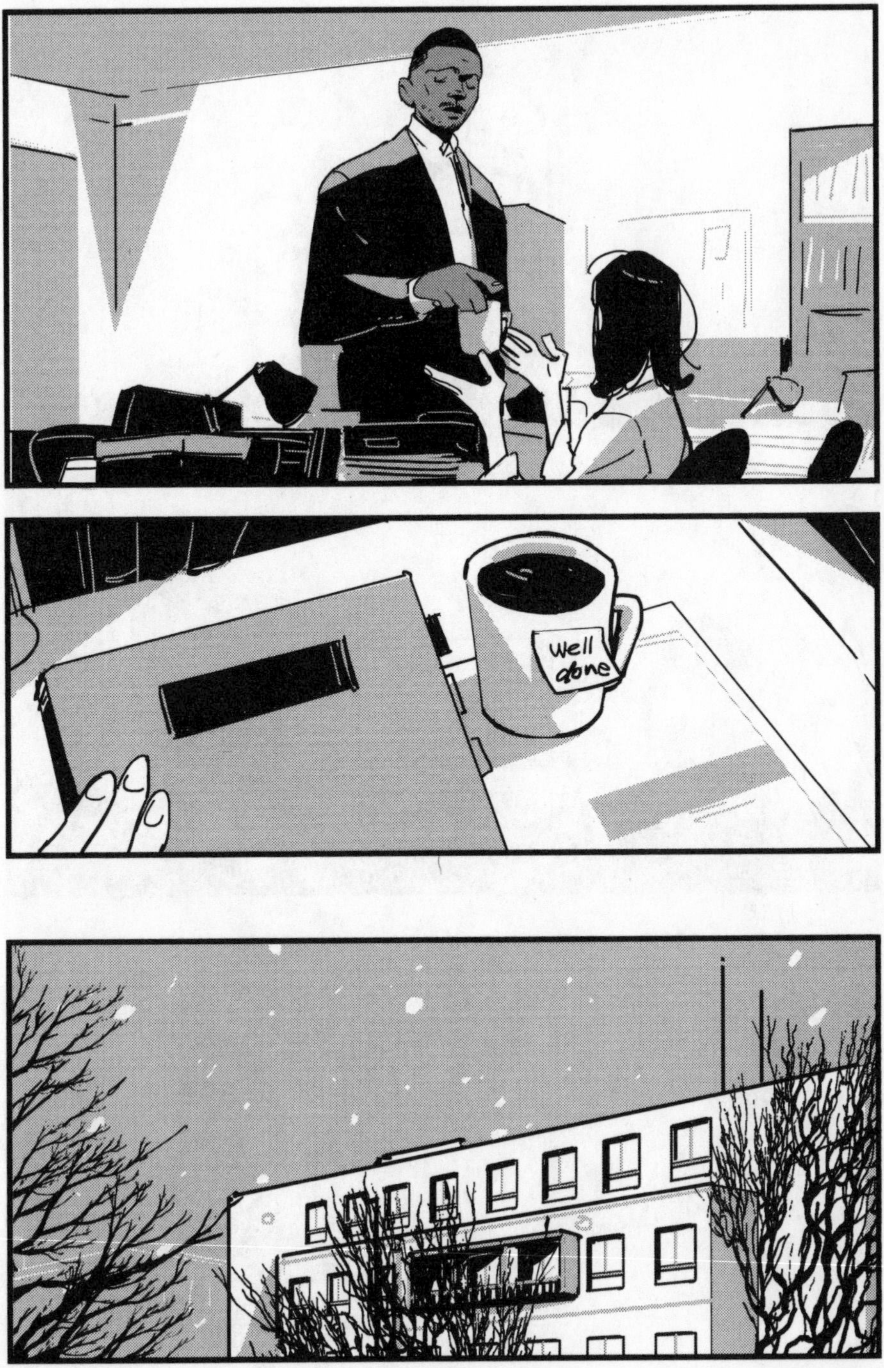
Well done

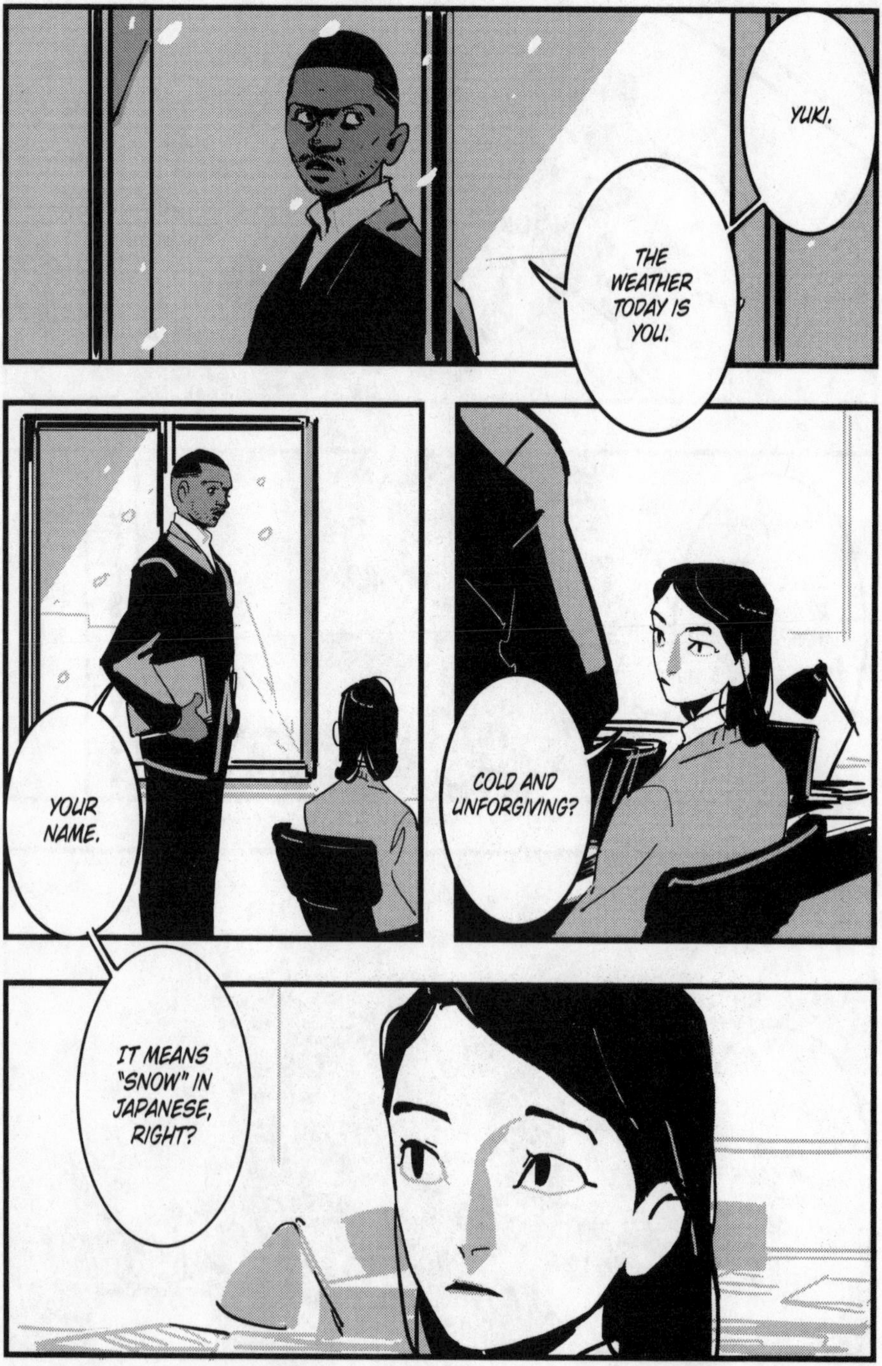
YUKI.
THE WEATHER TODAY IS YOU.
COLD AND UNFORGIVING?
YOUR NAME.
IT MEANS "SNOW" IN JAPANESE, RIGHT?

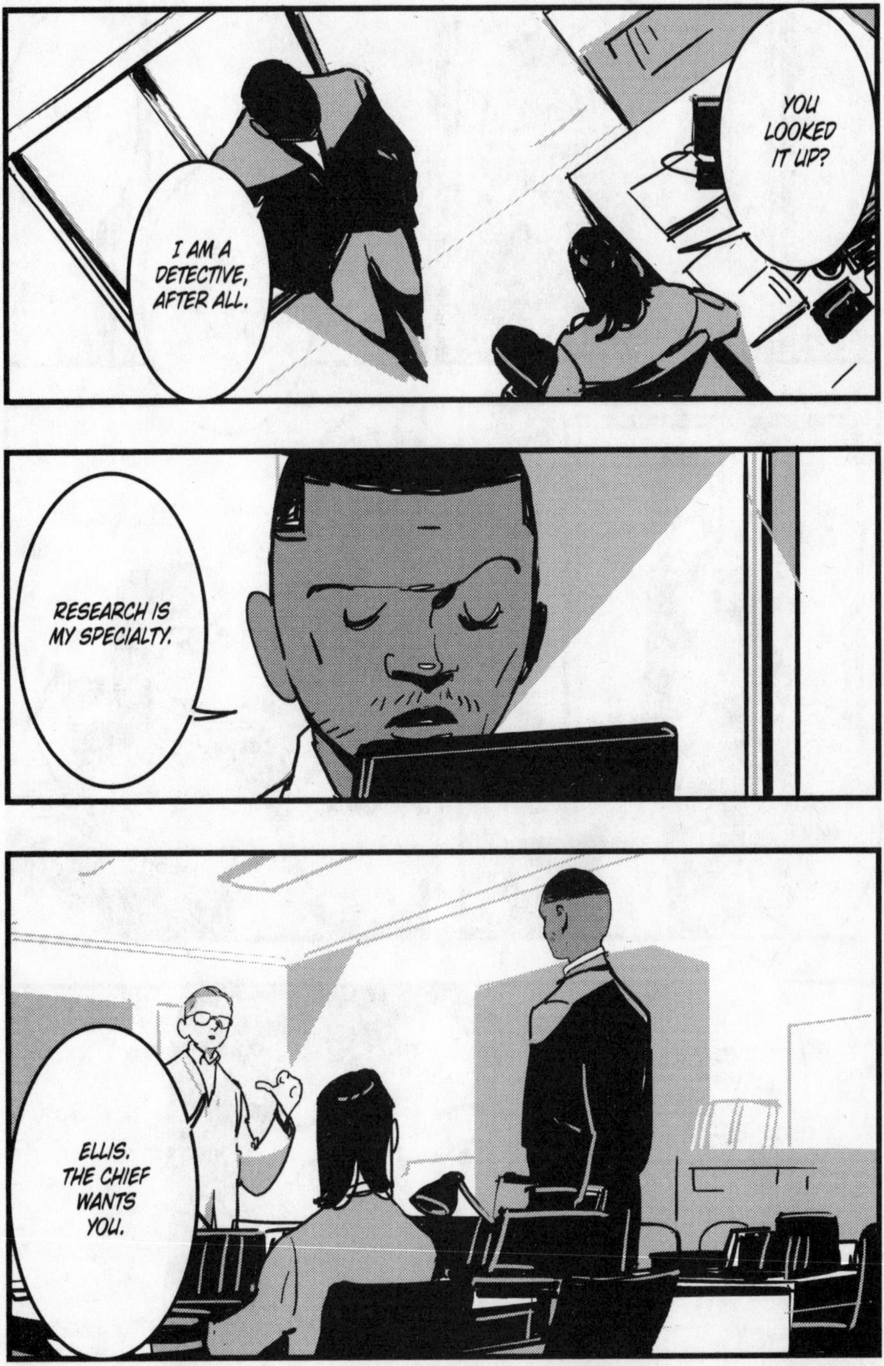
YOU LOOKED IT UP?
I AM A DETECTIVE, AFTER ALL.
RESEARCH IS MY SPECIALTY.
ELLIS. THE CHIEF WANTS YOU.

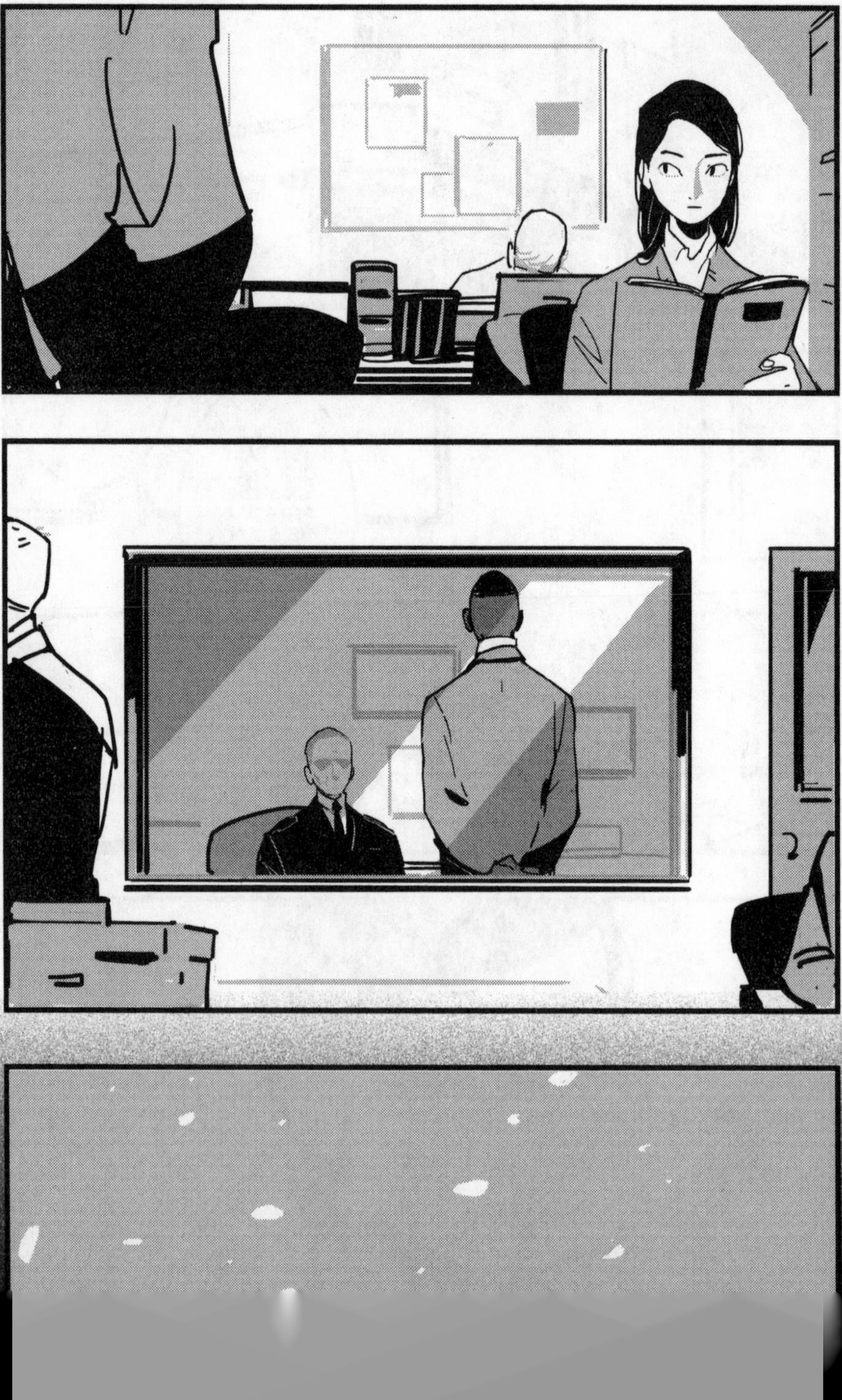

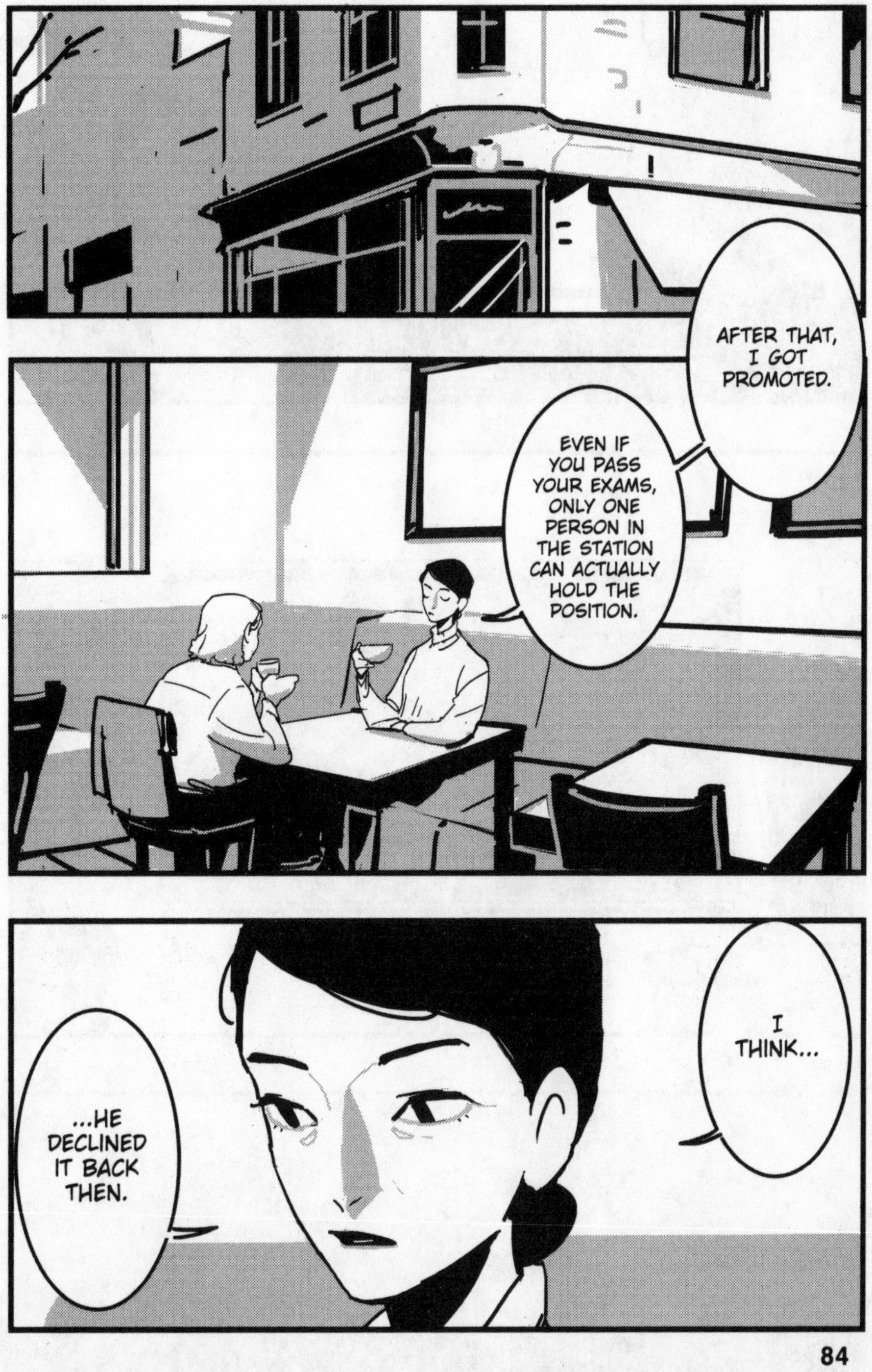
AFTER THAT, I GOT PROMOTED.
EVEN IF YOU PASS YOUR EXAMS, ONLY ONE PERSON IN THE STATION CAN ACTUALLY HOLD THE POSITION.
I THINK...
...HE DECLINED IT BACK THEN.

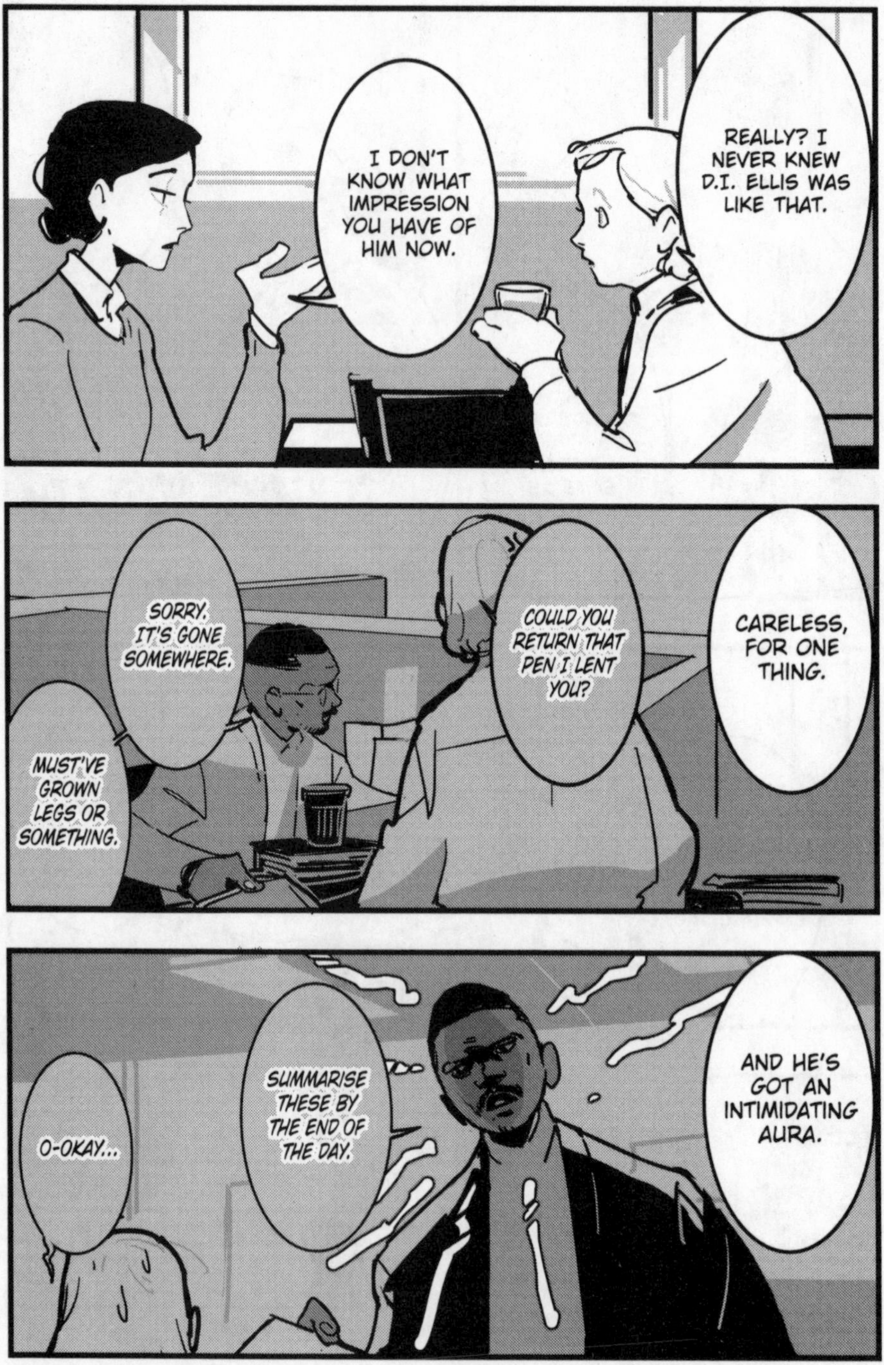
REALLY? I NEVER KNEW D.I. ELLIS WAS LIKE THAT.
I DON'T KNOW WHAT IMPRESSION YOU HAVE OF HIM NOW.
CARELESS, FOR ONE THING.
COULD YOU RETURN THAT PEN I LENT YOU?
SORRY. IT'S GONE SOMEWHERE.
MUST'VE GROWN LEGS OR SOMETHING.
AND HE'S GOT AN INTIMIDATING AURA.
SUMMARISE THESE BY THE END OF THE DAY.
O-OKAY...

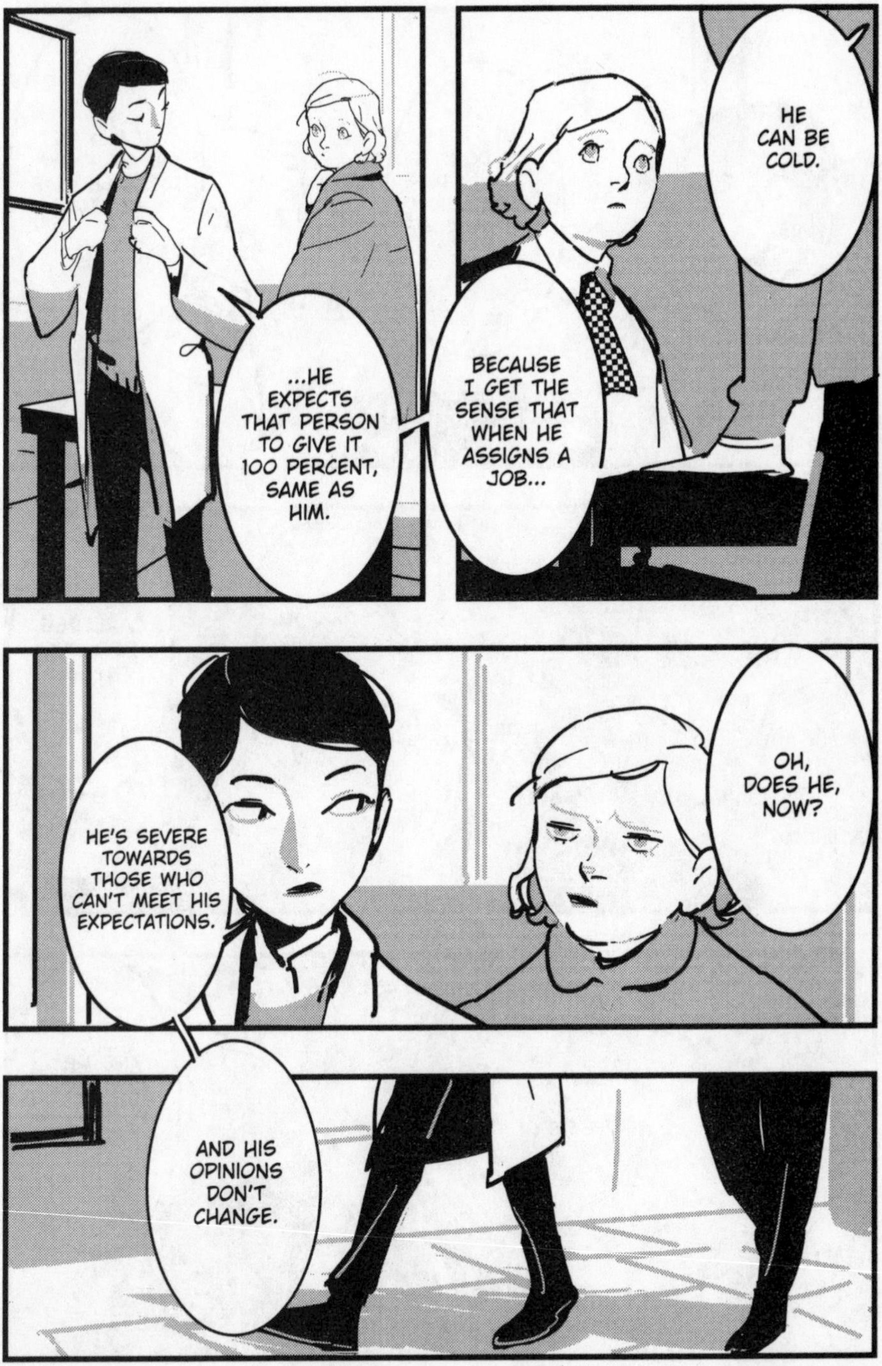
HE CAN BE COLD.
BECAUSE I GET THE SENSE THAT WHEN HE ASSIGNS A JOB...
...HE EXPECTS THAT PERSON TO GIVE IT 100 PERCENT, SAME AS HIM.
OH, DOES HE, NOW?
HE'S SEVERE TOWARDS THOSE WHO CAN'T MEET HIS EXPECTATIONS.
AND HIS OPINIONS DON'T CHANGE.

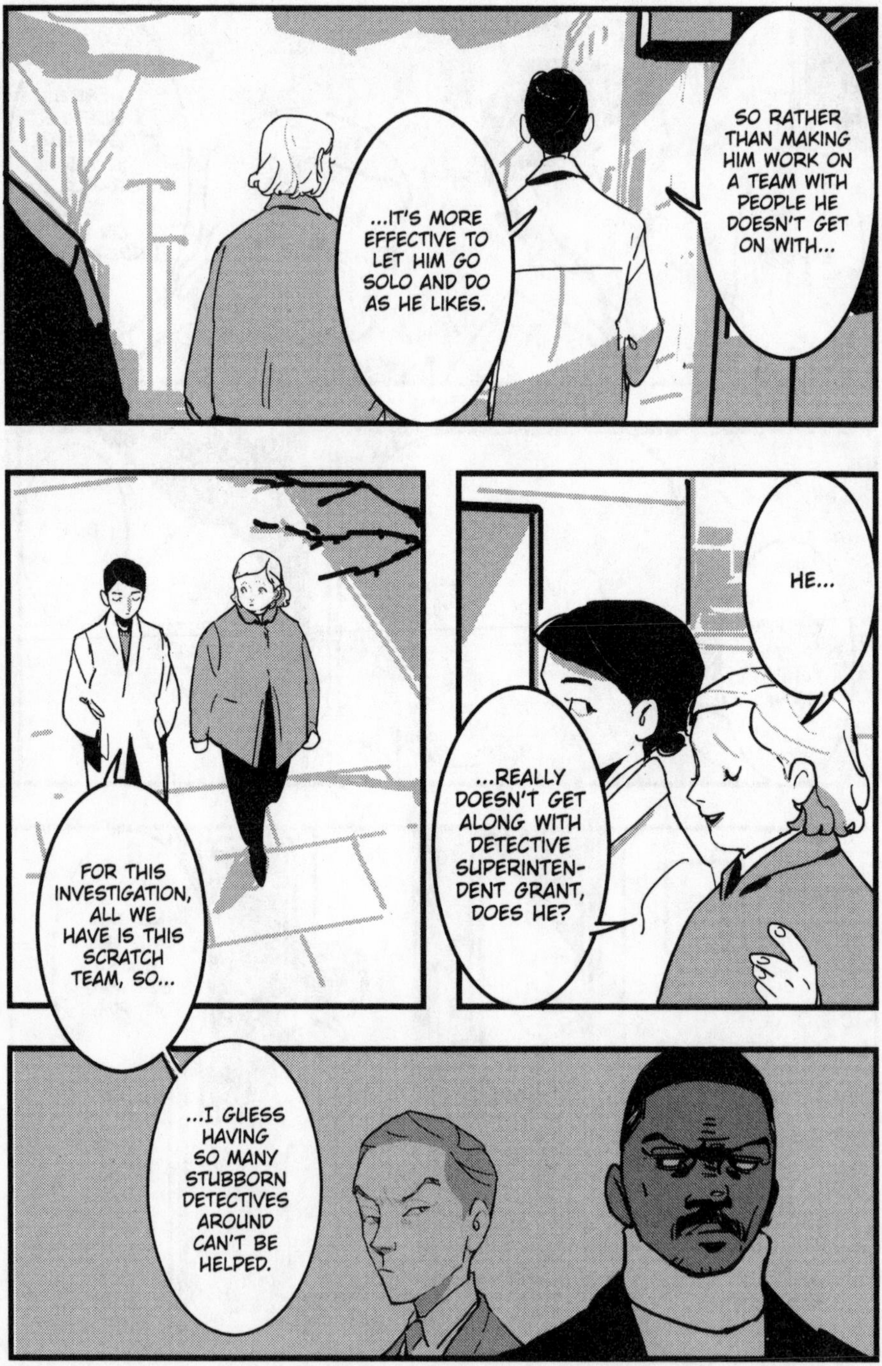
SO RATHER THAN MAKING HIM WORK ON A TEAM WITH PEOPLE HE DOESN'T GET ON WITH...
...IT'S MORE EFFECTIVE TO LET HIM GO SOLO AND DO AS HE LIKES.
HE...
...REALLY DOESN'T GET ALONG WITH DETECTIVE SUPERINTEN-DENT GRANT, DOES HE?
FOR THIS INVESTIGATION, ALL WE HAVE IS THIS SCRATCH TEAM, SO...
...I GUESS HAVING SO MANY STUBBORN DETECTIVES AROUND CAN'T BE HELPED.

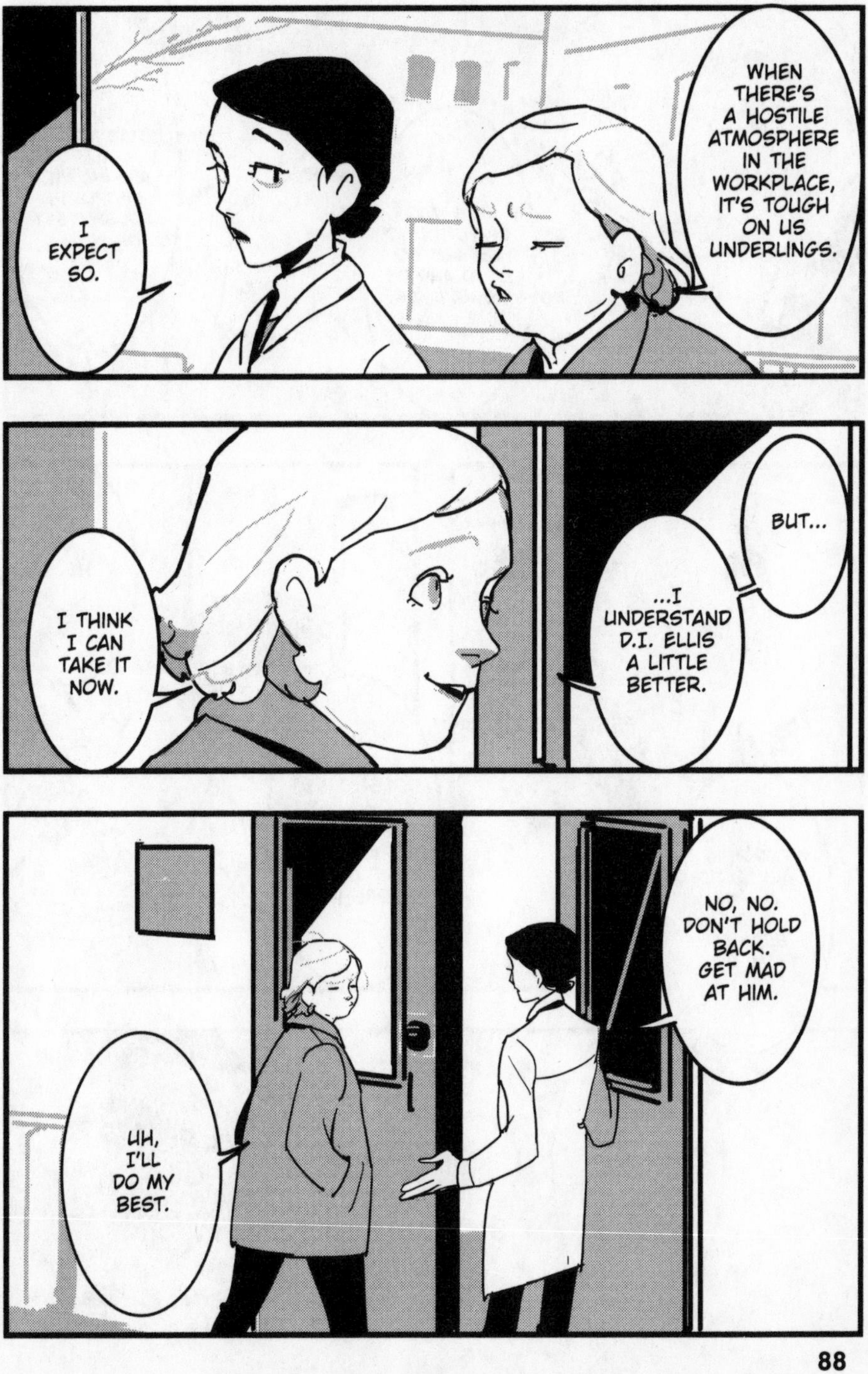
WHEN THERE'S A HOSTILE ATMOSPHERE IN THE WORKPLACE, IT'S TOUGH ON US UNDERLINGS.
I EXPECT SO.
BUT...
...I UNDERSTAND D.I. ELLIS A LITTLE BETTER.
I THINK I CAN TAKE IT NOW.
NO, NO. DON'T HOLD BACK. GET MAD AT HIM.
UH, I'LL DO MY BEST.

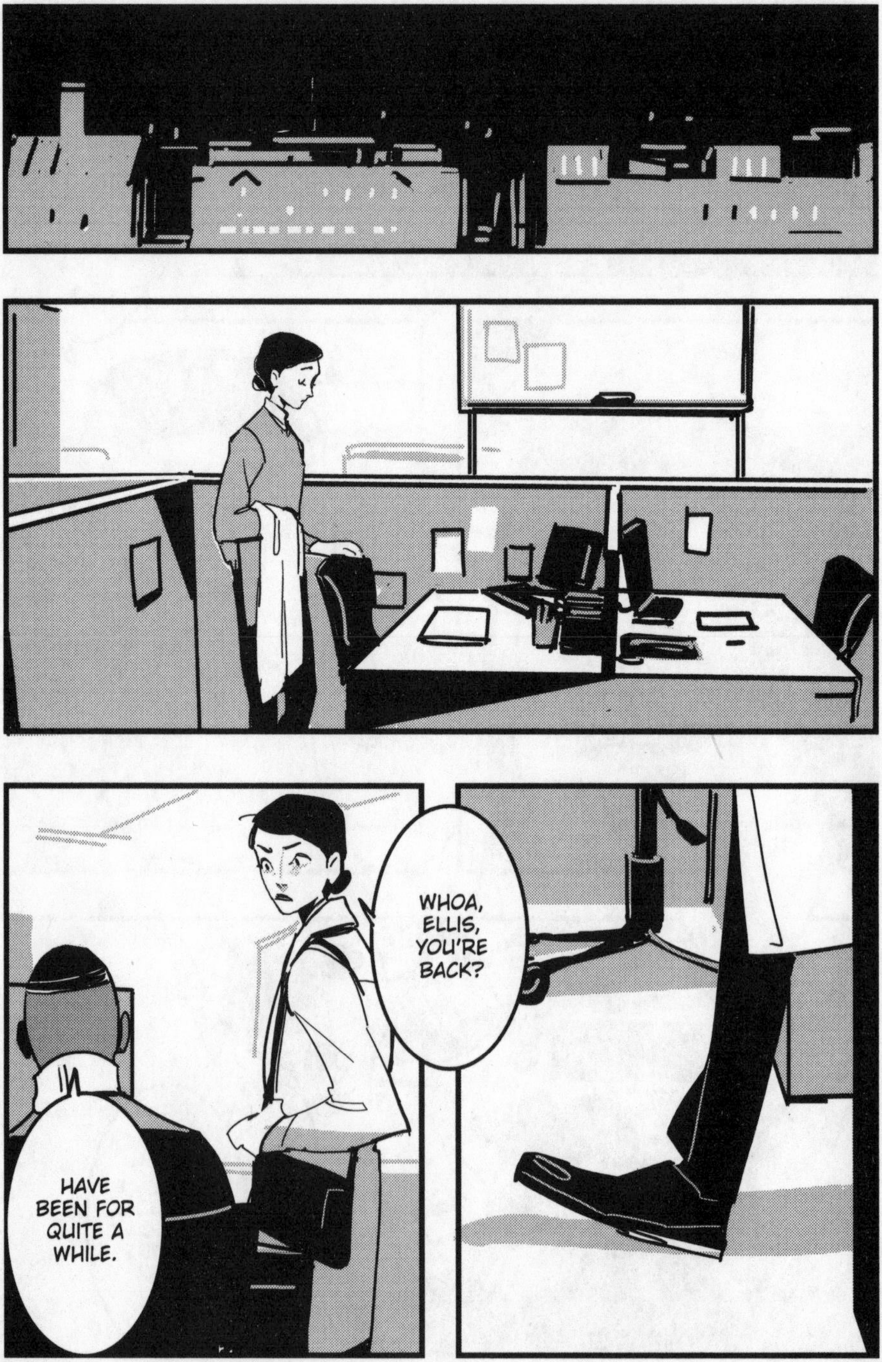
WHOA, ELLIS, YOU'RE BACK?
HAVE BEEN FOR QUITE A WHILE.

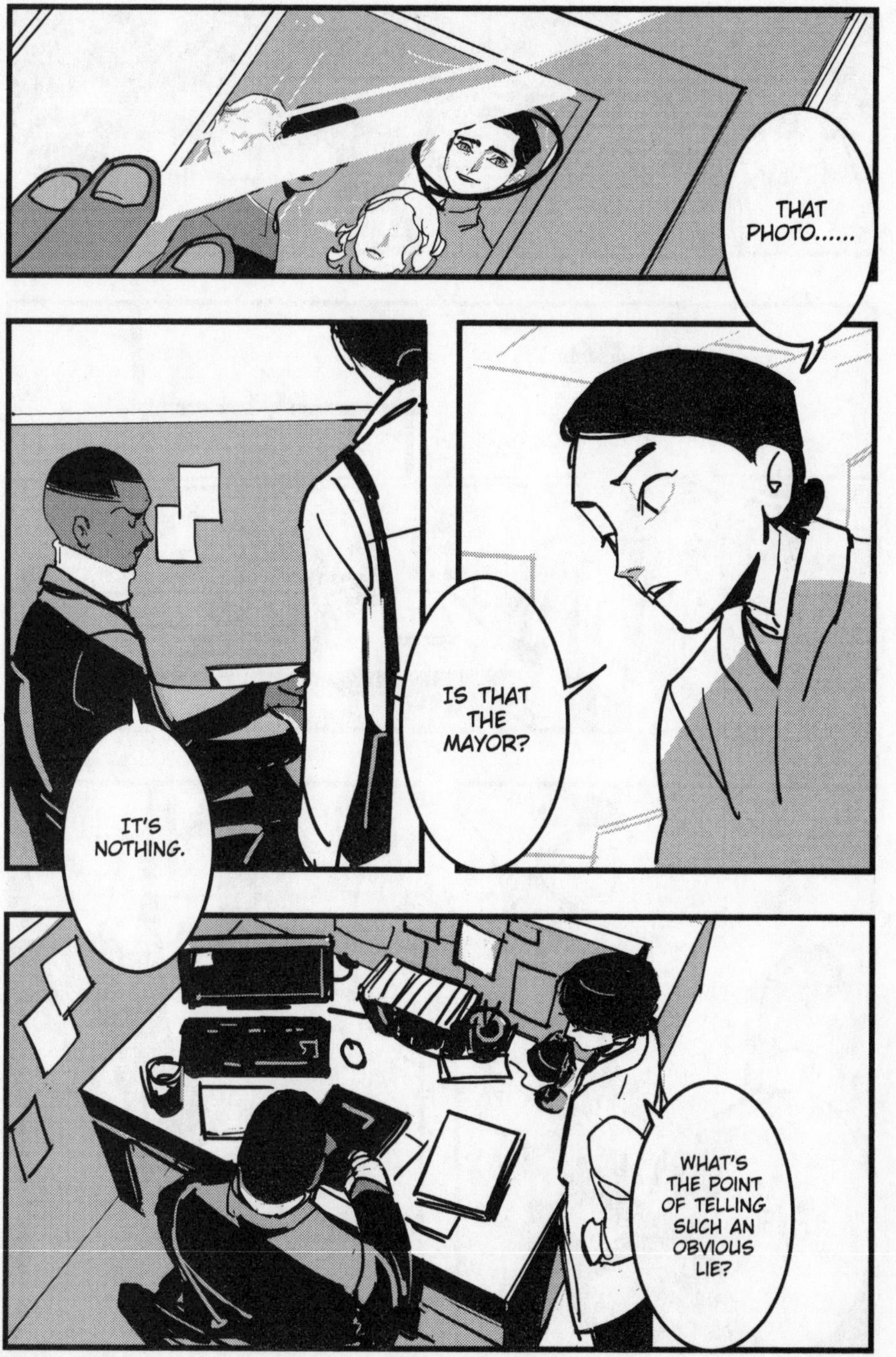
THAT PHOTO......
IS THAT THE MAYOR?
IT'S NOTHING.
WHAT'S THE POINT OF TELLING SUCH AN OBVIOUS LIE?

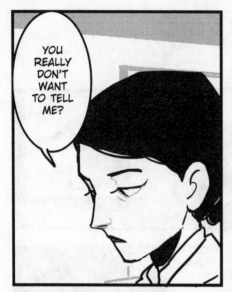

IT'S A LONG STORY.
YOU REALLY DON'T WANT TO TELL ME?
I'M COUNTING ON YOU.
SO...
...FOR NOW, PRETEND YOU DIDN'T SEE ANYTHING.

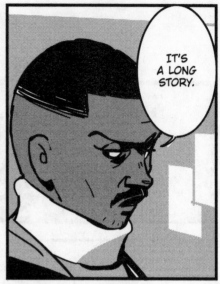

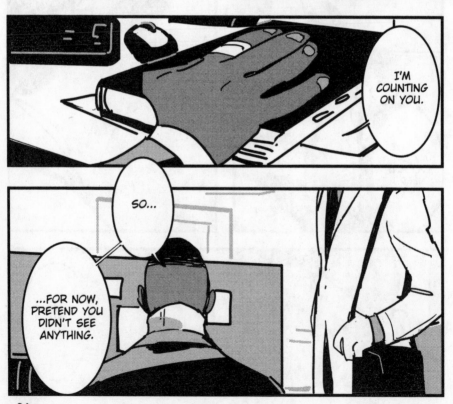

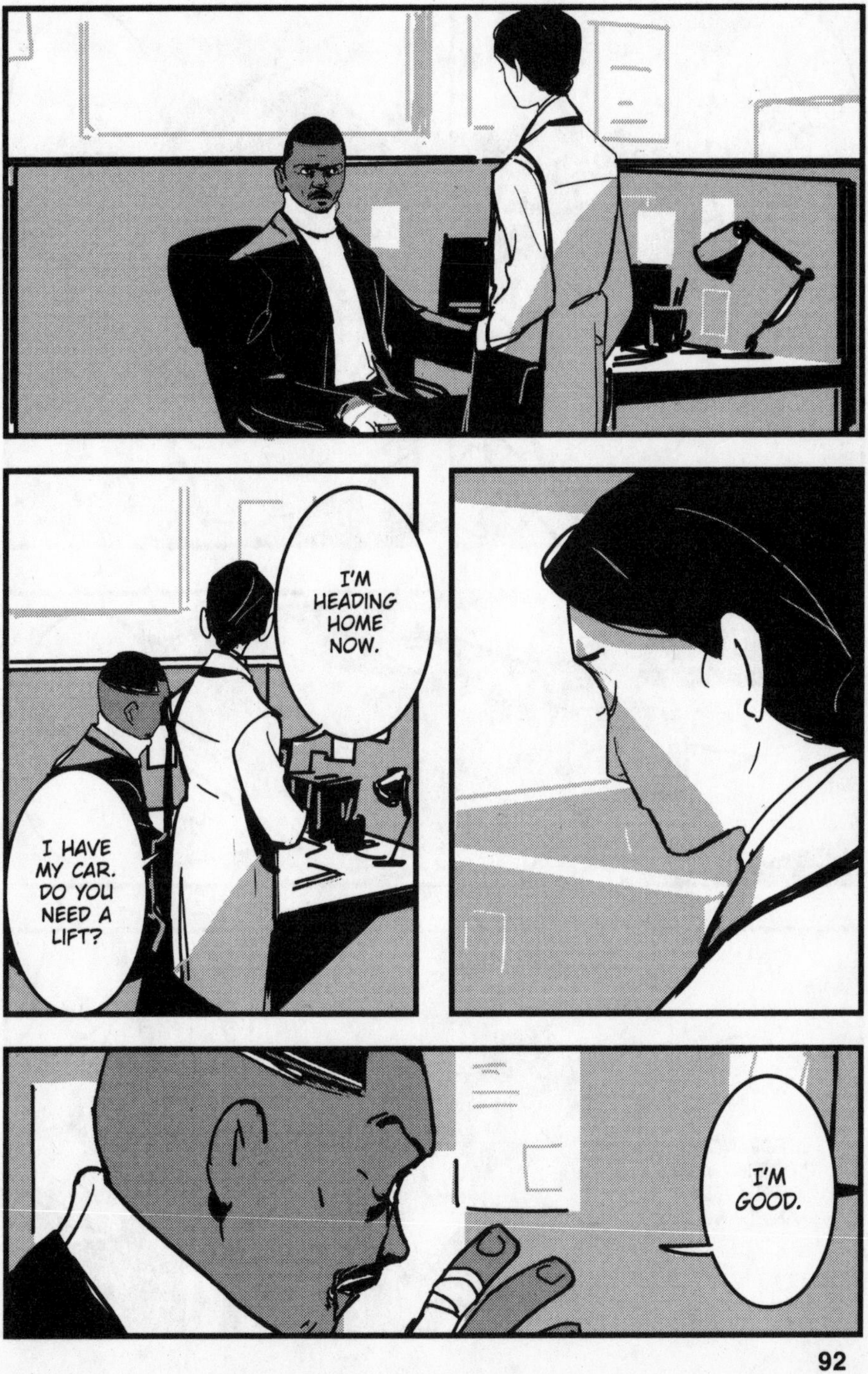
I'M HEADING HOME NOW.
I HAVE MY CAR. DO YOU NEED A LIFT?
I'M GOOD.

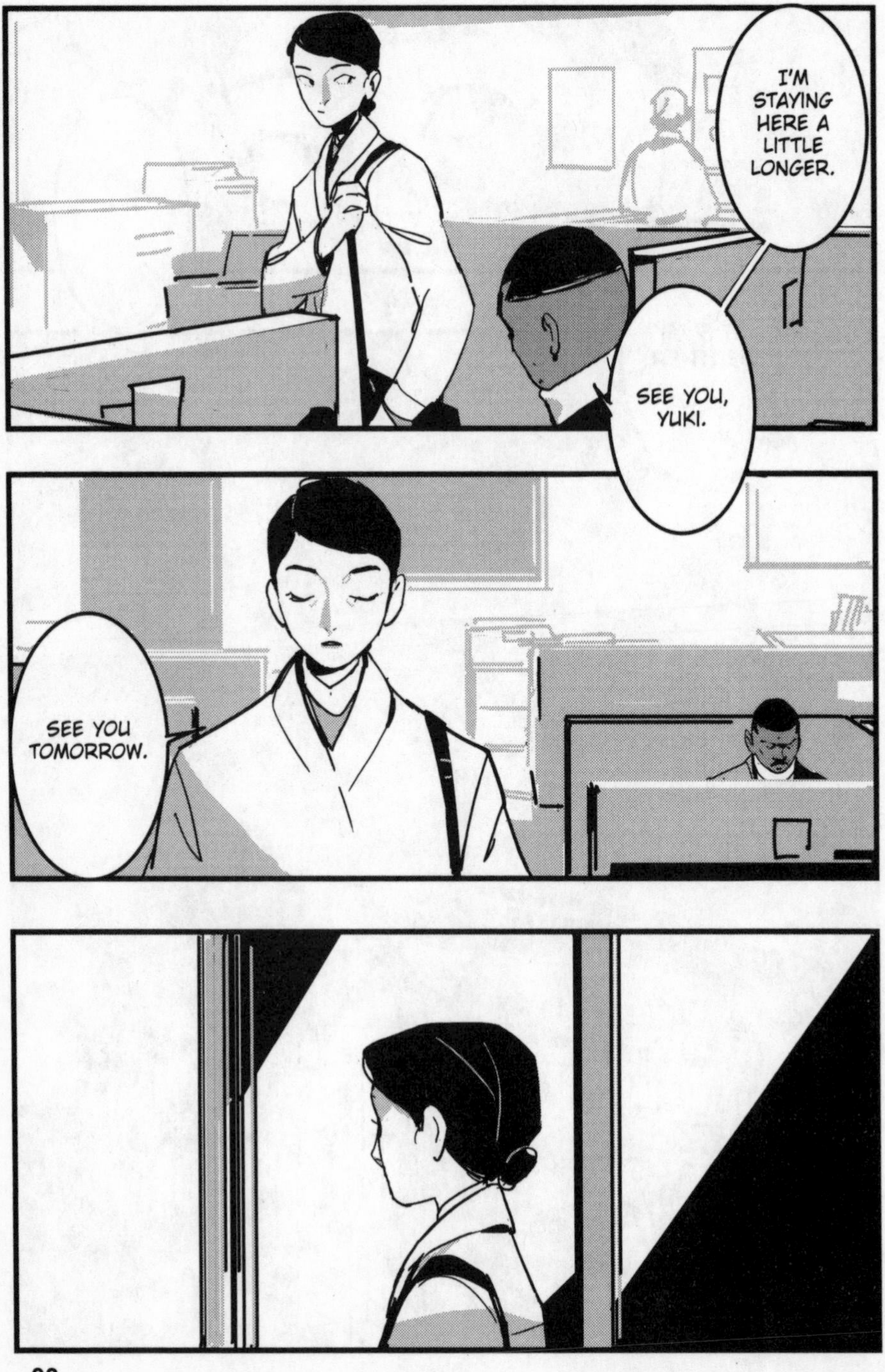
I'M STAYING HERE A LITTLE LONGER.
SEE YOU, YUKI.
SEE YOU TOMORROW.

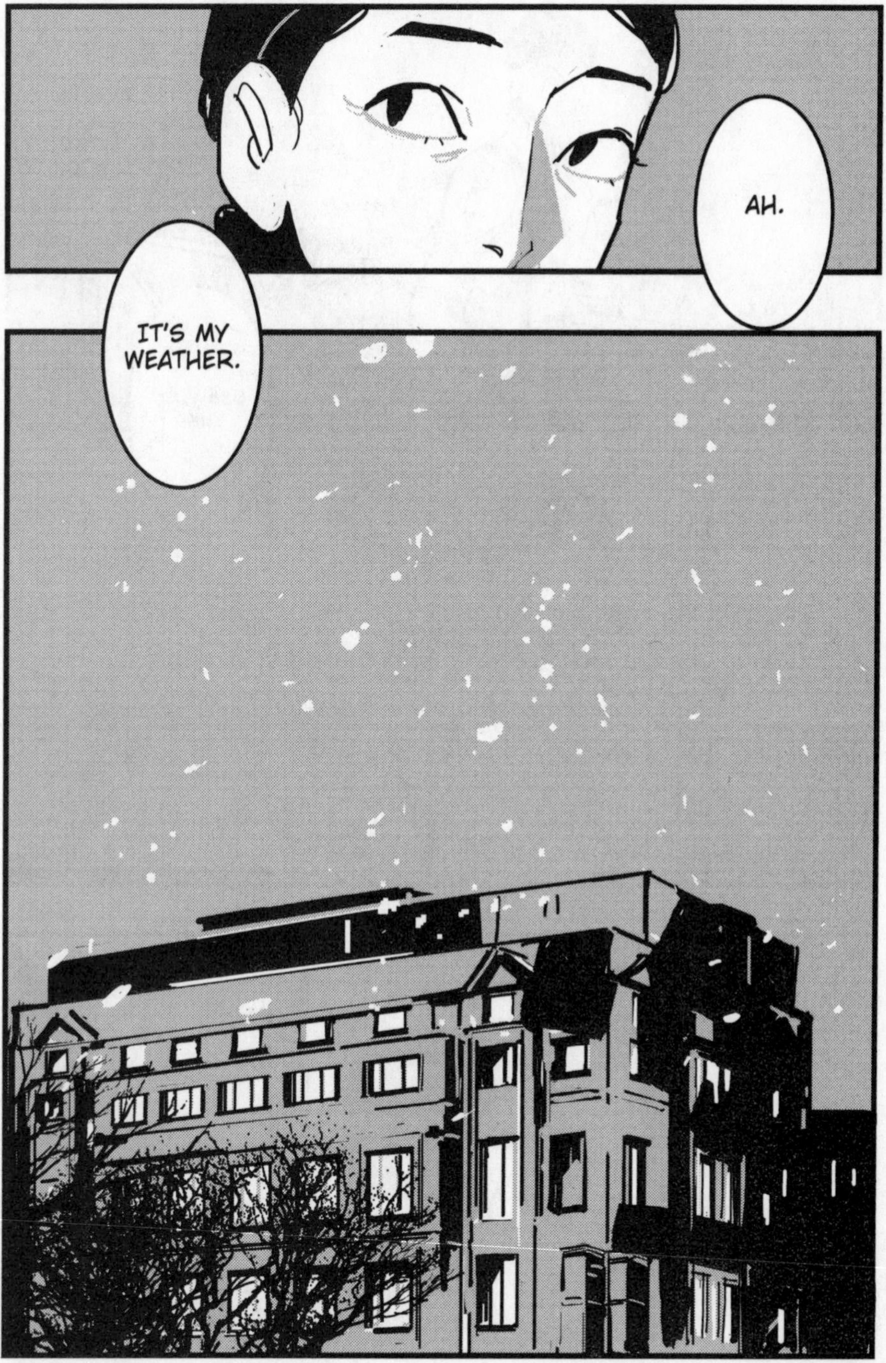
AH.
IT'S MY WEATHER.

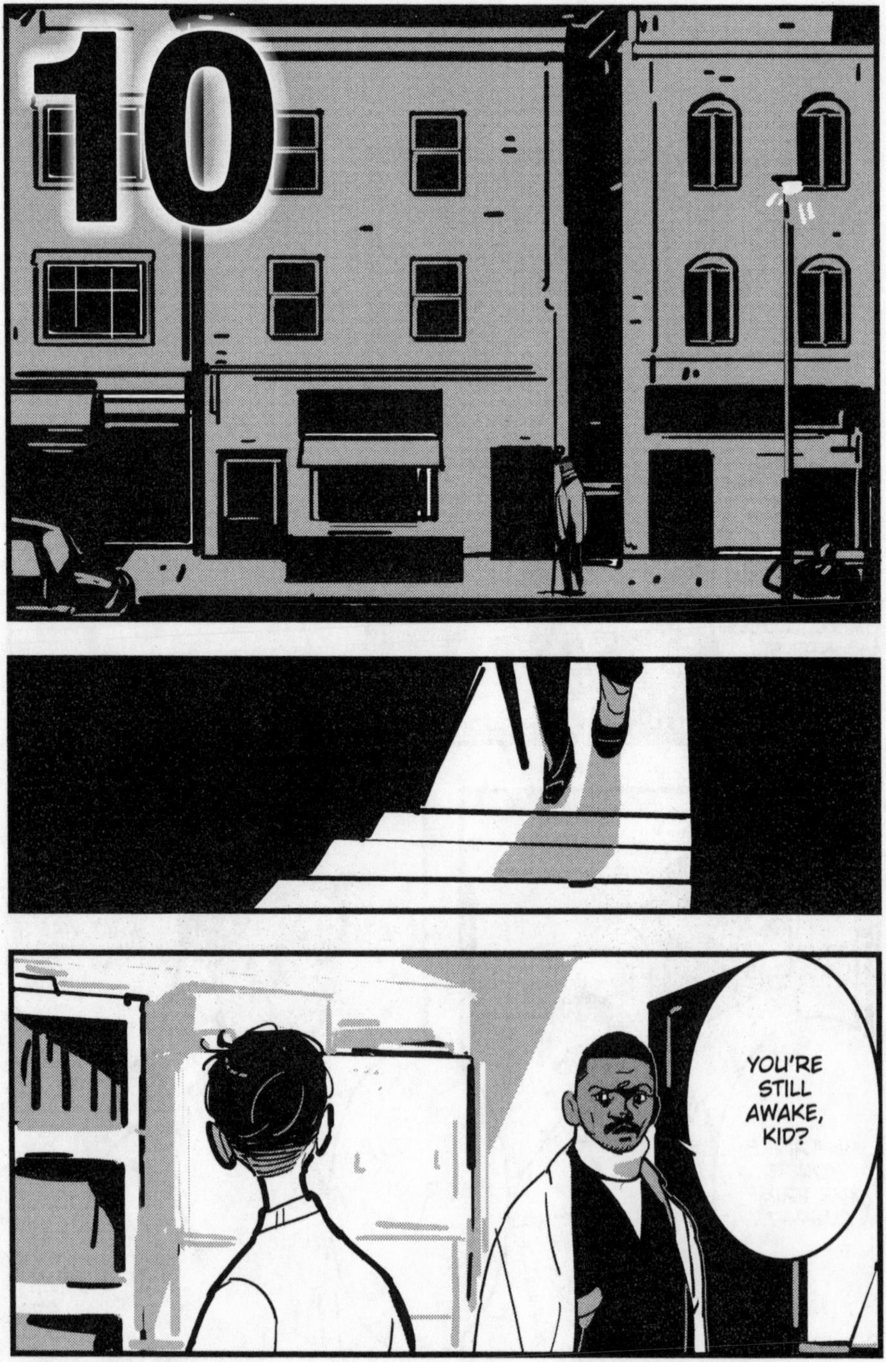
10
YOU'RE STILL AWAKE, KID?

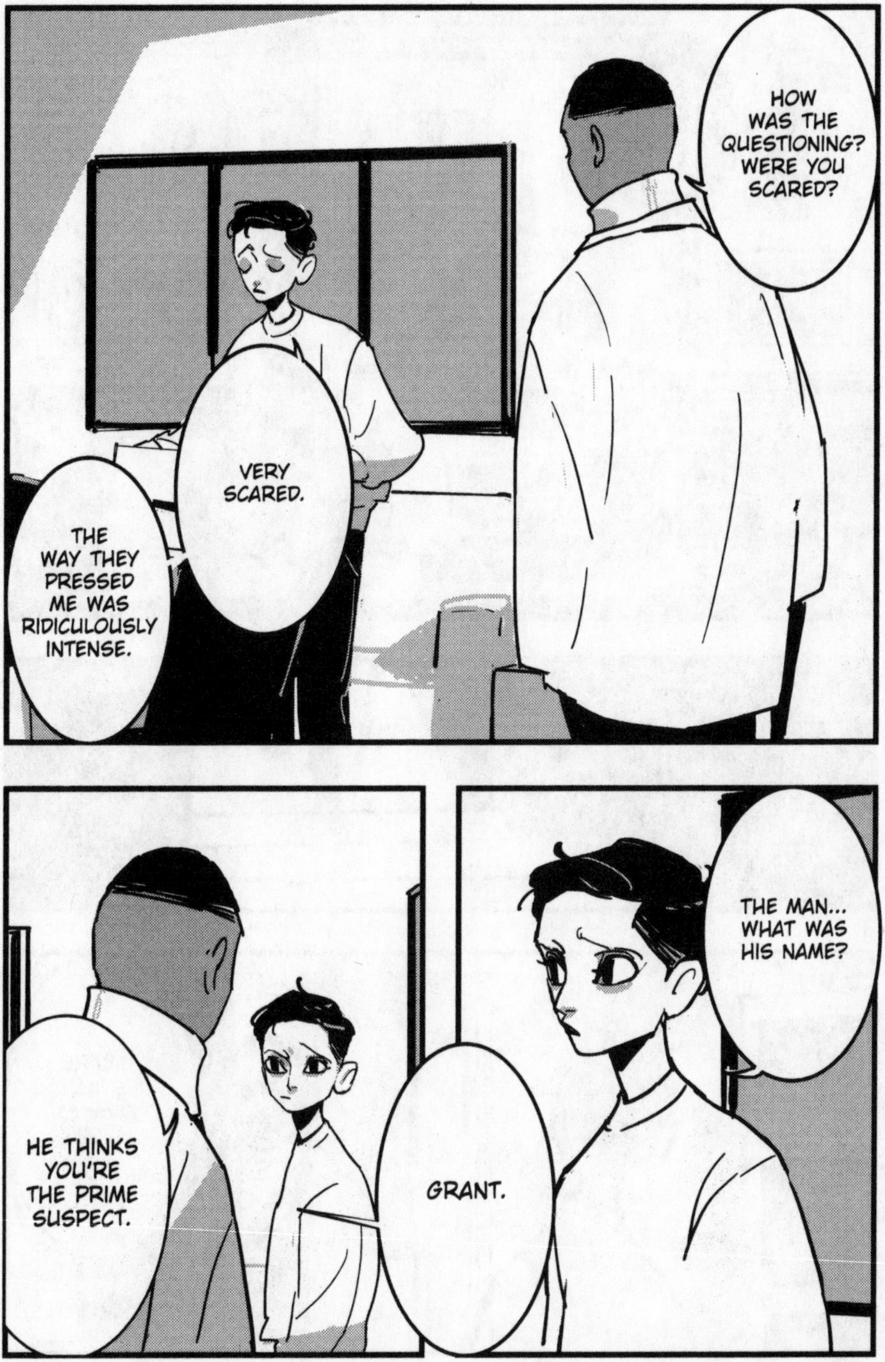
HOW WAS THE QUESTIONING? WERE YOU SCARED?
VERY SCARED.
THE WAY THEY PRESSED ME WAS RIDICULOUSLY INTENSE.
THE MAN... WHAT WAS HIS NAME?
GRANT.
HE THINKS YOU'RE THE PRIME SUSPECT.

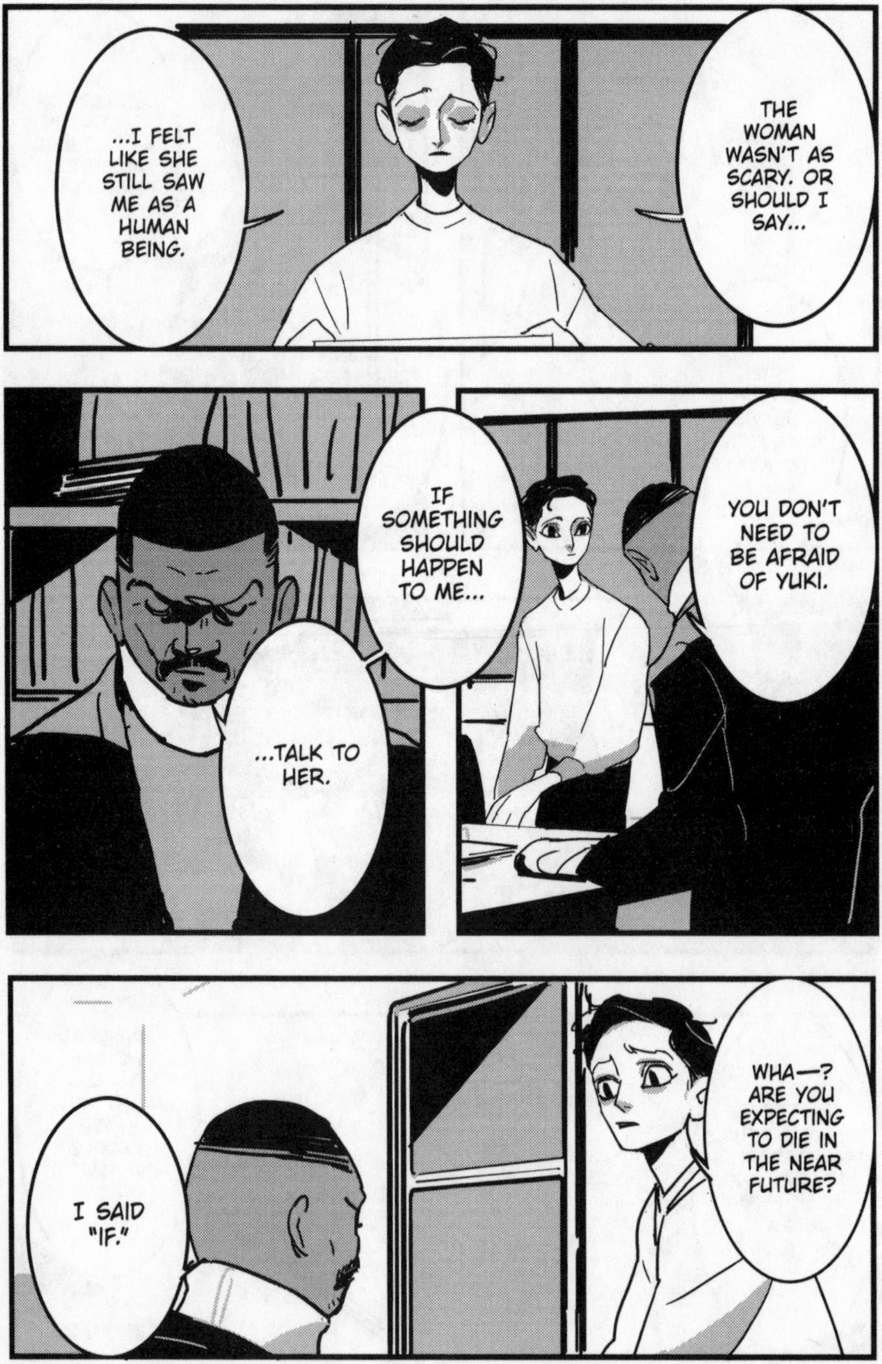
THE WOMAN WASN'T AS SCARY. OR SHOULD I SAY...
...I FELT LIKE SHE STILL SAW ME AS A HUMAN BEING.
YOU DON'T NEED TO BE AFRAID OF YUKI.
IF SOMETHING SHOULD HAPPEN TO ME...
...TALK TO HER.
WHA—? ARE YOU EXPECTING TO DIE IN THE NEAR FUTURE?
I SAID "IF."

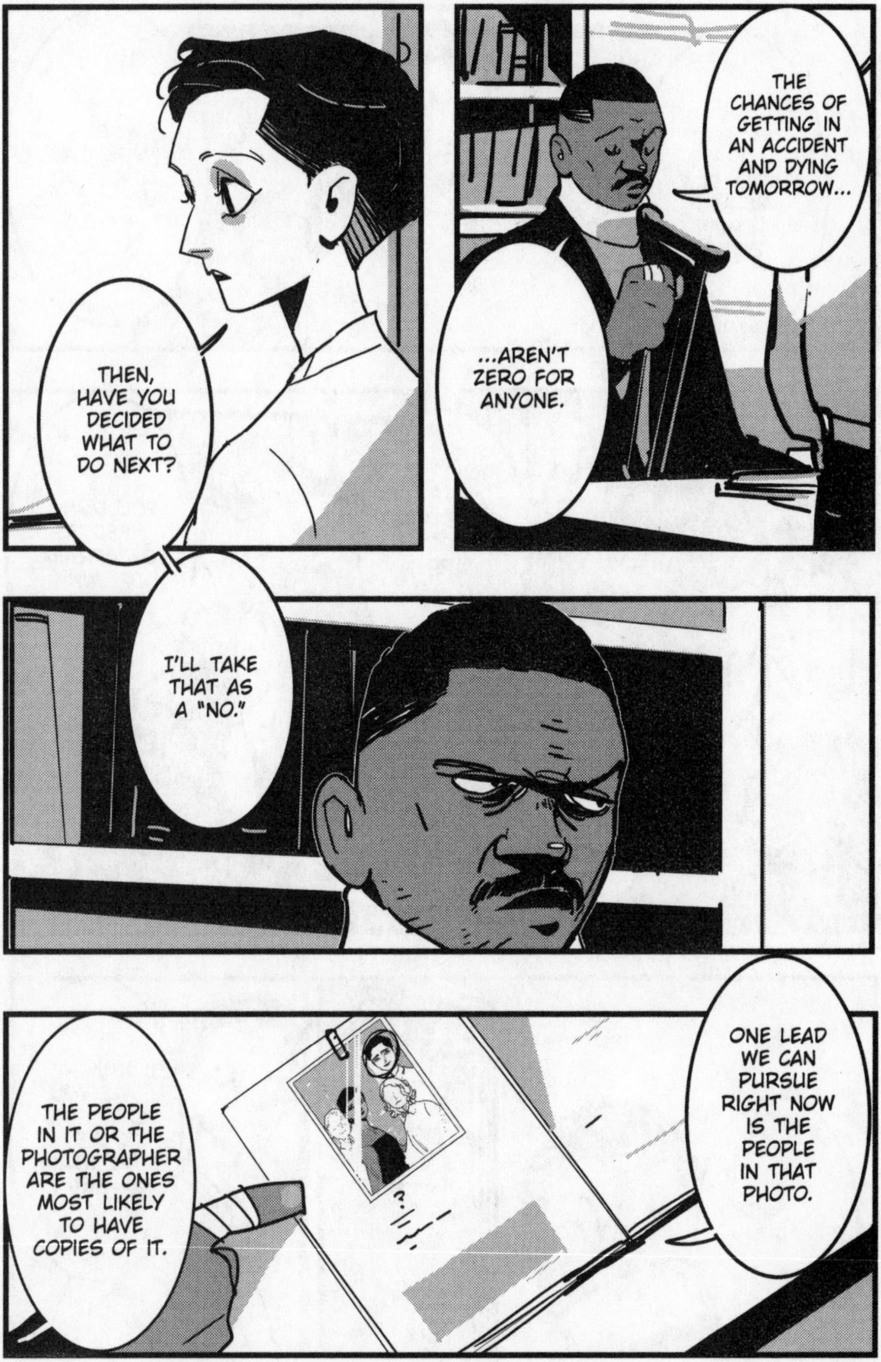
THE CHANCES OF GETTING IN AN ACCIDENT AND DYING TOMORROW...
...AREN'T ZERO FOR ANYONE.
THEN, HAVE YOU DECIDED WHAT TO DO NEXT?
I'LL TAKE THAT AS A "NO."
ONE LEAD WE CAN PURSUE RIGHT NOW IS THE PEOPLE IN THAT PHOTO.
THE PEOPLE IN IT OR THE PHOTOGRAPHER ARE THE ONES MOST LIKELY TO HAVE COPIES OF IT.

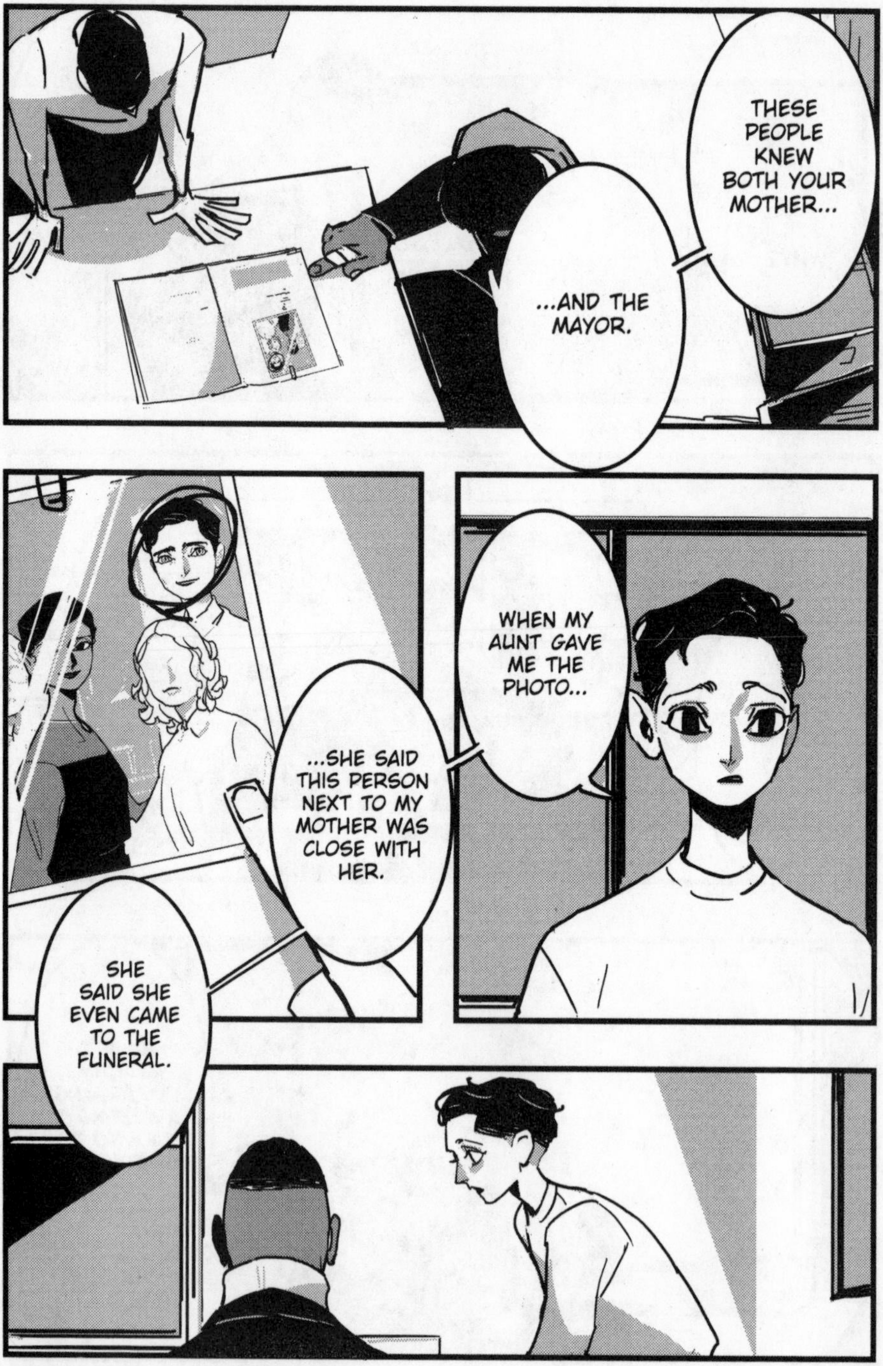
THESE PEOPLE KNEW BOTH YOUR MOTHER...
...AND THE MAYOR.
WHEN MY AUNT GAVE ME THE PHOTO...
...SHE SAID THIS PERSON NEXT TO MY MOTHER WAS CLOSE WITH HER.
SHE SAID SHE EVEN CAME TO THE FUNERAL.

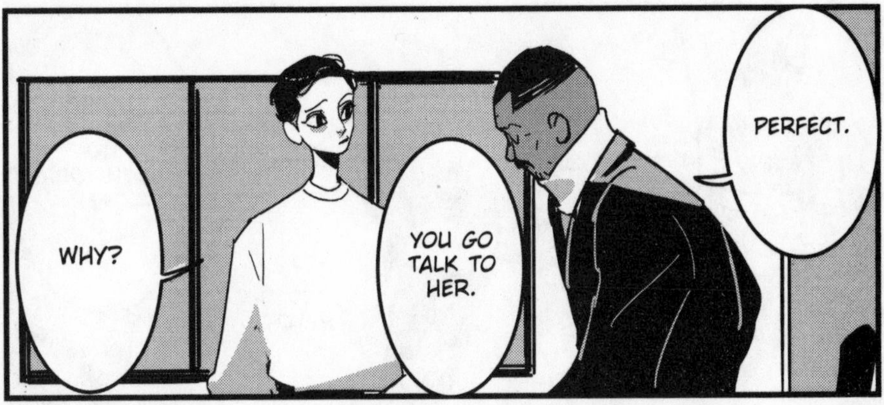
PERFECT.
YOU GO TALK TO HER.
WHY?

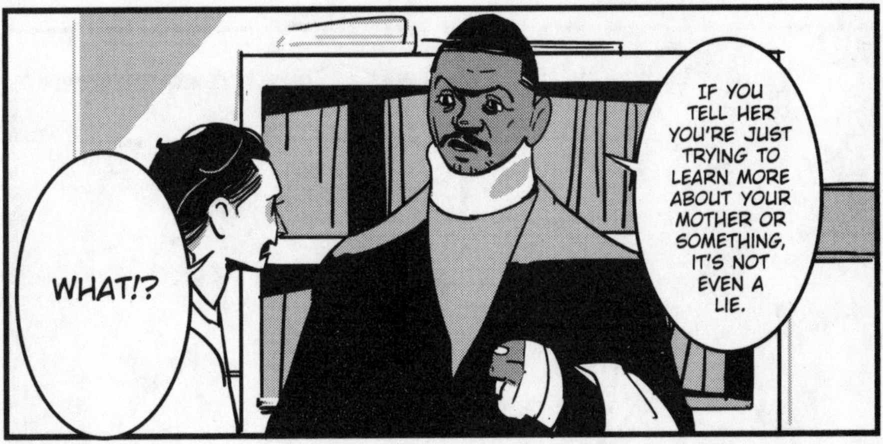
IF YOU TELL HER YOU'RE JUST TRYING TO LEARN MORE ABOUT YOUR MOTHER OR SOMETHING, IT'S NOT EVEN A LIE.
WHAT!?

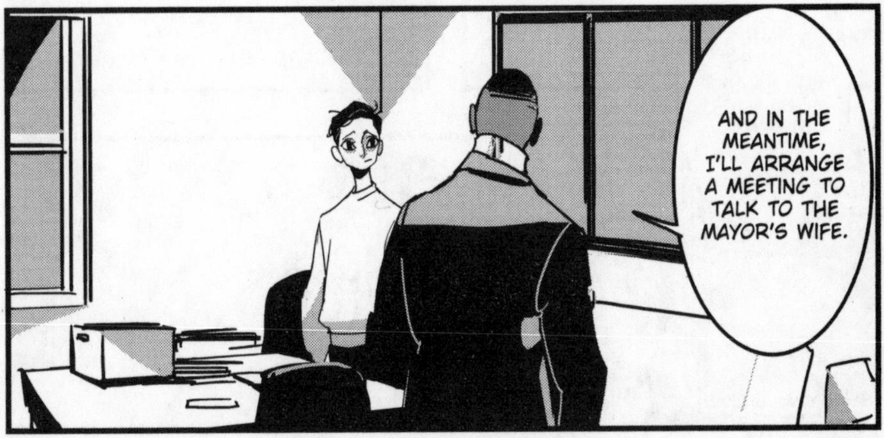
AND IN THE MEANTIME, I'LL ARRANGE A MEETING TO TALK TO THE MAYOR'S WIFE.

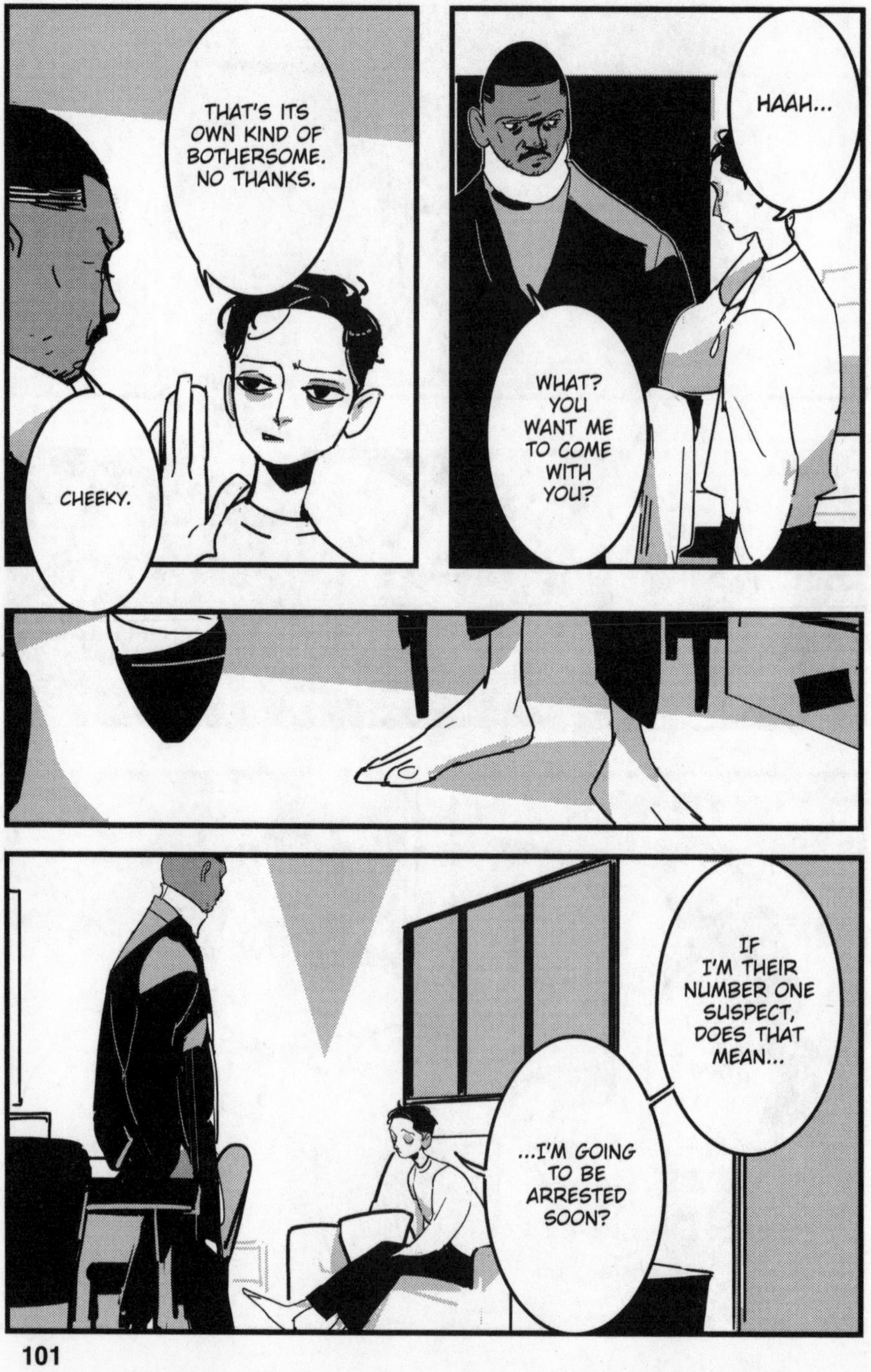
HAAH...
WHAT? YOU WANT ME TO COME WITH YOU?
THAT'S ITS OWN KIND OF BOTHERSOME. NO THANKS.
CHEEKY.
IF I'M THEIR NUMBER ONE SUSPECT, DOES THAT MEAN...
...I'M GOING TO BE ARRESTED SOON?

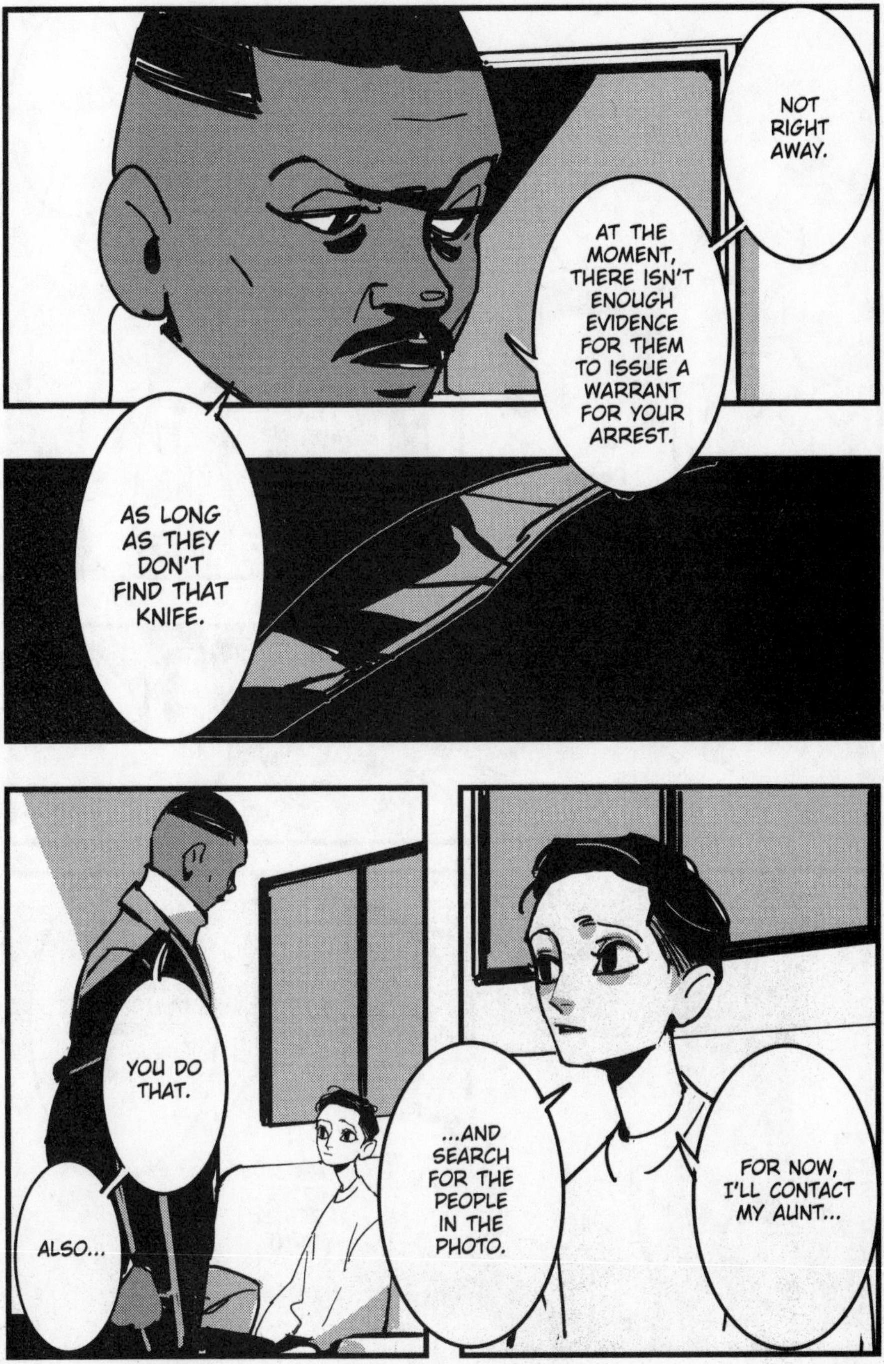
NOT RIGHT AWAY.
AT THE MOMENT, THERE ISN'T ENOUGH EVIDENCE FOR THEM TO ISSUE A WARRANT FOR YOUR ARREST.
AS LONG AS THEY DON'T FIND THAT KNIFE.
FOR NOW, I'LL CONTACT MY AUNT...
...AND SEARCH FOR THE PEOPLE IN THE PHOTO.
YOU DO THAT.
ALSO...

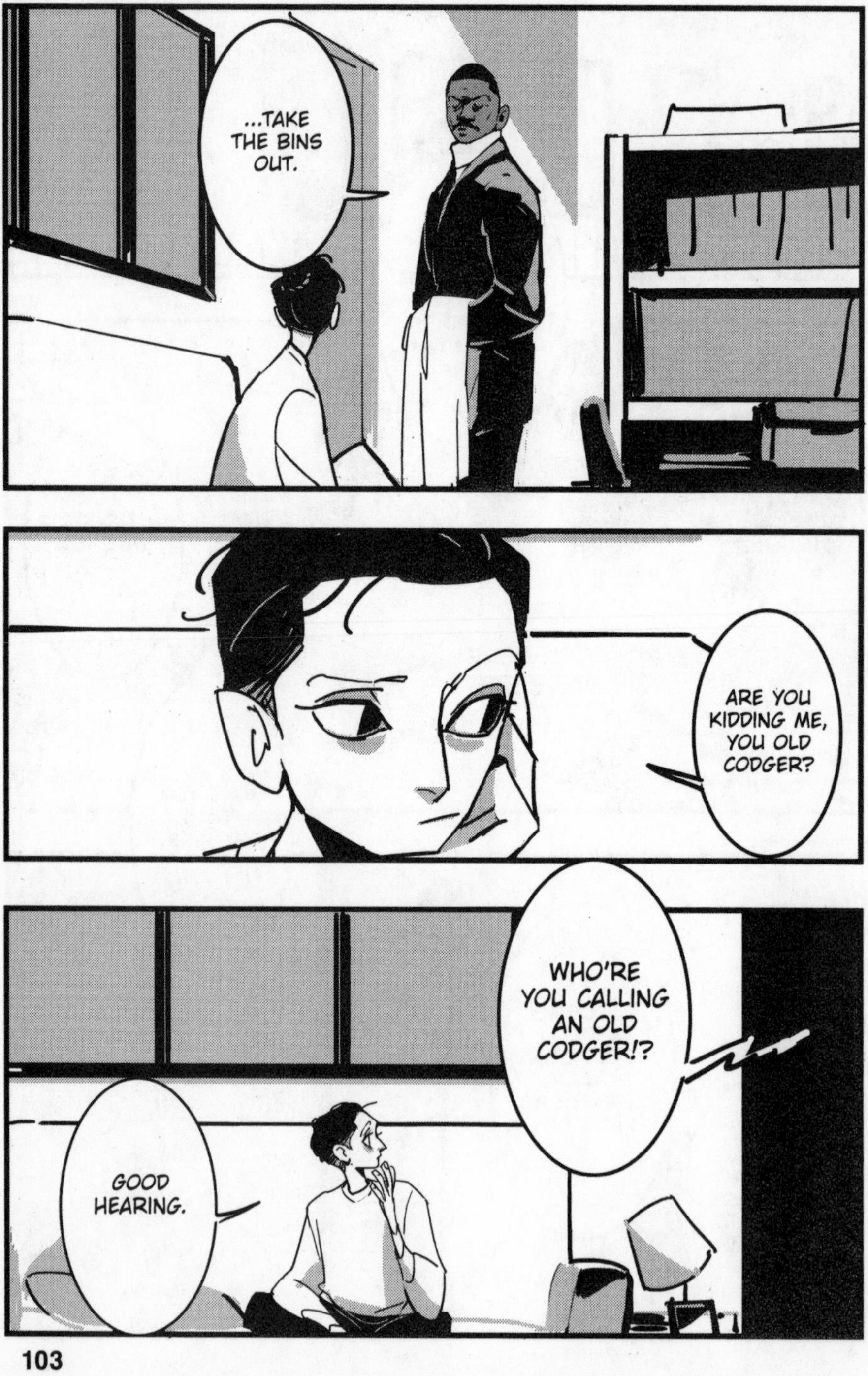
...TAKE THE BINS OUT.
ARE YOU KIDDING ME, YOU OLD CODGER?
WHO'RE YOU CALLING AN OLD CODGER!?
GOOD HEARING.

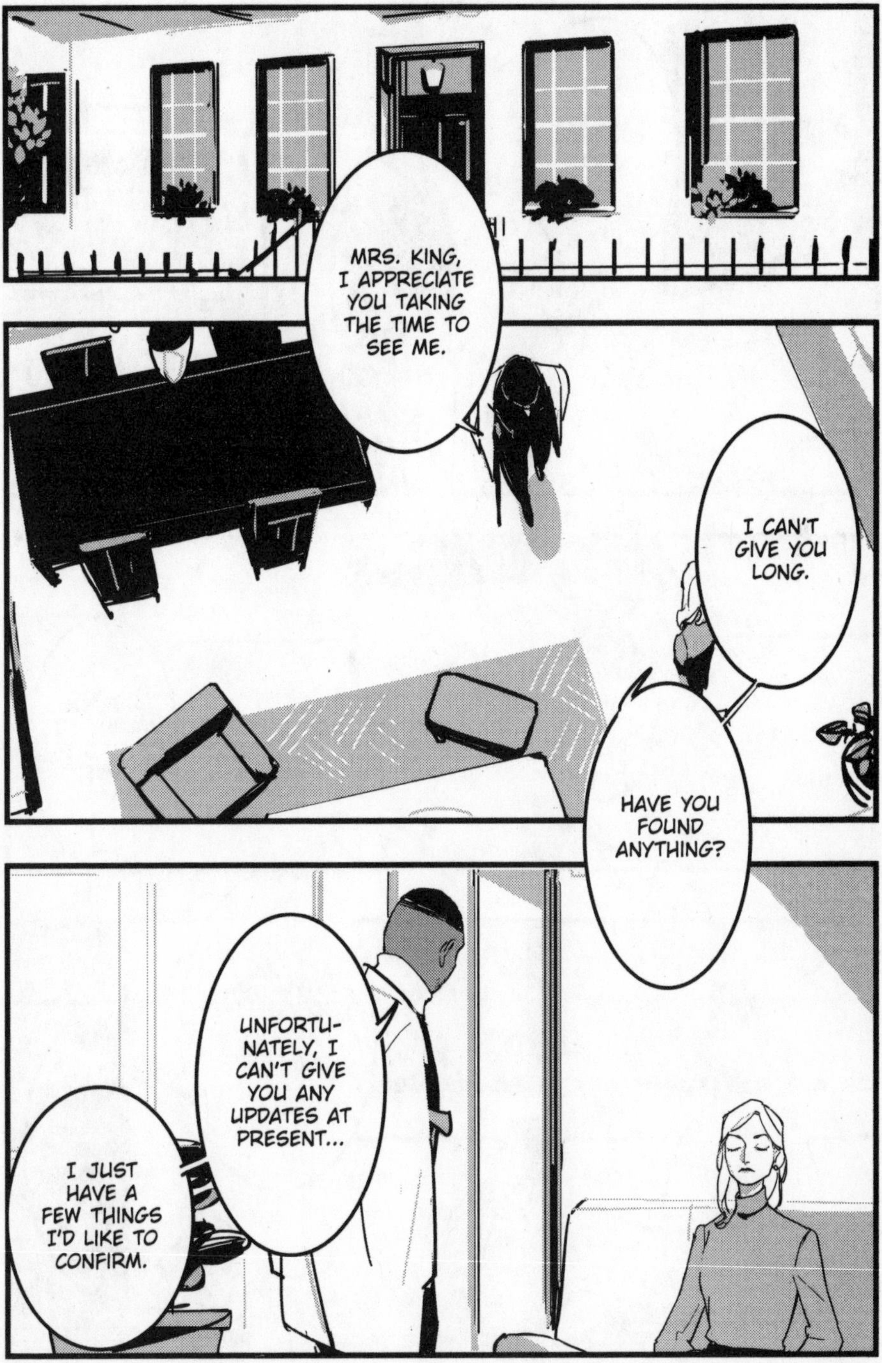
MRS. KING, I APPRECIATE YOU TAKING THE TIME TO SEE ME.
I CAN'T GIVE YOU LONG.
HAVE YOU FOUND ANYTHING?
UNFORTUNATELY, I CAN'T GIVE YOU ANY UPDATES AT PRESENT...
I JUST HAVE A FEW THINGS I'D LIKE TO CONFIRM.

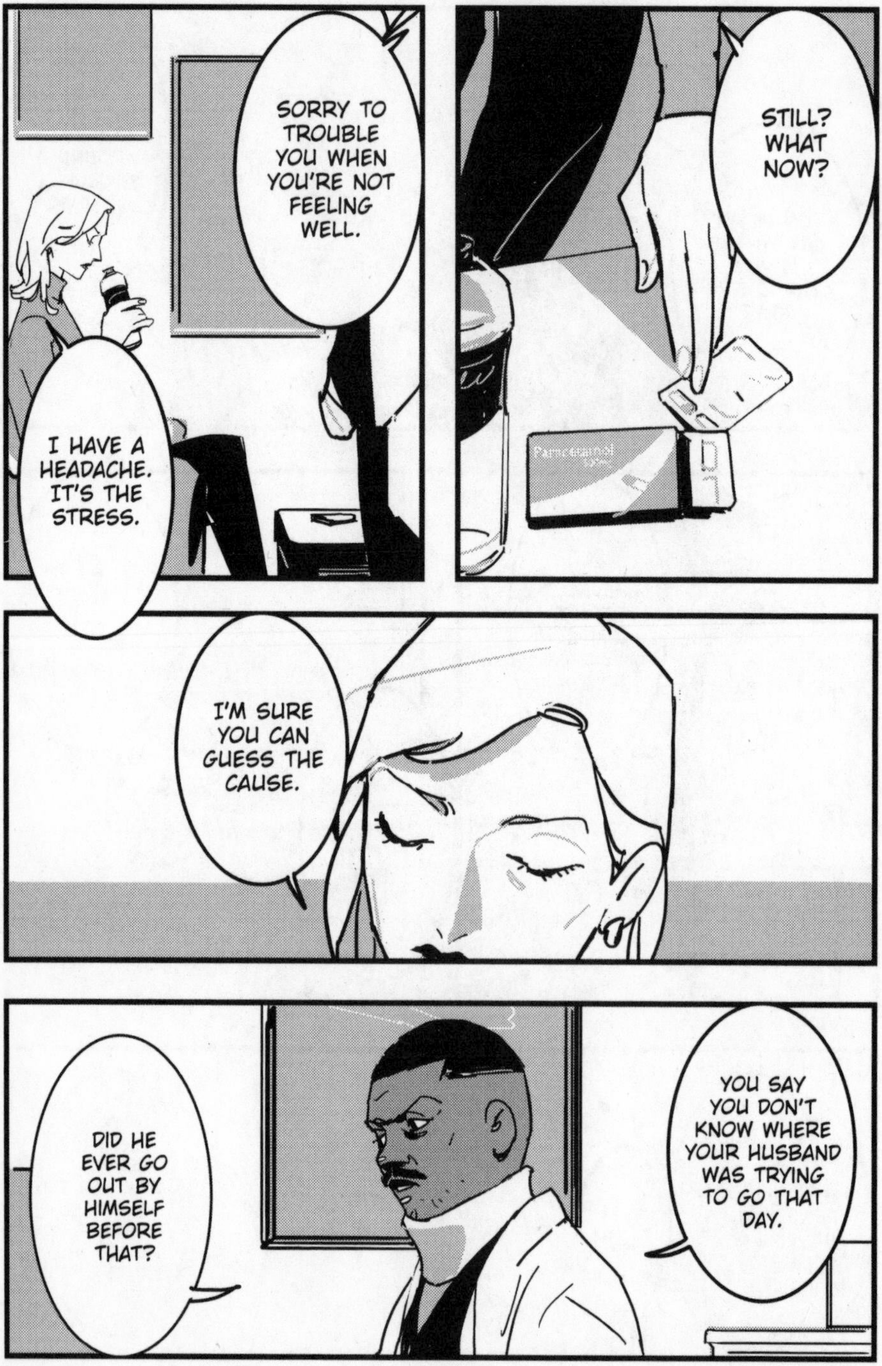
STILL? WHAT NOW?
SORRY TO TROUBLE YOU WHEN YOU'RE NOT FEELING WELL.
I HAVE A HEADACHE. IT'S THE STRESS.
I'M SURE YOU CAN GUESS THE CAUSE.
YOU SAY YOU DON'T KNOW WHERE YOUR HUSBAND WAS TRYING TO GO THAT DAY.
DID HE EVER GO OUT BY HIMSELF BEFORE THAT?

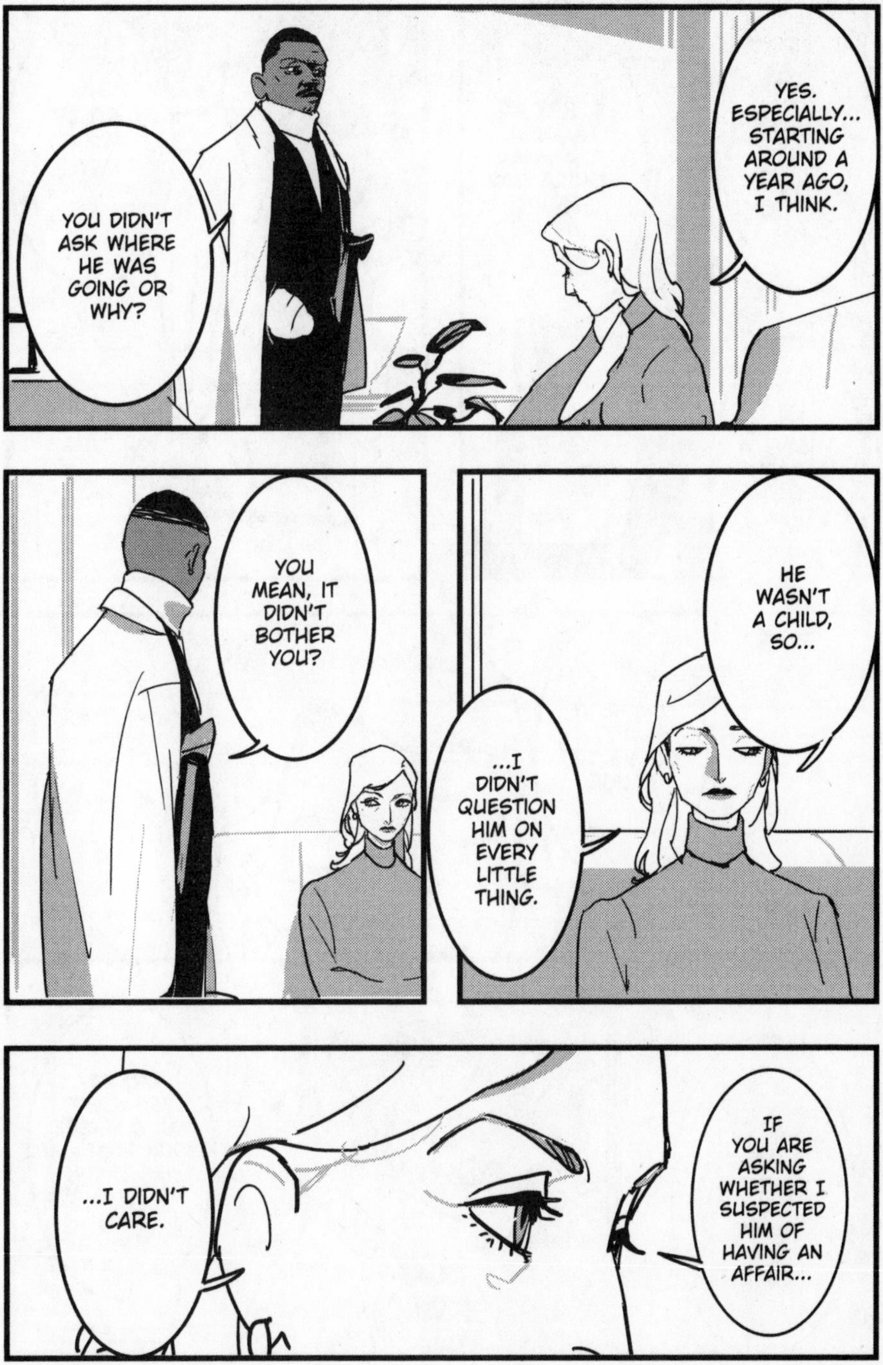
YES. ESPECIALLY... STARTING AROUND A YEAR AGO, I THINK.
YOU DIDN'T ASK WHERE HE WAS GOING OR WHY?
HE WASN'T A CHILD, SO...
...I DIDN'T QUESTION HIM ON EVERY LITTLE THING.
YOU MEAN, IT DIDN'T BOTHER YOU?
IF YOU ARE ASKING WHETHER I SUSPECTED HIM OF HAVING AN AFFAIR...
...I DIDN'T CARE.

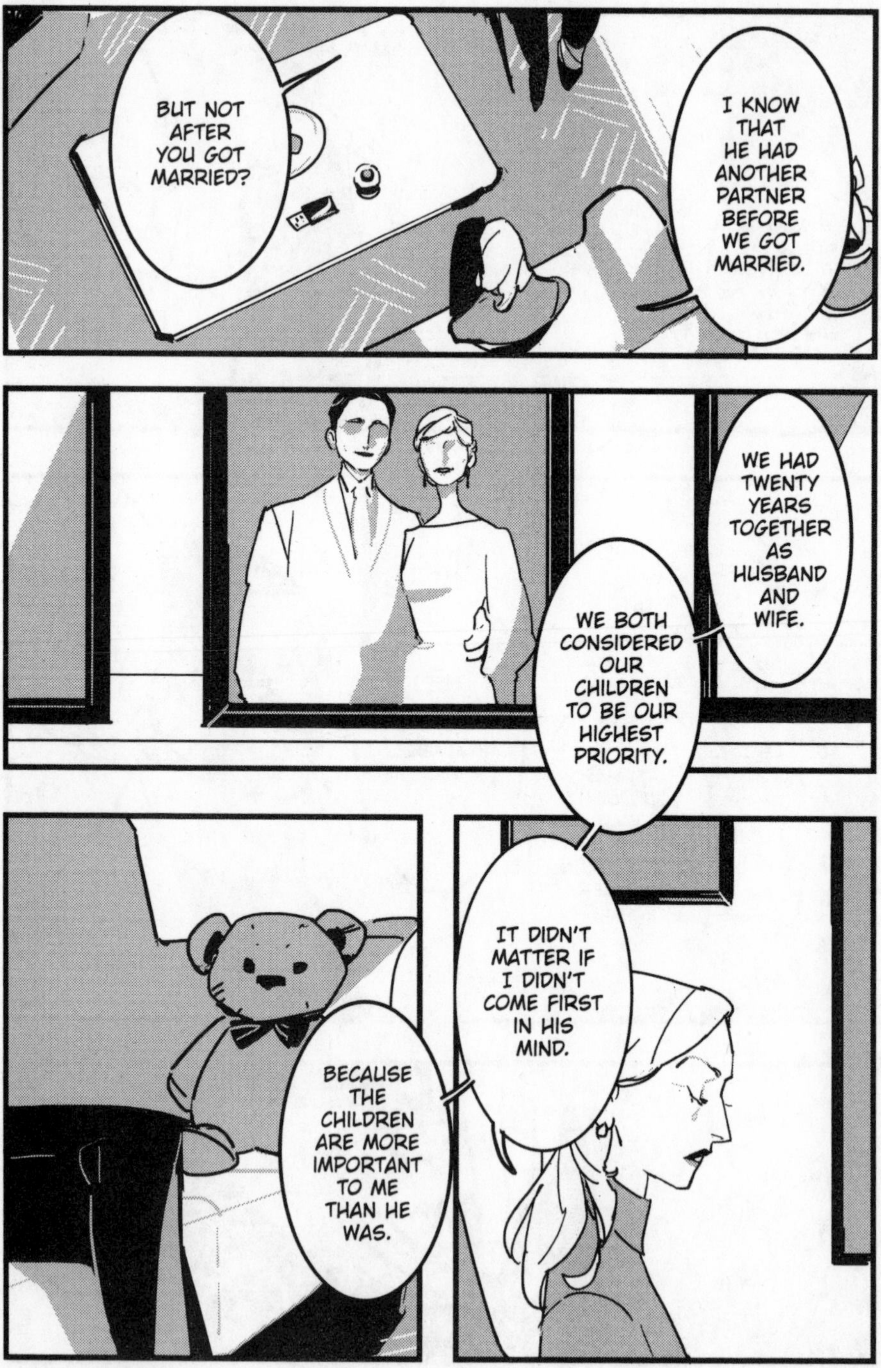
I KNOW THAT HE HAD ANOTHER PARTNER BEFORE WE GOT MARRIED.
BUT NOT AFTER YOU GOT MARRIED?
WE HAD TWENTY YEARS TOGETHER AS HUSBAND AND WIFE.
WE BOTH CONSIDERED OUR CHILDREN TO BE OUR HIGHEST PRIORITY.
IT DIDN'T MATTER IF I DIDN'T COME FIRST IN HIS MIND.
BECAUSE THE CHILDREN ARE MORE IMPORTANT TO ME THAN HE WAS.

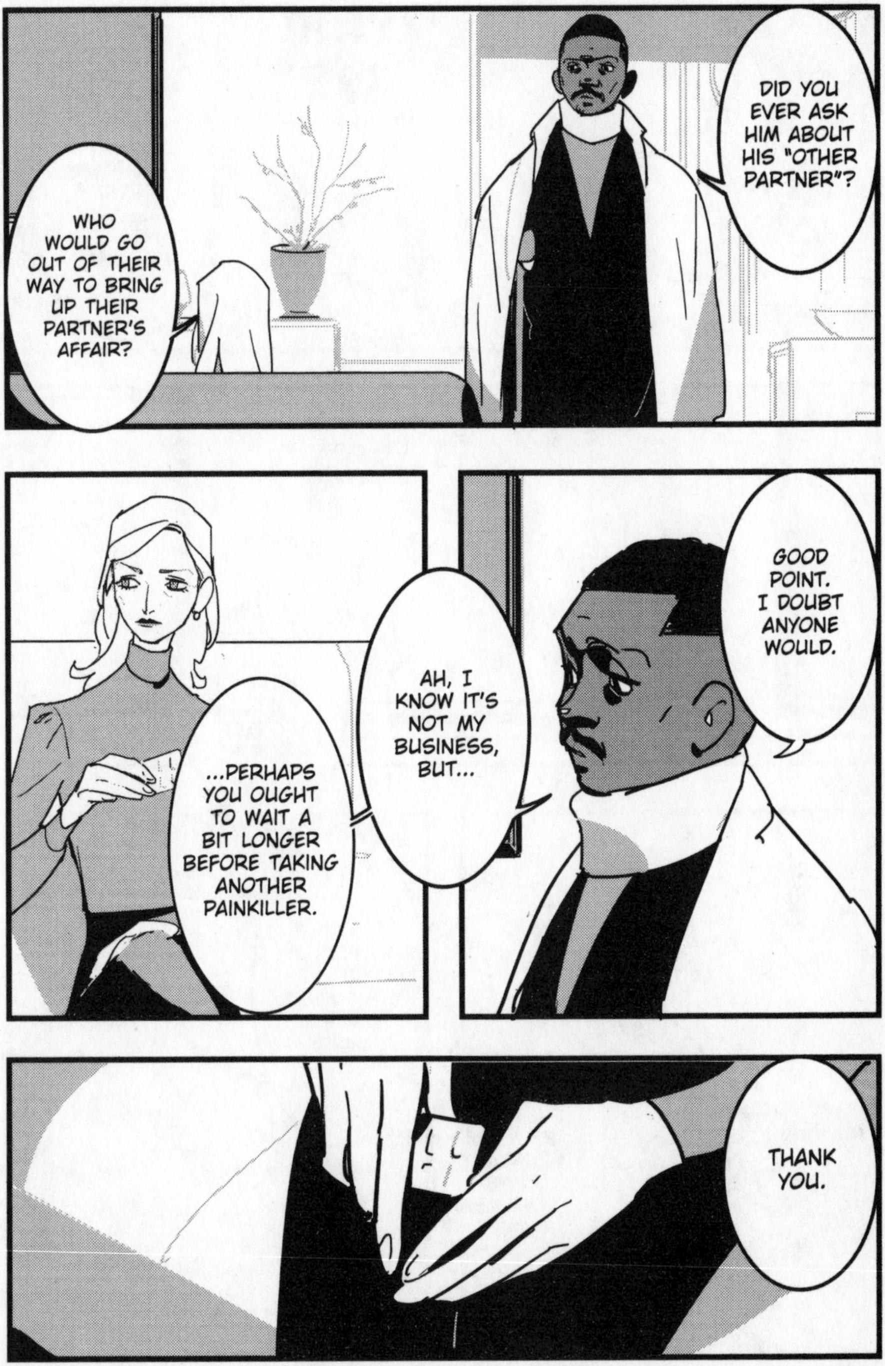
DID YOU EVER ASK HIM ABOUT HIS "OTHER PARTNER"?
WHO WOULD GO OUT OF THEIR WAY TO BRING UP THEIR PARTNER'S AFFAIR?
GOOD POINT. I DOUBT ANYONE WOULD.
AH, I KNOW IT'S NOT MY BUSINESS, BUT...
...PERHAPS YOU OUGHT TO WAIT A BIT LONGER BEFORE TAKING ANOTHER PAINKILLER.
THANK YOU.

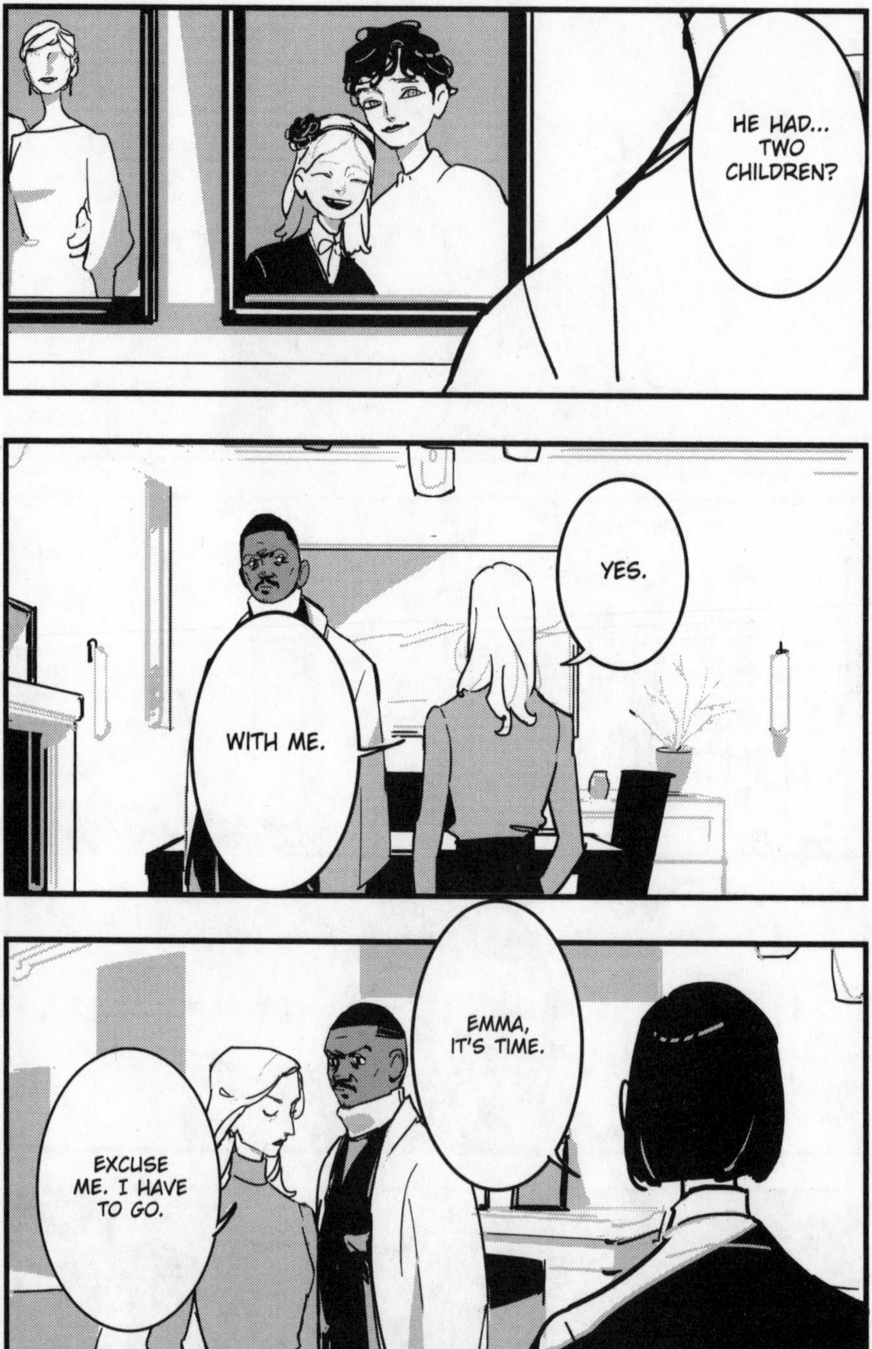
HE HAD... TWO CHILDREN?
YES.
WITH ME.
EMMA, IT'S TIME.
EXCUSE ME. I HAVE TO GO.

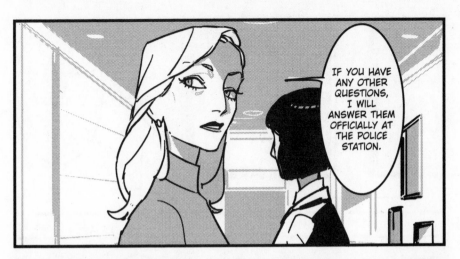

IF YOU HAVE ANY OTHER QUESTIONS, I WILL ANSWER THEM OFFICIALLY AT THE POLICE STATION.

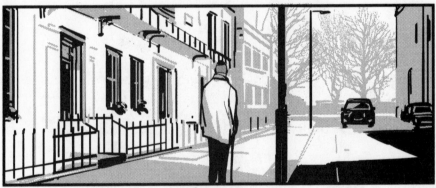

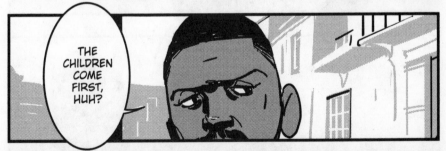

THE CHILDREN COME FIRST, HUH?

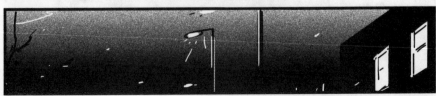

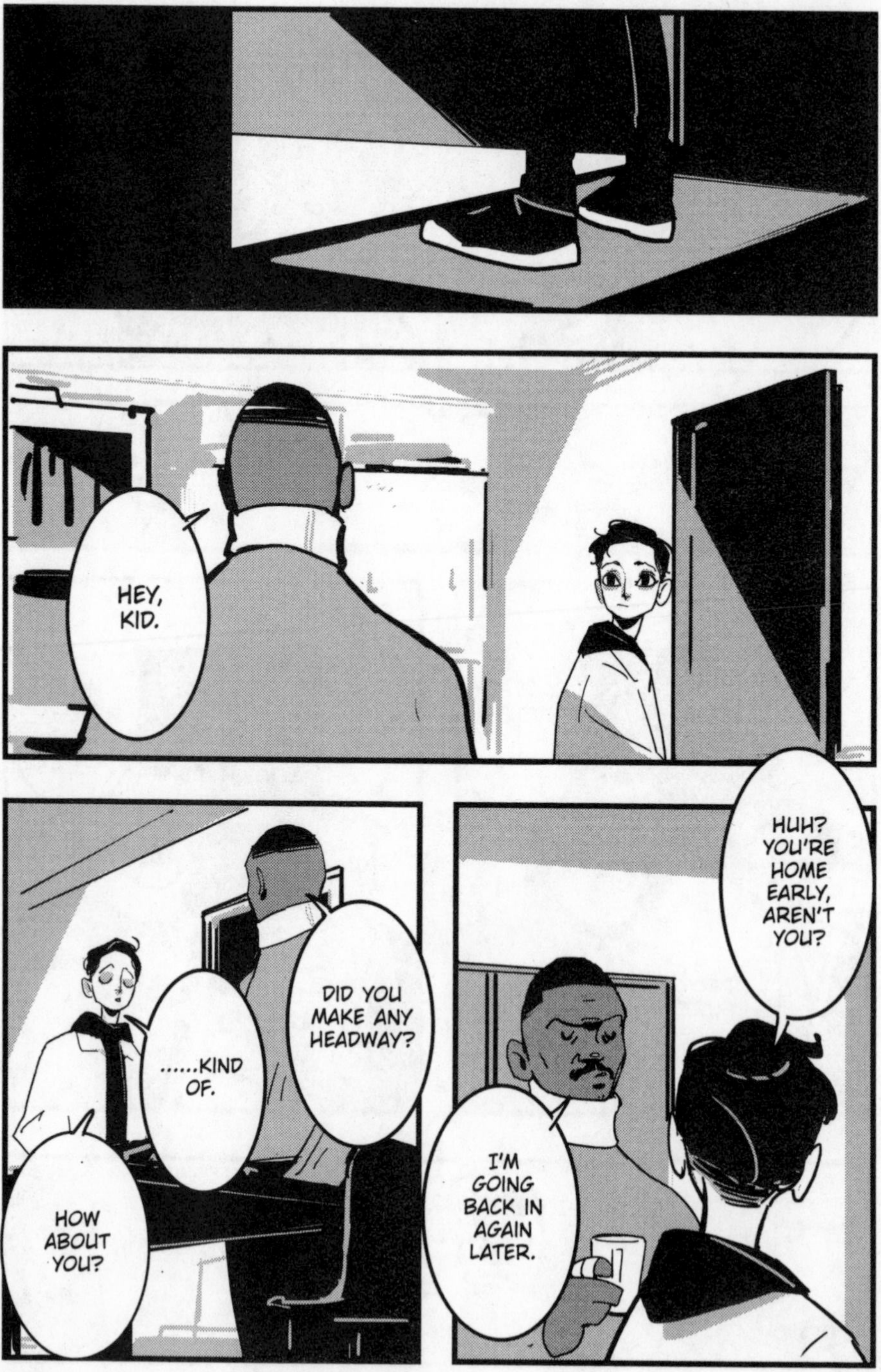
HEY, KID.
HUH? YOU'RE HOME EARLY, AREN'T YOU?
I'M GOING BACK IN AGAIN LATER.
DID YOU MAKE ANY HEADWAY?
......KIND OF.
HOW ABOUT YOU?

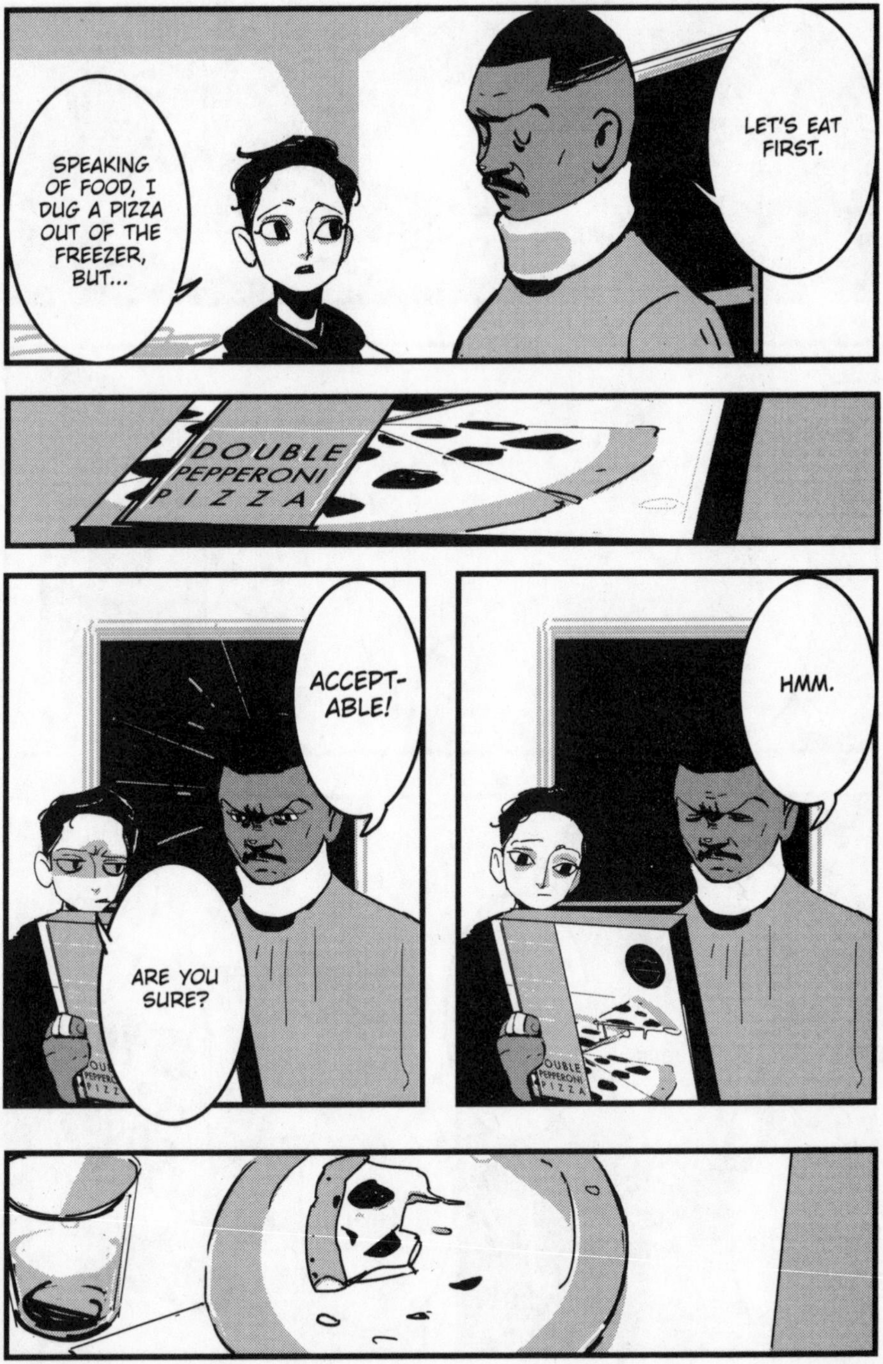
LET'S EAT FIRST.
SPEAKING OF FOOD, I DUG A PIZZA OUT OF THE FREEZER, BUT...
DOUBLE PEPPERONI PIZZA
HMM.
DOUBLE PEPPERONI PIZZA
ACCEPT-ABLE!
ARE YOU SURE?
DOUBLE PEPPERONI PIZZA

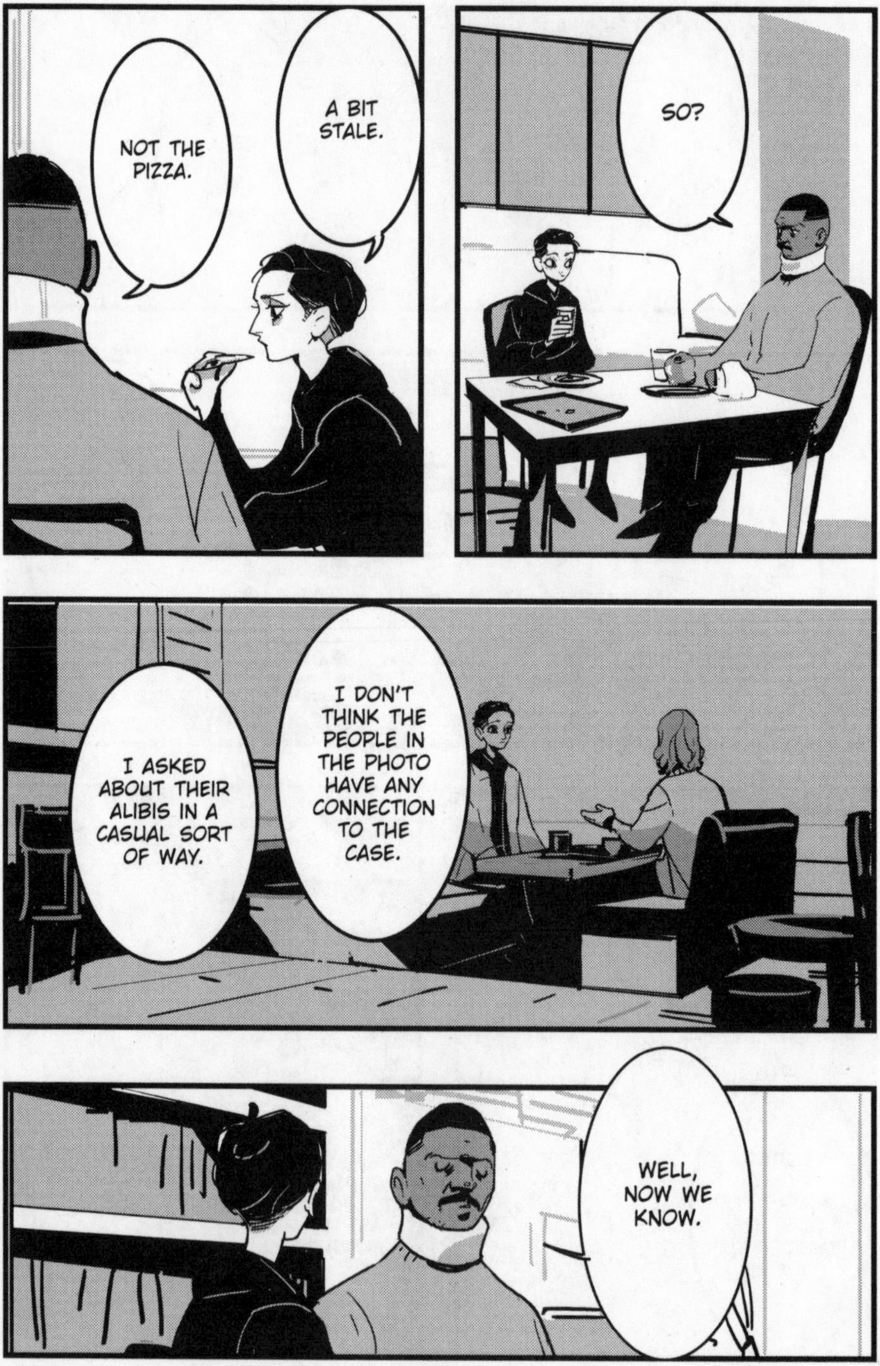
SO?
A BIT STALE.
NOT THE PIZZA.
I DON'T THINK THE PEOPLE IN THE PHOTO HAVE ANY CONNECTION TO THE CASE.
I ASKED ABOUT THEIR ALIBIS IN A CASUAL SORT OF WAY.
WELL, NOW WE KNOW.

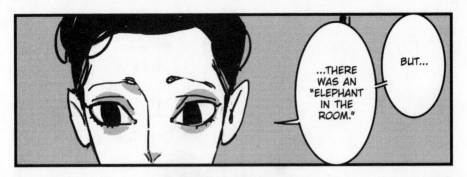

BUT...
...THERE WAS AN "ELEPHANT IN THE ROOM."
SOMETHING THEY WERE PRETENDING NOT TO SEE?
I'M ABOUT 99 PERCENT SURE AT THIS POINT THAT THE MAYOR WAS MY BIOLOGICAL FATHER.
YEAH, I CAN HAZARD A GUESS AS TO HIS REASON FOR HANGING AROUND YOU.
BUT MY MOTHER...
I STILL DON'T UNDERSTAND WHY SHE DECIDED TO HAVE ME.

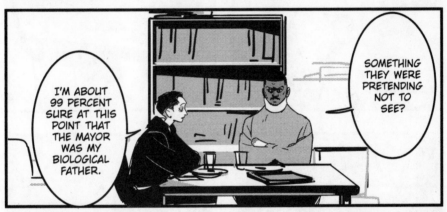

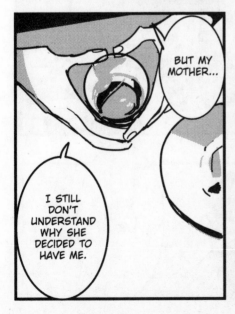

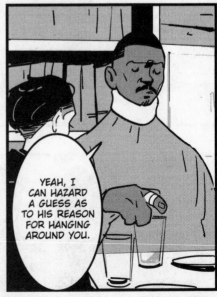

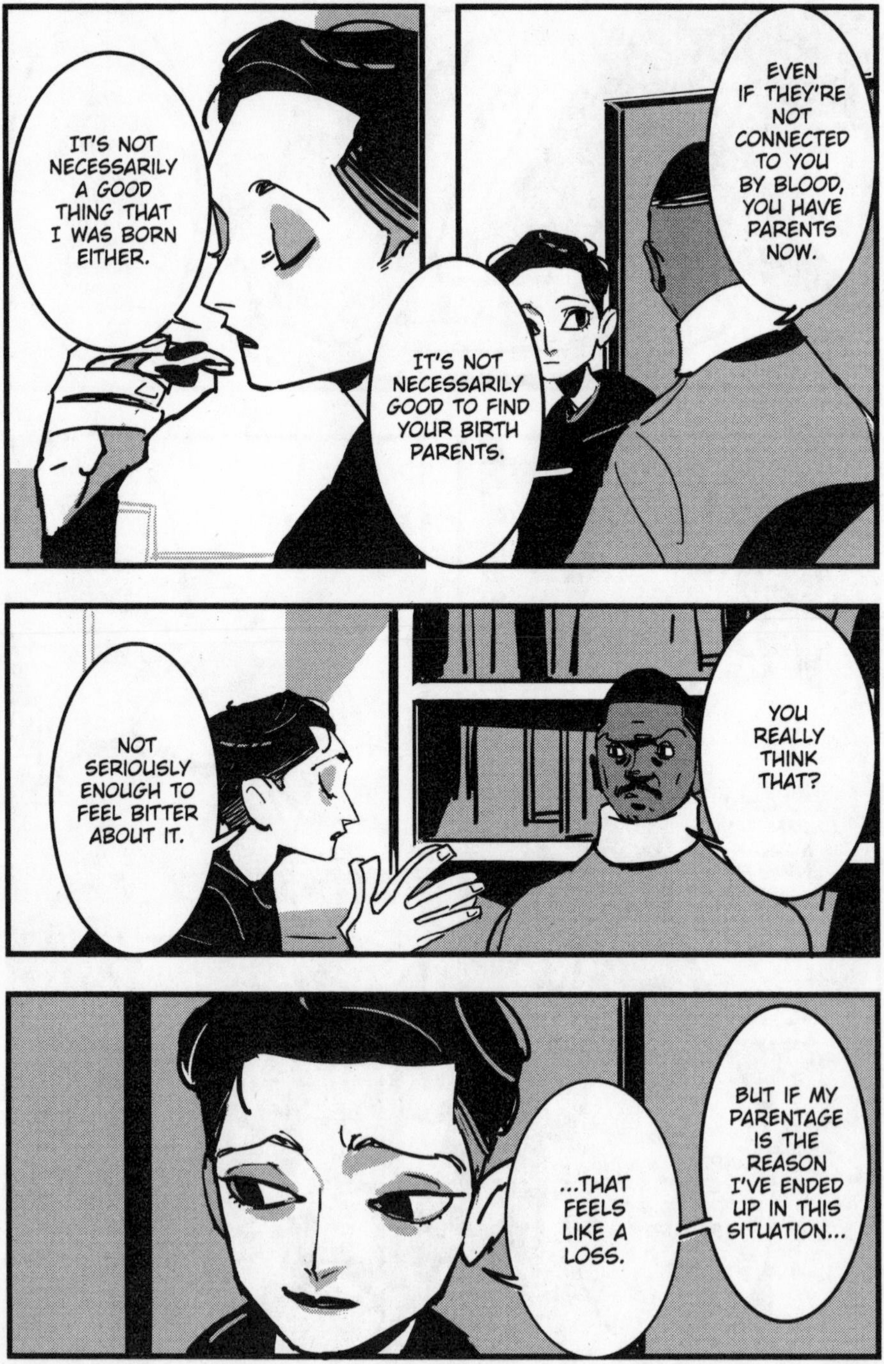
EVEN IF THEY'RE NOT CONNECTED TO YOU BY BLOOD, YOU HAVE PARENTS NOW.
IT'S NOT NECESSARILY GOOD TO FIND YOUR BIRTH PARENTS.
IT'S NOT NECESSARILY A GOOD THING THAT I WAS BORN EITHER.
YOU REALLY THINK THAT?
NOT SERIOUSLY ENOUGH TO FEEL BITTER ABOUT IT.
BUT IF MY PARENTAGE IS THE REASON I'VE ENDED UP IN THIS SITUATION...
...THAT FEELS LIKE A LOSS.

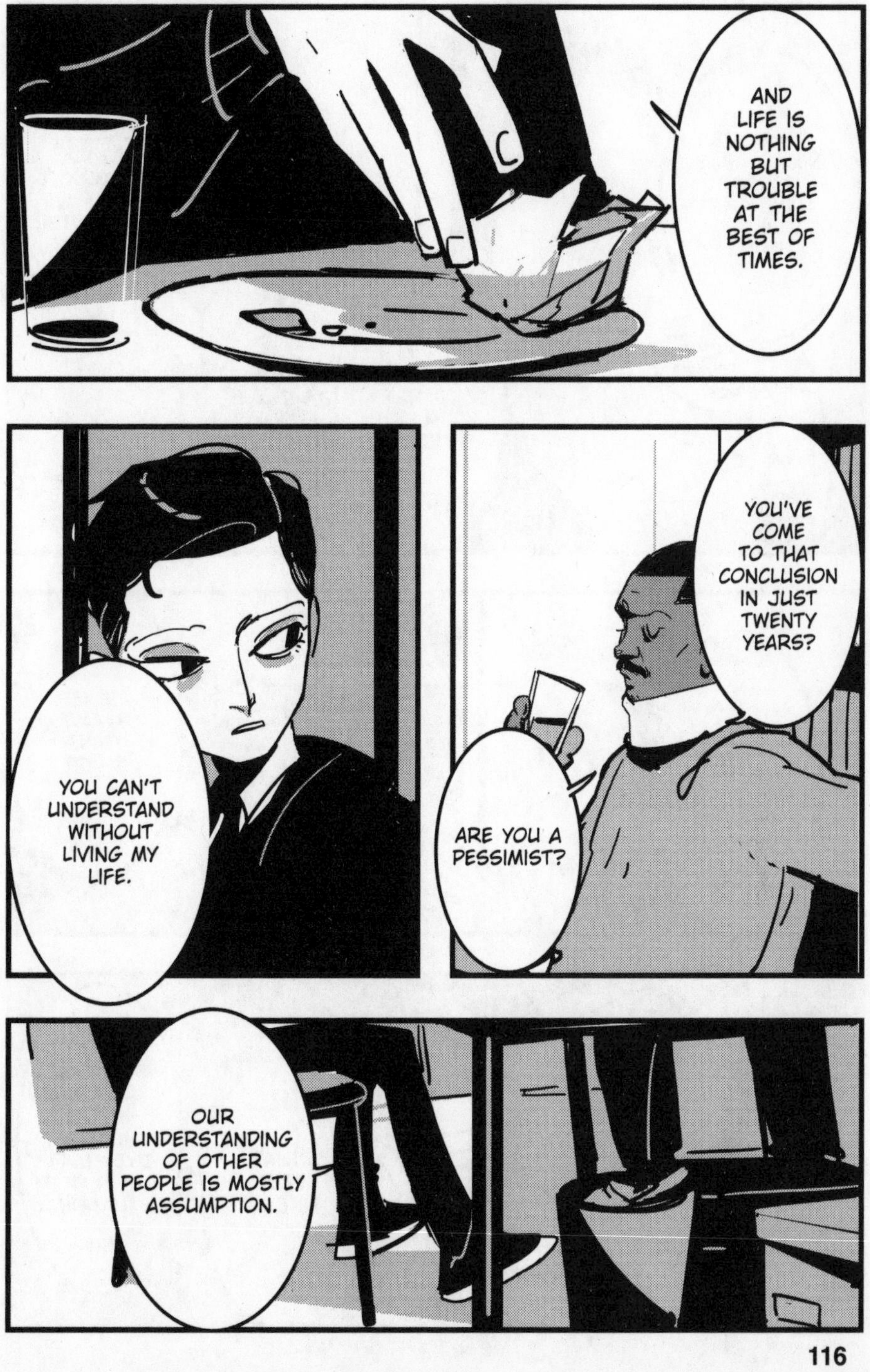
AND LIFE IS NOTHING BUT TROUBLE AT THE BEST OF TIMES.
YOU'VE COME TO THAT CONCLUSION IN JUST TWENTY YEARS?
ARE YOU A PESSIMIST?
YOU CAN'T UNDERSTAND WITHOUT LIVING MY LIFE.
OUR UNDERSTANDING OF OTHER PEOPLE IS MOSTLY ASSUMPTION.

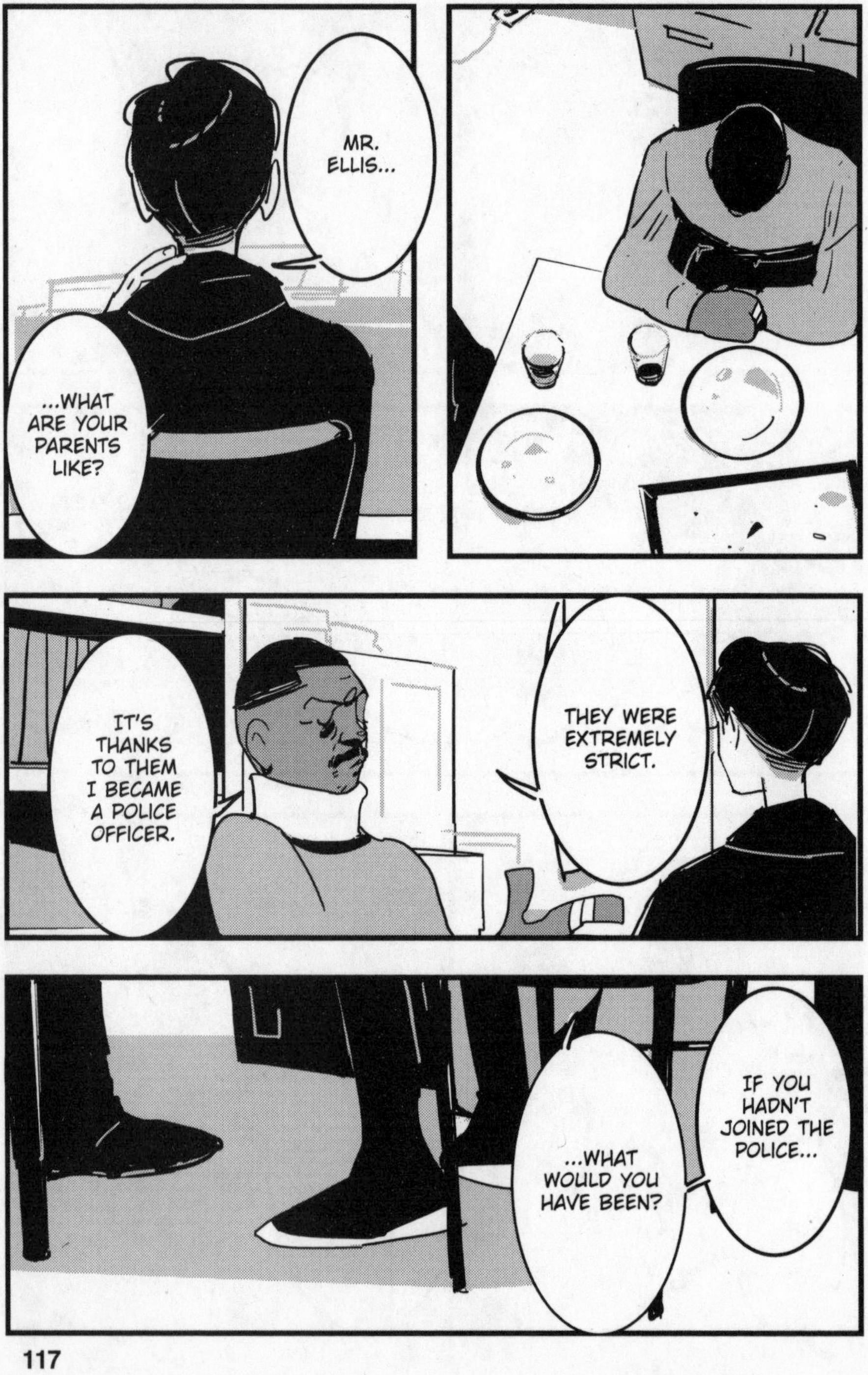
MR. ELLIS...
...WHAT ARE YOUR PARENTS LIKE?
THEY WERE EXTREMELY STRICT.
IT'S THANKS TO THEM I BECAME A POLICE OFFICER.
IF YOU HADN'T JOINED THE POLICE...
...WHAT WOULD YOU HAVE BEEN?

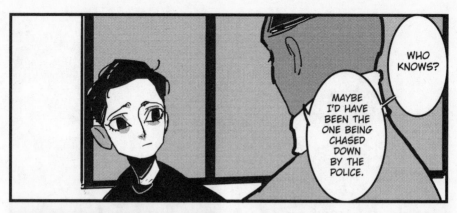

WHO KNOWS?
MAYBE I'D HAVE BEEN THE ONE BEING CHASED DOWN BY THE POLICE.
TO KEEP ME FROM ENDING UP LIKE THAT...
...I WAS TOLD OVER AND OVER AGAIN TO "CONTRIBUTE TO SOCIETY."
LOOKING BACK ON IT NOW...
...THEY REASONED THAT ANY LAW-ABIDING AND USEFUL CITIZEN MIGHT BE ABLE TO GET A ROYAL PARDON, EVEN IF THEY DIDN'T HAVE BLUE EYES.
THAT'S JUST THE WAY IT IS.
BUT......

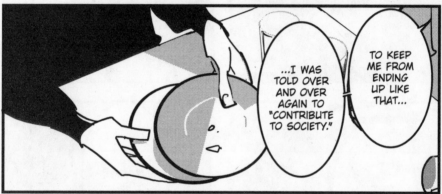

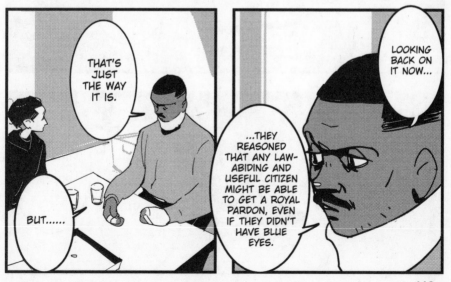

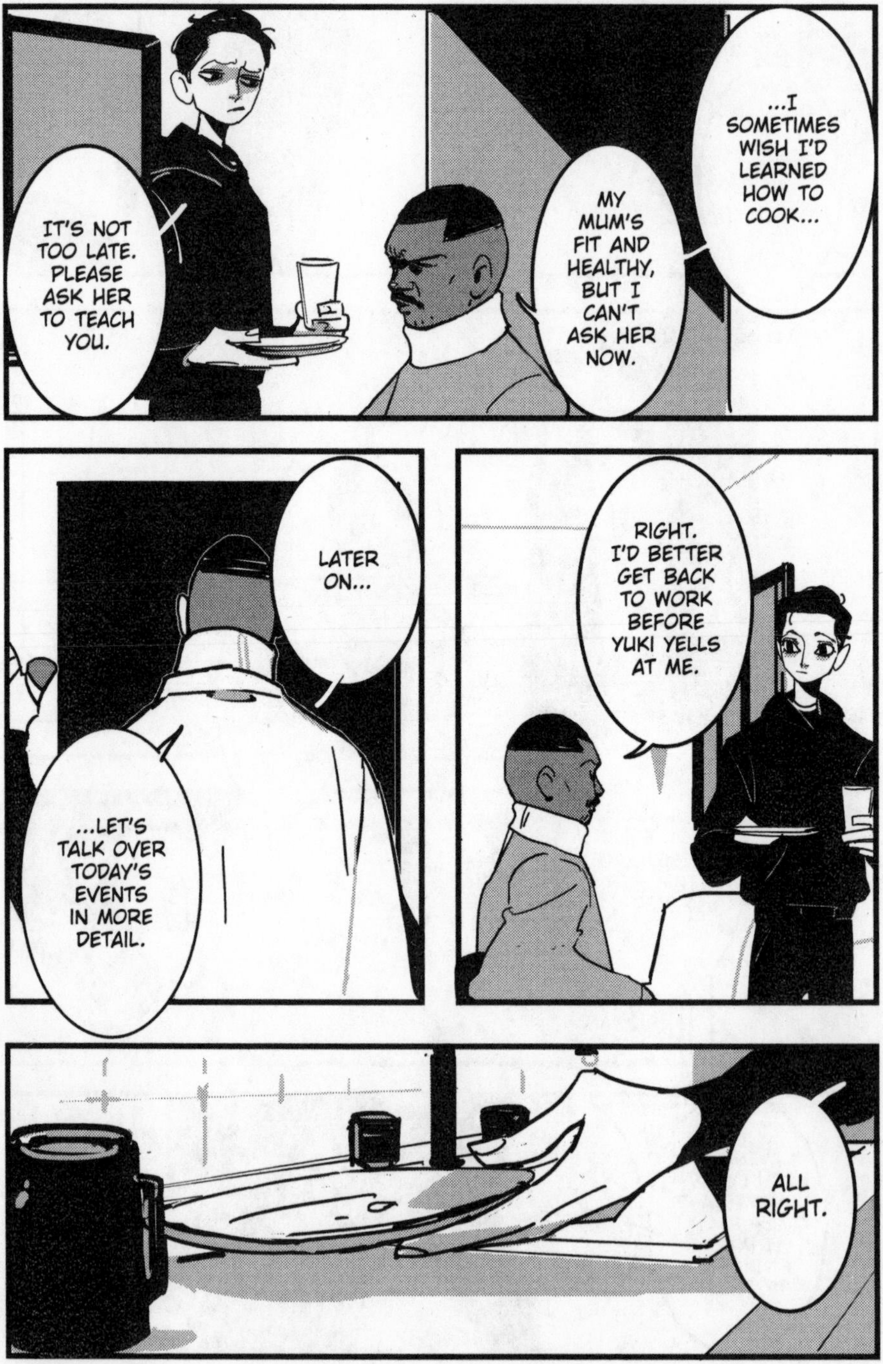
...I SOMETIMES WISH I'D LEARNED HOW TO COOK...
MY MUM'S FIT AND HEALTHY, BUT I CAN'T ASK HER NOW.
IT'S NOT TOO LATE. PLEASE ASK HER TO TEACH YOU.
RIGHT. I'D BETTER GET BACK TO WORK BEFORE YUKI YELLS AT ME.
LATER ON...
...LET'S TALK OVER TODAY'S EVENTS IN MORE DETAIL.
ALL RIGHT.

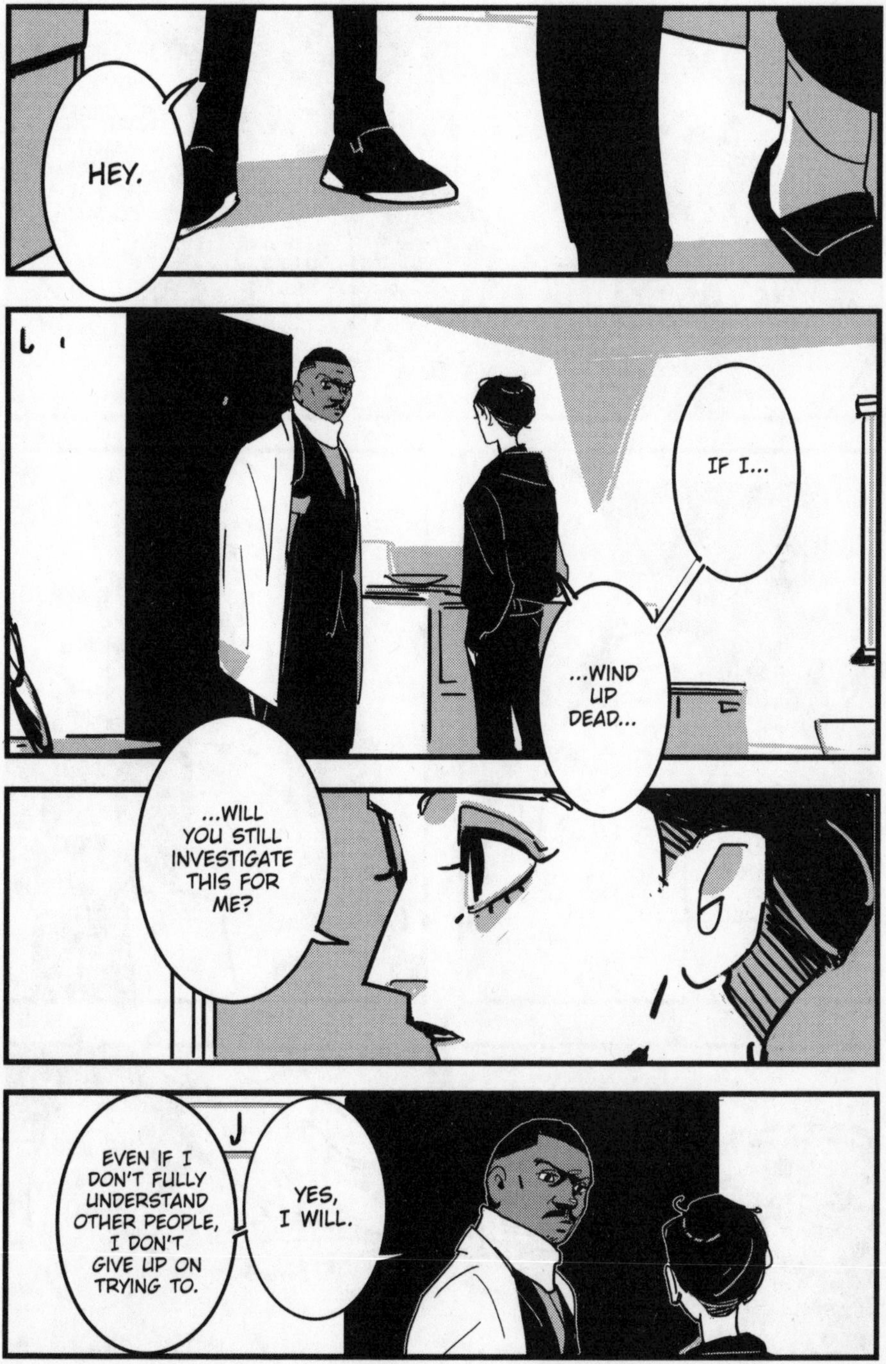
HEY.
IF I...
...WIND UP DEAD...
...WILL YOU STILL INVESTIGATE THIS FOR ME?
YES, I WILL.
EVEN IF I DON'T FULLY UNDERSTAND OTHER PEOPLE, I DON'T GIVE UP ON TRYING TO.

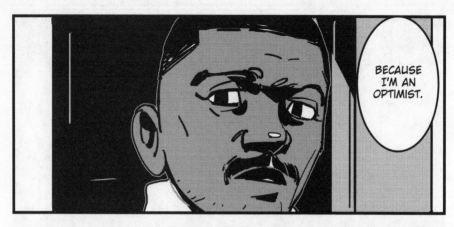

BECAUSE I'M AN OPTIMIST.

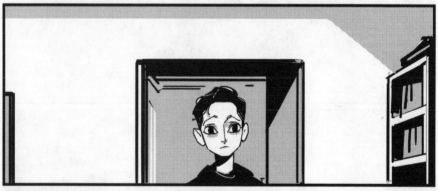

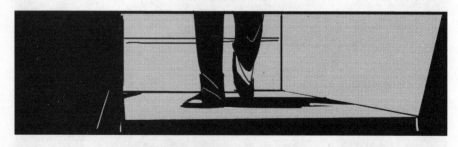

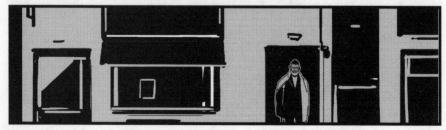

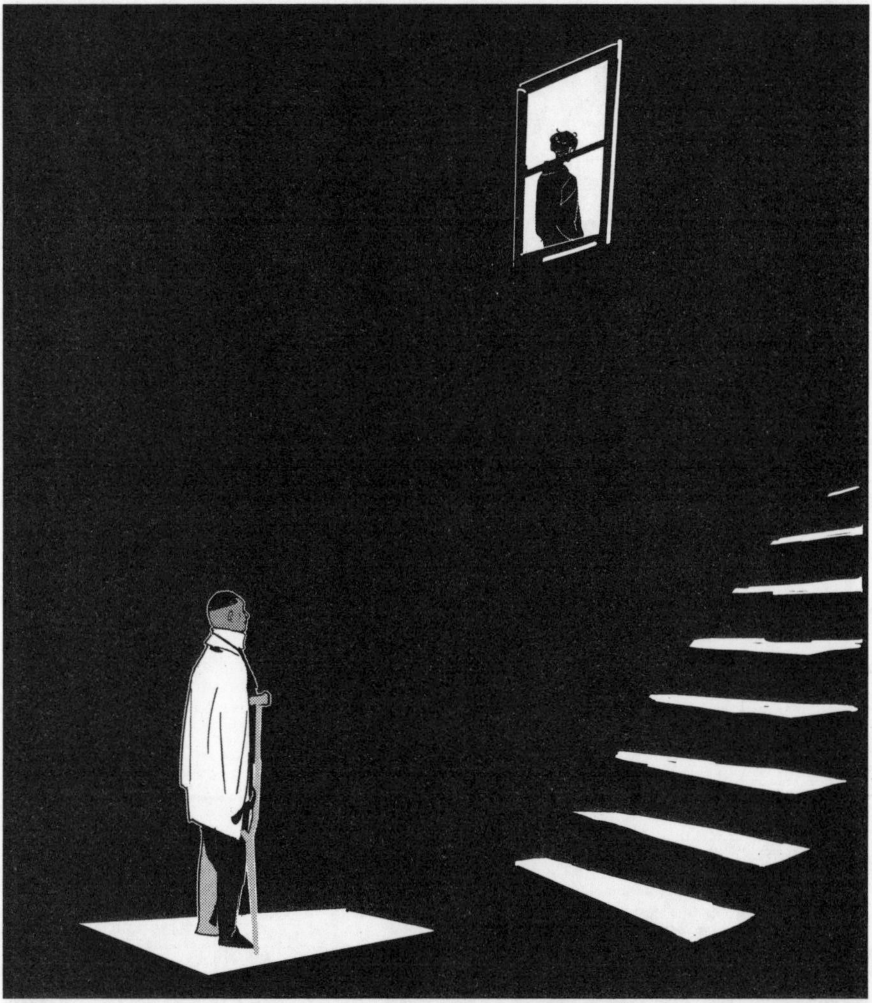
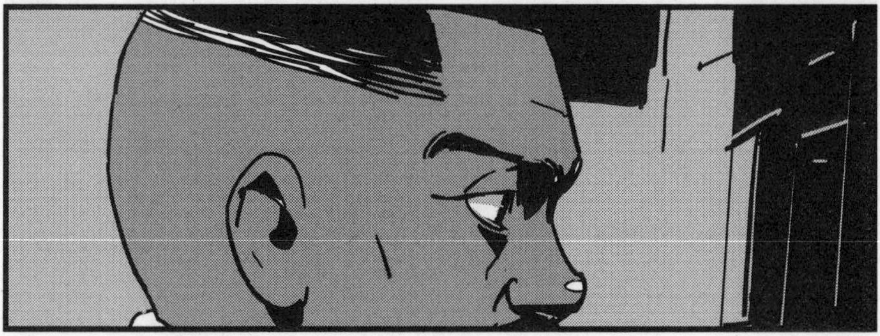

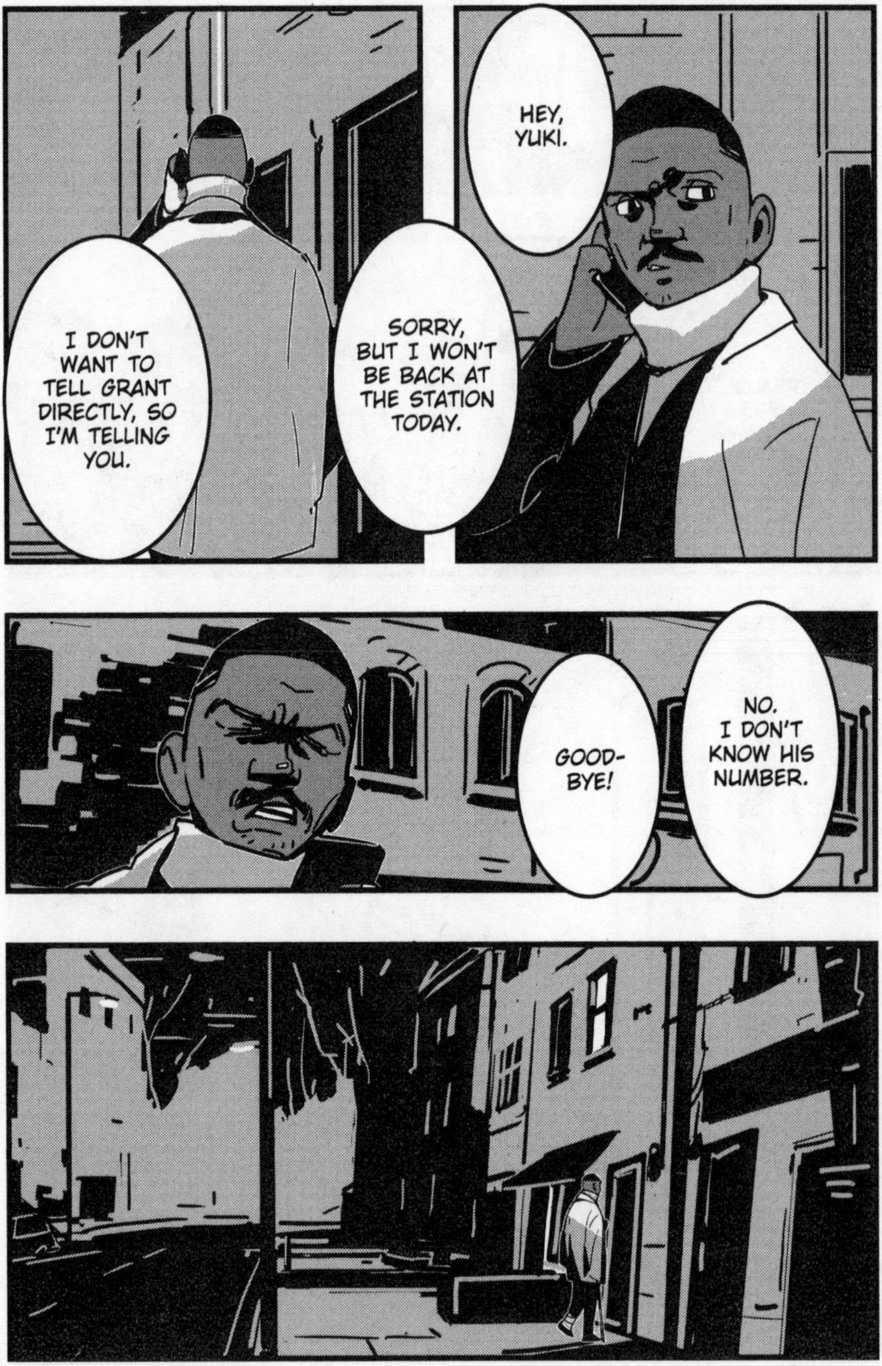
HEY, YUKI.
SORRY, BUT I WON'T BE BACK AT THE STATION TODAY.
I DON'T WANT TO TELL GRANT DIRECTLY, SO I'M TELLING YOU.
NO. I DON'T KNOW HIS NUMBER.
GOOD-BYE!

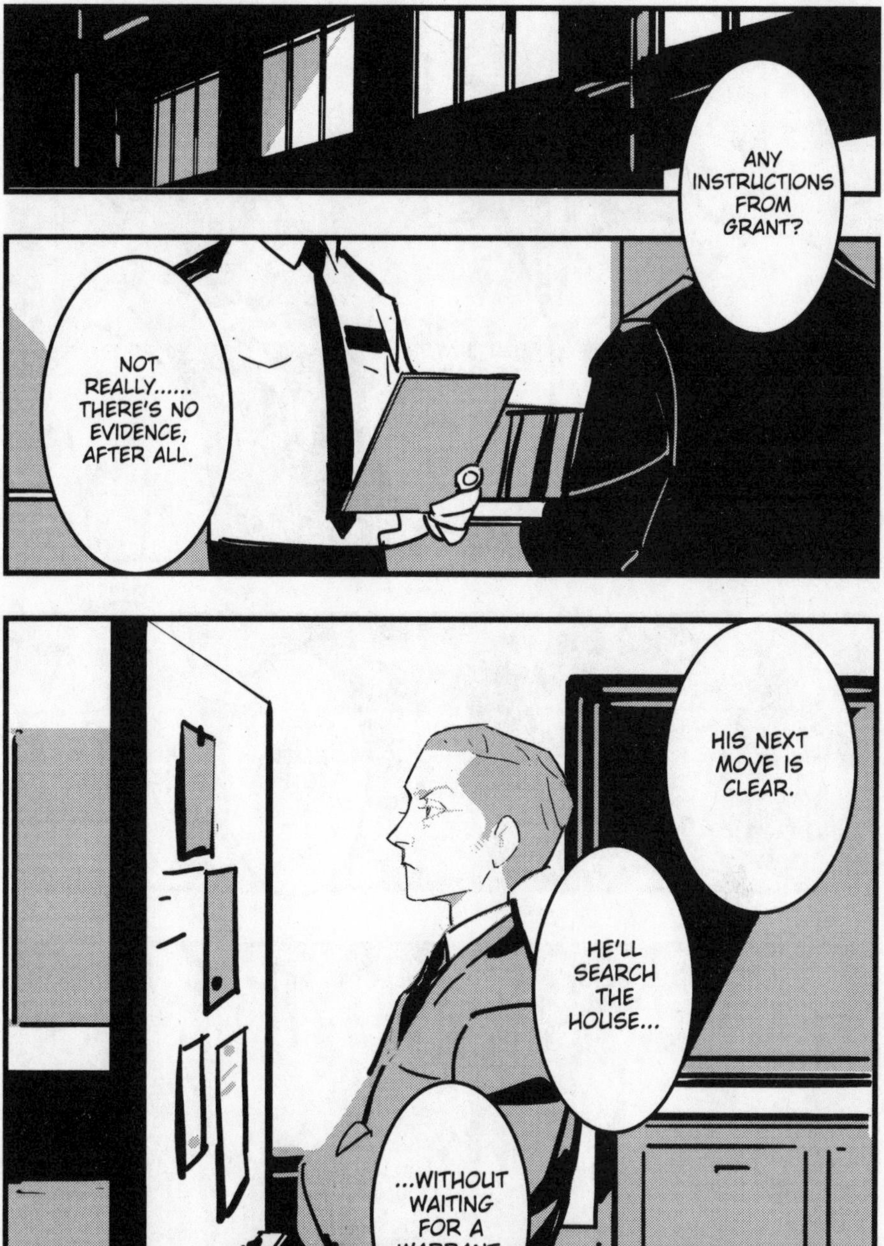
ANY INSTRUCTIONS FROM GRANT?
NOT REALLY...... THERE'S NO EVIDENCE, AFTER ALL.
HIS NEXT MOVE IS CLEAR.
HE'LL SEARCH THE HOUSE...
...WITHOUT WAITING FOR A WARRANT.

Lost
Lad
London

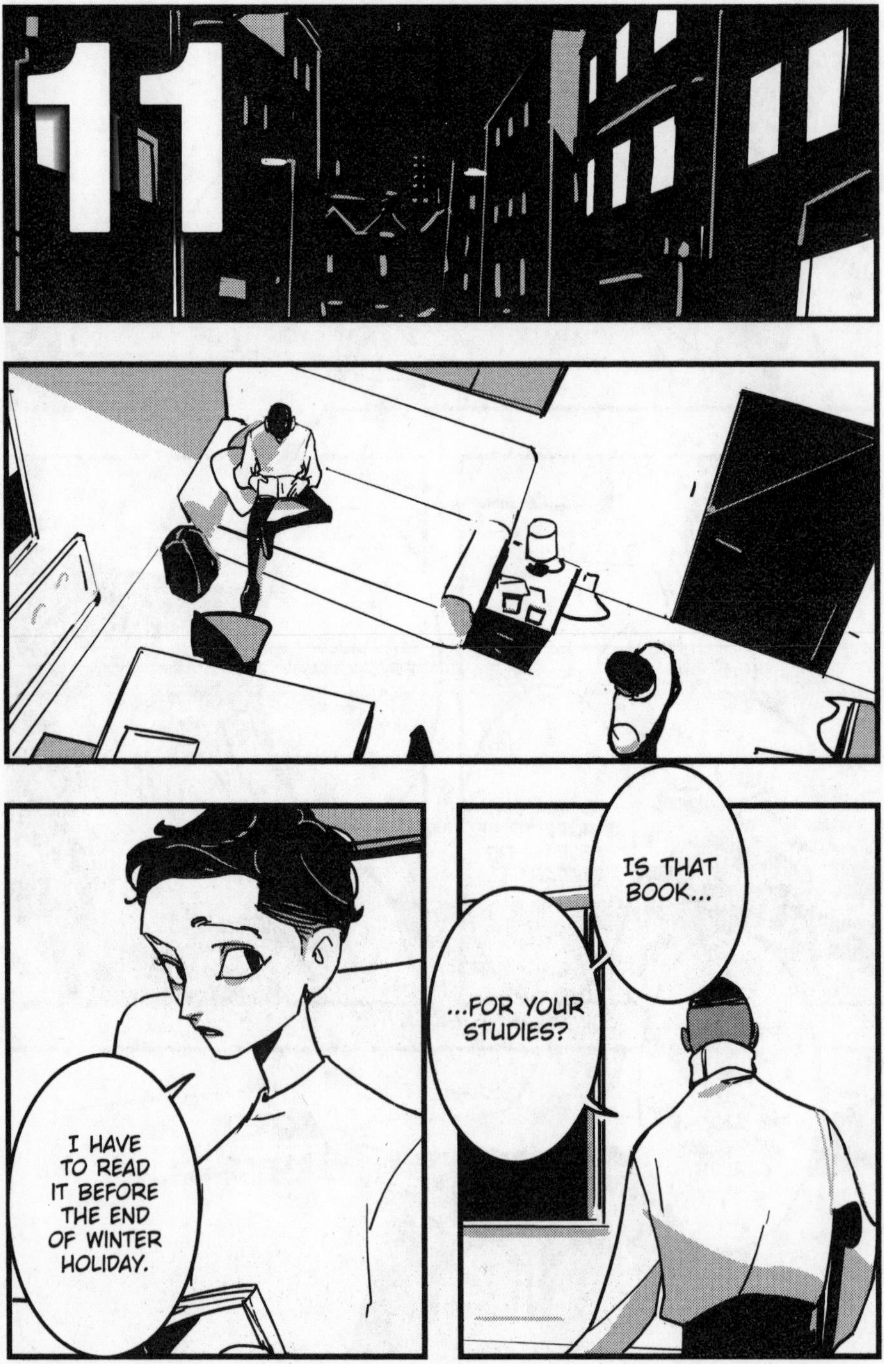
IS THAT BOOK...
...FOR YOUR STUDIES?
I HAVE TO READ IT BEFORE THE END OF WINTER HOLIDAY.

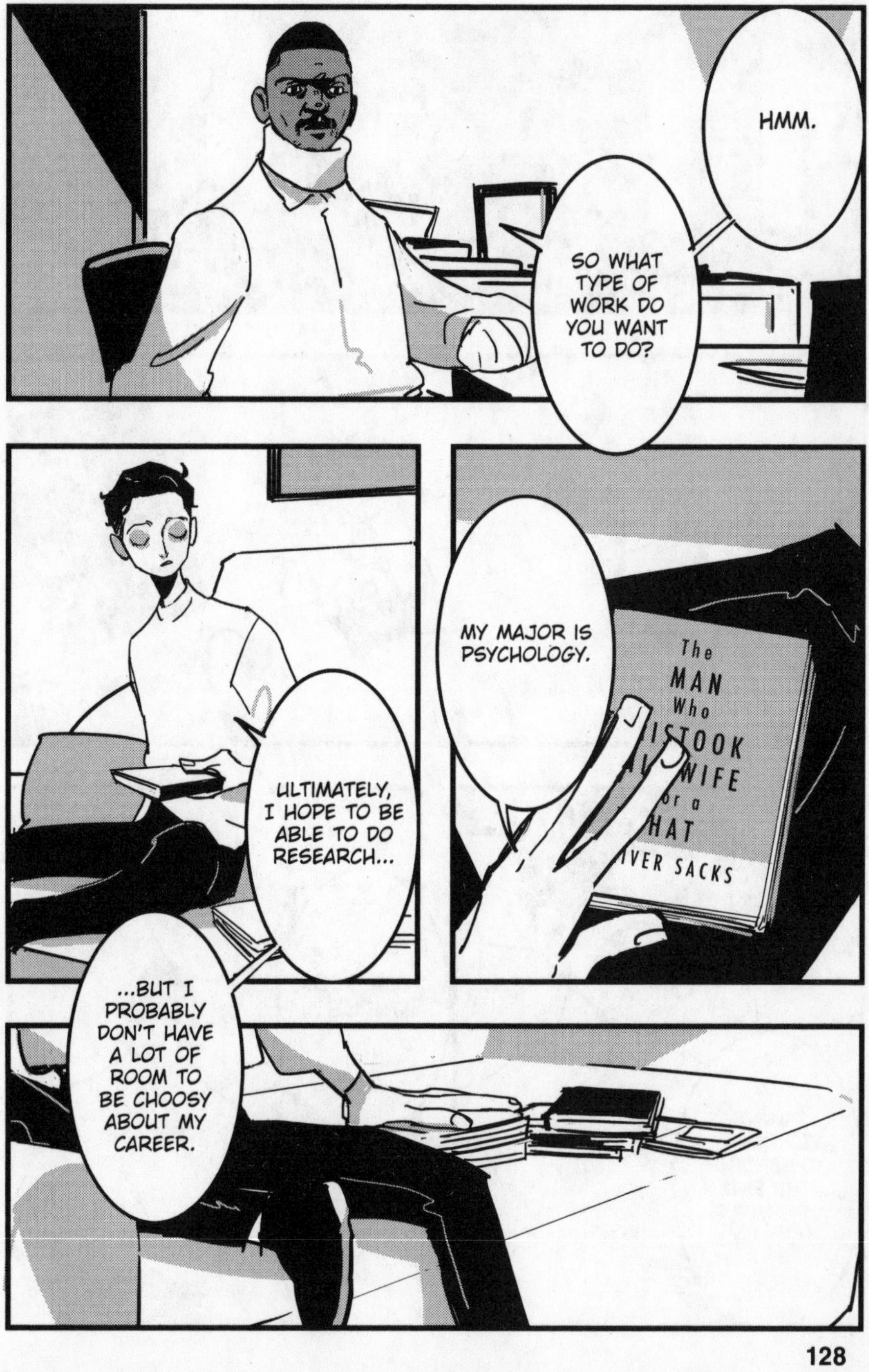
HMM.
SO WHAT TYPE OF WORK DO YOU WANT TO DO?
MY MAJOR IS PSYCHOLOGY.
The MAN Who
IVER SACKS
ULTIMATELY, I HOPE TO BE ABLE TO DO RESEARCH...
...BUT I PROBABLY DON'T HAVE A LOT OF ROOM TO BE CHOOSY ABOUT MY CAREER.

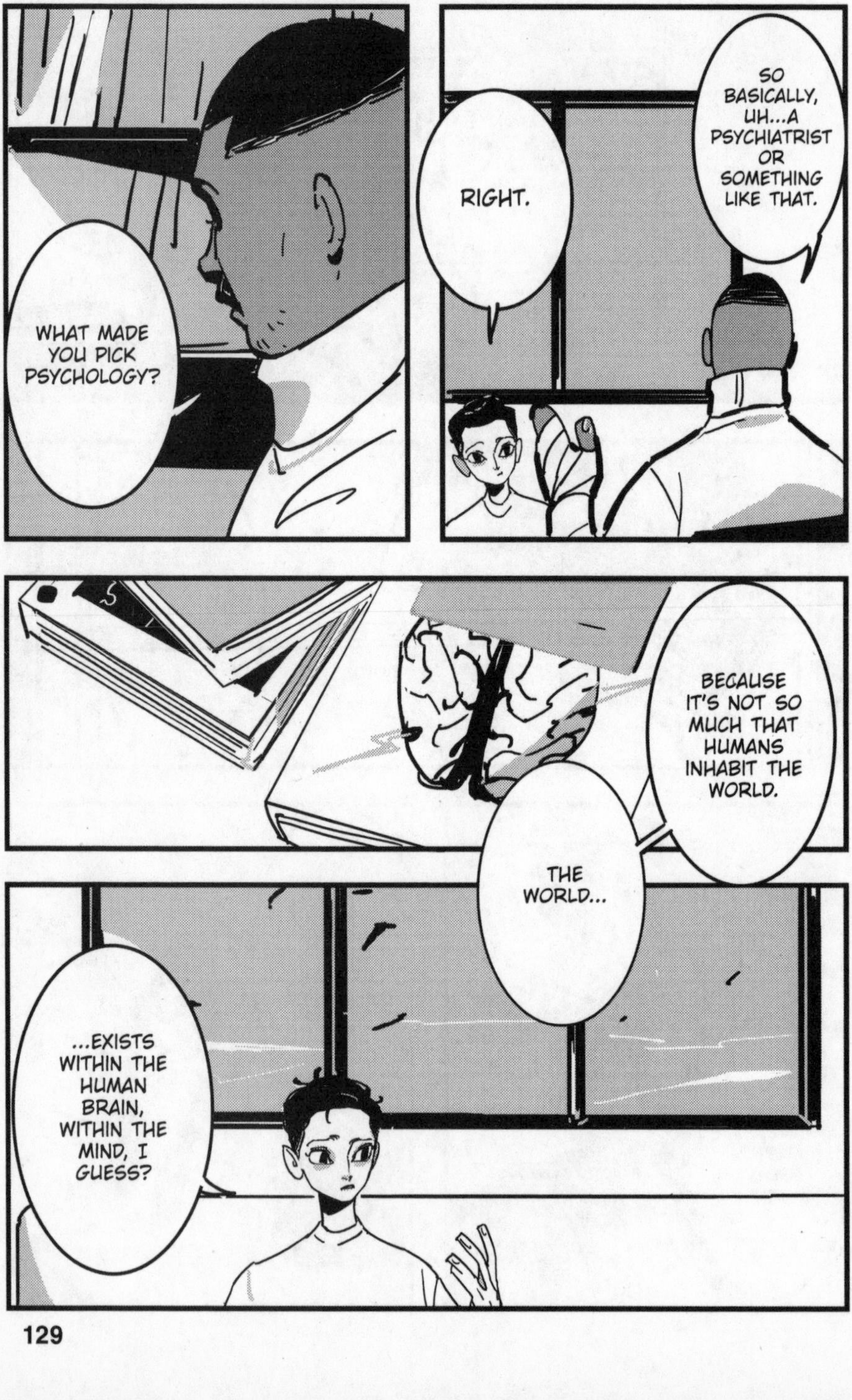
SO BASICALLY, UH...A PSYCHIATRIST OR SOMETHING LIKE THAT.
RIGHT.
WHAT MADE YOU PICK PSYCHOLOGY?
BECAUSE IT'S NOT SO MUCH THAT HUMANS INHABIT THE WORLD.
THE WORLD...
...EXISTS WITHIN THE HUMAN BRAIN, WITHIN THE MIND, I GUESS?

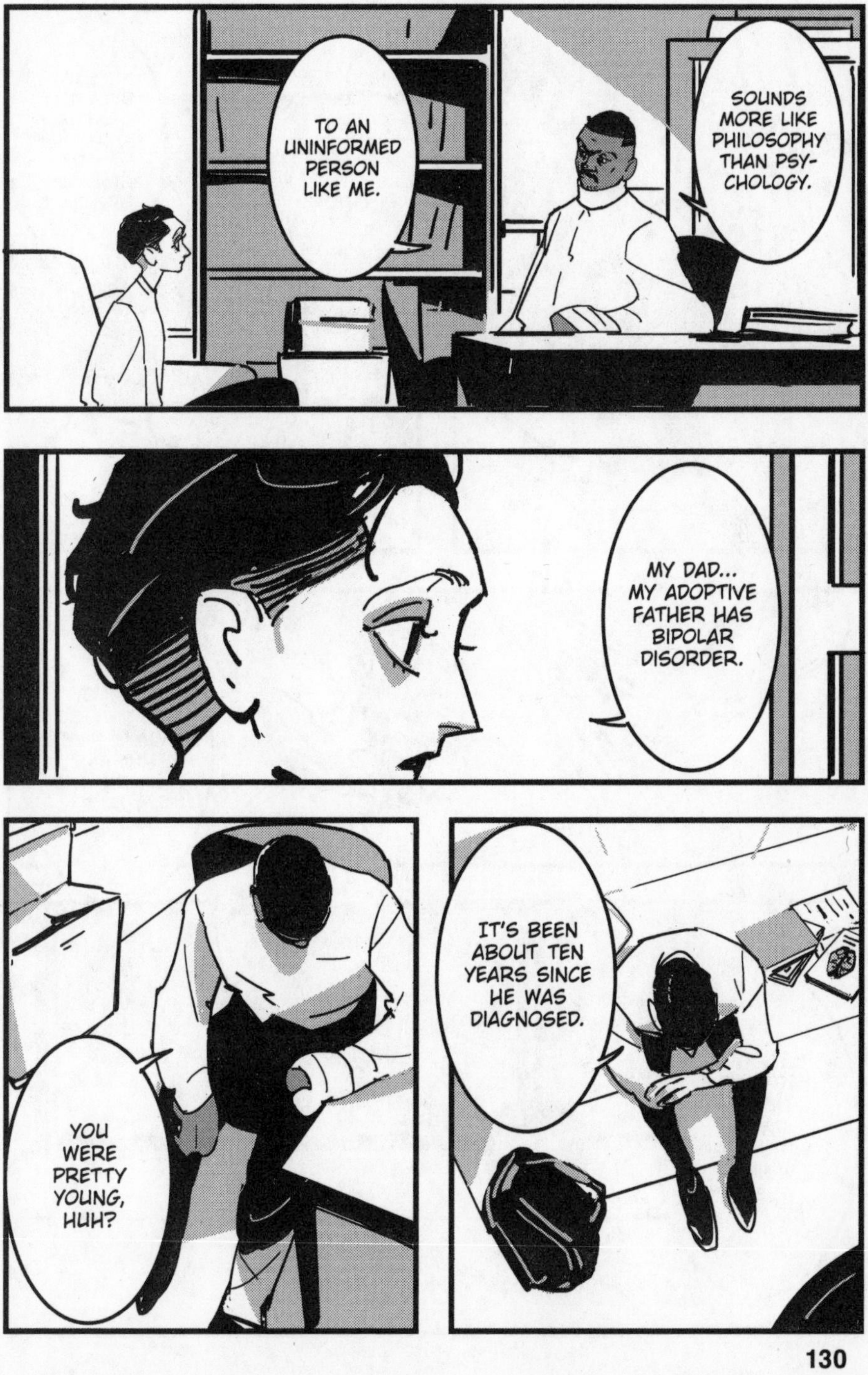
SOUNDS MORE LIKE PHILOSOPHY THAN PSY-CHOLOGY.
TO AN UNINFORMED PERSON LIKE ME.
MY DAD... MY ADOPTIVE FATHER HAS BIPOLAR DISORDER.
IT'S BEEN ABOUT TEN YEARS SINCE HE WAS DIAGNOSED.
YOU WERE PRETTY YOUNG, HUH?

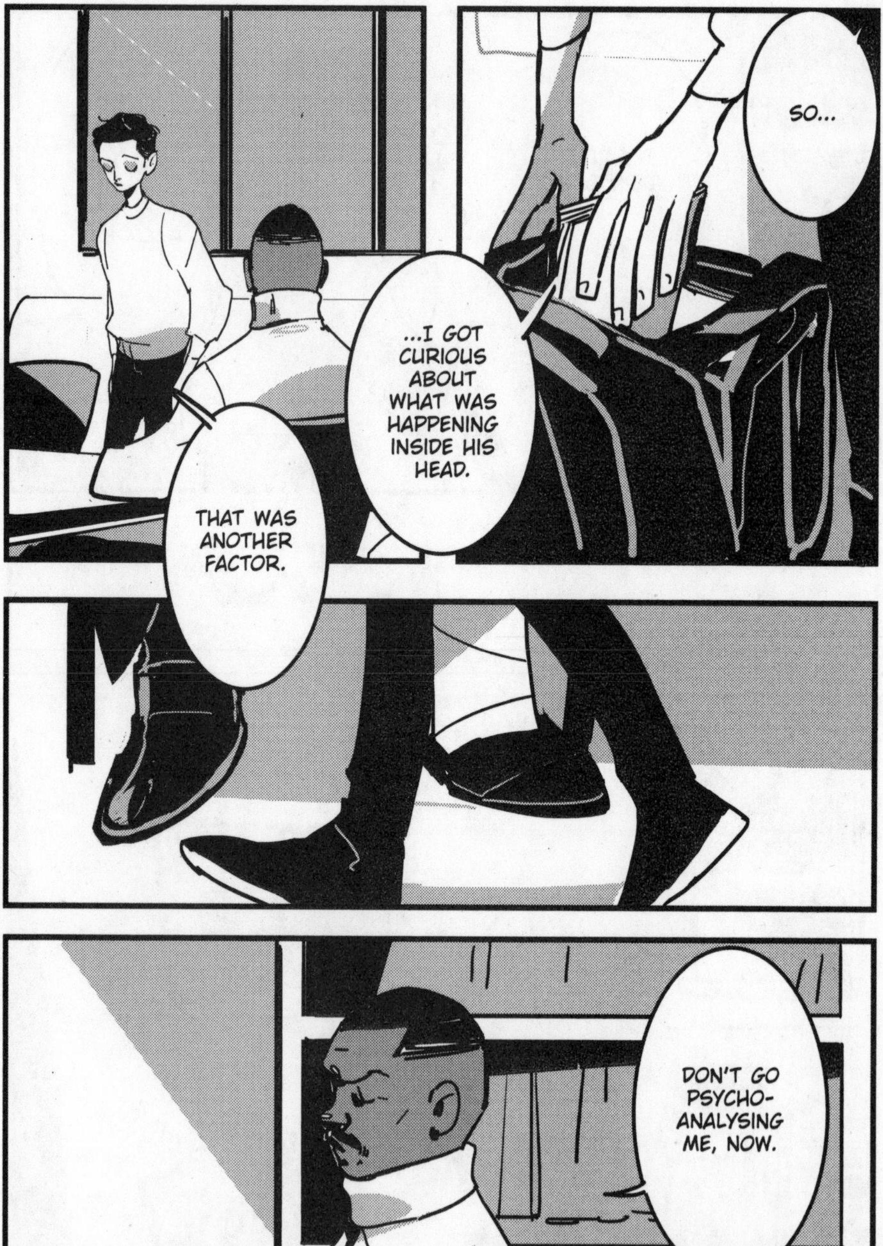
SO...
...I GOT CURIOUS ABOUT WHAT WAS HAPPENING INSIDE HIS HEAD.
THAT WAS ANOTHER FACTOR.
DON'T GO PSYCHO-ANALYSING ME, NOW.

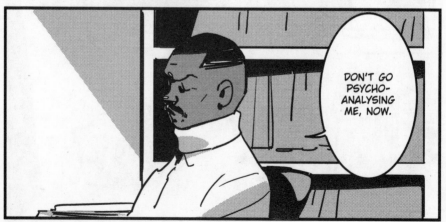

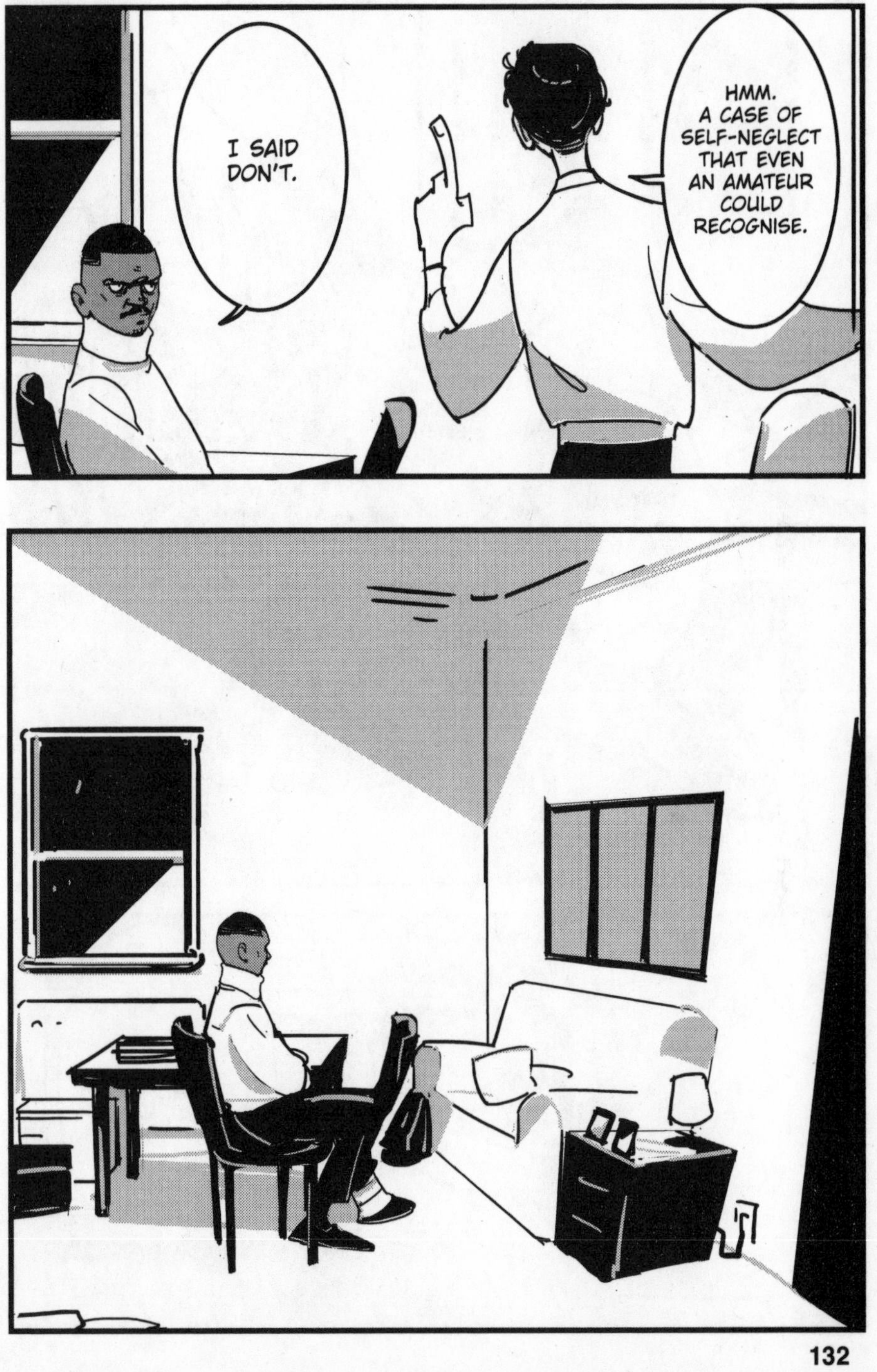
HMM. A CASE OF SELF-NEGLECT THAT EVEN AN AMATEUR COULD RECOGNISE.
I SAID DON'T.

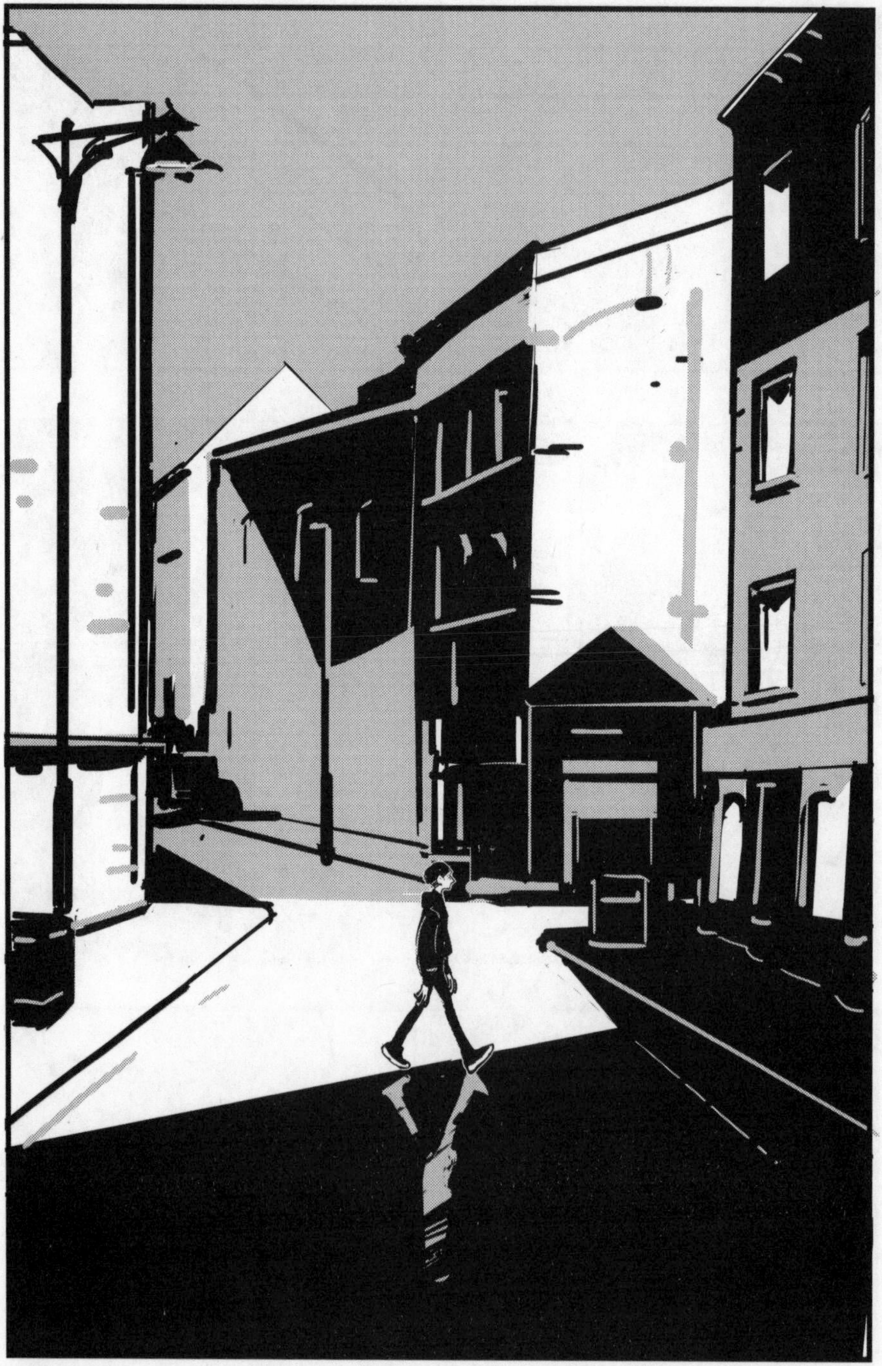

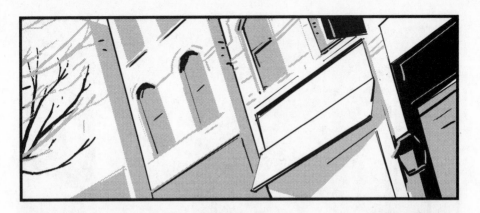

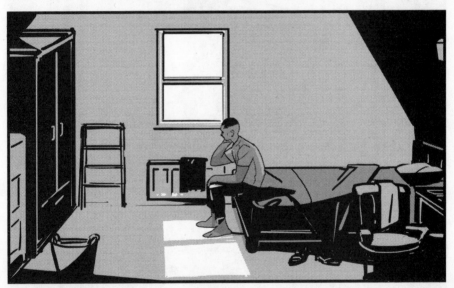

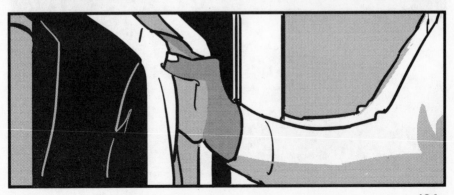

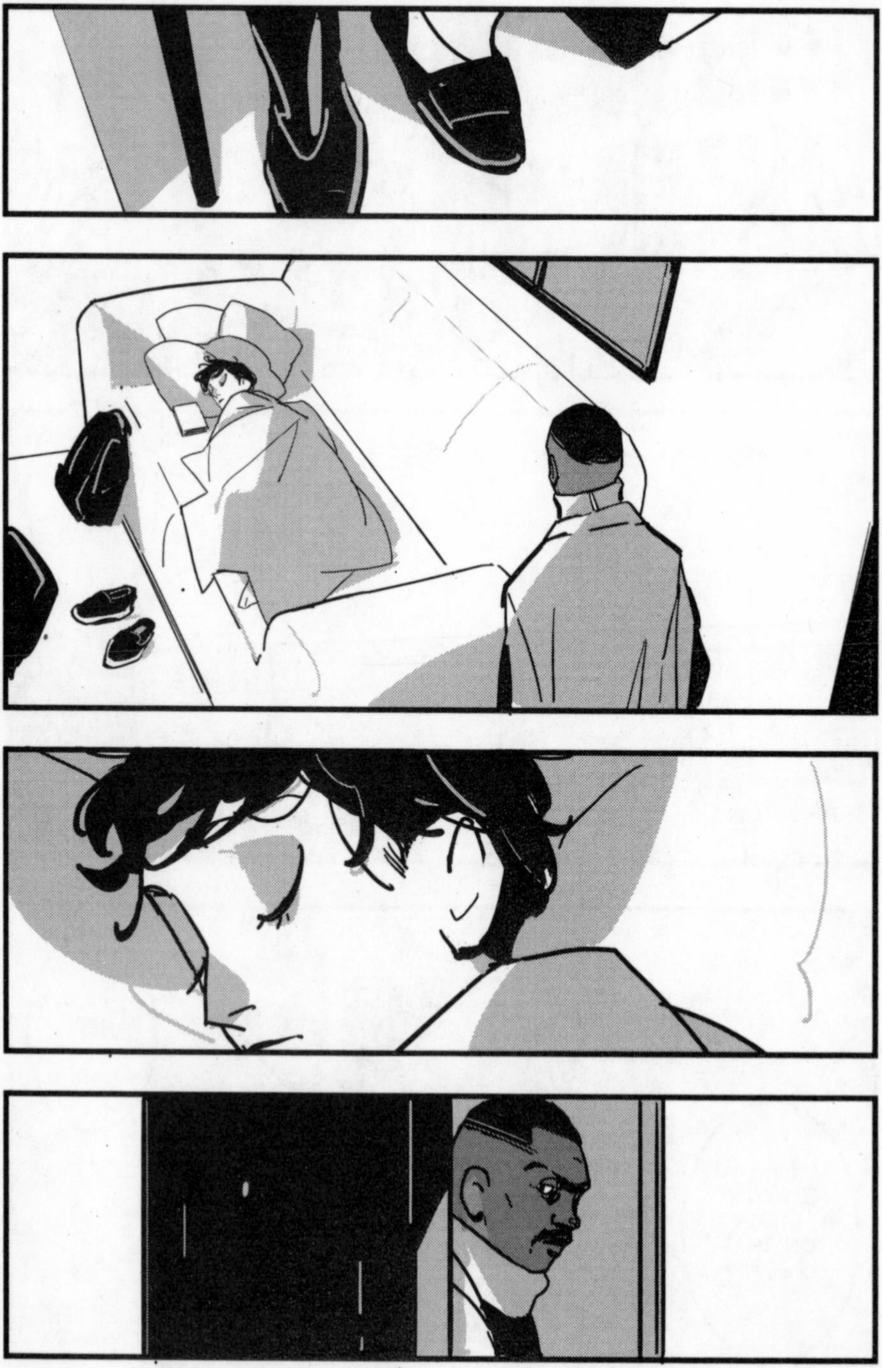

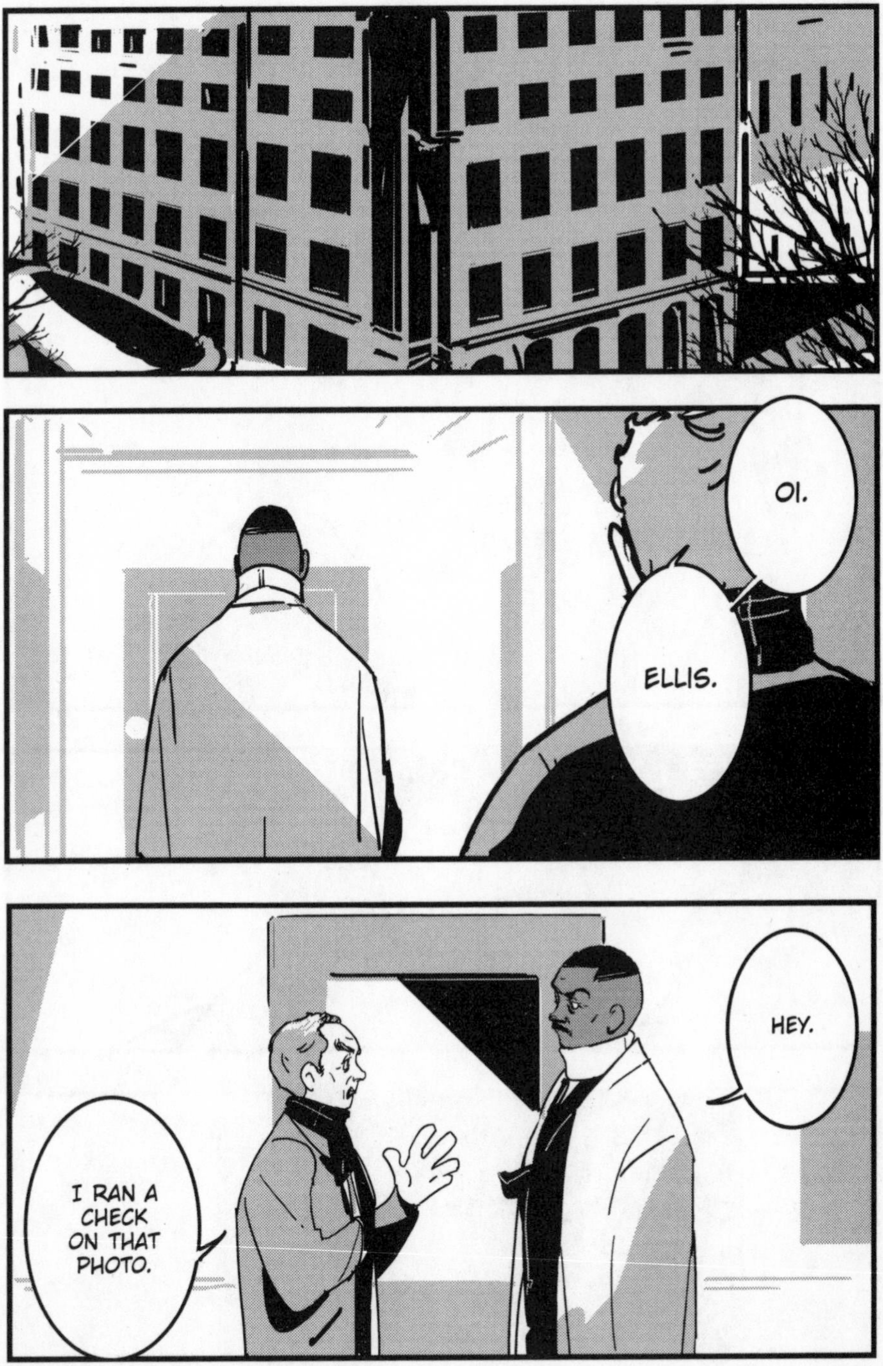
OI.
ELLIS.
HEY.
I RAN A CHECK ON THAT PHOTO.

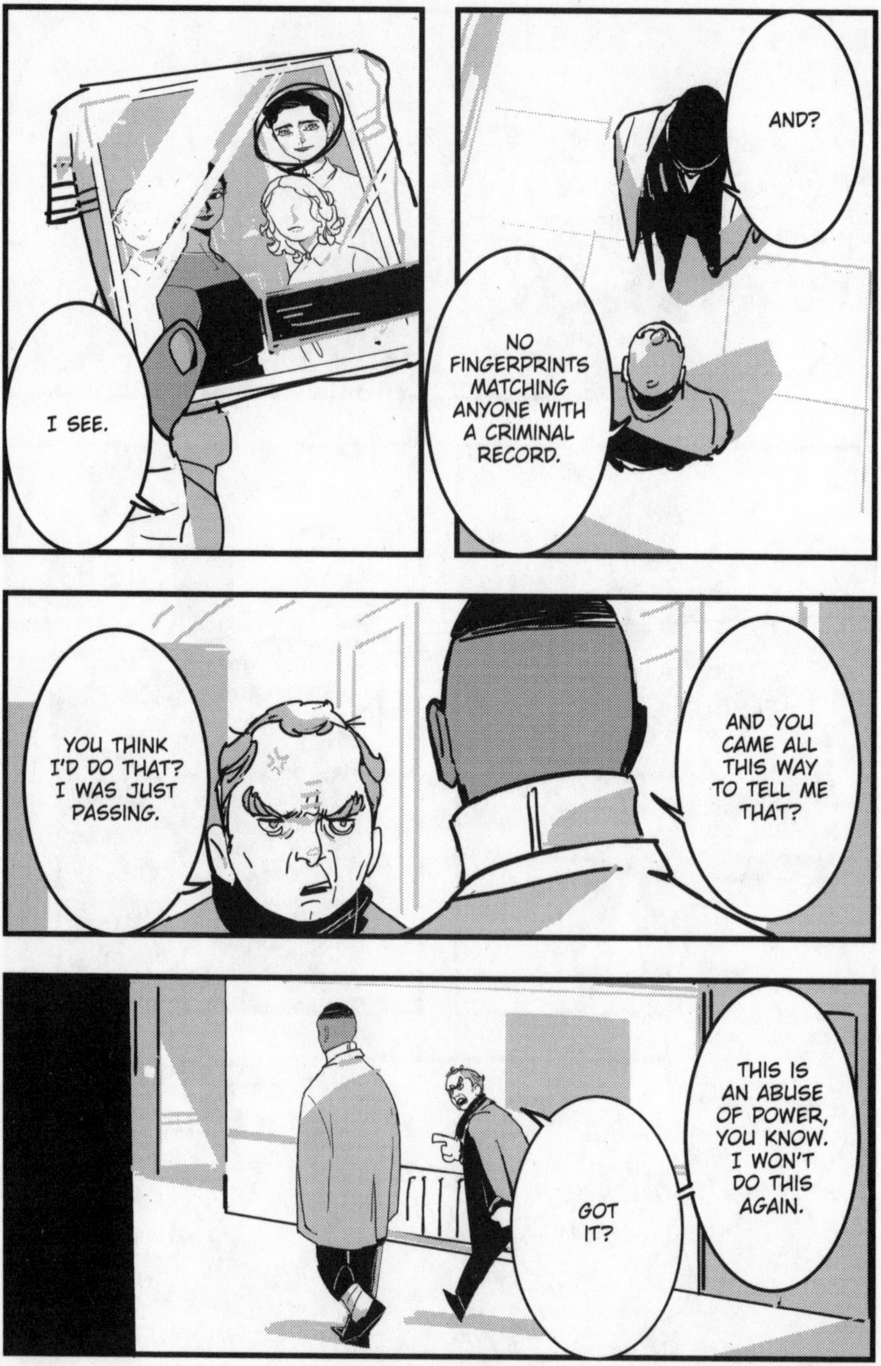
AND?
NO FINGERPRINTS MATCHING ANYONE WITH A CRIMINAL RECORD.
I SEE.
AND YOU CAME ALL THIS WAY TO TELL ME THAT?
YOU THINK I'D DO THAT? I WAS JUST PASSING.
THIS IS AN ABUSE OF POWER, YOU KNOW. I WON'T DO THIS AGAIN.
GOT IT?

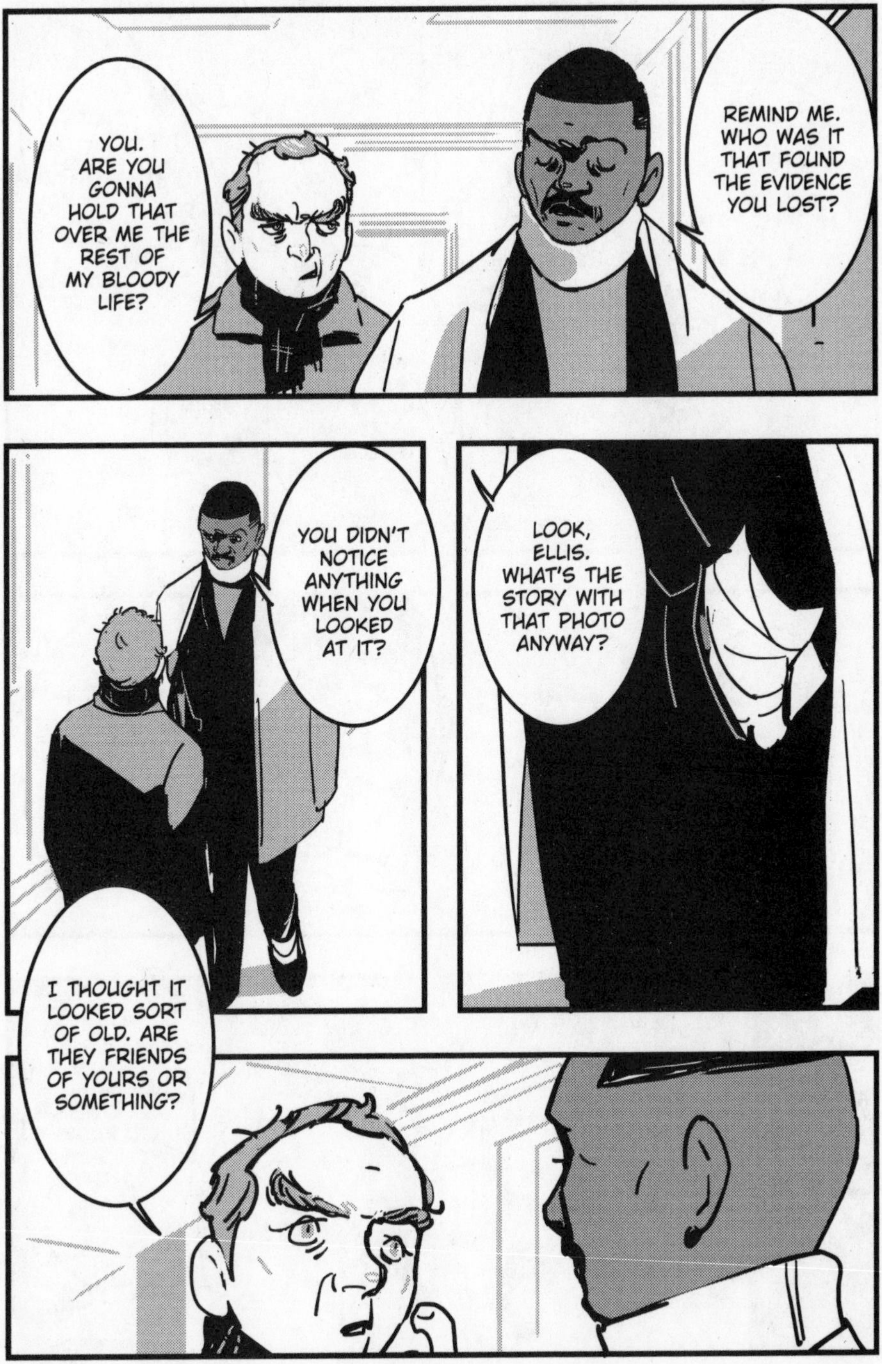
REMIND ME. WHO WAS IT THAT FOUND THE EVIDENCE YOU LOST?
YOU. ARE YOU GONNA HOLD THAT OVER ME THE REST OF MY BLOODY LIFE?
LOOK, ELLIS. WHAT'S THE STORY WITH THAT PHOTO ANYWAY?
YOU DIDN'T NOTICE ANYTHING WHEN YOU LOOKED AT IT?
I THOUGHT IT LOOKED SORT OF OLD. ARE THEY FRIENDS OF YOURS OR SOMETHING?

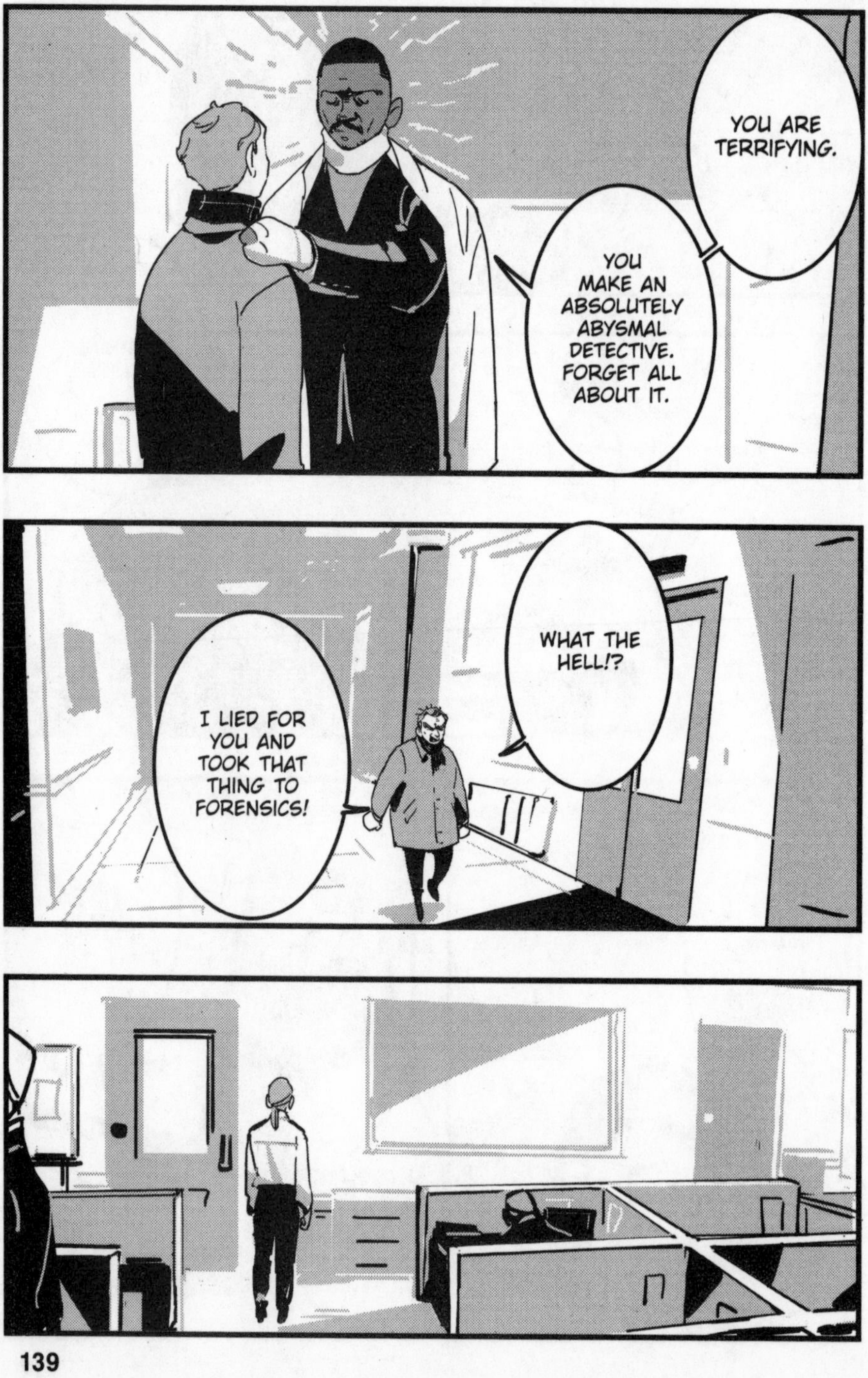
YOU ARE TERRIFYING.
YOU MAKE AN ABSOLUTELY ABYSMAL DETECTIVE. FORGET ALL ABOUT IT.
WHAT THE HELL!?
I LIED FOR YOU AND TOOK THAT THING TO FORENSICS!

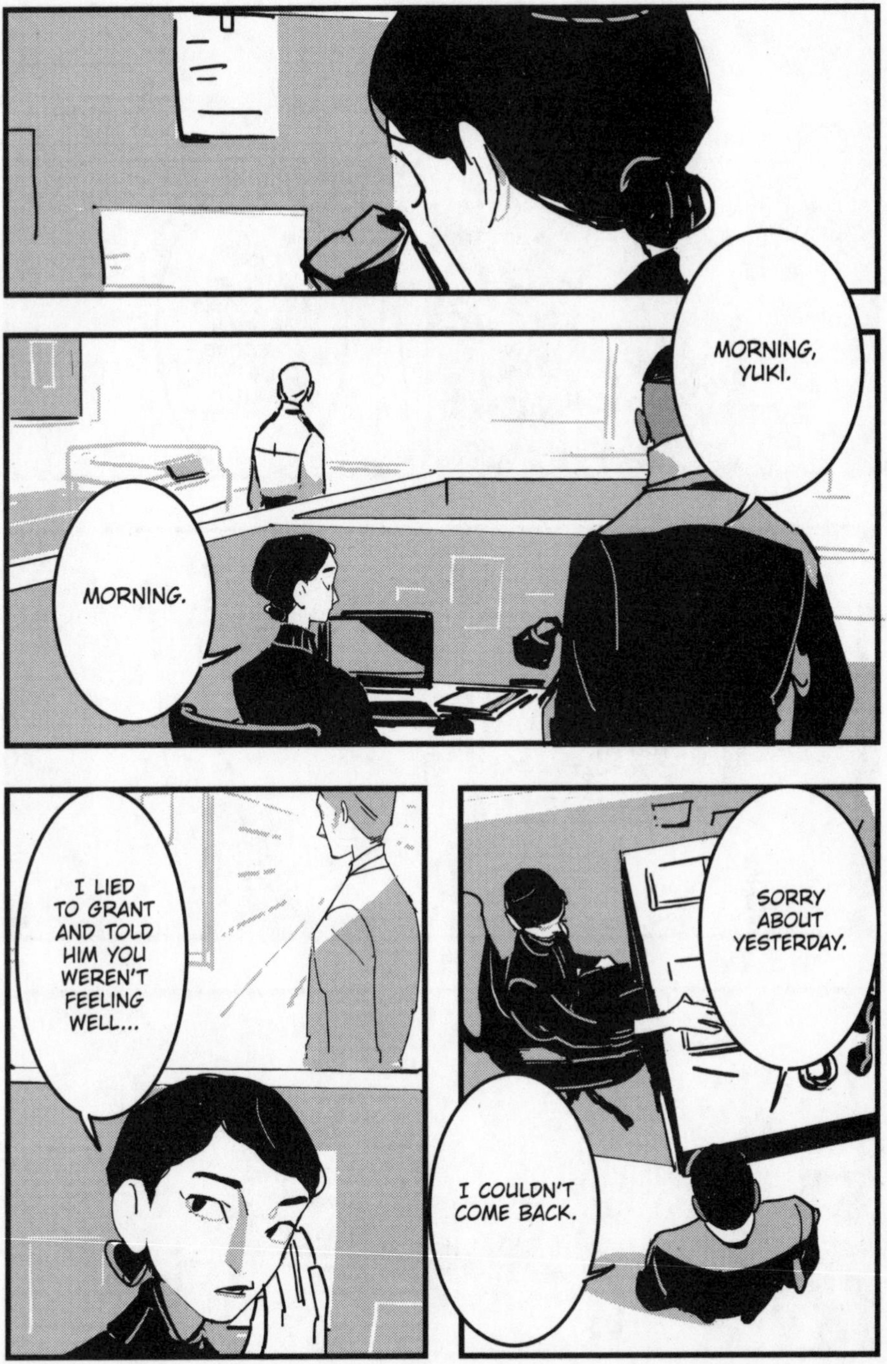
MORNING, YUKI.
MORNING.
SORRY ABOUT YESTERDAY.
I COULDN'T COME BACK.
I LIED TO GRANT AND TOLD HIM YOU WEREN'T FEELING WELL...

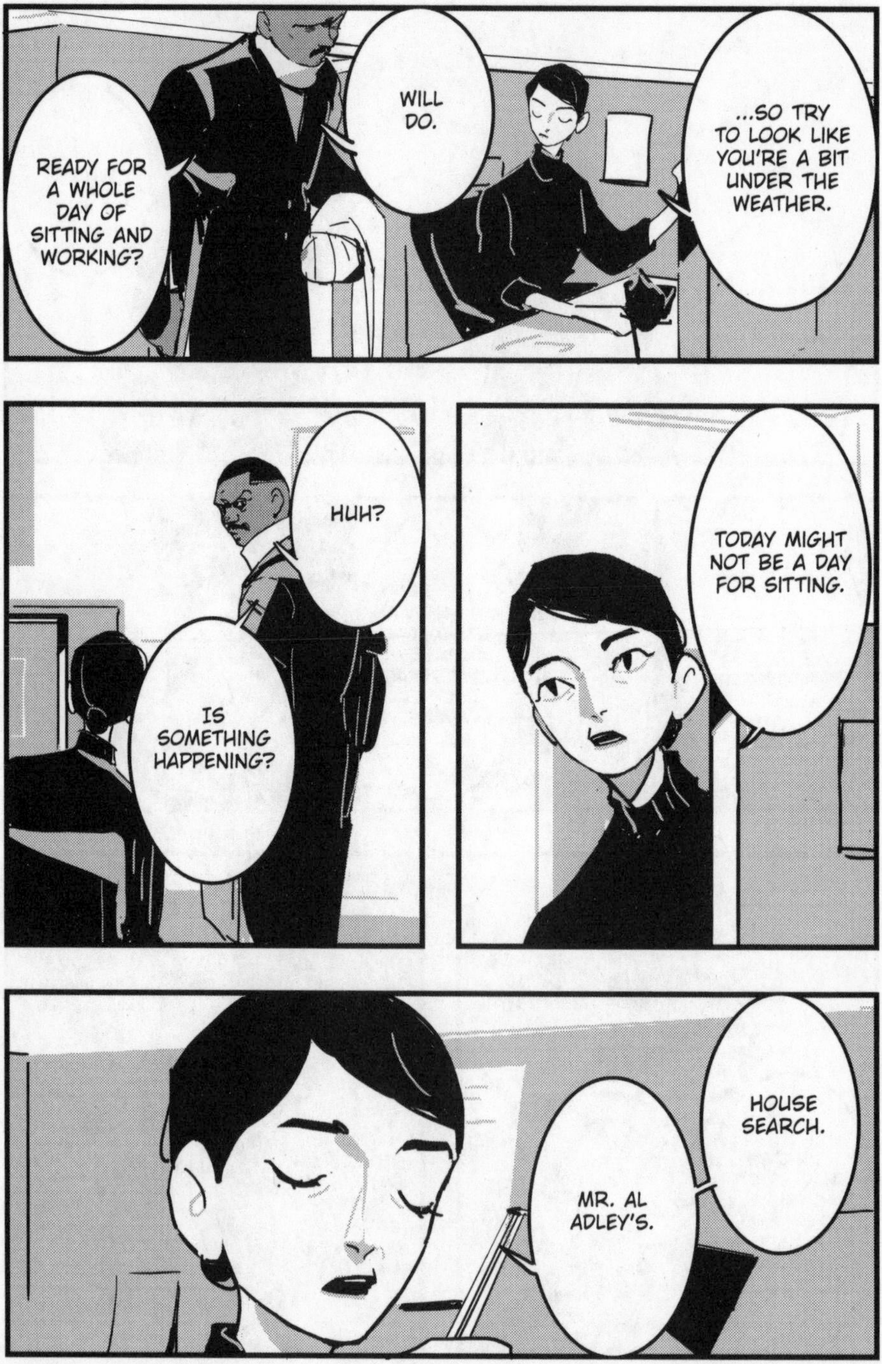
...SO TRY TO LOOK LIKE YOU'RE A BIT UNDER THE WEATHER.
WILL DO.
READY FOR A WHOLE DAY OF SITTING AND WORKING?
TODAY MIGHT NOT BE A DAY FOR SITTING.
HUH?
IS SOMETHING HAPPENING?
HOUSE SEARCH.
MR. AL ADLEY'S.

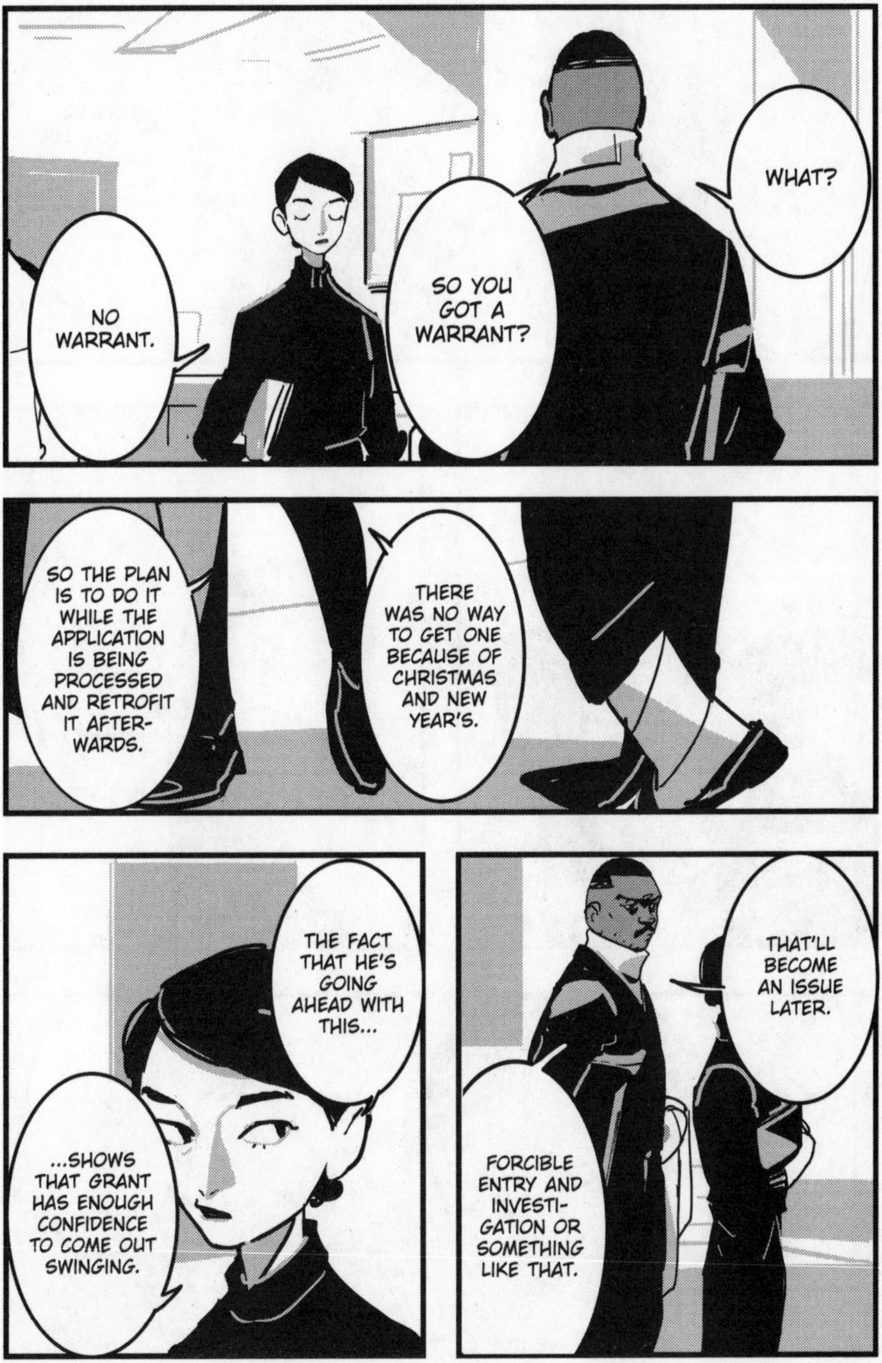
WHAT?
SO YOU GOT A WARRANT?
NO WARRANT.
THERE WAS NO WAY TO GET ONE BECAUSE OF CHRISTMAS AND NEW YEAR'S.
SO THE PLAN IS TO DO IT WHILE THE APPLICATION IS BEING PROCESSED AND RETROFIT IT AFTER-WARDS.
THAT'LL BECOME AN ISSUE LATER.
FORCIBLE ENTRY AND INVESTI-GATION OR SOMETHING LIKE THAT.
THE FACT THAT HE'S GOING AHEAD WITH THIS...
...SHOWS THAT GRANT HAS ENOUGH CONFIDENCE TO COME OUT SWINGING.

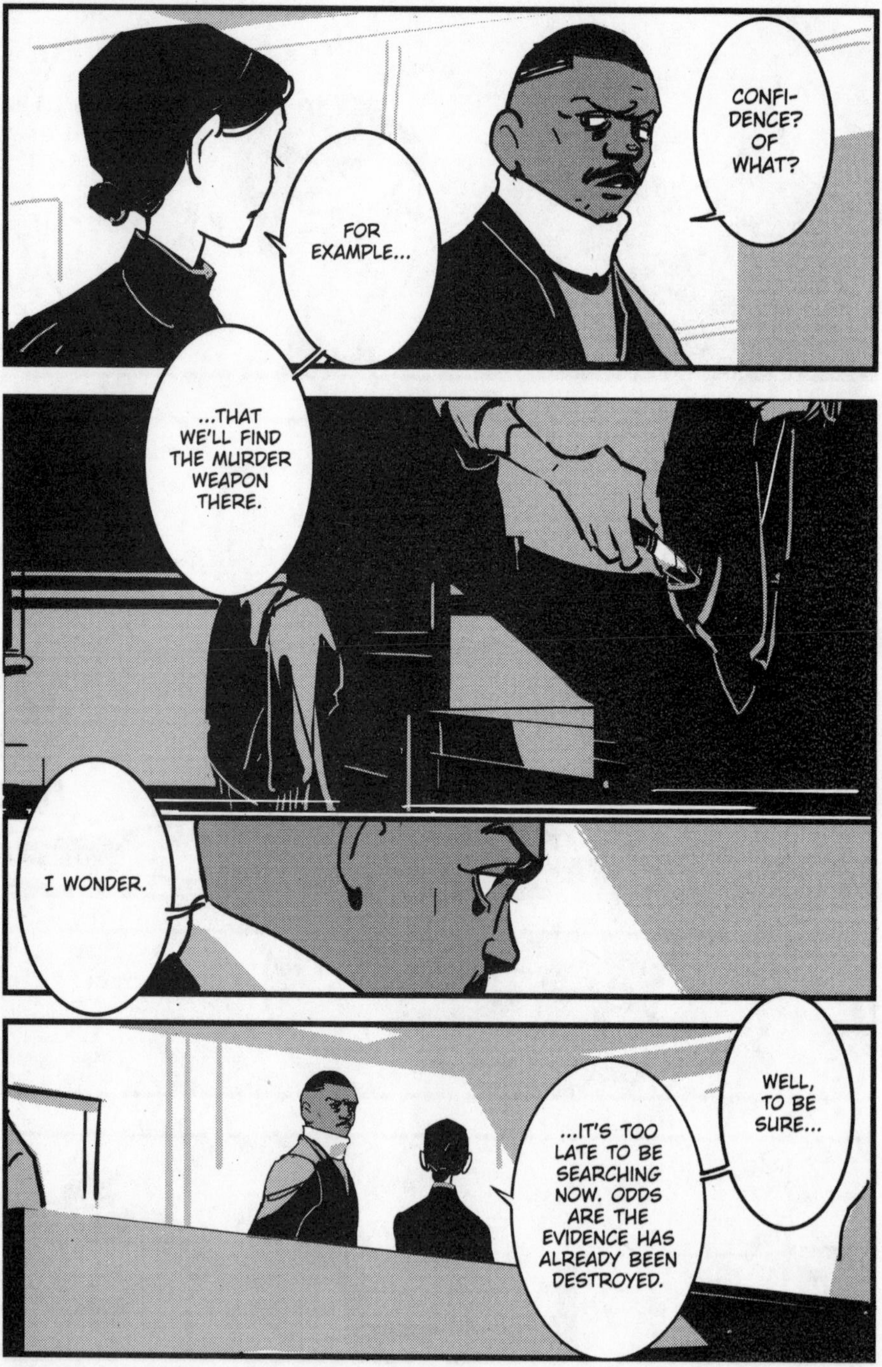
CONFI-
DENCE?
OF
WHAT?
FOR EXAMPLE...
...THAT WE'LL FIND THE MURDER WEAPON THERE.
I WONDER.
WELL, TO BE SURE...
...IT'S TOO LATE TO BE SEARCHING NOW. ODDS ARE THE EVIDENCE HAS ALREADY BEEN DESTROYED.

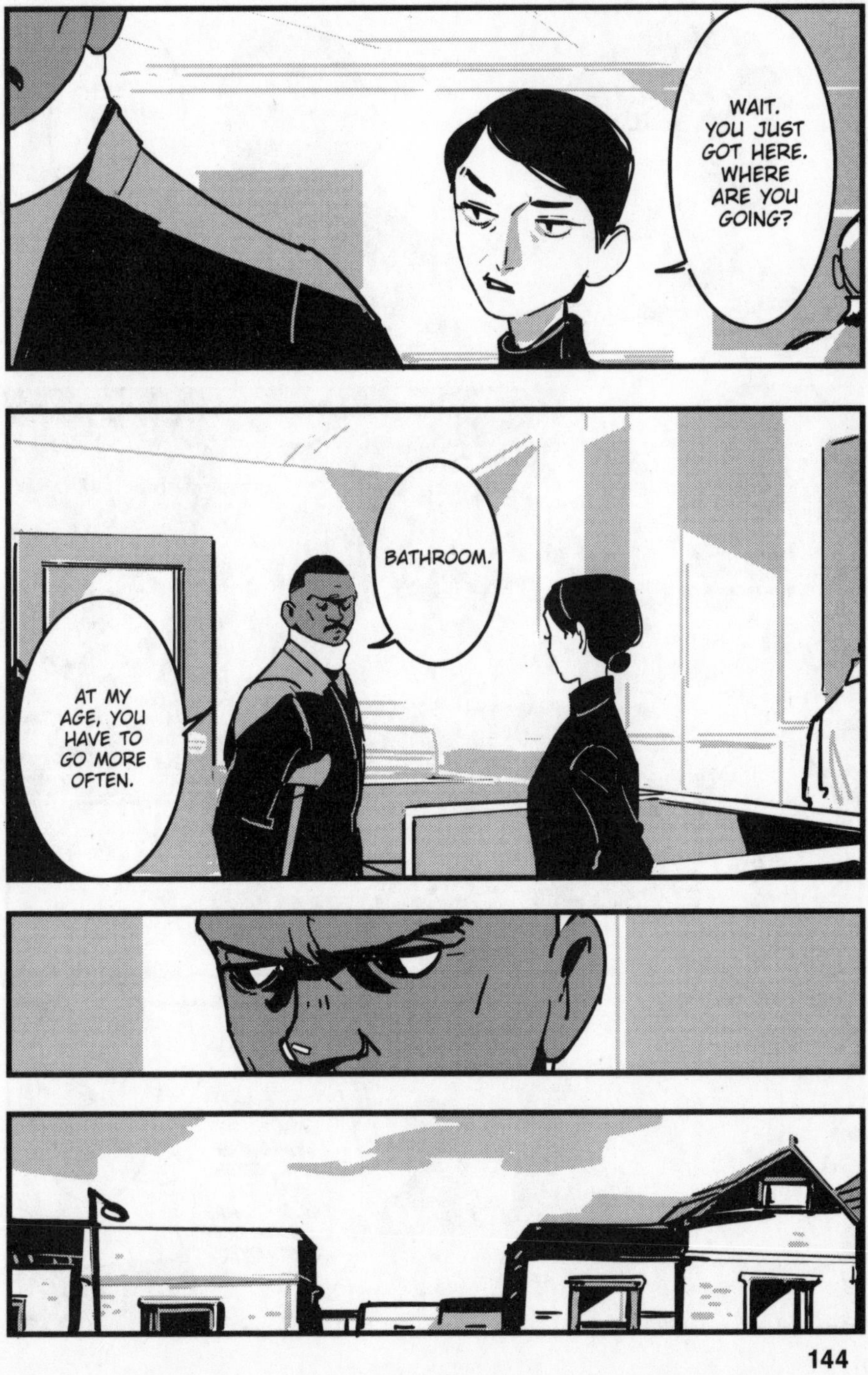
WAIT. YOU JUST GOT HERE. WHERE ARE YOU GOING?
BATHROOM.
AT MY AGE, YOU HAVE TO GO MORE OFTEN.

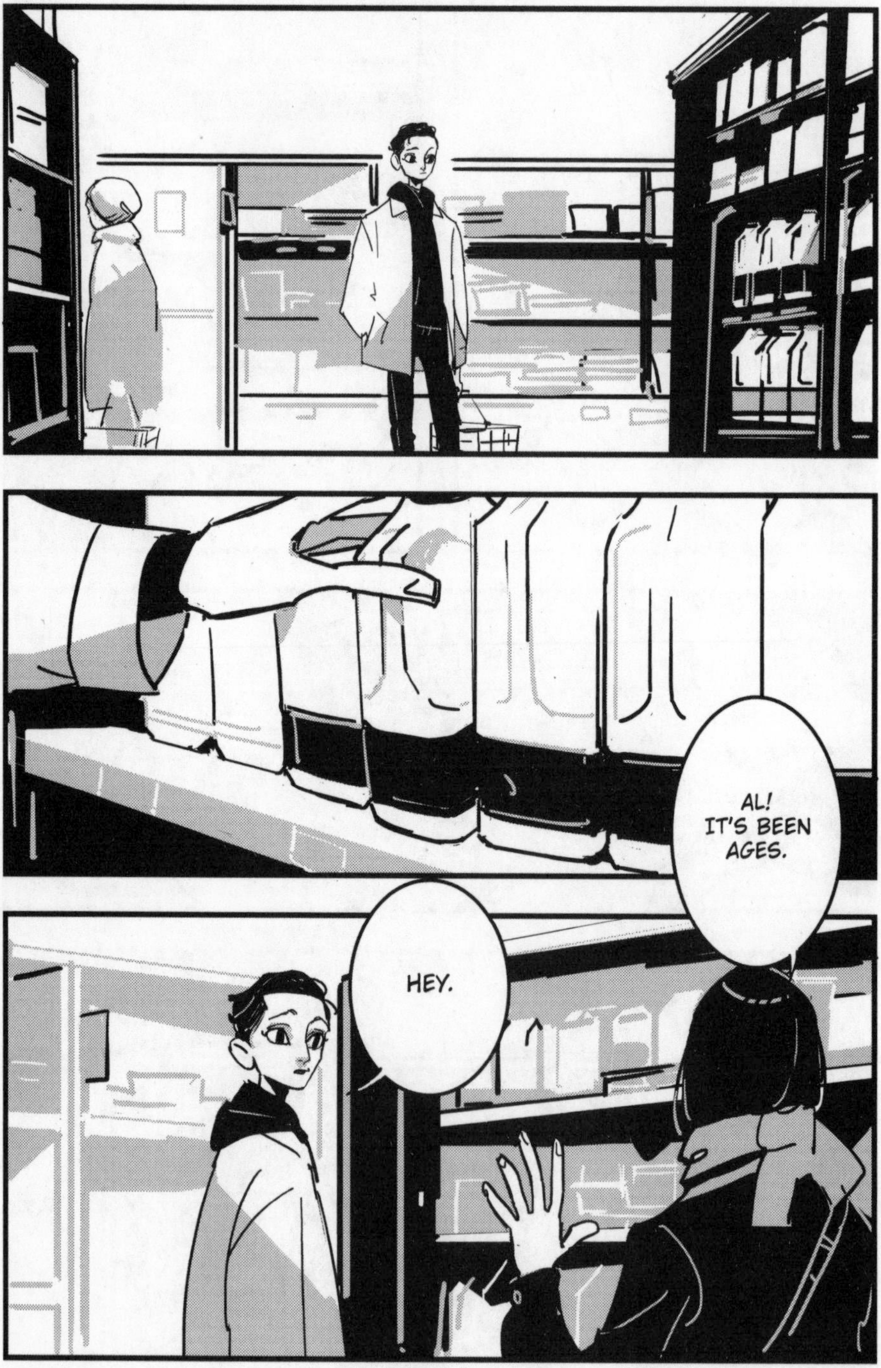
AL! IT'S BEEN AGES.
HEY.

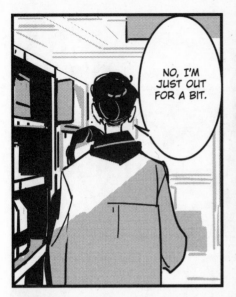

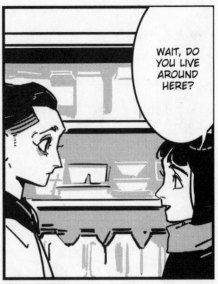

WAIT, DO YOU LIVE AROUND HERE?
NO, I'M JUST OUT FOR A BIT.
HOW ARE YOU?
I HAVEN'T SEEN YOU SINCE THE END OF TERM.
YOU DIDN'T EVEN COME TO THE HOLIDAY PARTY.
SOME STUFF HAPPENED... I'M SURE YOU HEARD ABOUT IT.

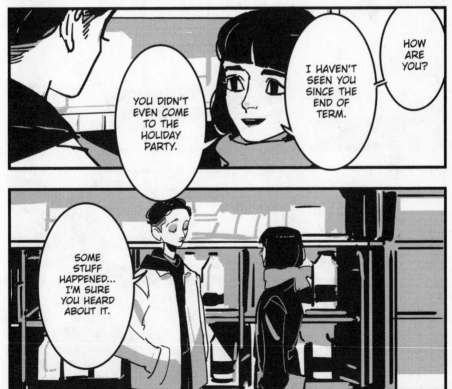

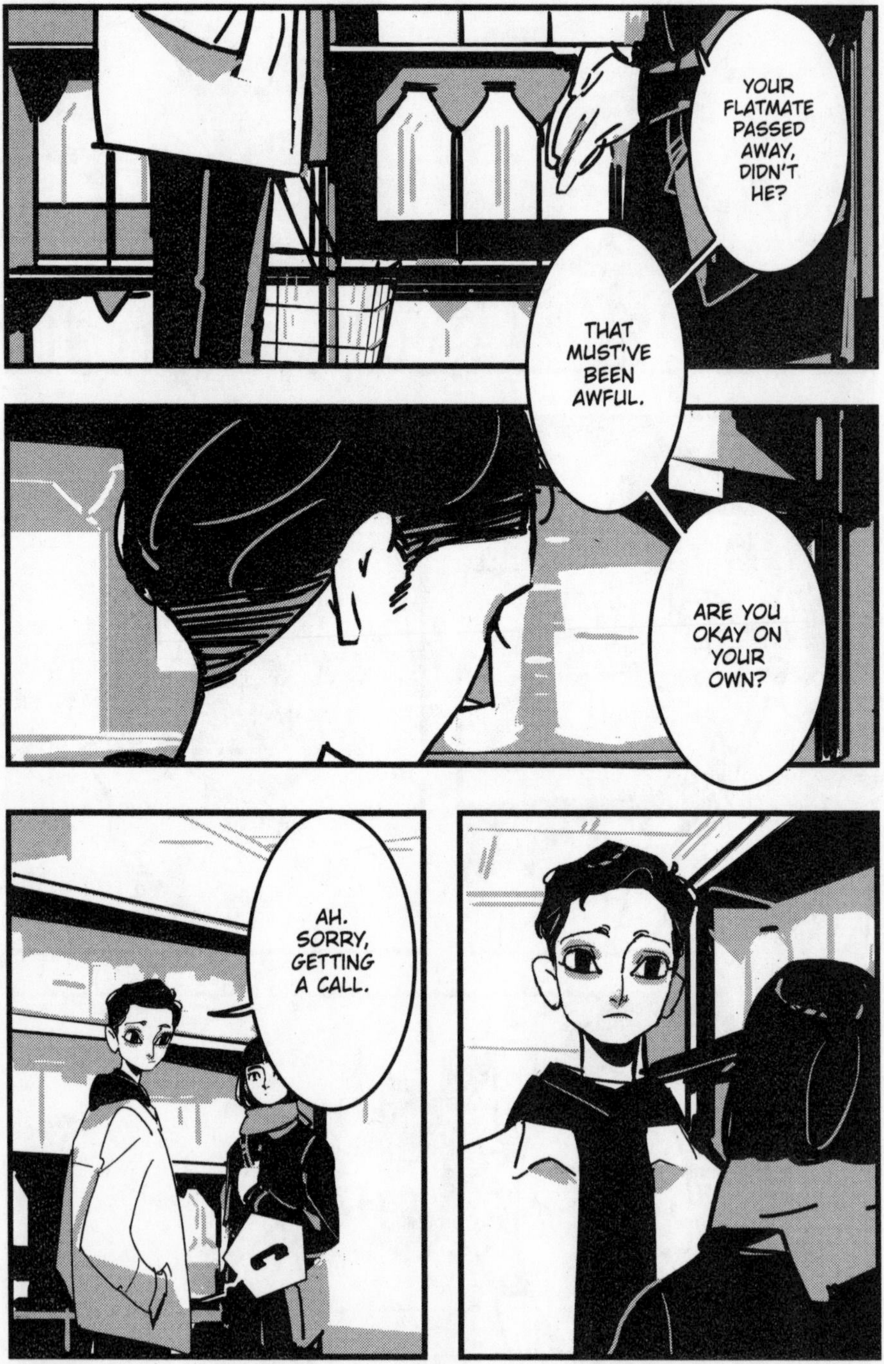
YOUR FLATMATE PASSED AWAY, DIDN'T HE?
THAT MUST'VE BEEN AWFUL.
ARE YOU OKAY ON YOUR OWN?
AH. SORRY, GETTING A CALL.

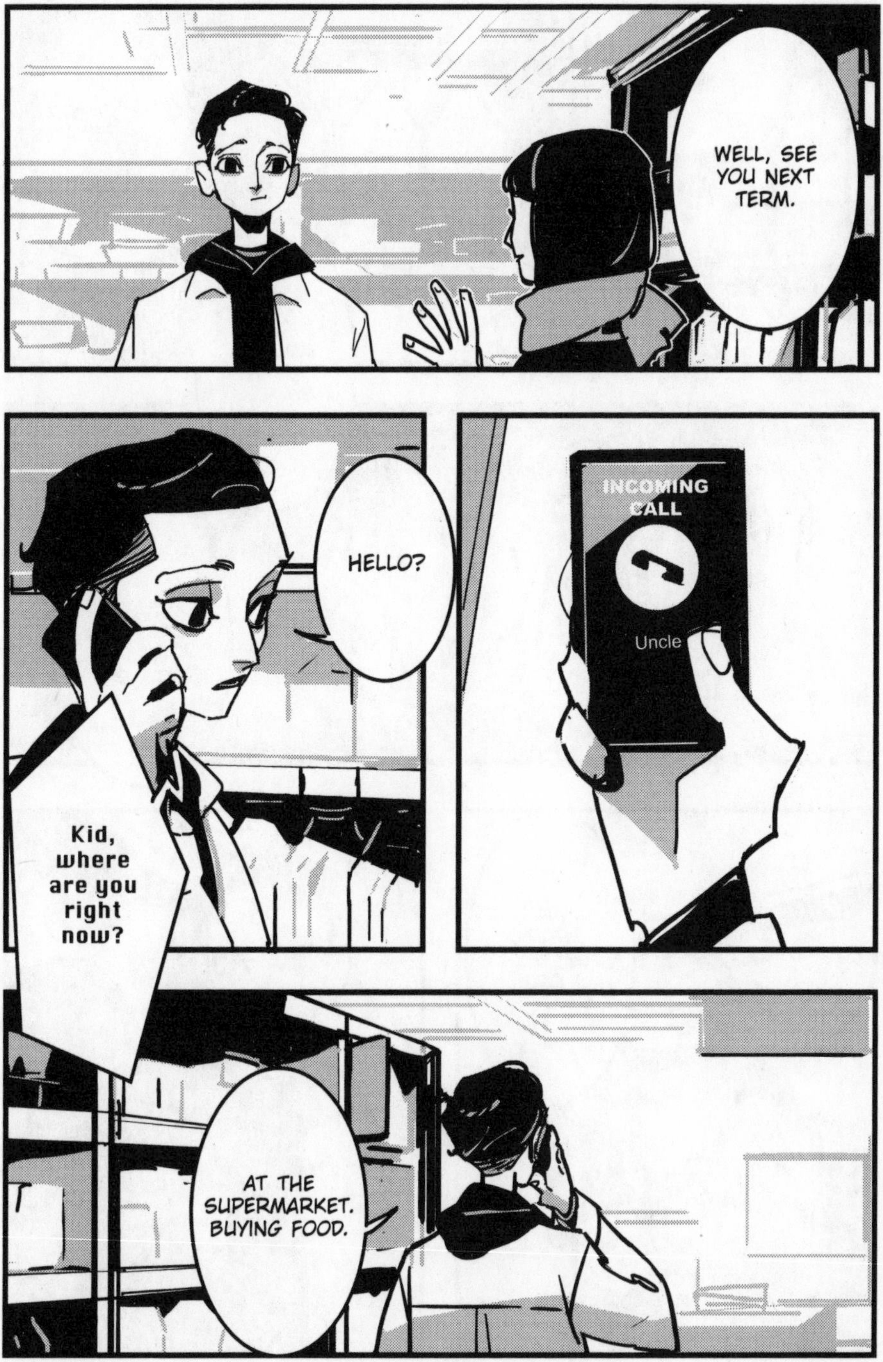
WELL, SEE YOU NEXT TERM.
INCOMING CALL
Uncle
HELLO?
Kid, where are you right now?
AT THE SUPERMARKET. BUYING FOOD.

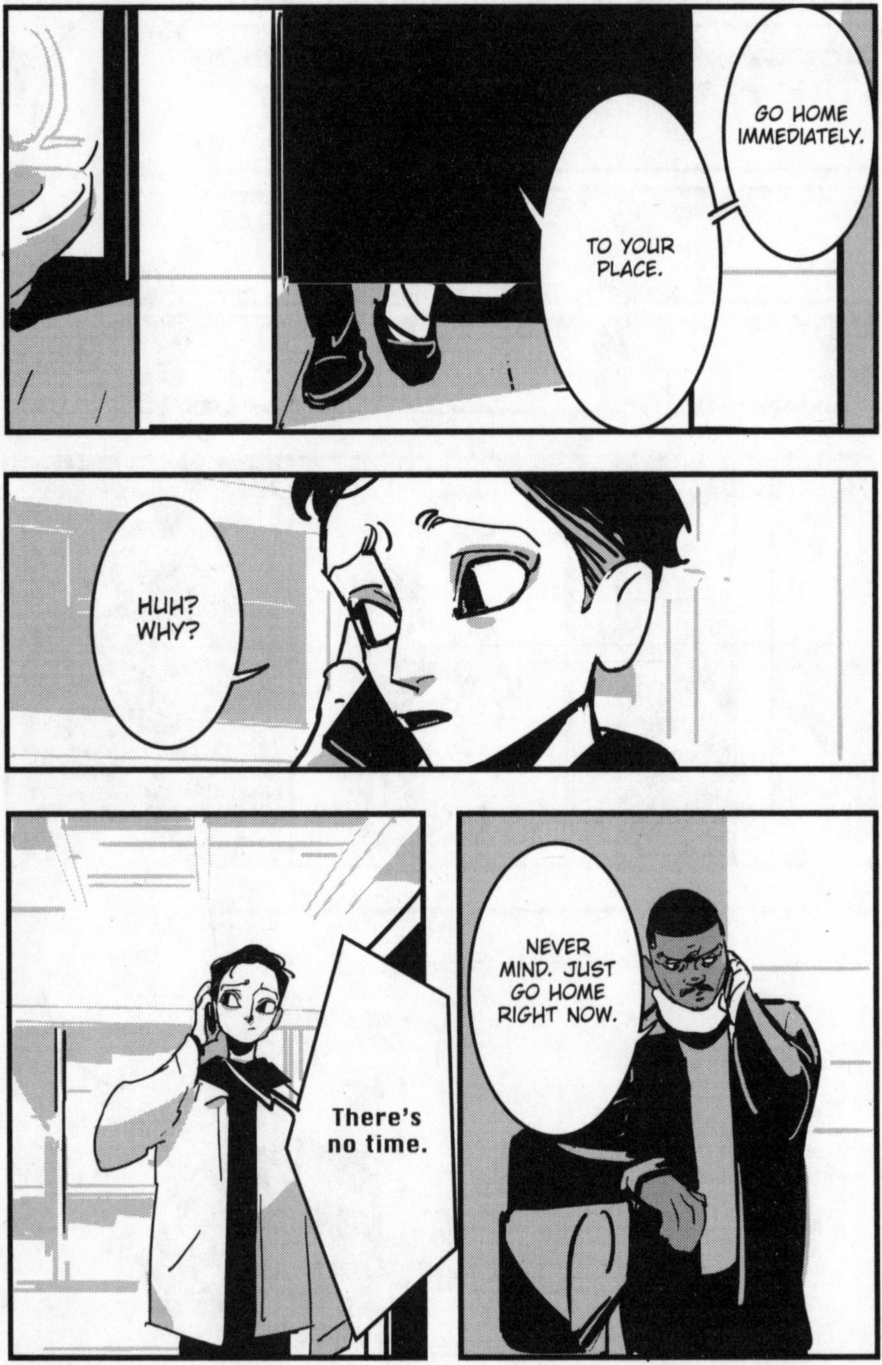
GO HOME IMMEDIATELY.
TO YOUR PLACE.
HUH? WHY?
NEVER MIND. JUST GO HOME RIGHT NOW.
There's no time.

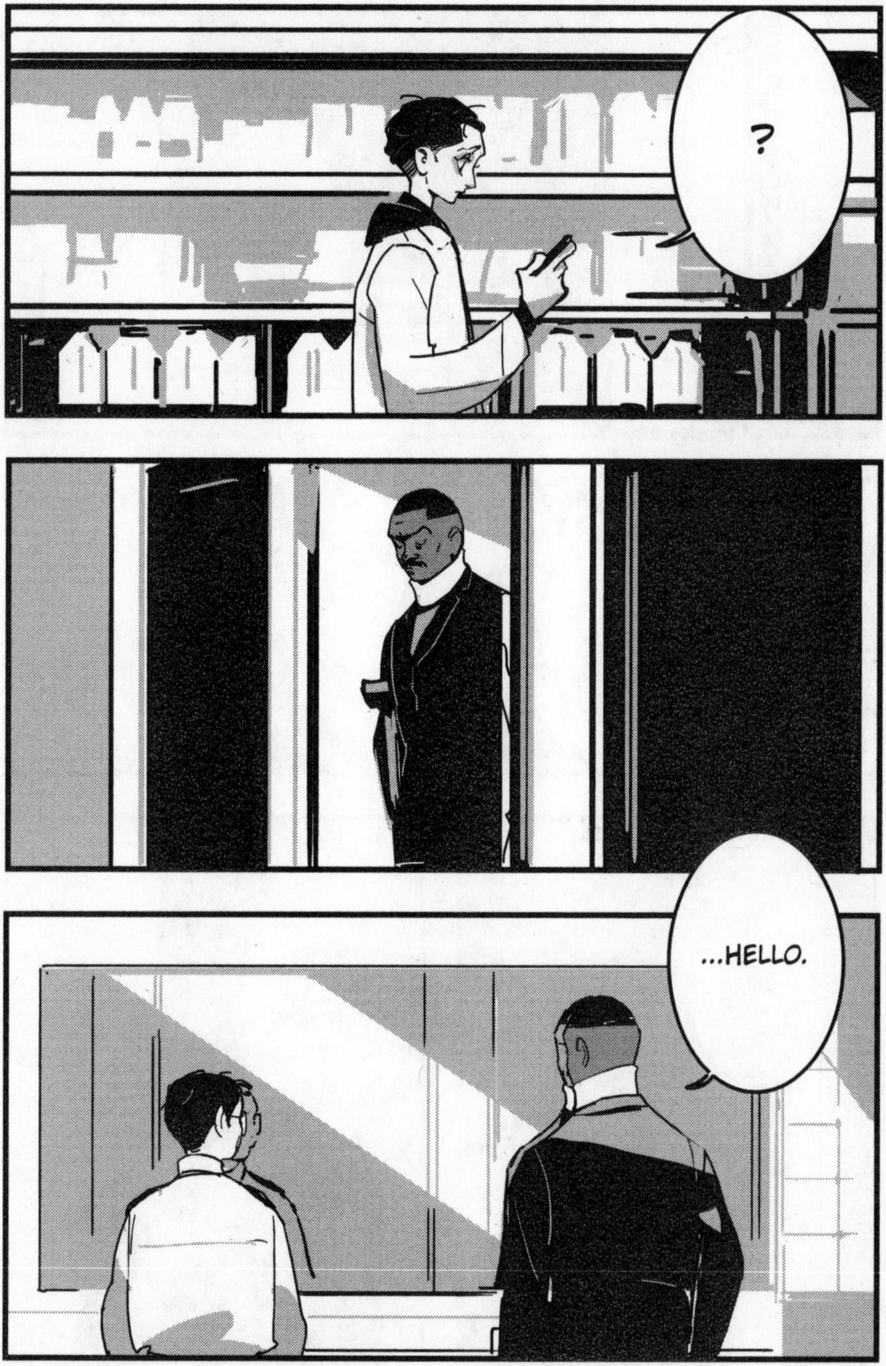
?
...HELLO.

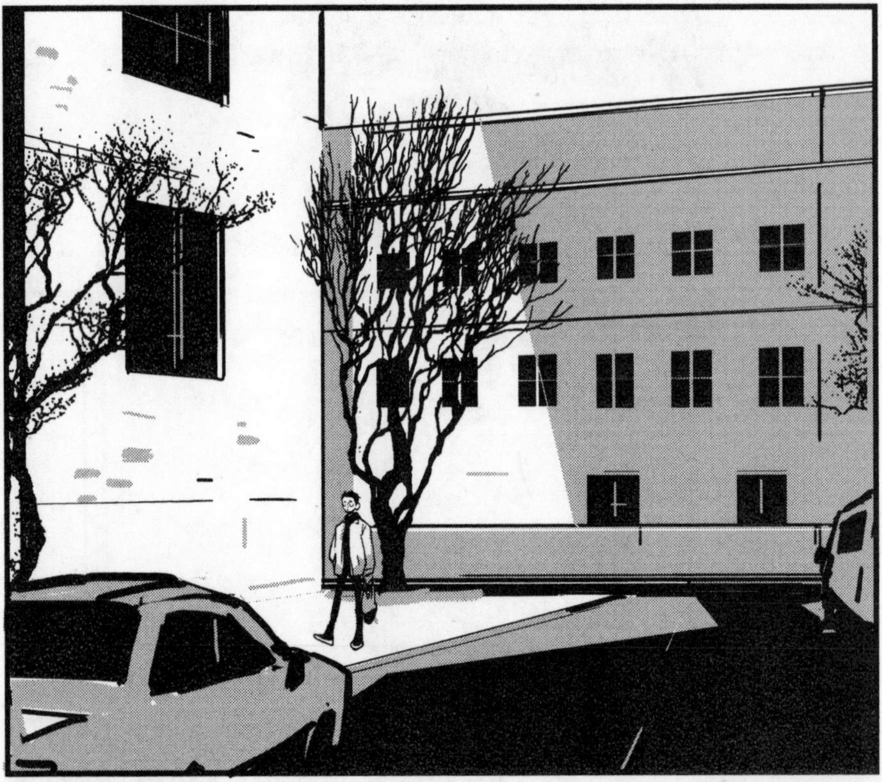

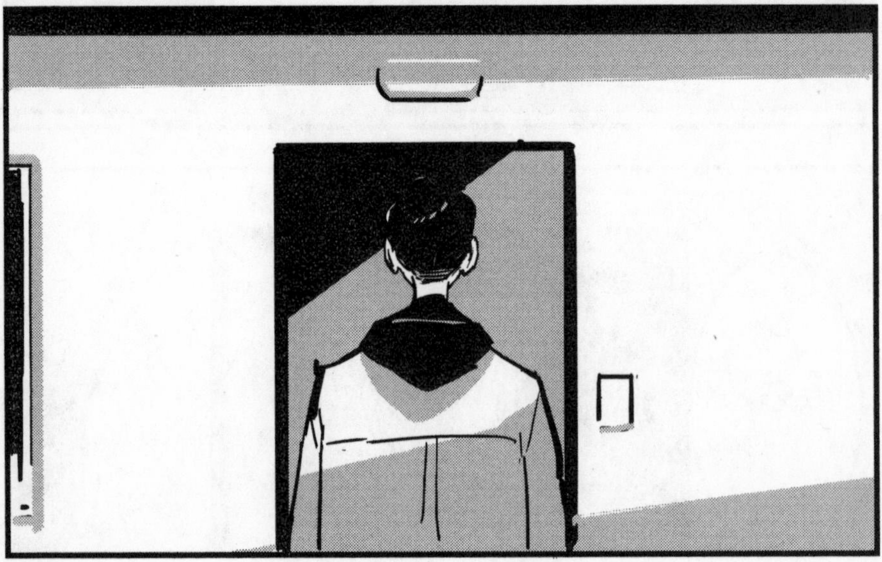

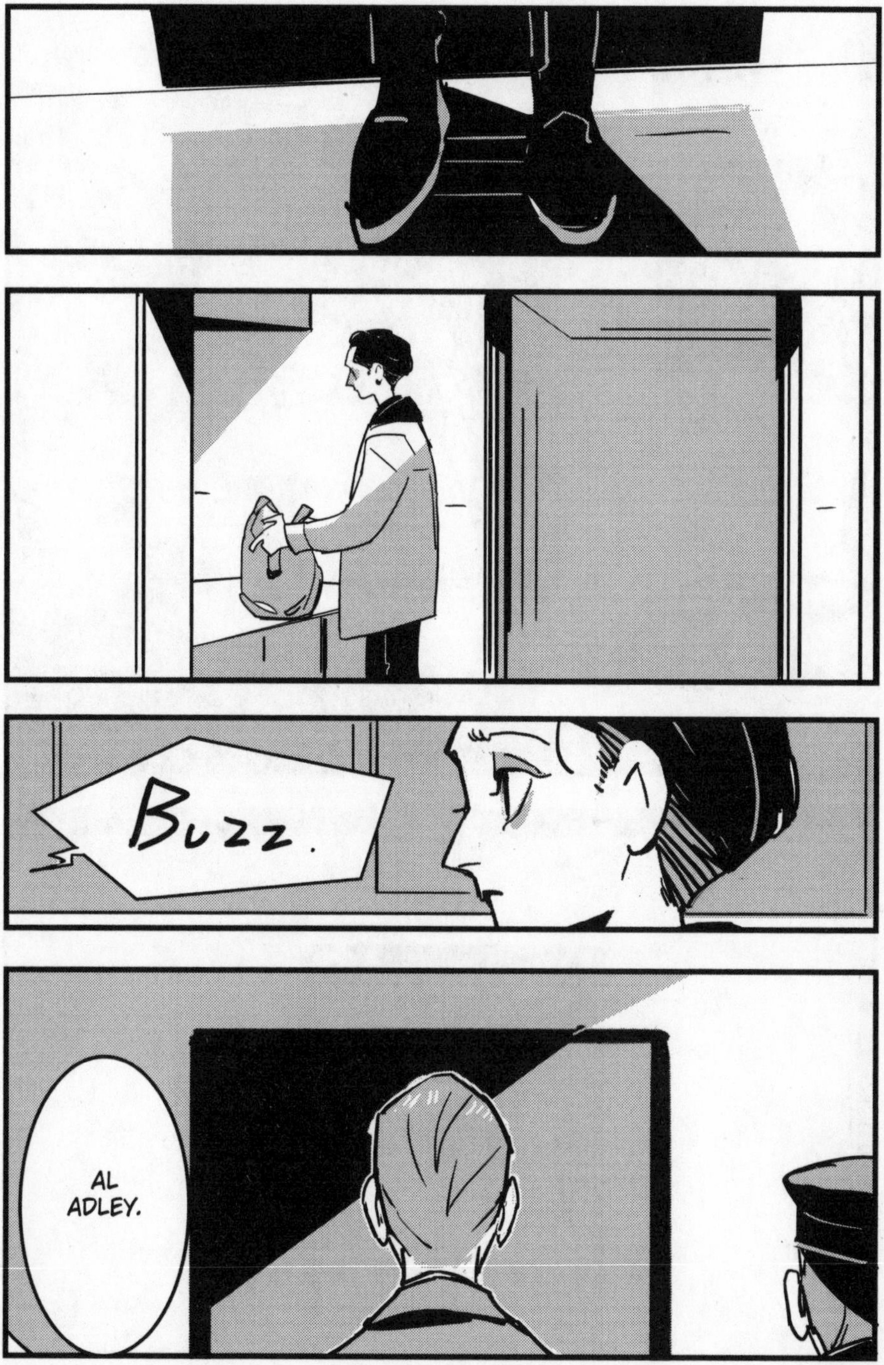
BUZZ.
AL ADLEY.

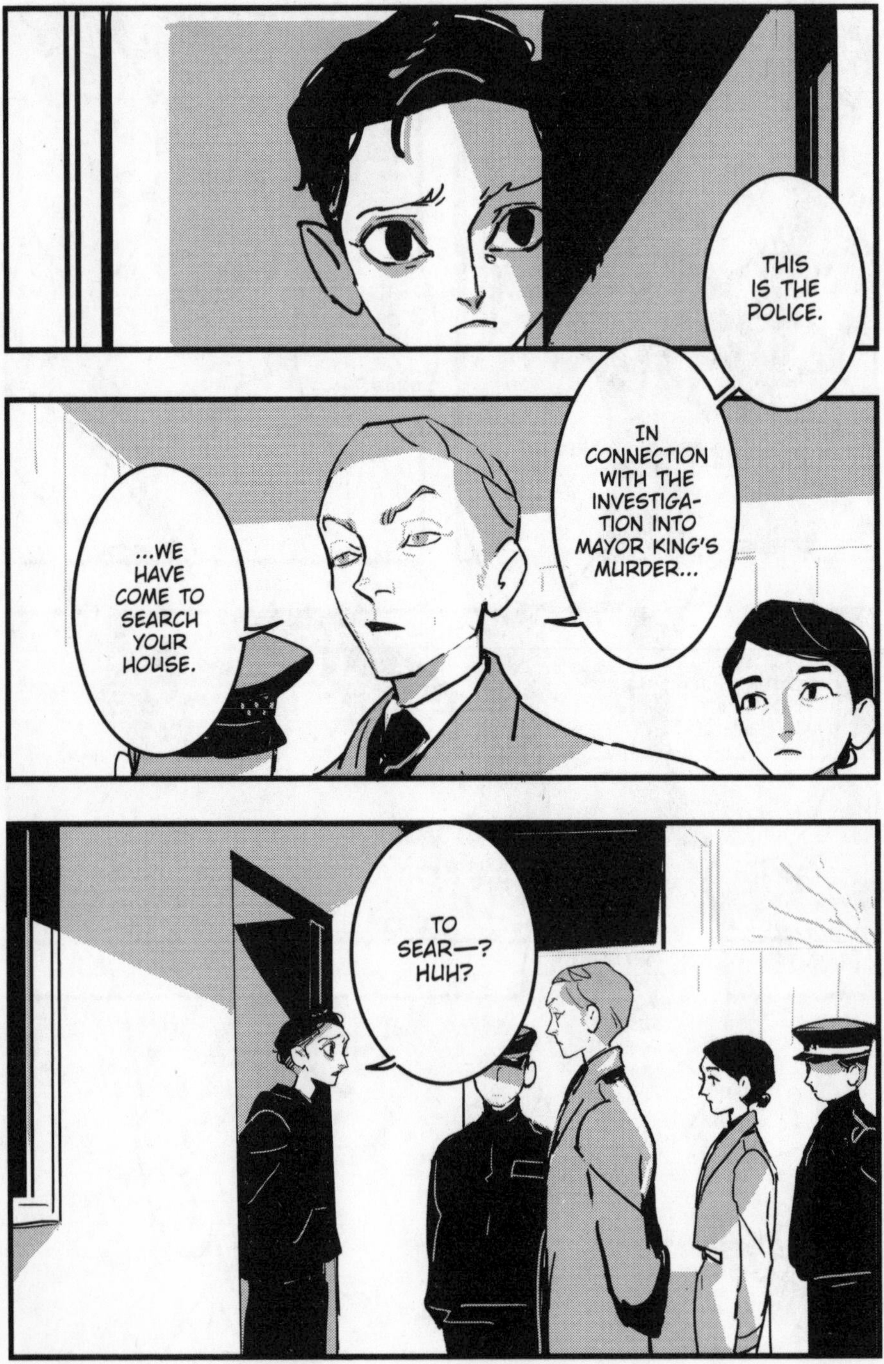
THIS IS THE POLICE.
IN CONNECTION WITH THE INVESTIGATION INTO MAYOR KING'S MURDER...
...WE HAVE COME TO SEARCH YOUR HOUSE.
TO SEAR—? HUH?

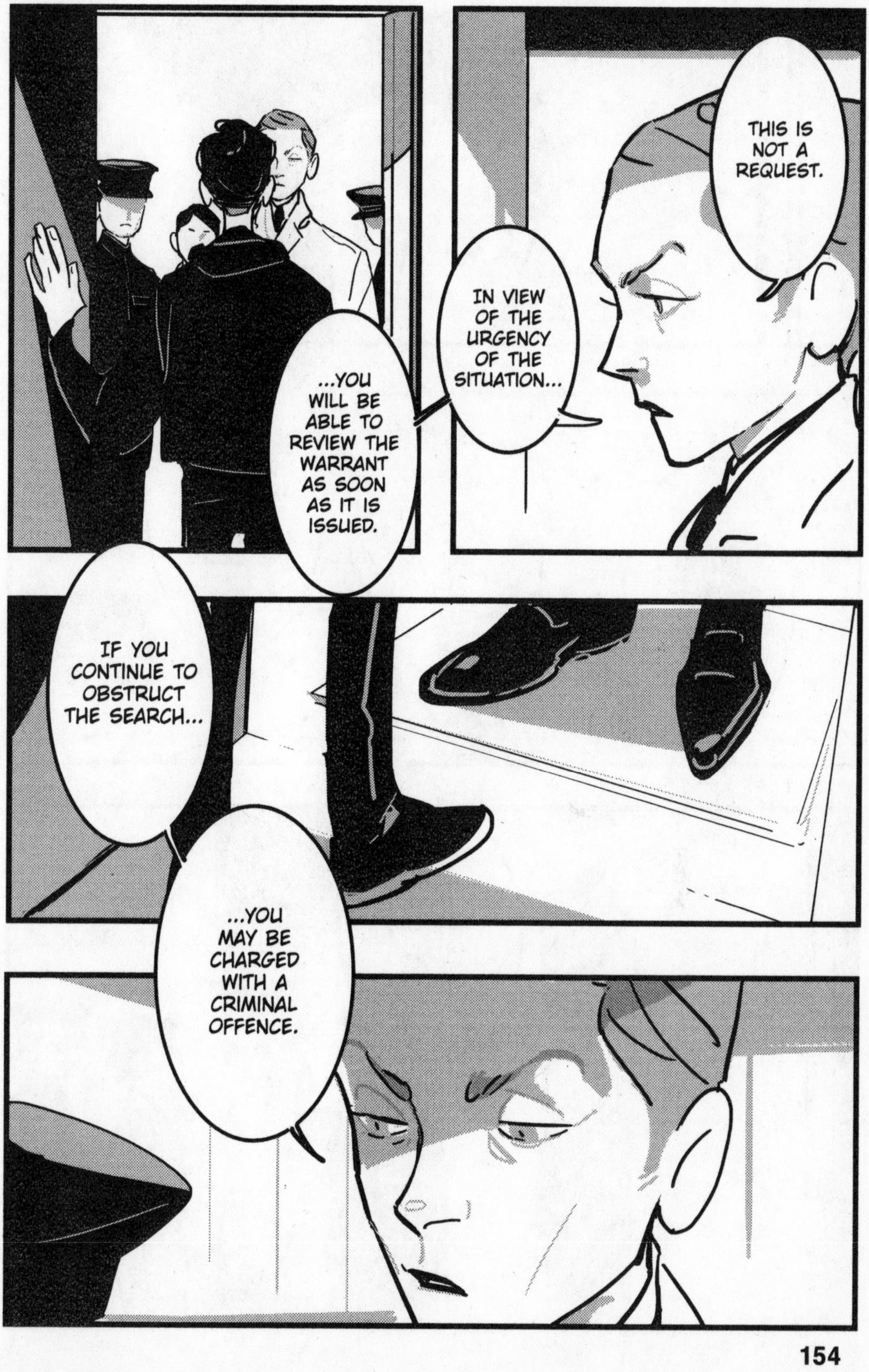
THIS IS NOT A REQUEST.
IN VIEW OF THE URGENCY OF THE SITUATION...
...YOU WILL BE ABLE TO REVIEW THE WARRANT AS SOON AS IT IS ISSUED.
IF YOU CONTINUE TO OBSTRUCT THE SEARCH...
...YOU MAY BE CHARGED WITH A CRIMINAL OFFENCE.

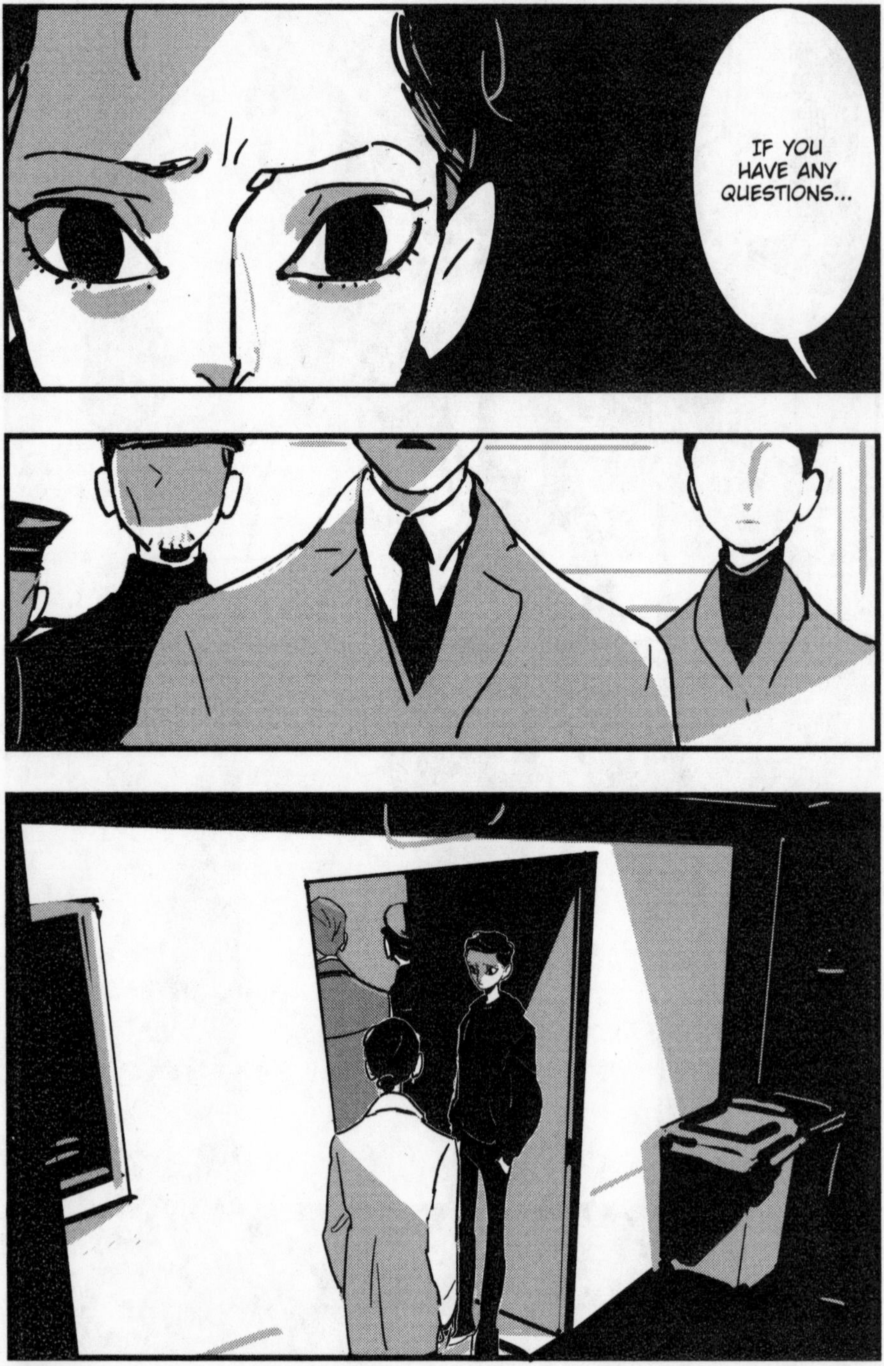
IF YOU HAVE ANY QUESTIONS...

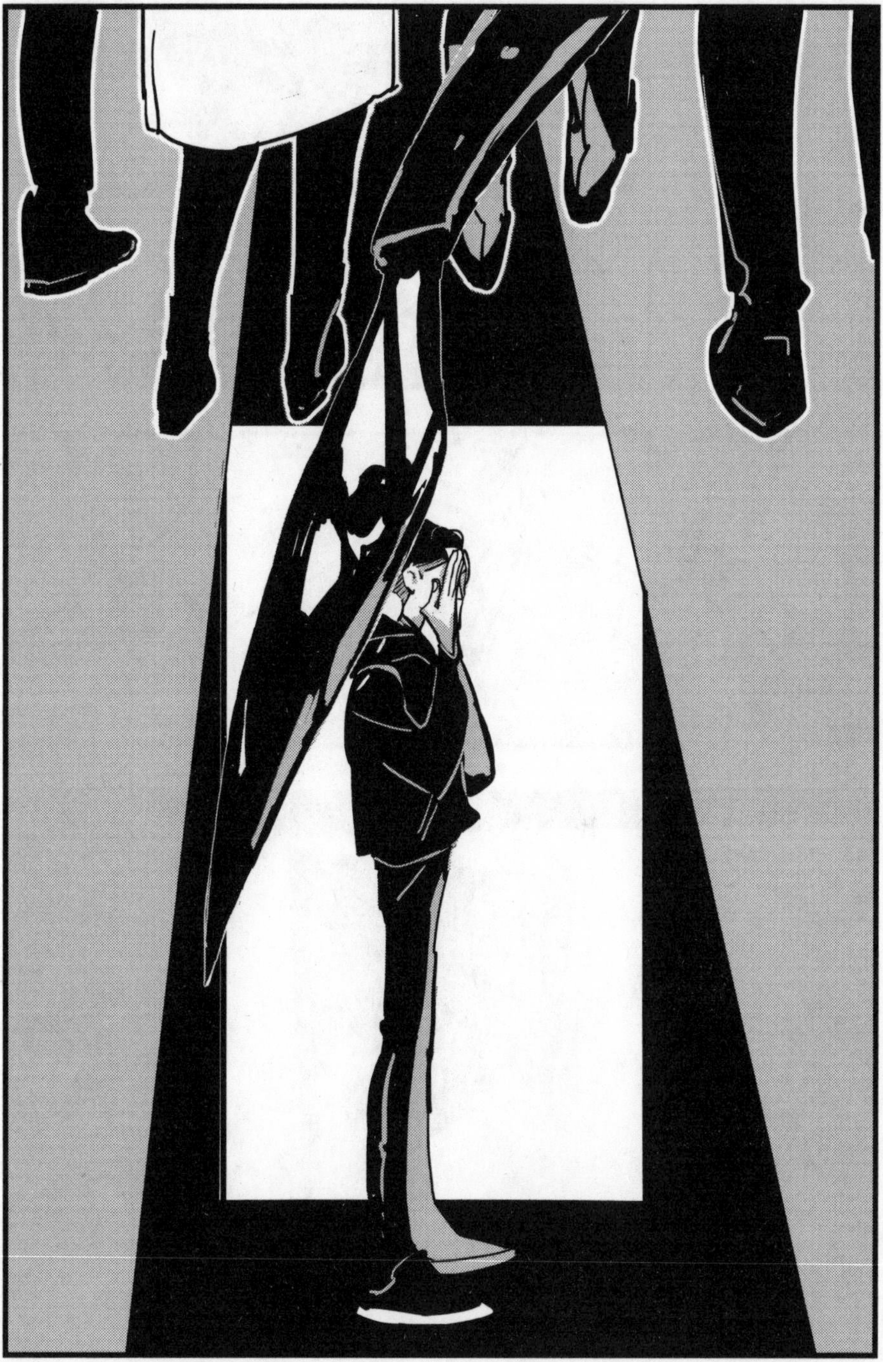

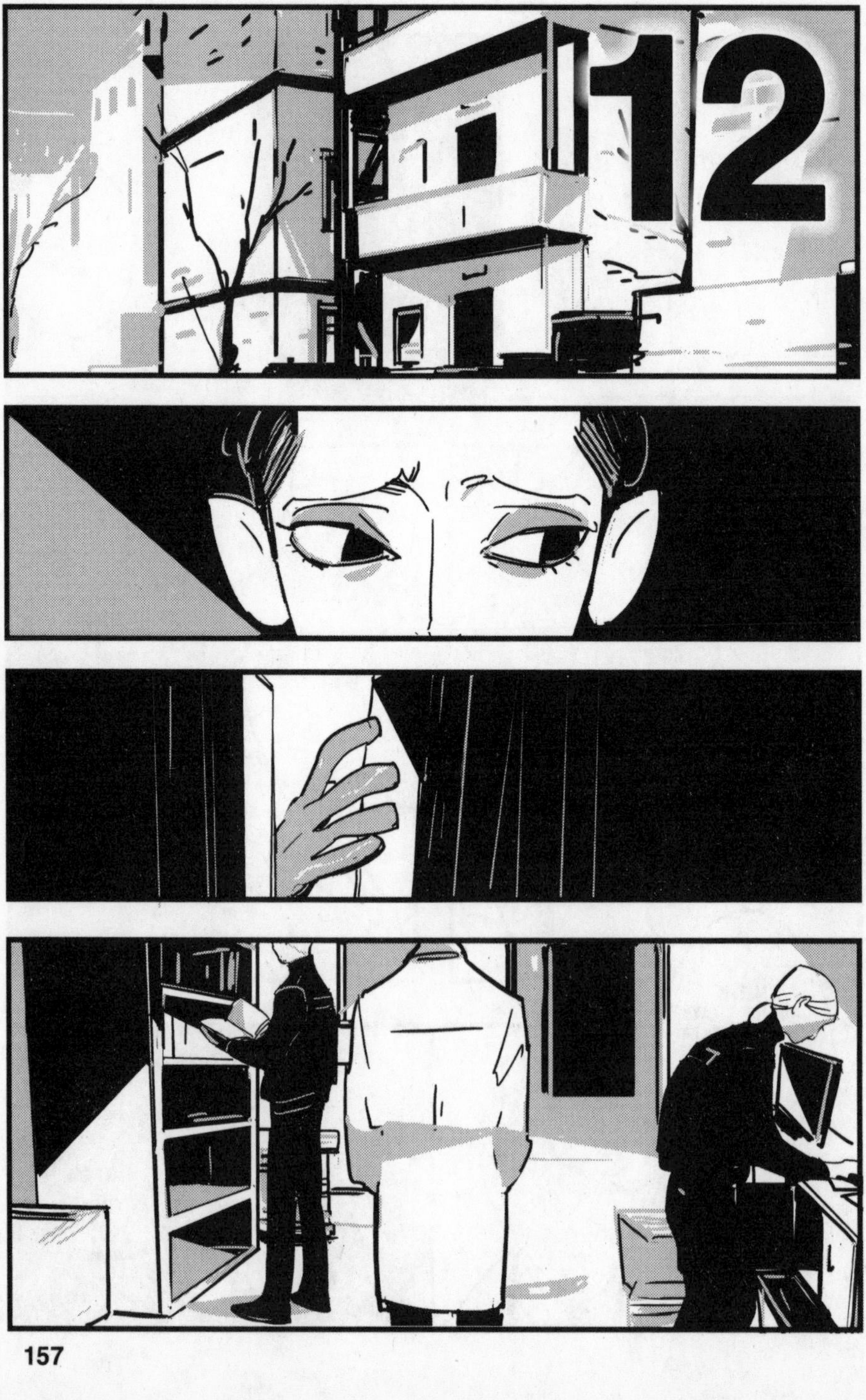
12

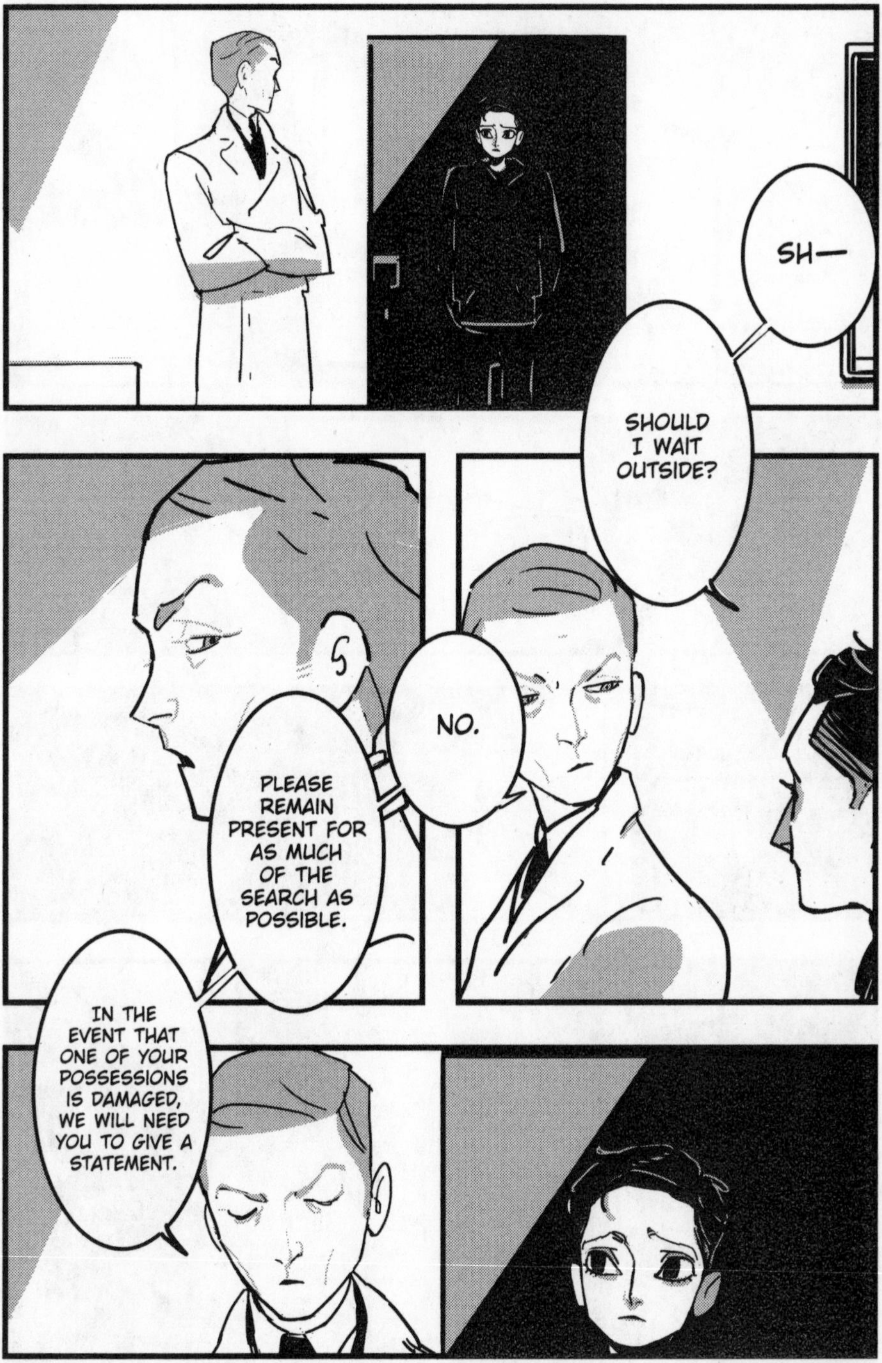
SH—
SHOULD I WAIT OUTSIDE?
NO.
PLEASE REMAIN PRESENT FOR AS MUCH OF THE SEARCH AS POSSIBLE.
IN THE EVENT THAT ONE OF YOUR POSSESSIONS IS DAMAGED, WE WILL NEED YOU TO GIVE A STATEMENT.

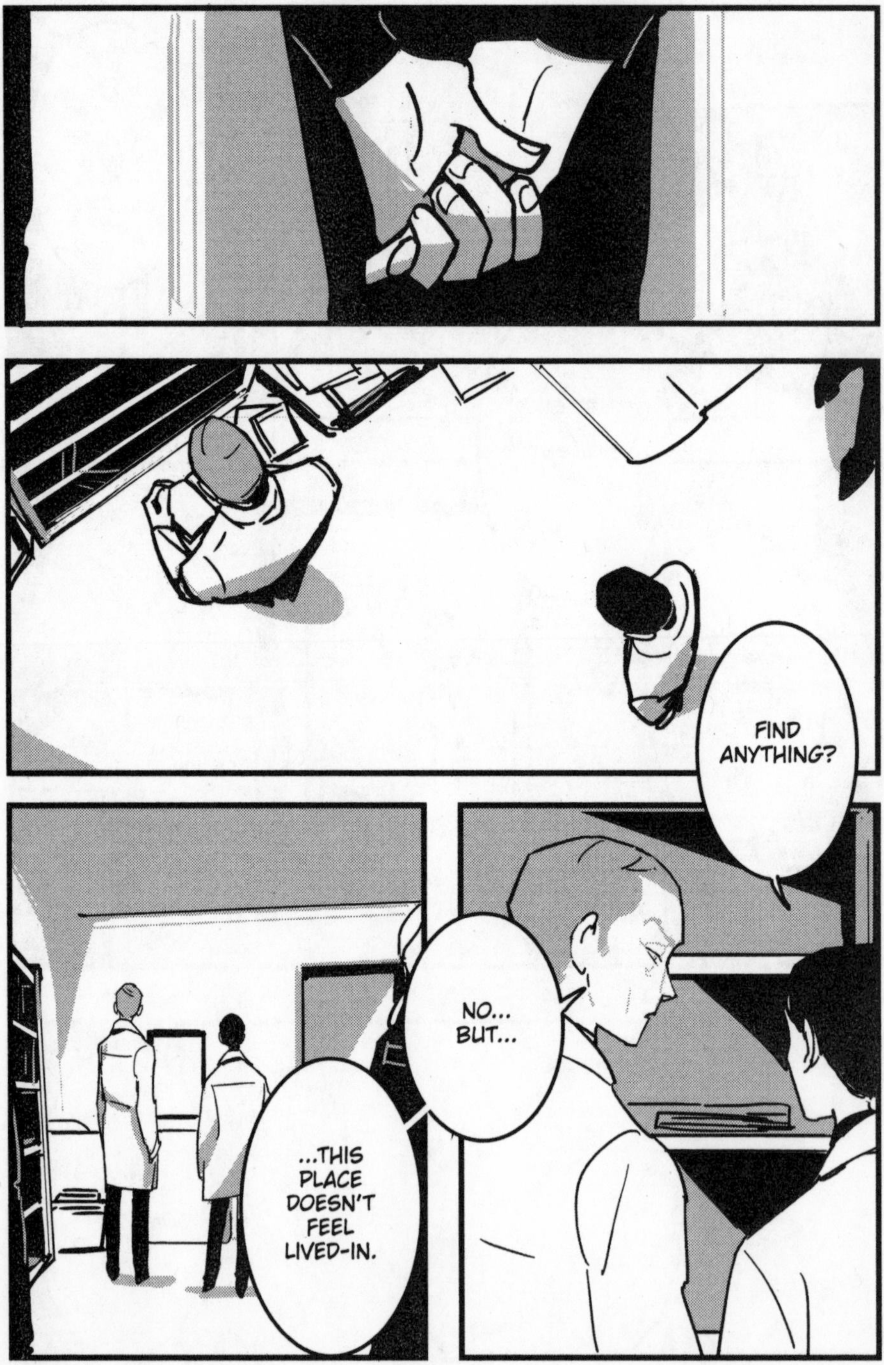
FIND ANYTHING?
NO... BUT...
...THIS PLACE DOESN'T FEEL LIVED-IN.

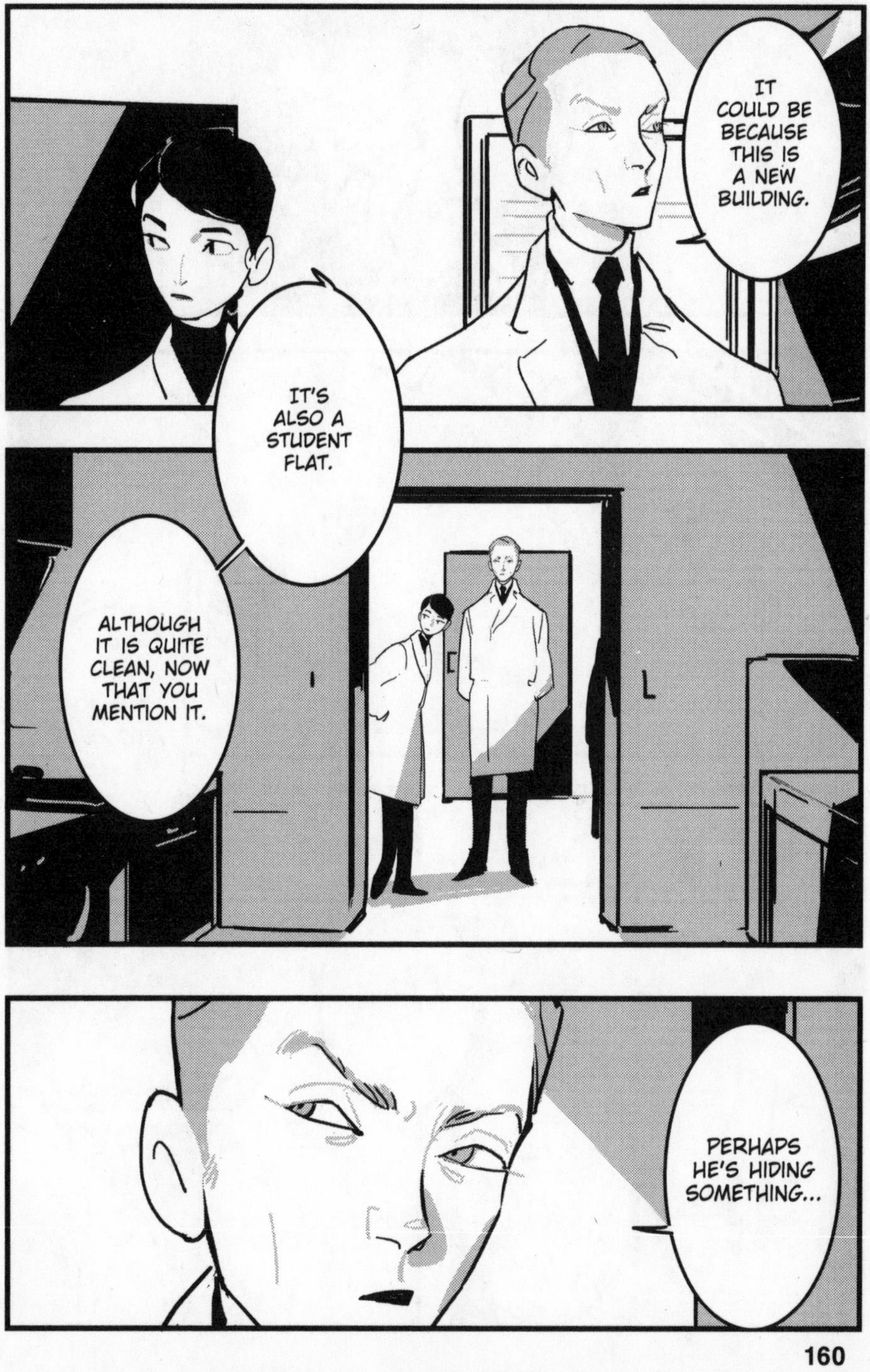
IT COULD BE BECAUSE THIS IS A NEW BUILDING.
IT'S ALSO A STUDENT FLAT.
ALTHOUGH IT IS QUITE CLEAN, NOW THAT YOU MENTION IT.
PERHAPS HE'S HIDING SOMETHING...

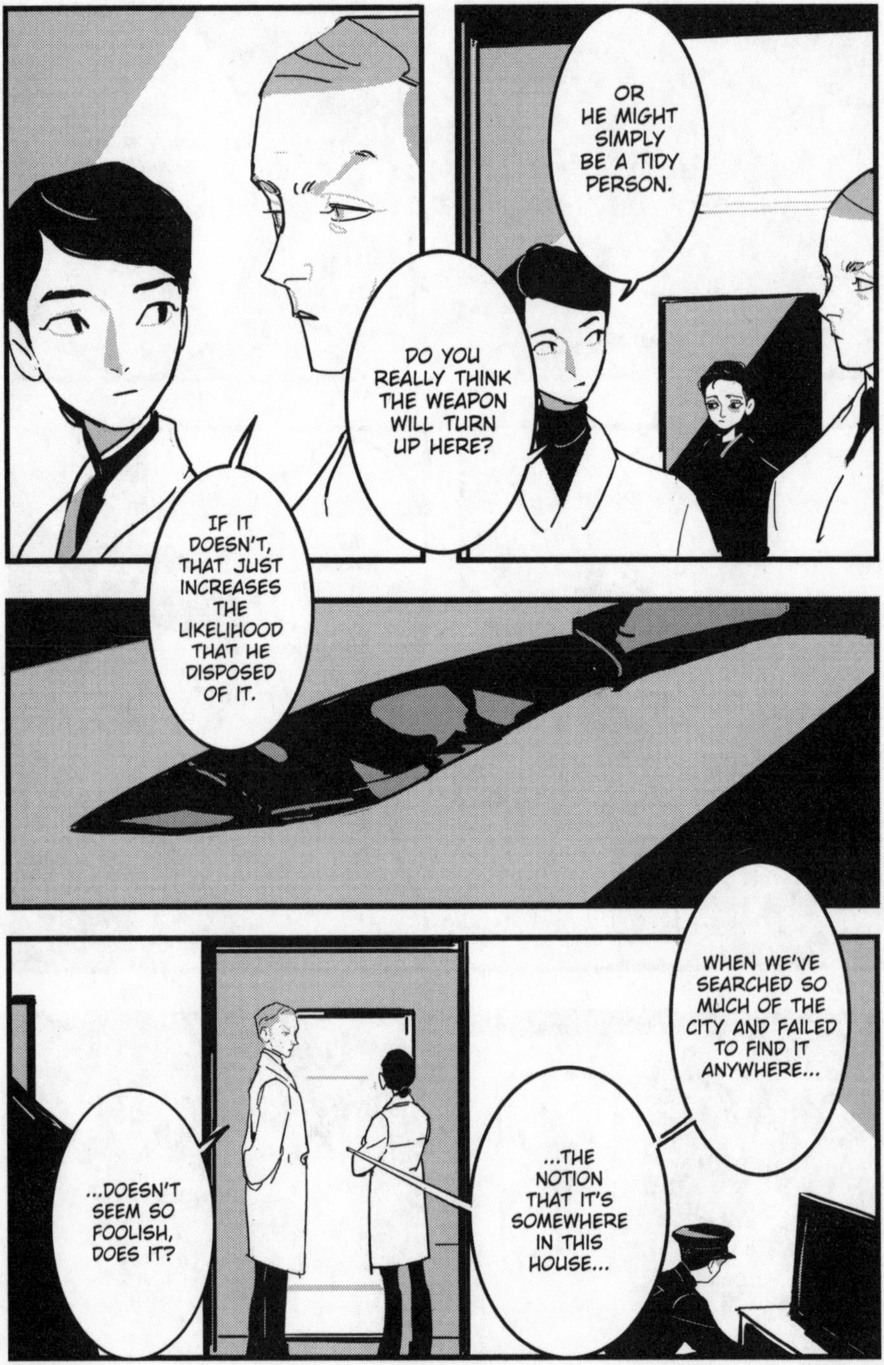

OR HE MIGHT SIMPLY BE A TIDY PERSON.
DO YOU REALLY THINK THE WEAPON WILL TURN UP HERE?
IF IT DOESN'T, THAT JUST INCREASES THE LIKELIHOOD THAT HE DISPOSED OF IT.
WHEN WE'VE SEARCHED SO MUCH OF THE CITY AND FAILED TO FIND IT ANYWHERE...
...THE NOTION THAT IT'S SOMEWHERE IN THIS HOUSE...
...DOESN'T SEEM SO FOOLISH, DOES IT?

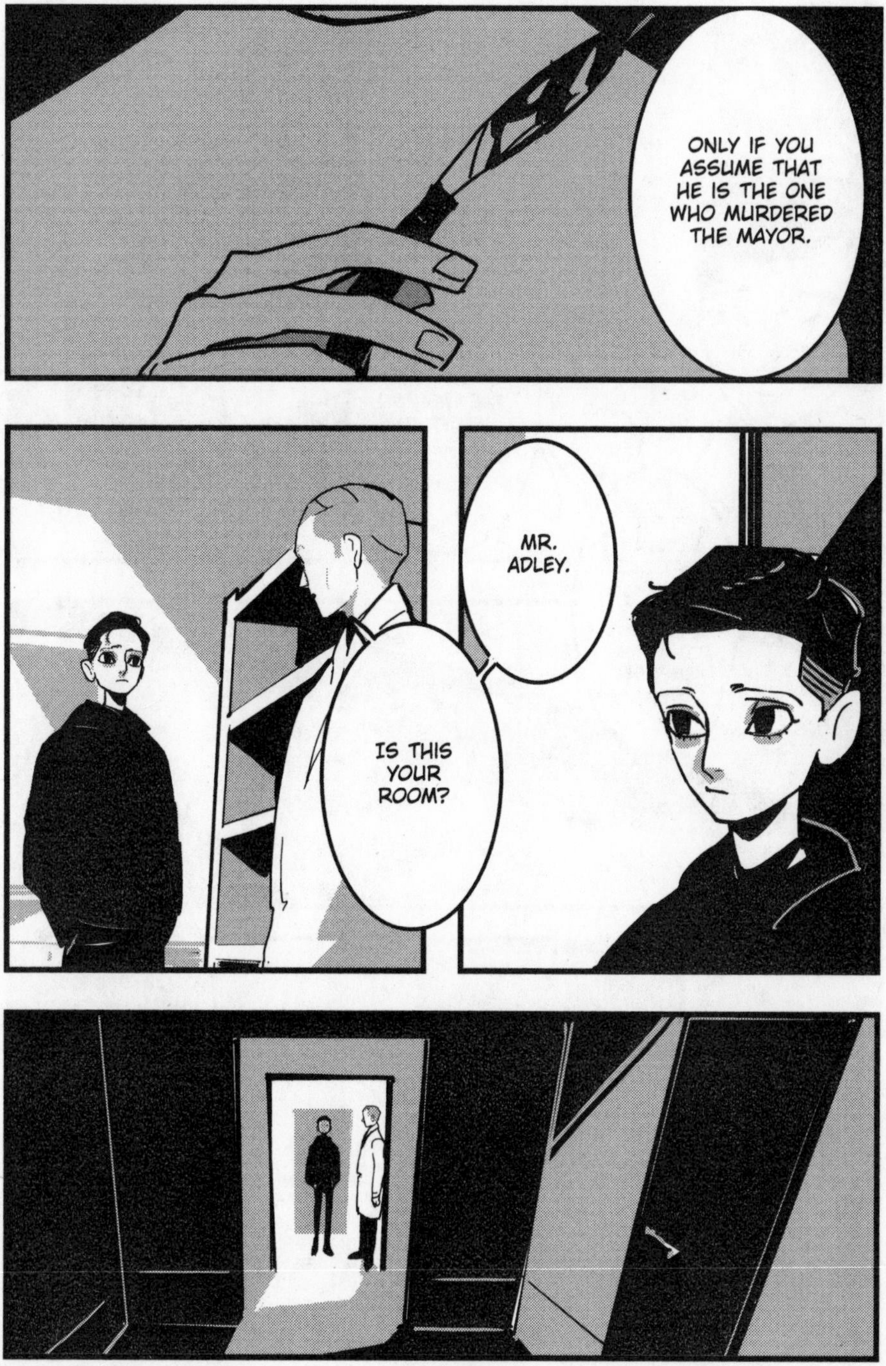
ONLY IF YOU ASSUME THAT HE IS THE ONE WHO MURDERED THE MAYOR.
MR. ADLEY.
IS THIS YOUR ROOM?

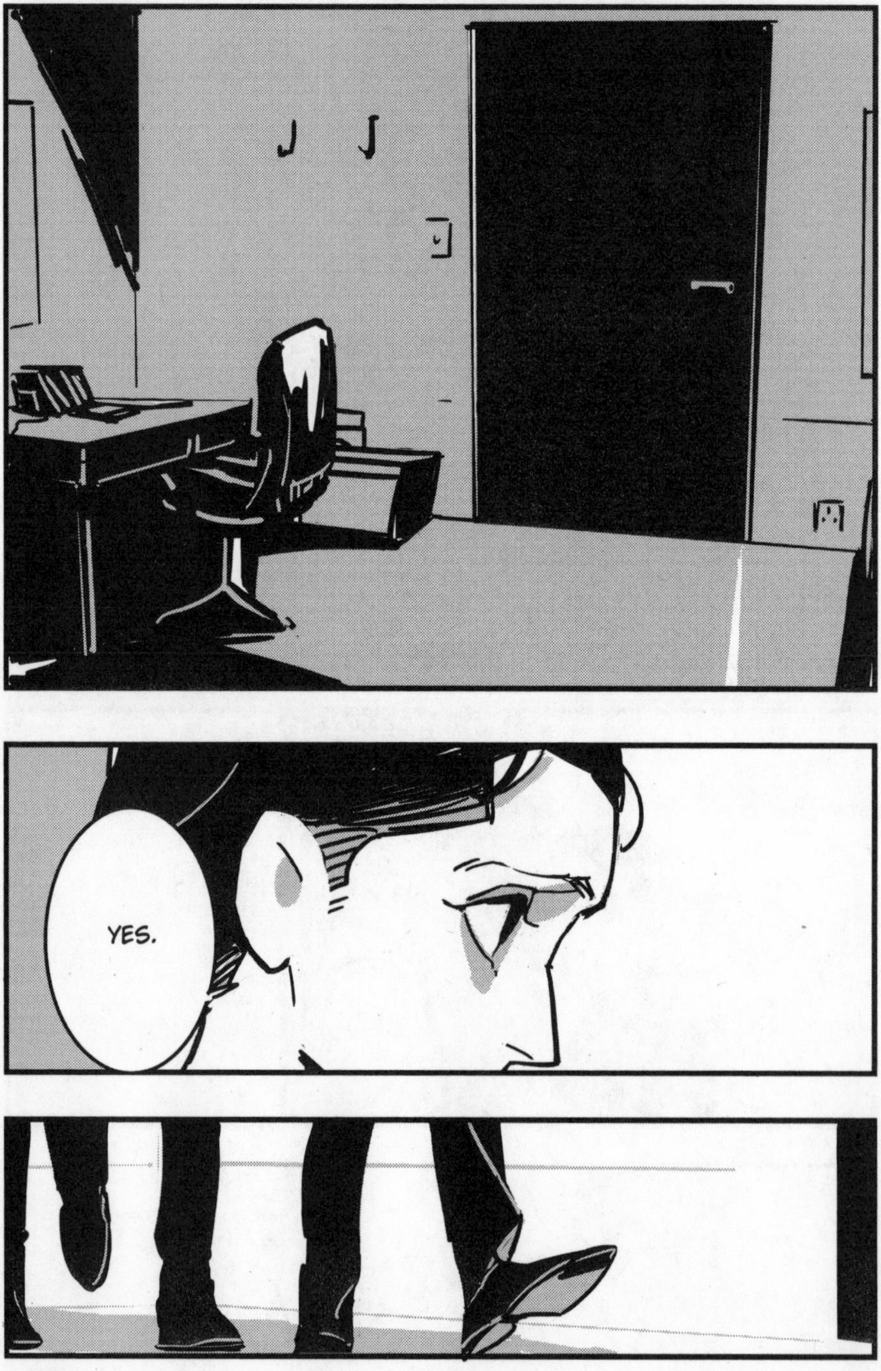
YES.

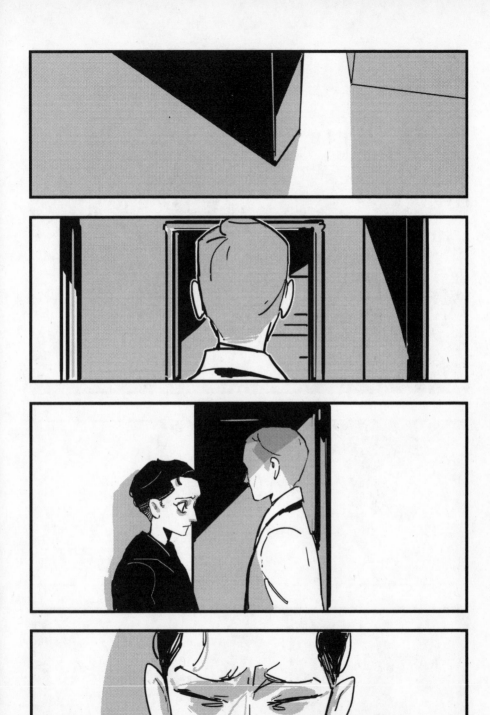

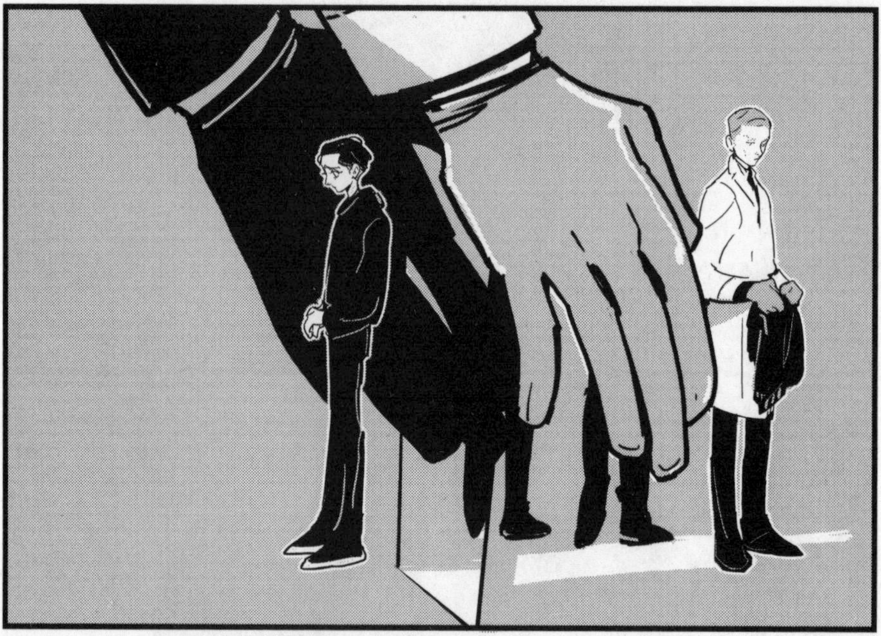
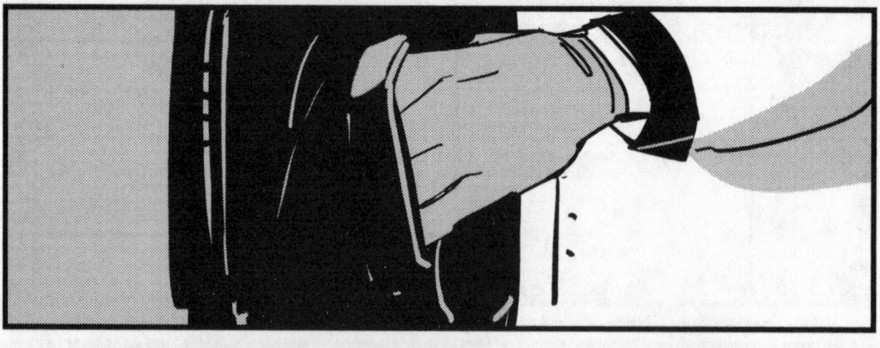
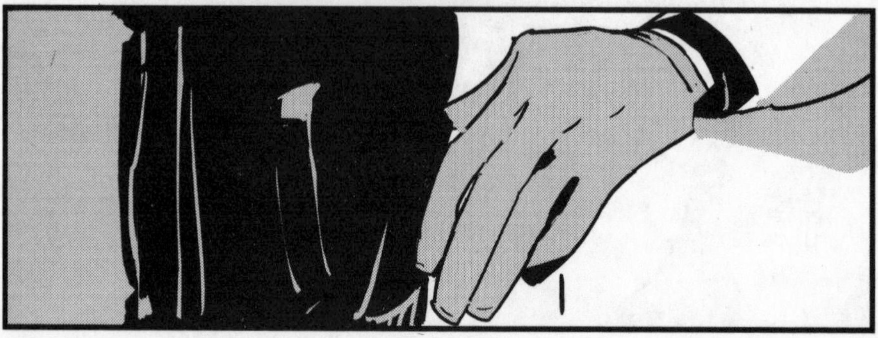

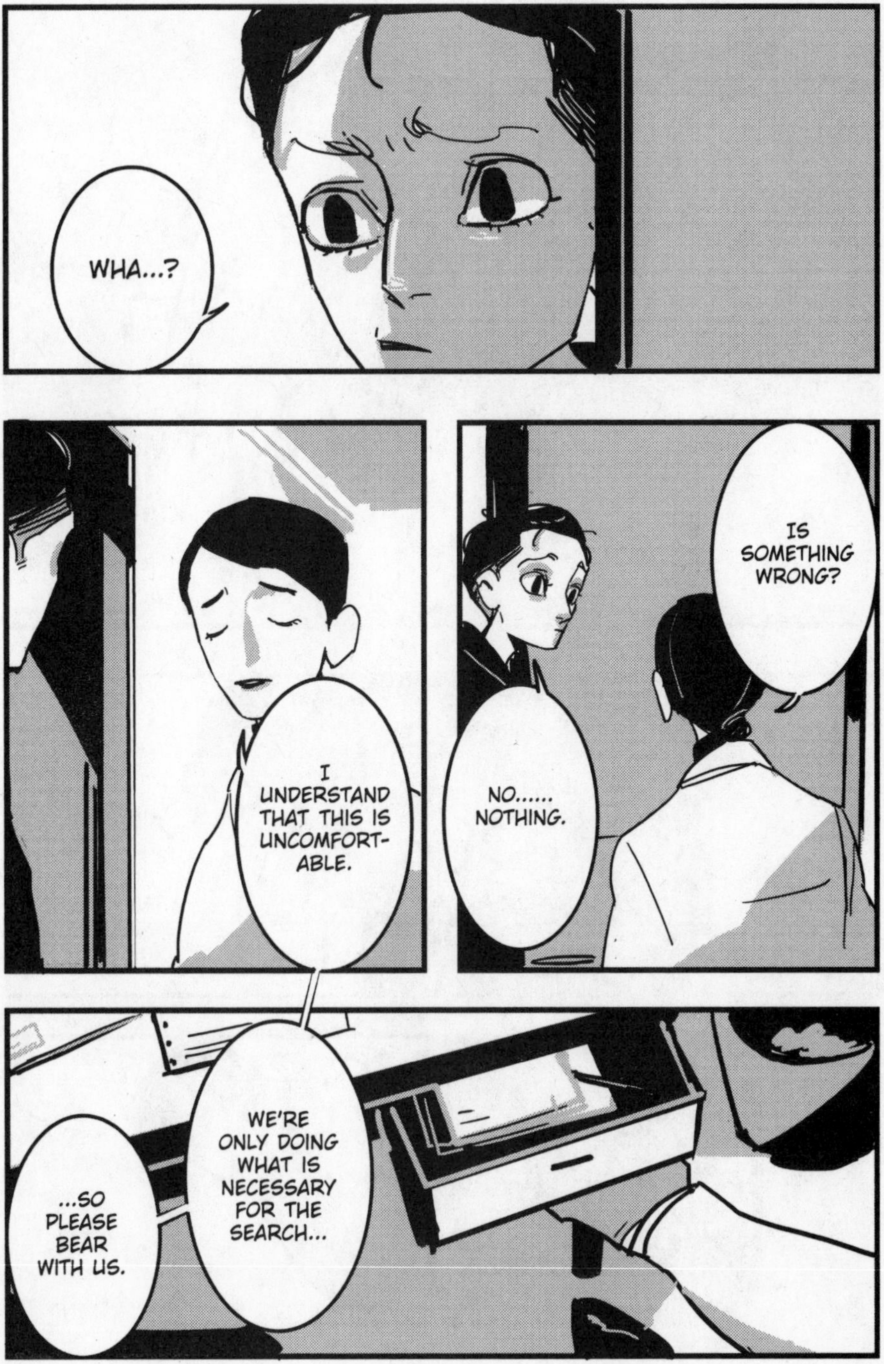
WHA...?
IS SOMETHING WRONG?
NO...... NOTHING.
I UNDERSTAND THAT THIS IS UNCOMFORT-ABLE.
WE'RE ONLY DOING WHAT IS NECESSARY FOR THE SEARCH...
...SO PLEASE BEAR WITH US.

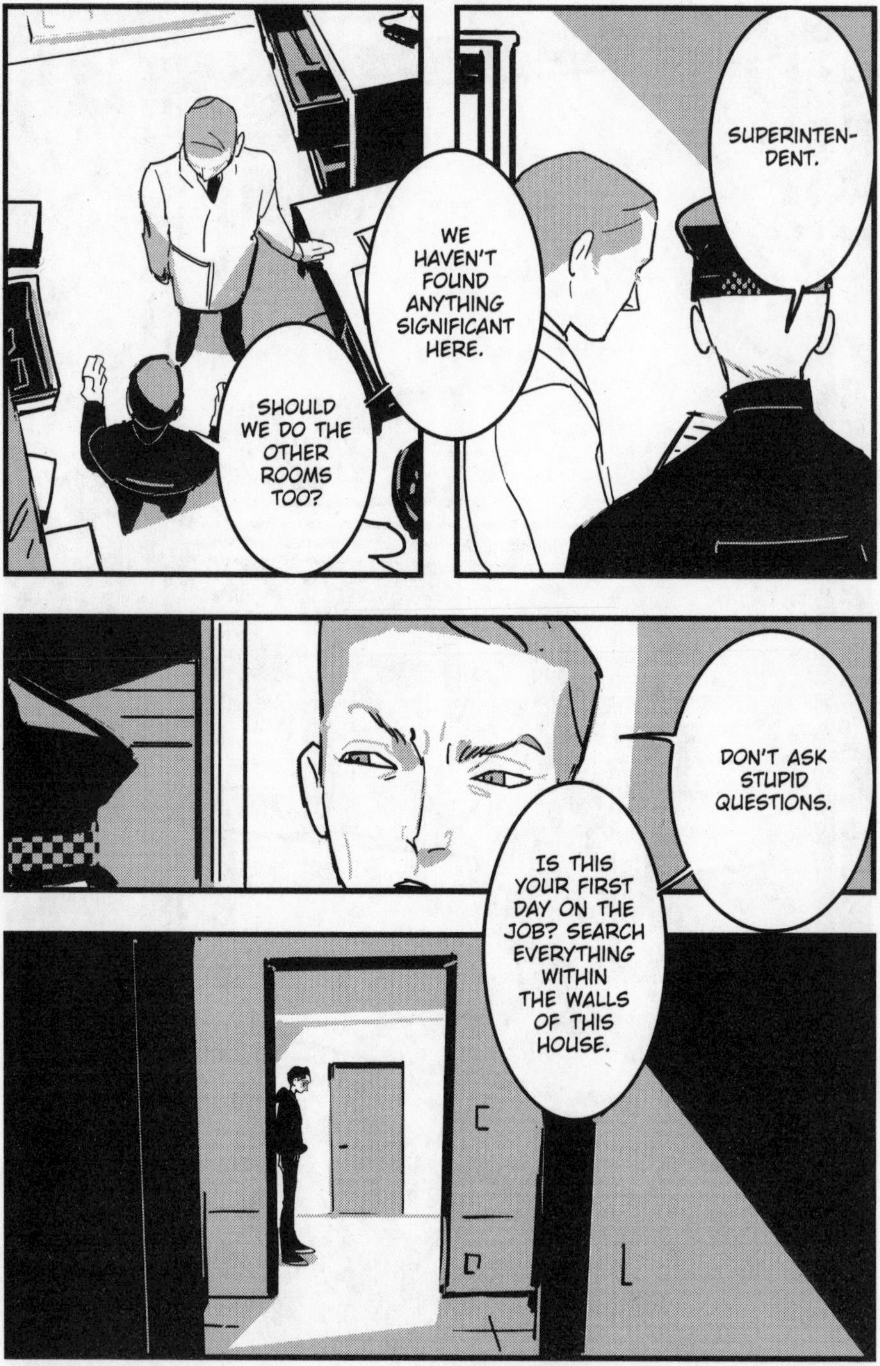
SUPERINTEN-DENT.
WE HAVEN'T FOUND ANYTHING SIGNIFICANT HERE.
SHOULD WE DO THE OTHER ROOMS TOO?
DON'T ASK STUPID QUESTIONS.
IS THIS YOUR FIRST DAY ON THE JOB? SEARCH EVERYTHING WITHIN THE WALLS OF THIS HOUSE.

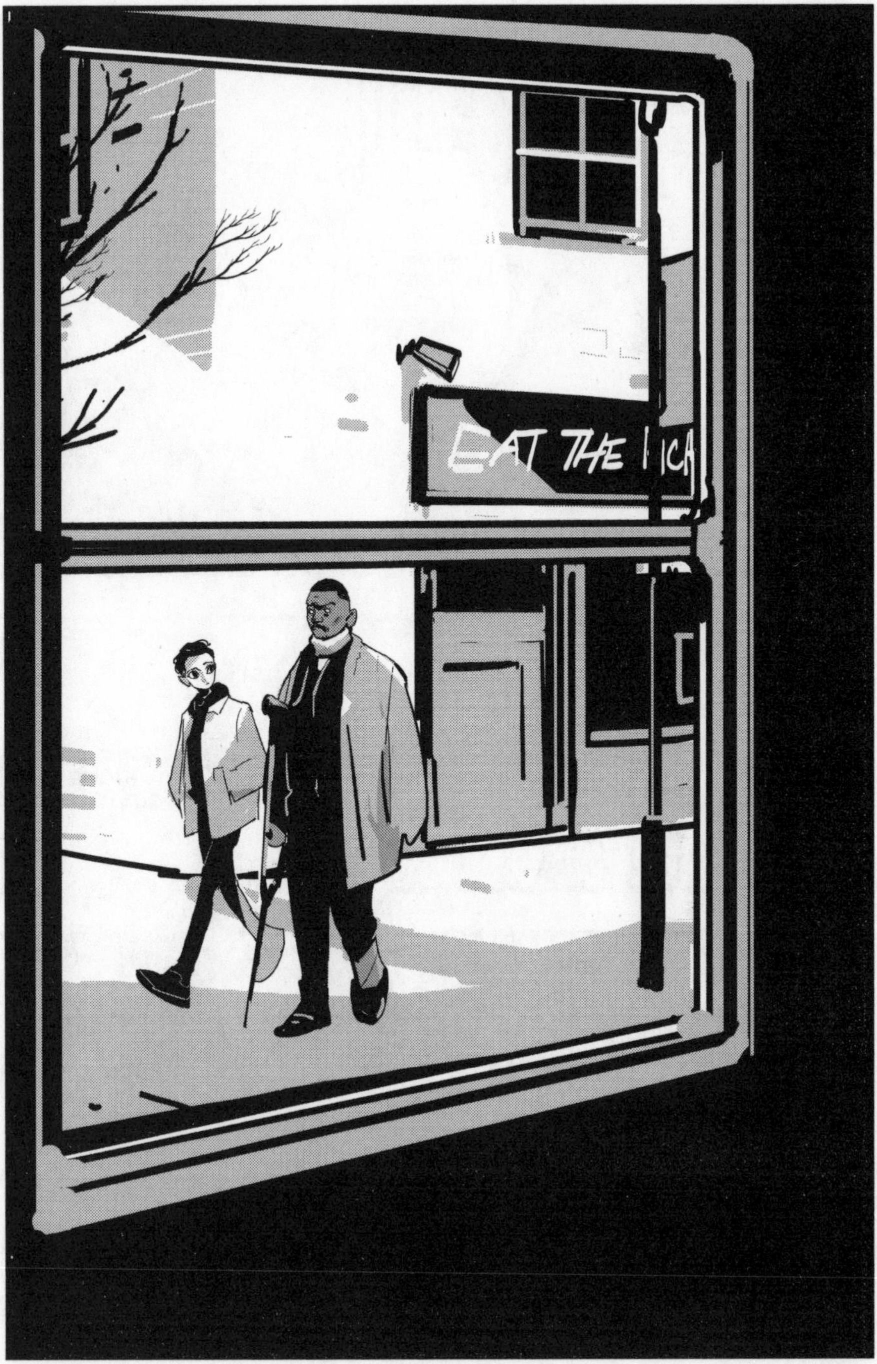
EAT THE

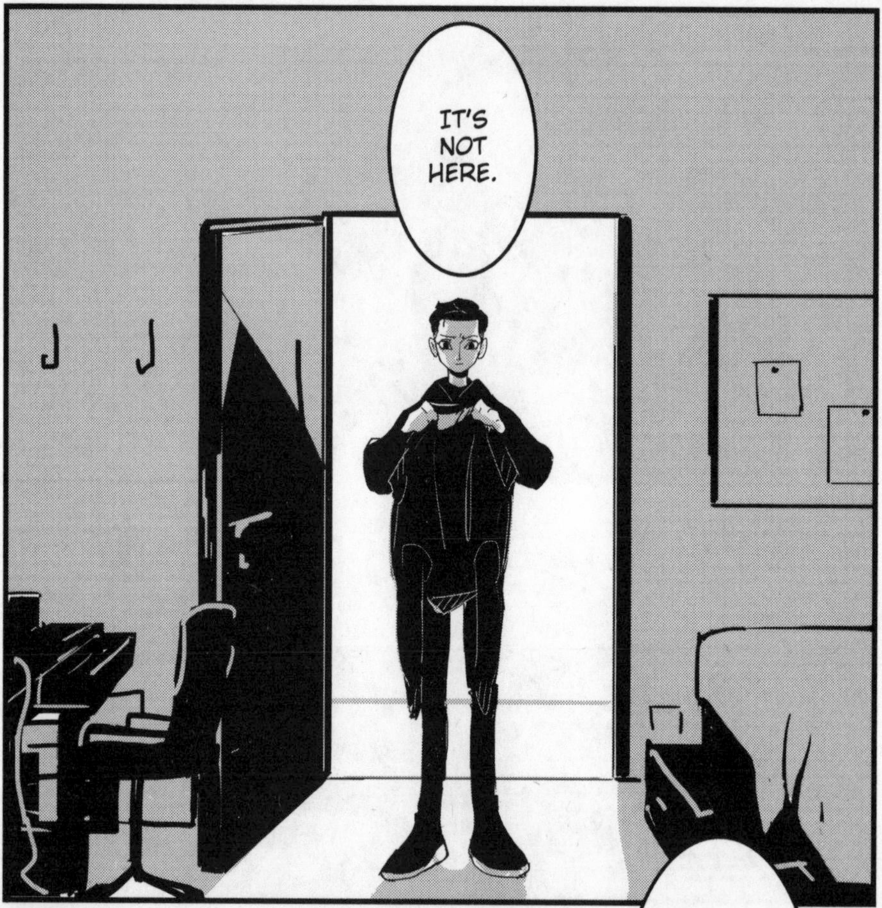
IT'S NOT HERE.

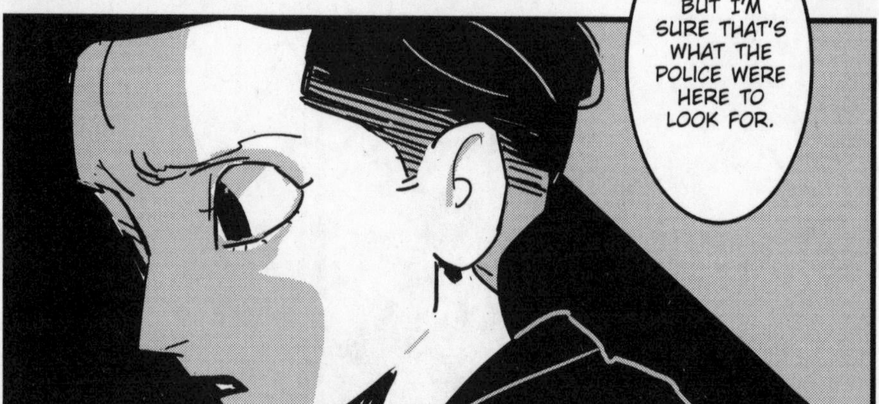
BUT I'M SURE THAT'S WHAT THE POLICE WERE HERE TO LOOK FOR.

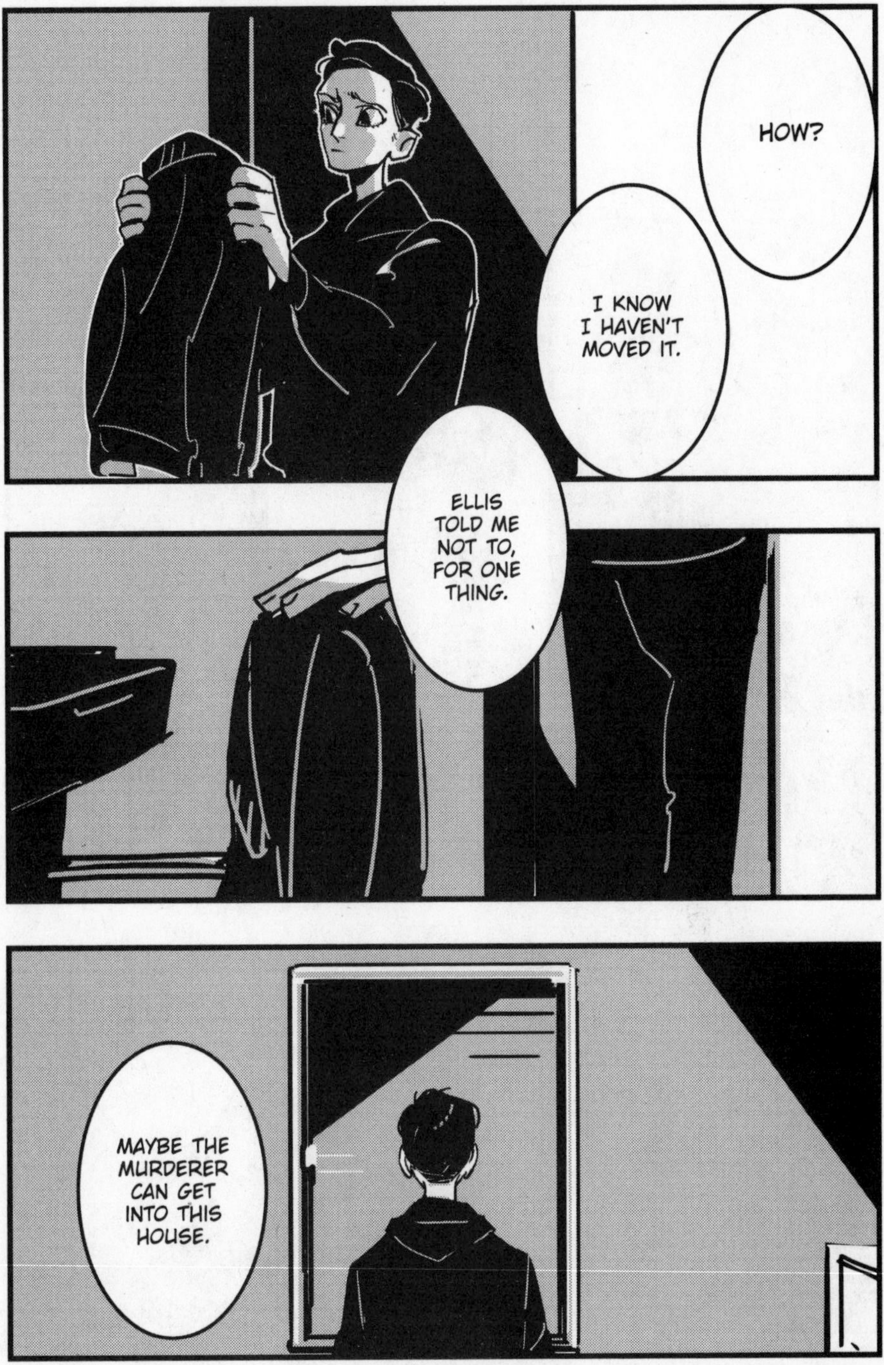
HOW?
I KNOW I HAVEN'T MOVED IT.
ELLIS TOLD ME NOT TO, FOR ONE THING.
MAYBE THE MURDERER CAN GET INTO THIS HOUSE.

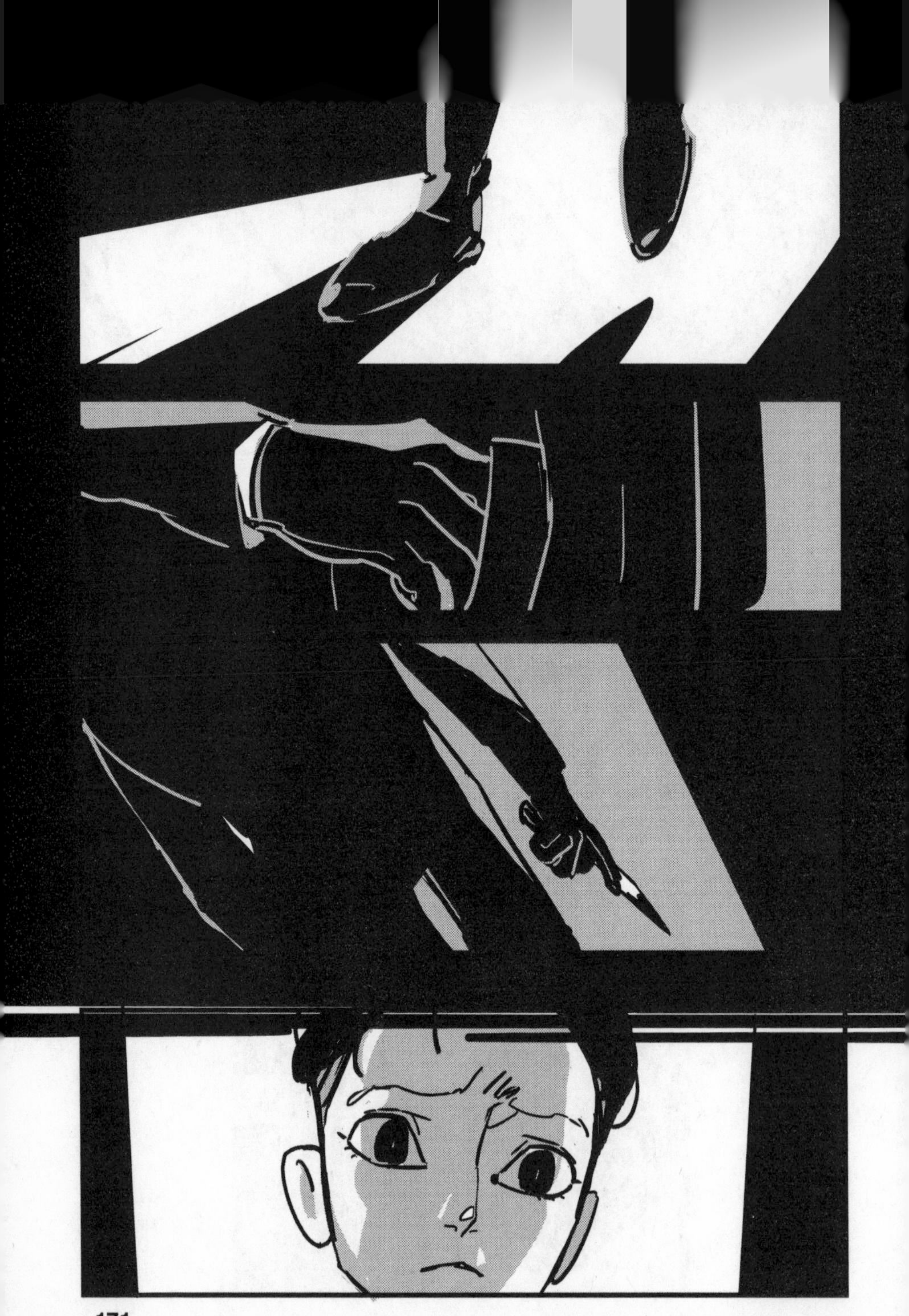

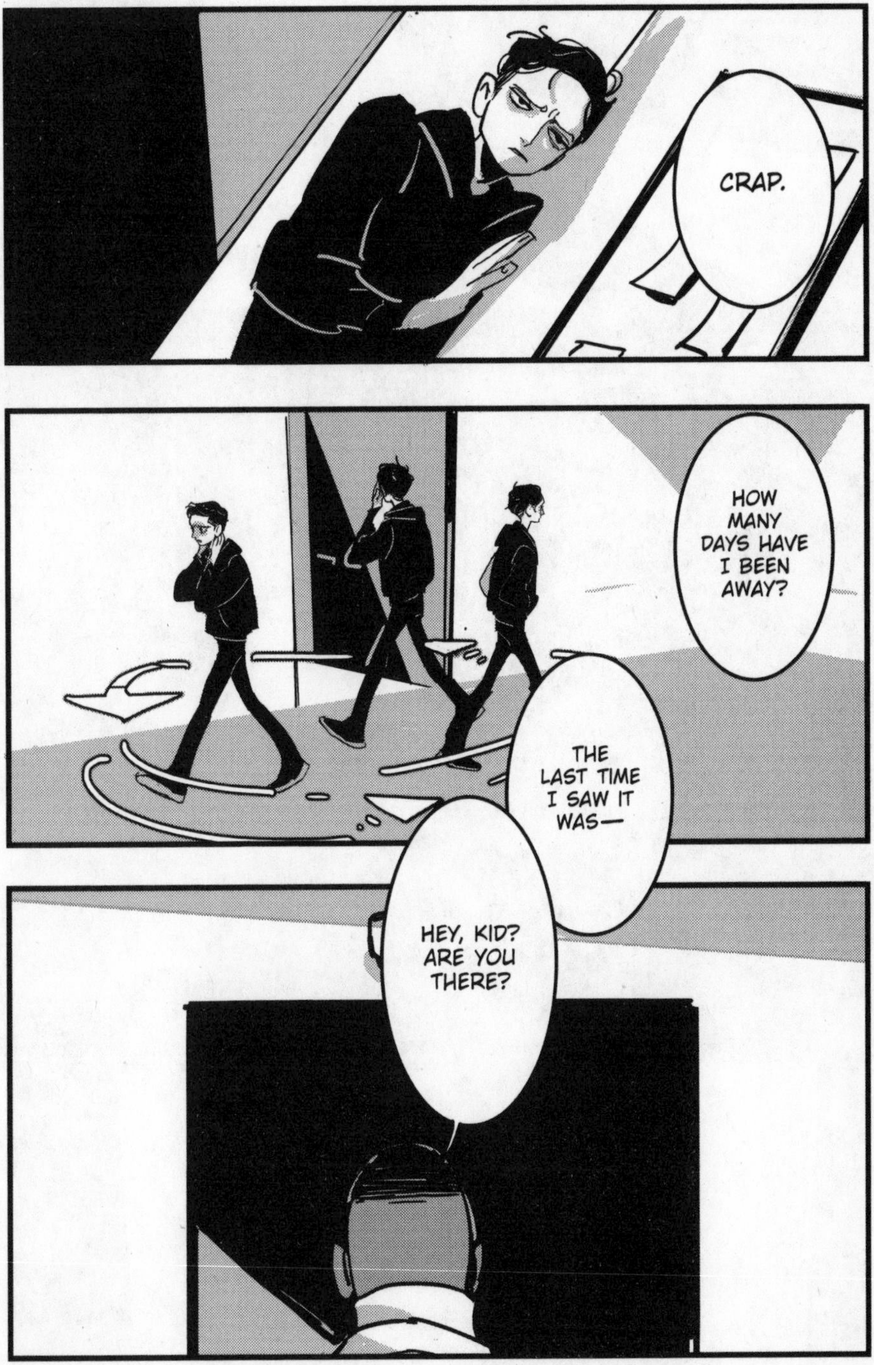
CRAP.
HOW MANY DAYS HAVE I BEEN AWAY?
THE LAST TIME I SAW IT WAS—
HEY, KID? ARE YOU THERE?

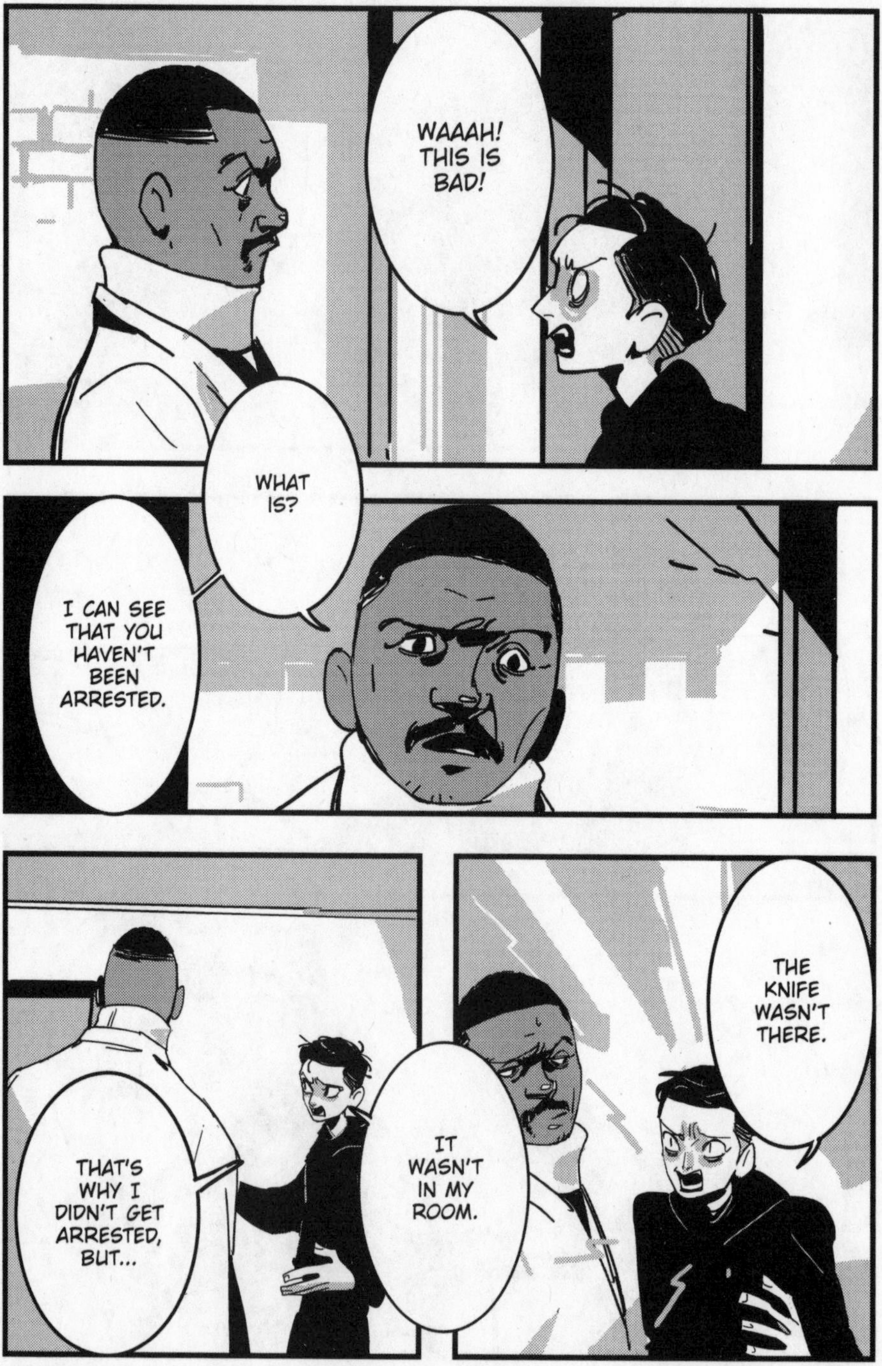
WAAAH! THIS IS BAD!
WHAT IS?
I CAN SEE THAT YOU HAVEN'T BEEN ARRESTED.
THE KNIFE WASN'T THERE.
IT WASN'T IN MY ROOM.
THAT'S WHY I DIDN'T GET ARRESTED, BUT...

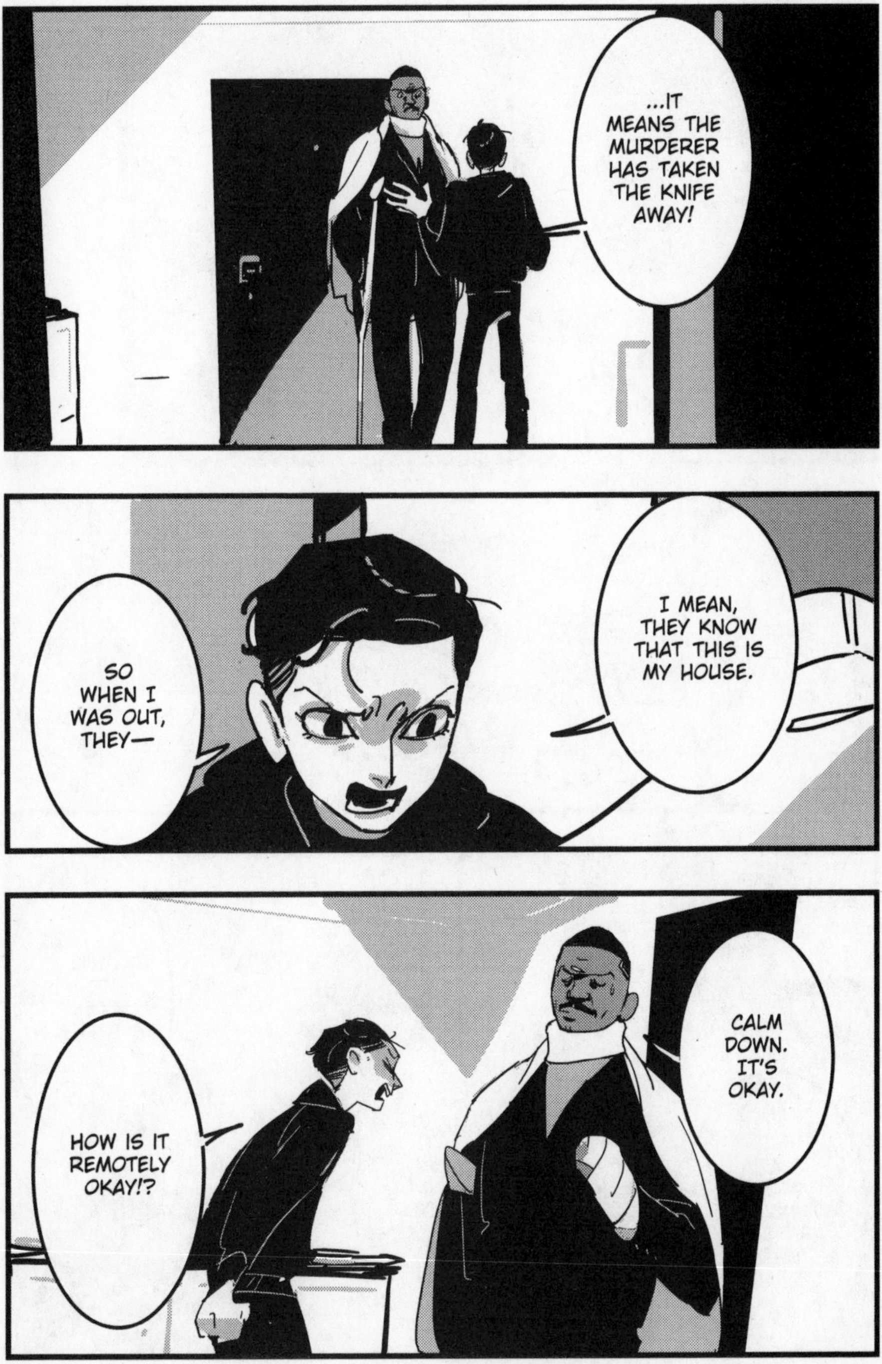
...IT MEANS THE MURDERER HAS TAKEN THE KNIFE AWAY!
I MEAN, THEY KNOW THAT THIS IS MY HOUSE.
SO WHEN I WAS OUT, THEY—
CALM DOWN. IT'S OKAY.
HOW IS IT REMOTELY OKAY!?

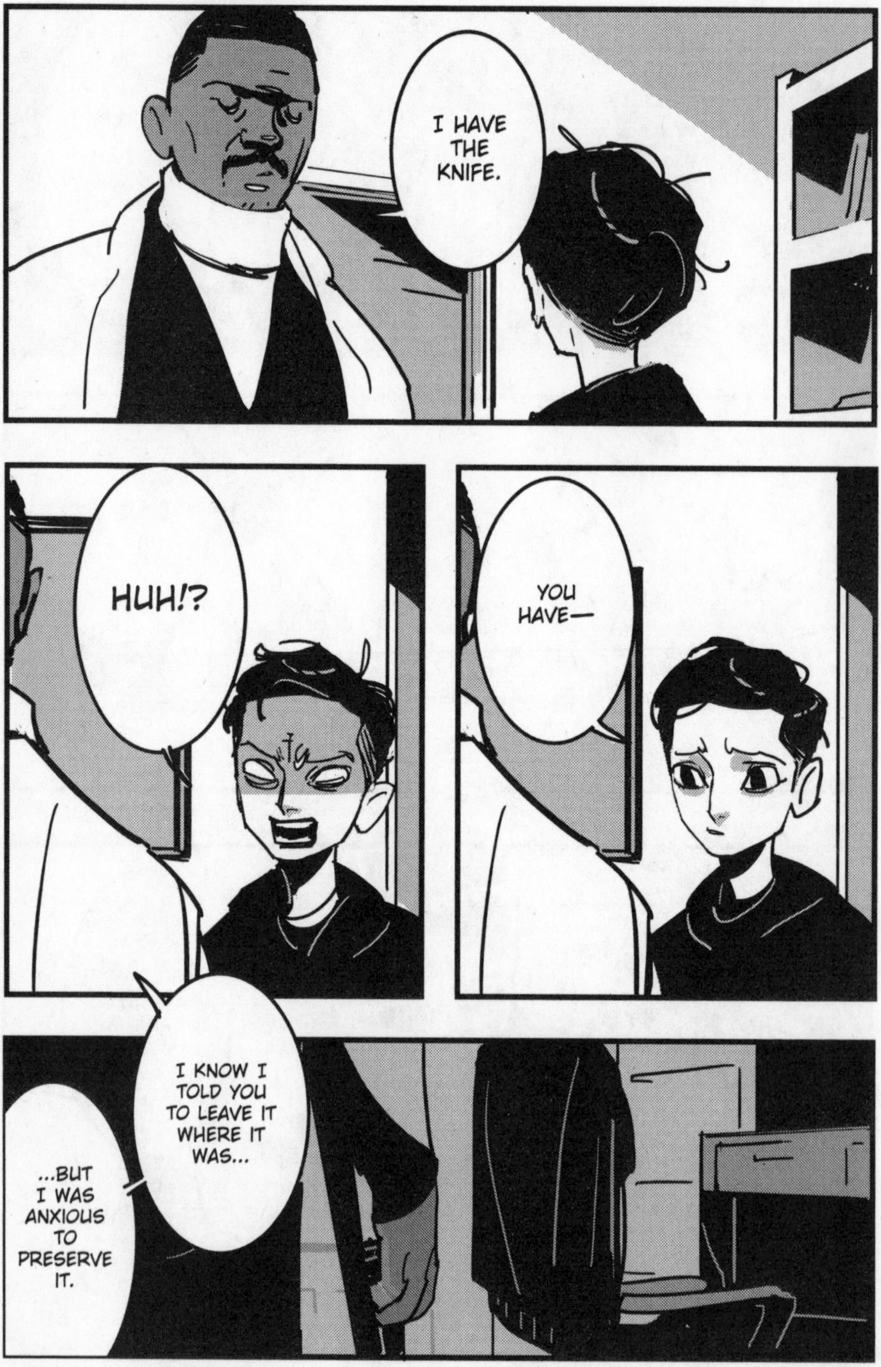
I HAVE THE KNIFE.
YOU HAVE—
HUH!?
I KNOW I TOLD YOU TO LEAVE IT WHERE IT WAS...
...BUT I WAS ANXIOUS TO PRESERVE IT.

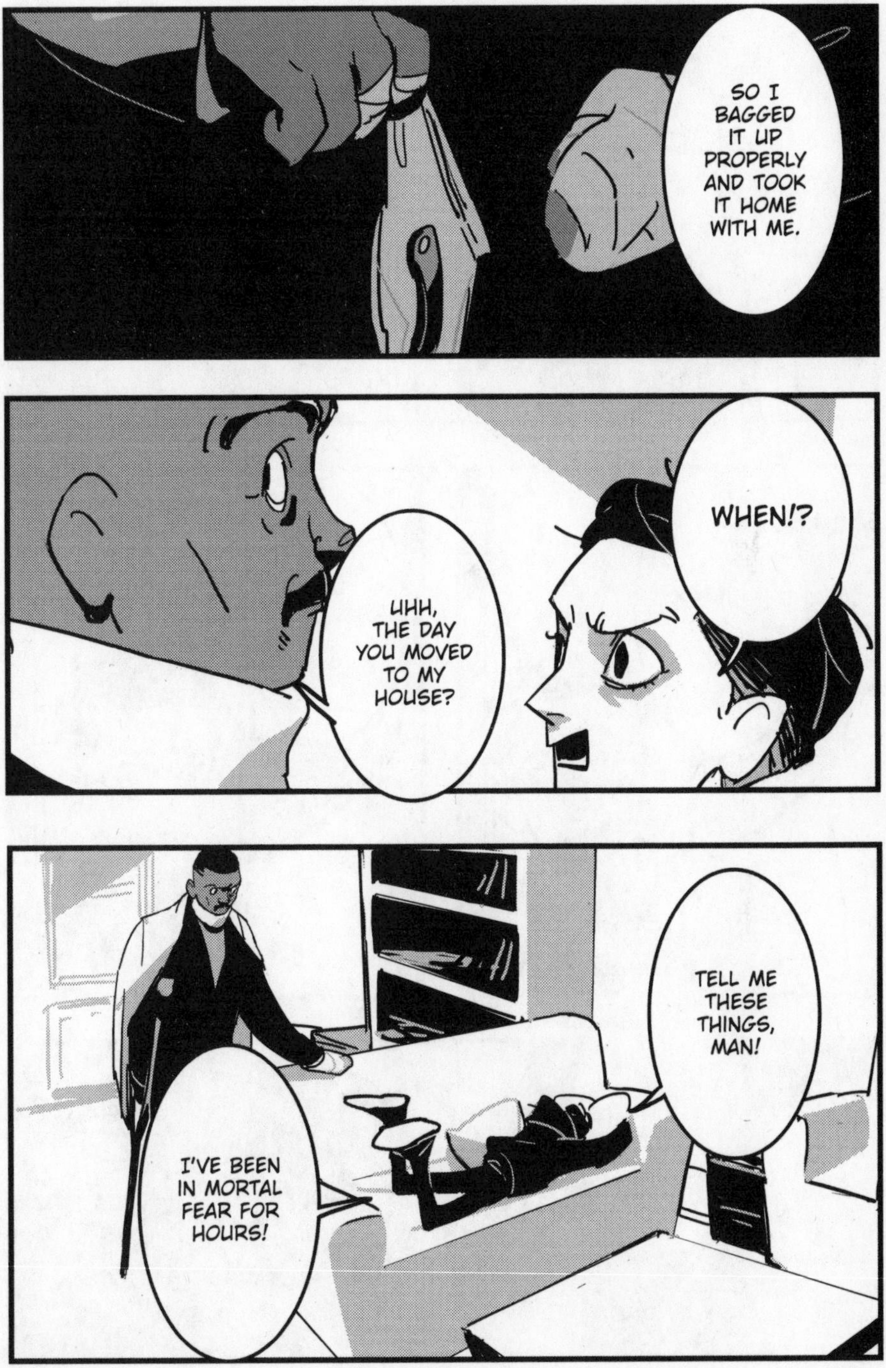
SO I BAGGED IT UP PROPERLY AND TOOK IT HOME WITH ME.
WHEN!?
UHH, THE DAY YOU MOVED TO MY HOUSE?
TELL ME THESE THINGS, MAN!
I'VE BEEN IN MORTAL FEAR FOR HOURS!

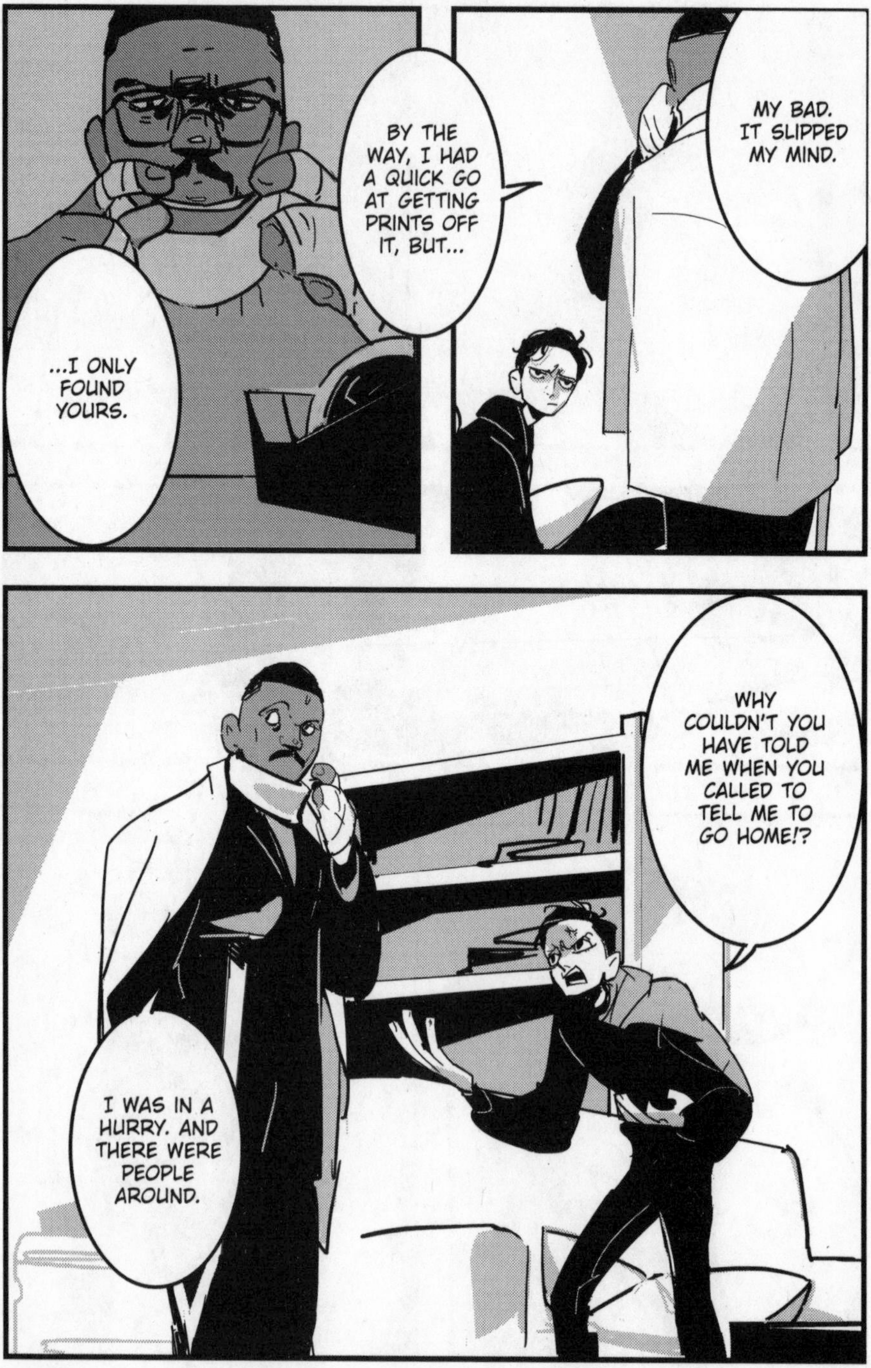
BY THE WAY, I HAD A QUICK GO AT GETTING PRINTS OFF IT, BUT...
...I ONLY FOUND YOURS.
MY BAD. IT SLIPPED MY MIND.
WHY COULDN'T YOU HAVE TOLD ME WHEN YOU CALLED TO TELL ME TO GO HOME!?
I WAS IN A HURRY. AND THERE WERE PEOPLE AROUND.

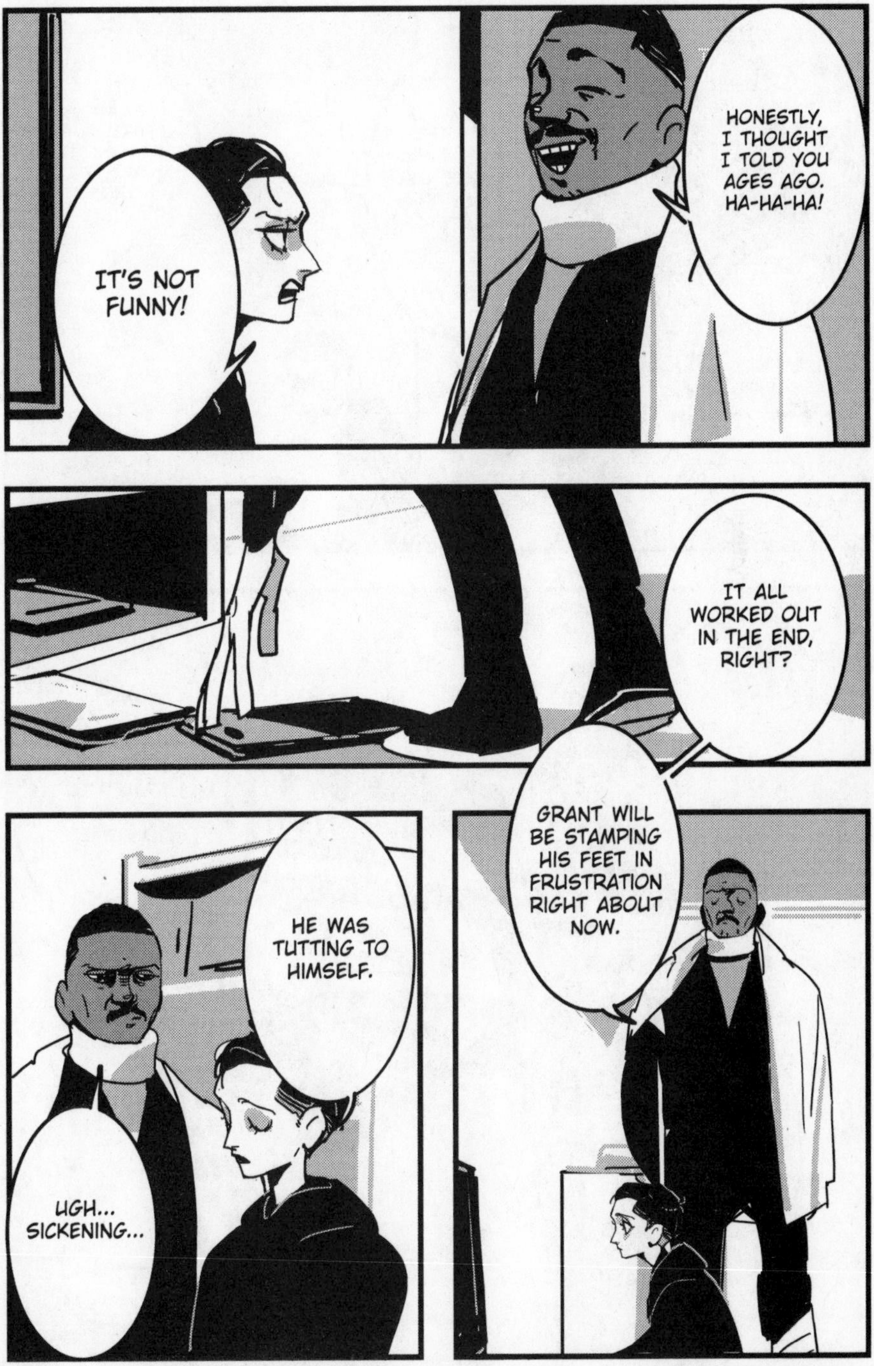
HONESTLY, I THOUGHT I TOLD YOU AGES AGO. HA-HA-HA!
IT'S NOT FUNNY!
IT ALL WORKED OUT IN THE END, RIGHT?
GRANT WILL BE STAMPING HIS FEET IN FRUSTRATION RIGHT ABOUT NOW.
HE WAS TUTTING TO HIMSELF.
UGH... SICKENING...

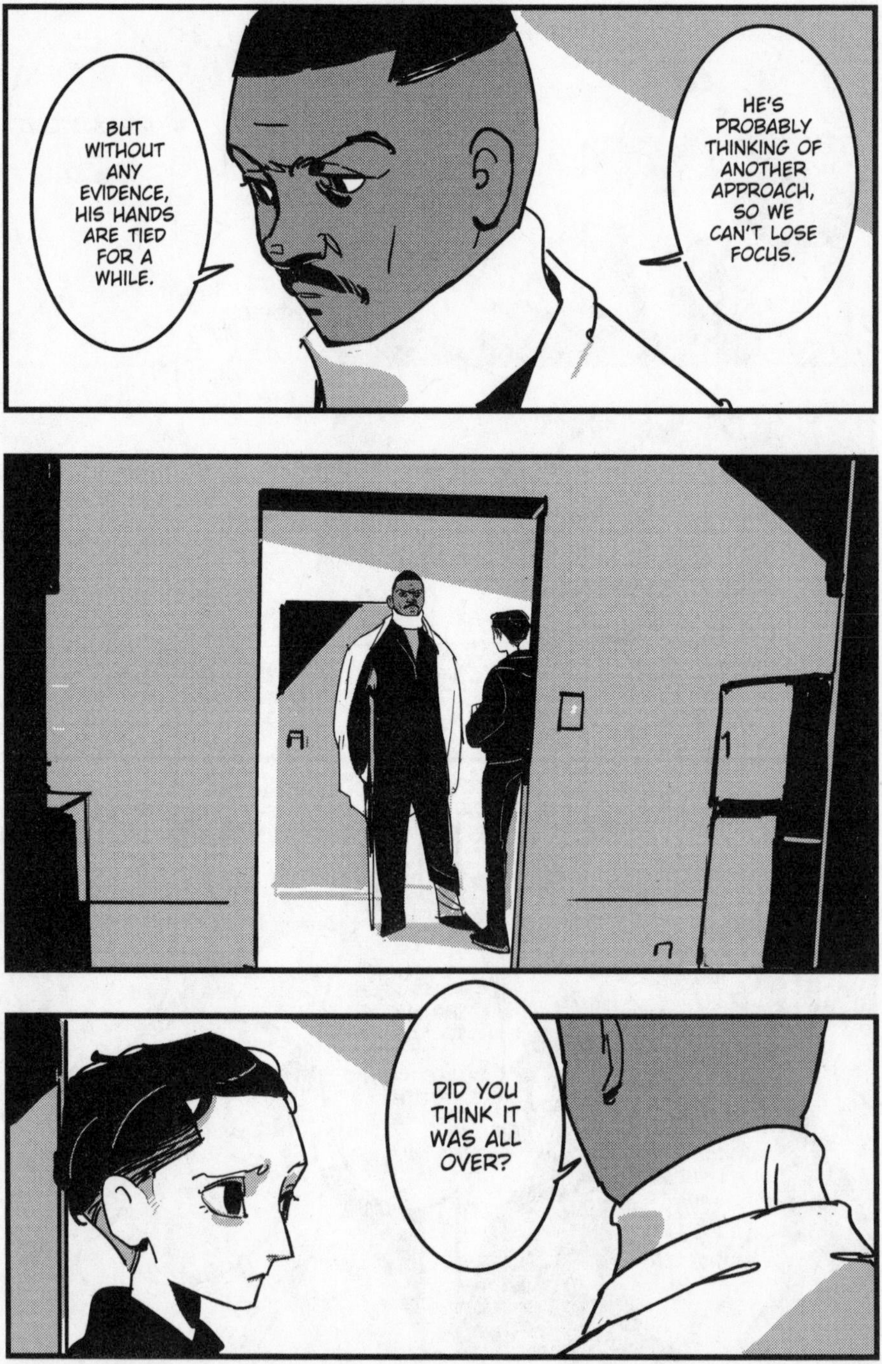
HE'S PROBABLY THINKING OF ANOTHER APPROACH, SO WE CAN'T LOSE FOCUS.
BUT WITHOUT ANY EVIDENCE, HIS HANDS ARE TIED FOR A WHILE.
DID YOU THINK IT WAS ALL OVER?

ABSOLUTELY! 200 PERCENT!
I FEEL SO GUILTY ABOUT SOMETHING I DIDN'T EVEN DO.
AND IT'S NO WALK IN THE PARK TO BE MADE TO FEEL LIKE I'VE BEEN CORNERED.
SO IF YOU...
...HAD BEEN KIND ENOUGH TO TELL ME THAT THE KNIFE WASN'T IN THE HOUSE...
IF YOU'RE GONNA HAVE A GRUDGE AGAINST ANYONE, IT SHOULD BE THE MURDERER, NOT ME.

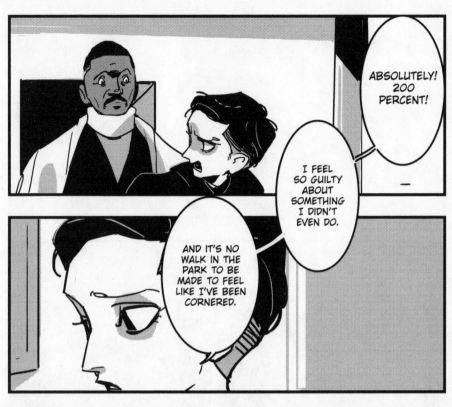

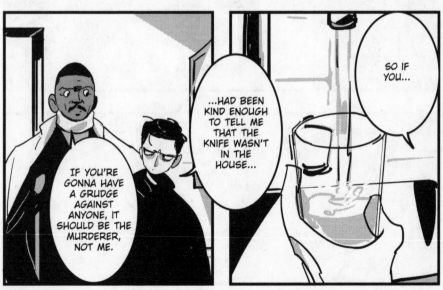

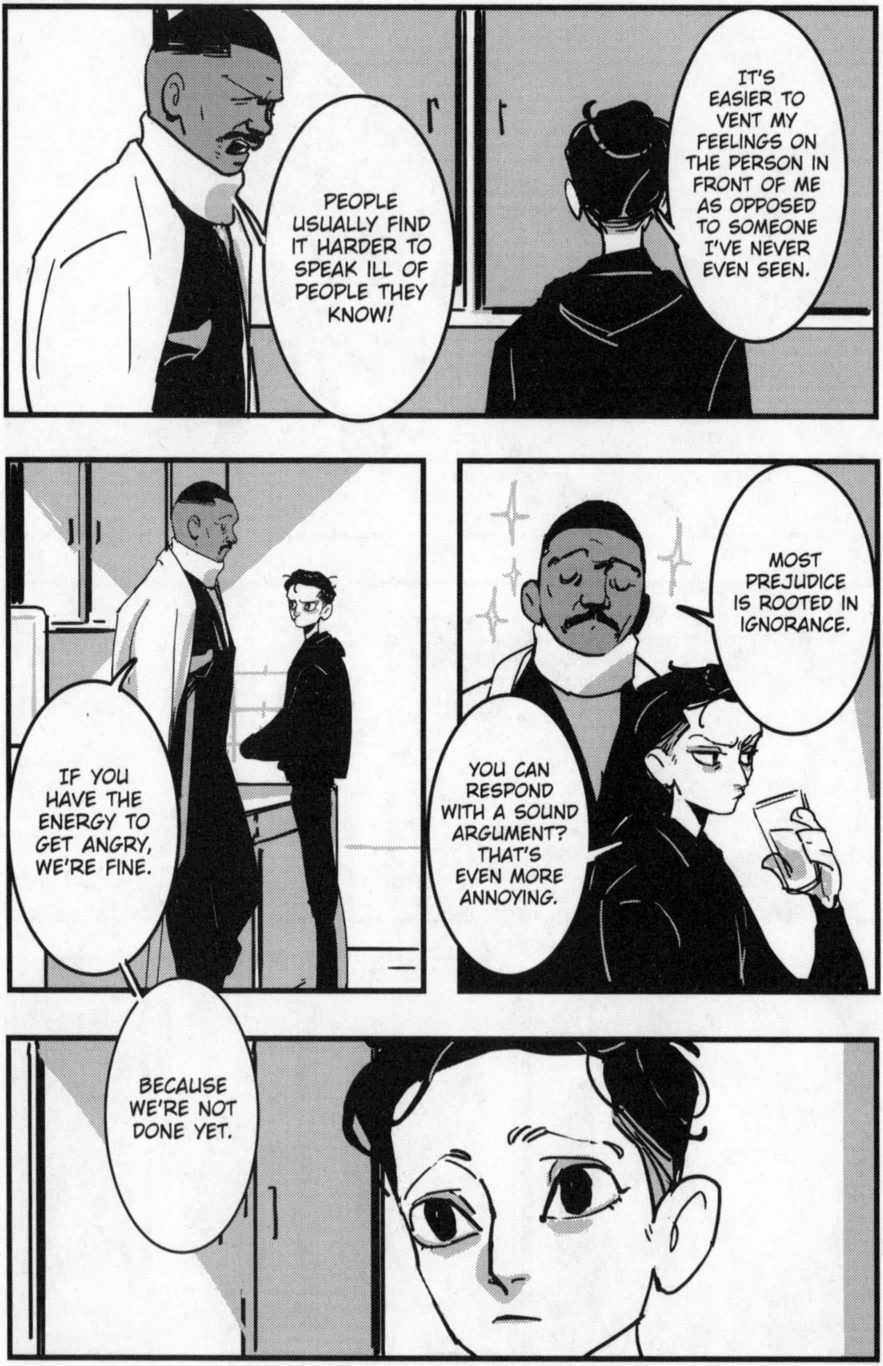
IT'S EASIER TO VENT MY FEELINGS ON THE PERSON IN FRONT OF ME AS OPPOSED TO SOMEONE I'VE NEVER EVEN SEEN.
PEOPLE USUALLY FIND IT HARDER TO SPEAK ILL OF PEOPLE THEY KNOW!
MOST PREJUDICE IS ROOTED IN IGNORANCE.
YOU CAN RESPOND WITH A SOUND ARGUMENT? THAT'S EVEN MORE ANNOYING.
IF YOU HAVE THE ENERGY TO GET ANGRY, WE'RE FINE.
BECAUSE WE'RE NOT DONE YET.

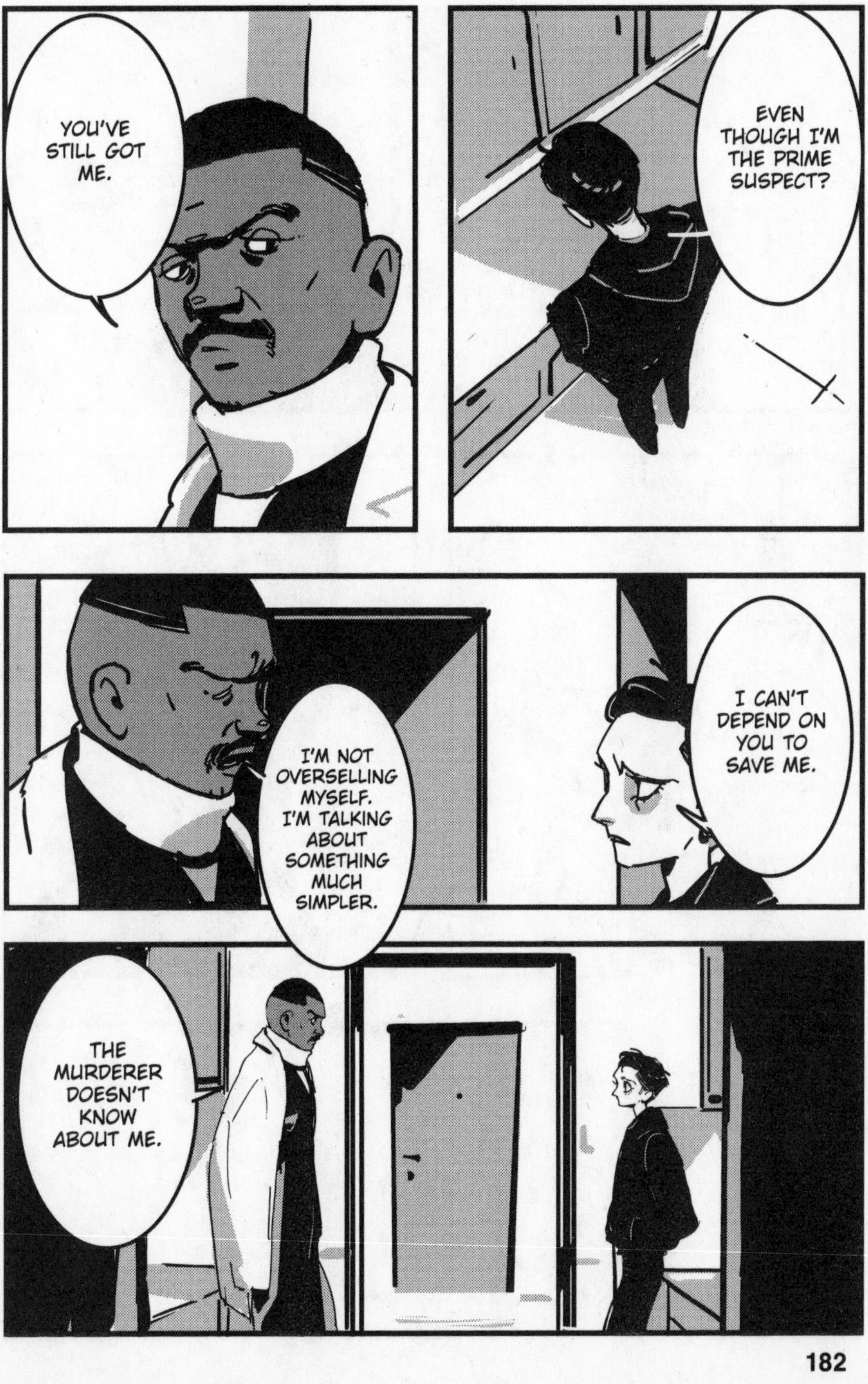
EVEN THOUGH I'M THE PRIME SUSPECT?
YOU'VE STILL GOT ME.
I CAN'T DEPEND ON YOU TO SAVE ME.
I'M NOT OVERSELLING MYSELF. I'M TALKING ABOUT SOMETHING MUCH SIMPLER.
THE MURDERER DOESN'T KNOW ABOUT ME.

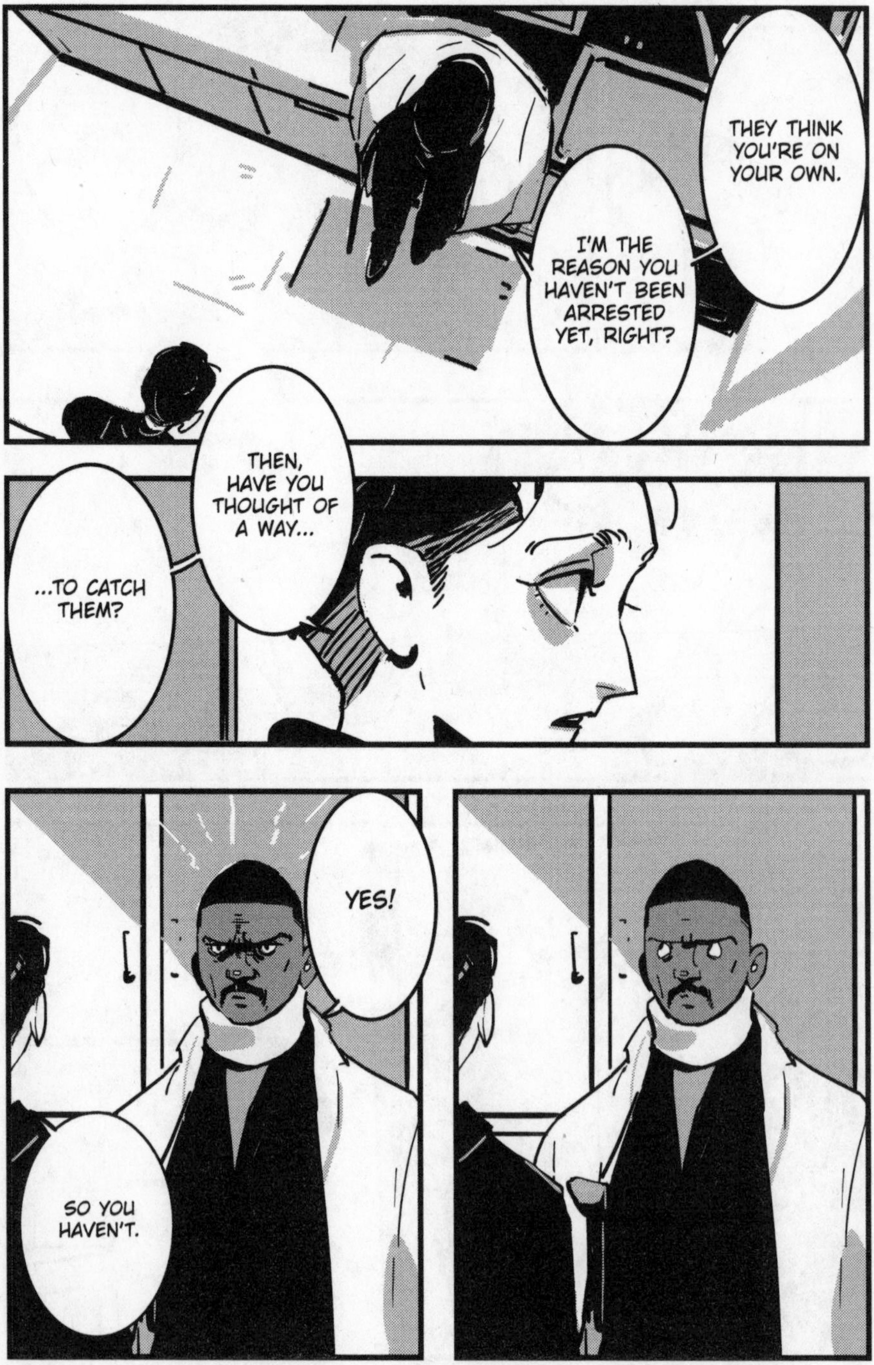
THEY THINK YOU'RE ON YOUR OWN.
I'M THE REASON YOU HAVEN'T BEEN ARRESTED YET, RIGHT?
THEN, HAVE YOU THOUGHT OF A WAY...
...TO CATCH THEM?
YES!
SO YOU HAVEN'T.

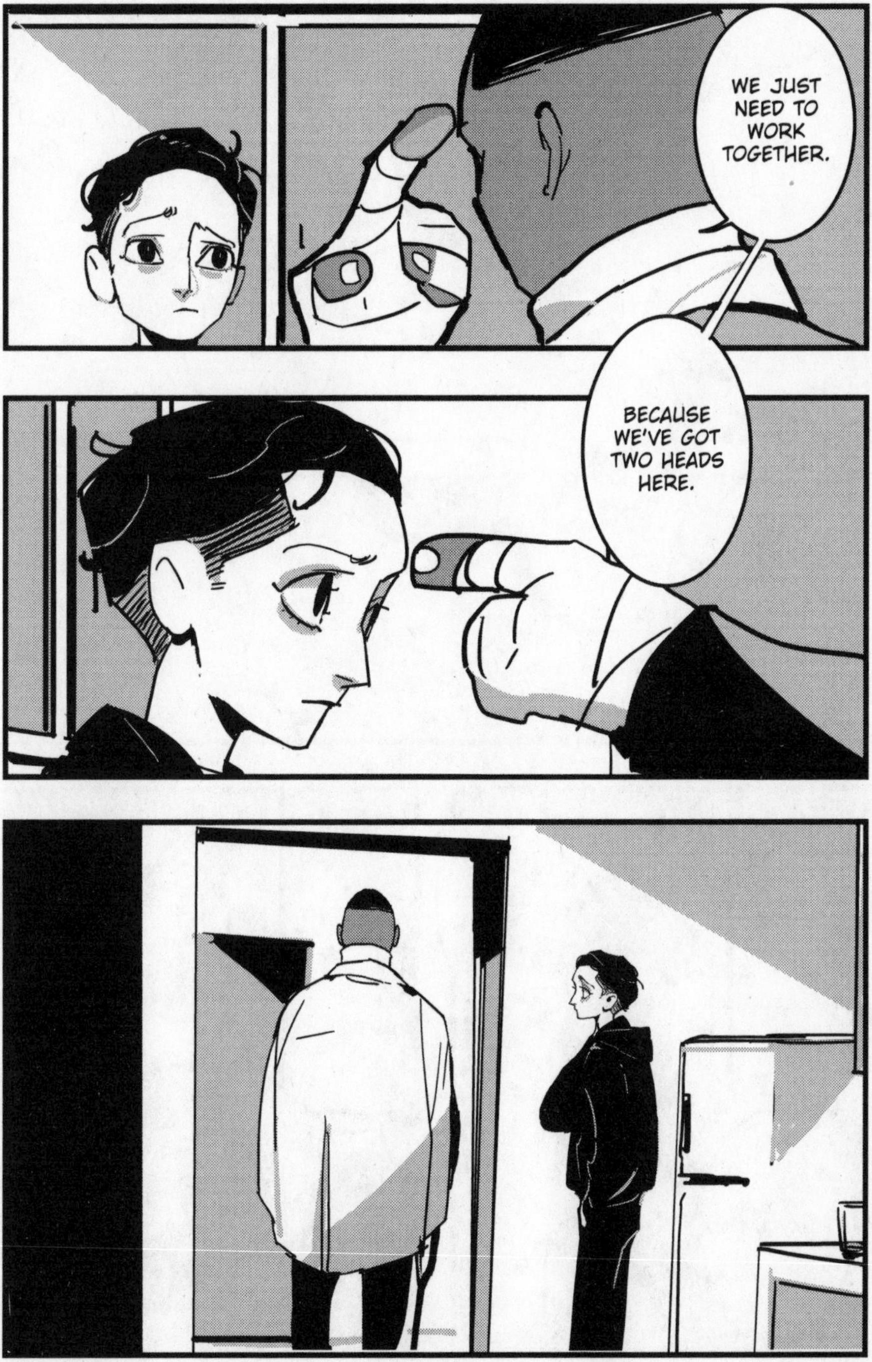
WE JUST NEED TO WORK TOGETHER.
BECAUSE WE'VE GOT TWO HEADS HERE.

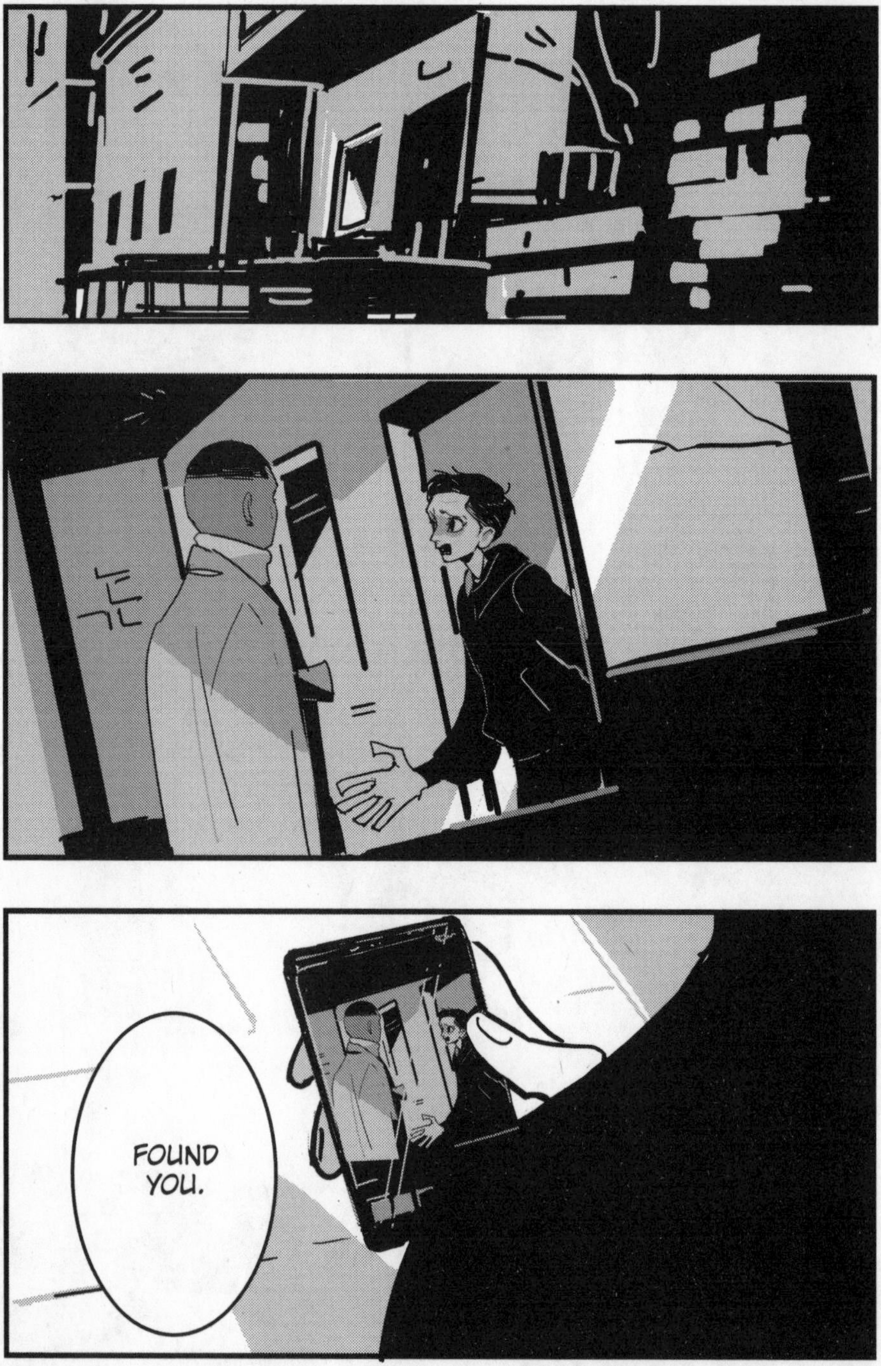
FOUND YOU.

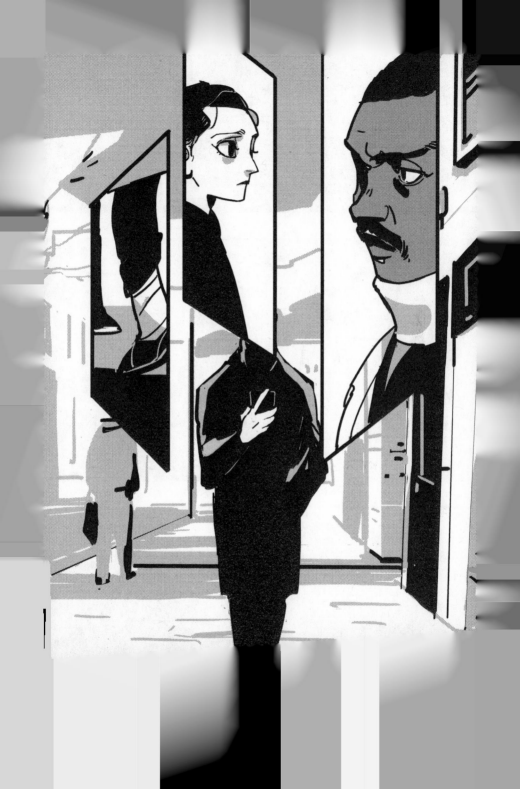

Lost
Lad
London

To be continued in Volume 3

EARLY CHARACTER DESIGNS

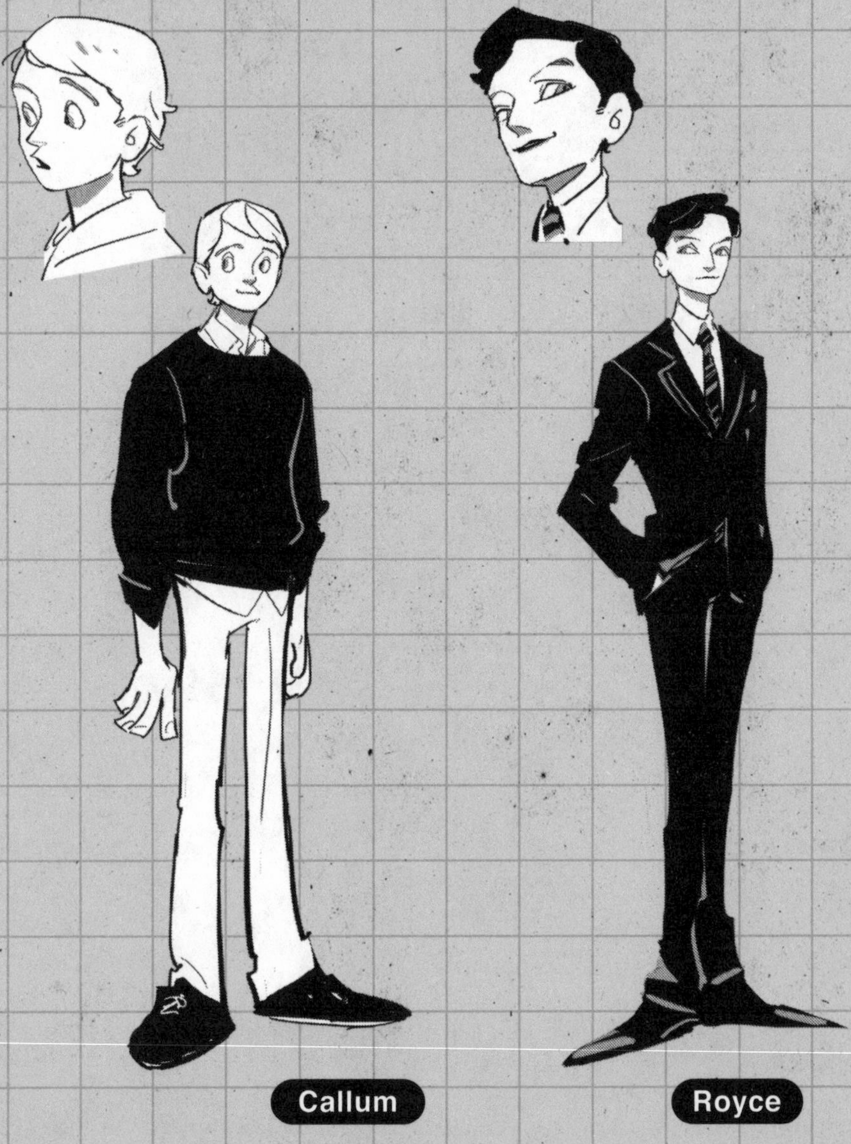
Callum
Royce

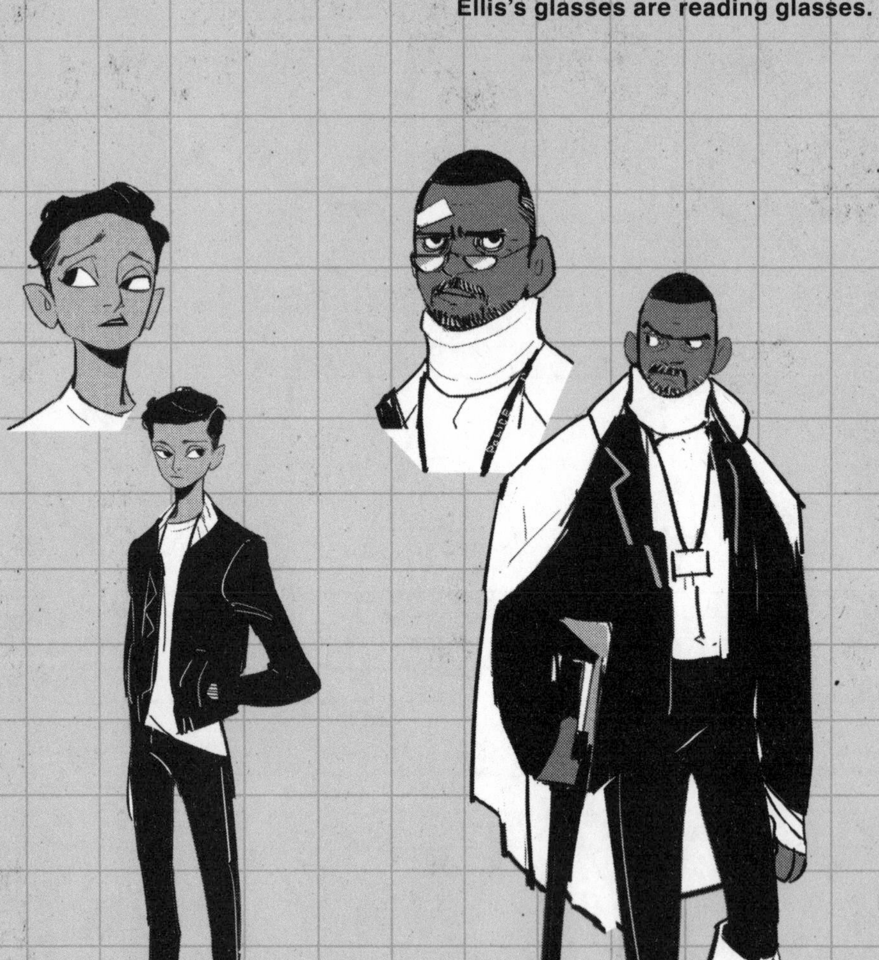
Ellis's glasses are reading glasses.
Al
Ellis

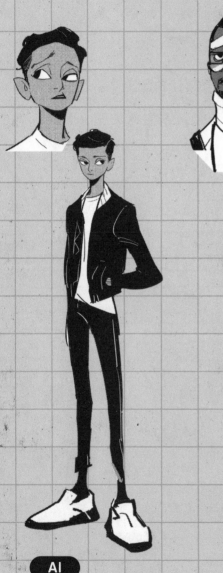

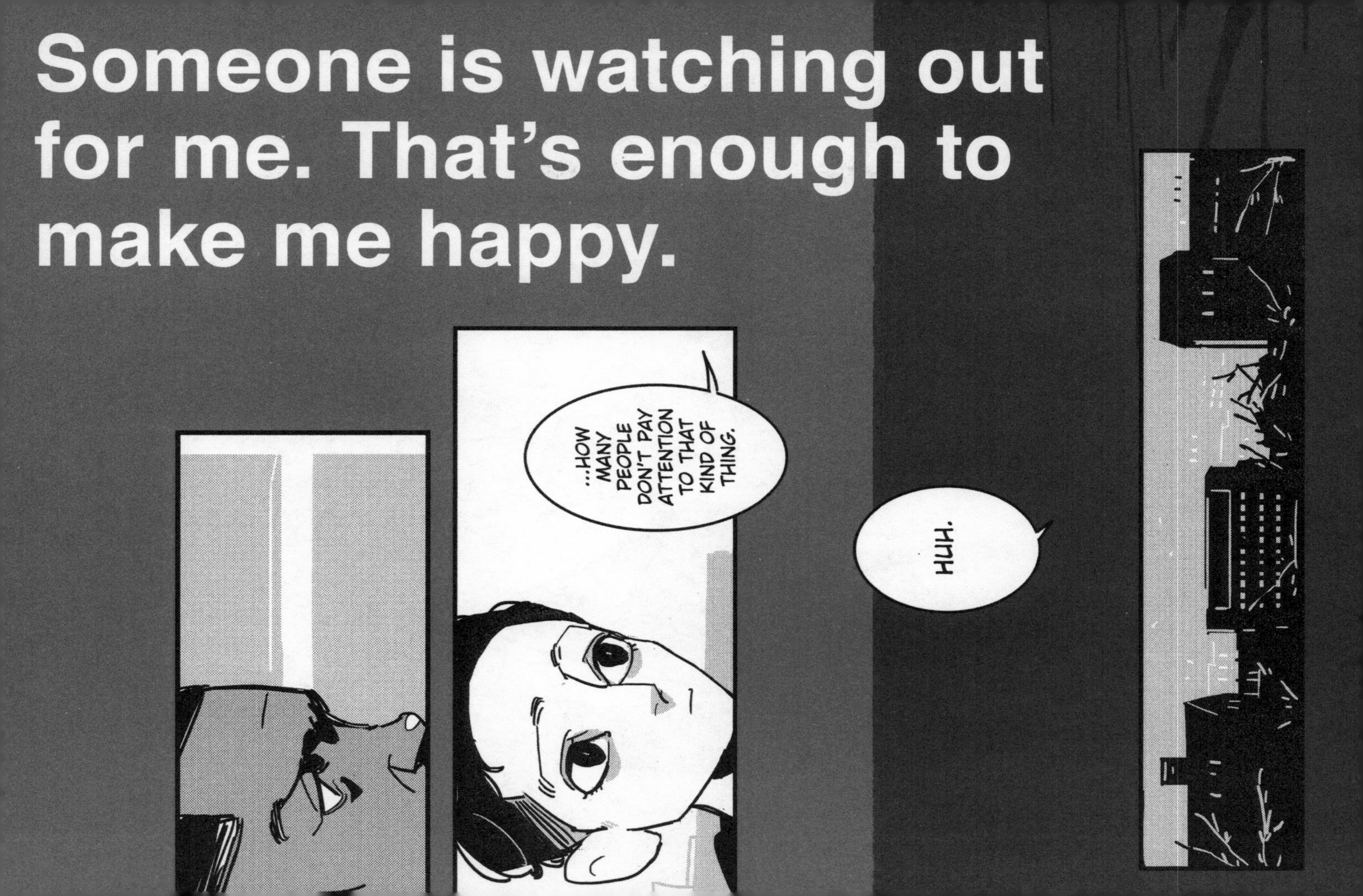
Someone is watching out for me. That's enough to make me happy.
...HOW MANY PEOPLE DON'T PAY ATTENTION TO THAT KIND OF THING.
HUH.

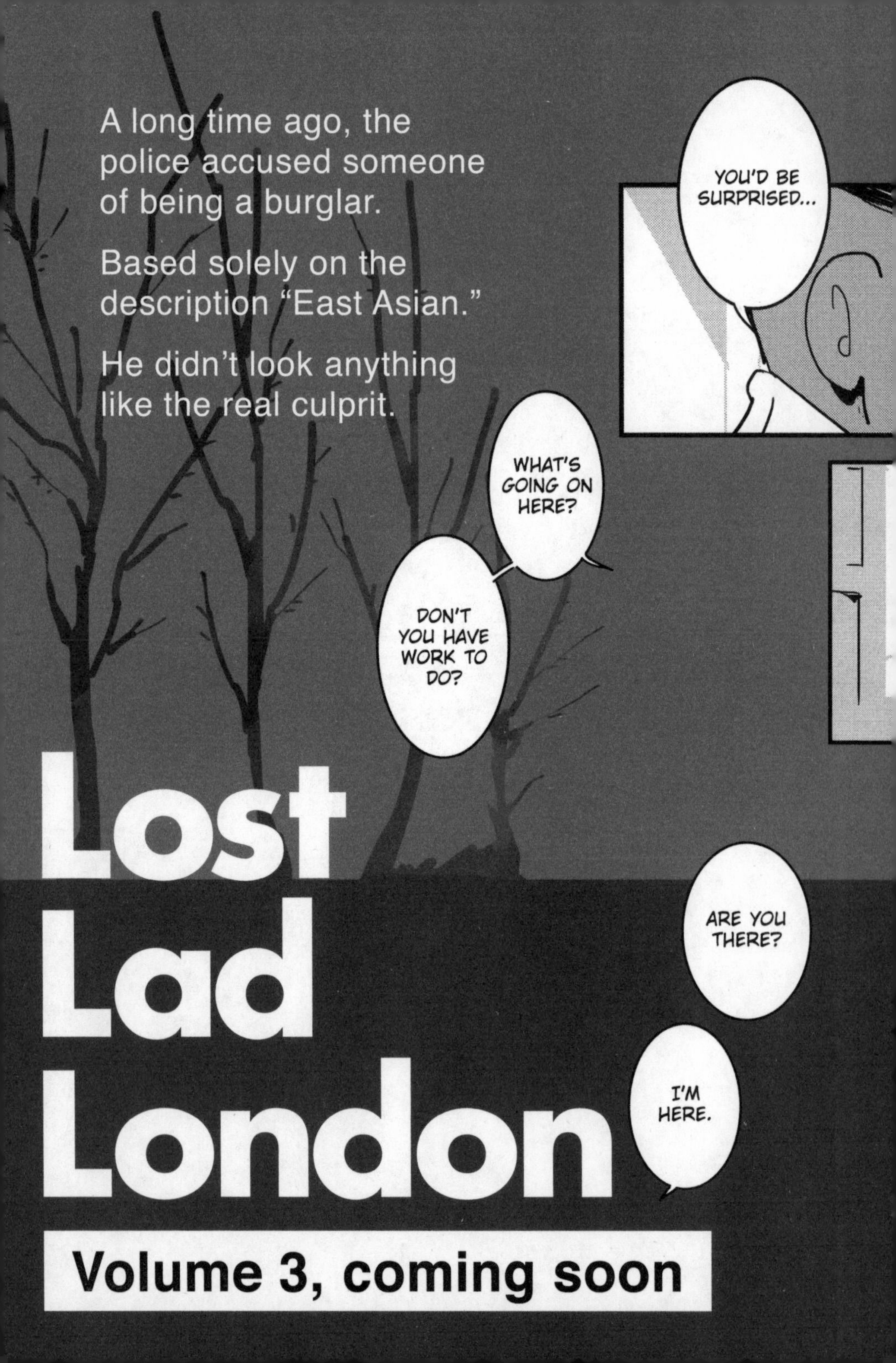

A long time ago, the police accused someone of being a burglar.
Based solely on the description "East Asian."
He didn't look anything like the real culprit.
YOU'D BE SURPRISED...
WHAT'S GOING ON HERE?
DON'T YOU HAVE WORK TO DO?
ARE YOU THERE?
I'M HERE.
Lost Lad London
Volume 3, coming soon

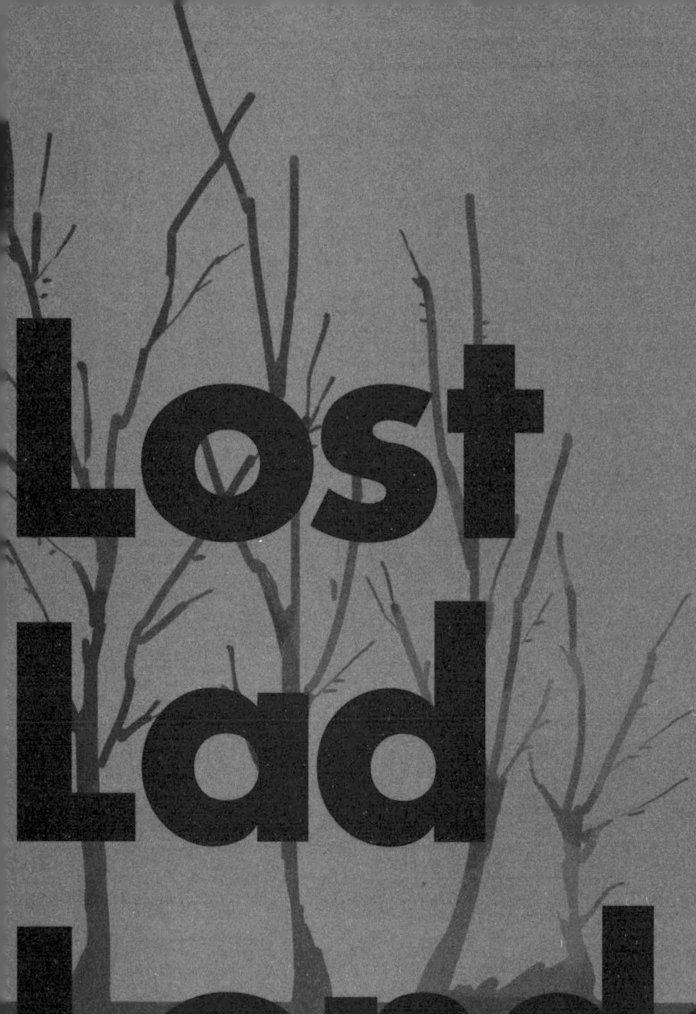

Lost Lad London

Lost Lad London ❷

SHIMA SHINYA

Translation: ELEANOR RUTH SUMMERS
Lettering: ABIGAIL BLACKMAN

LOST LAD LONDON Volume 2
© Shima Shinya 2021
First published in Japan in 2021 by KADOKAWA CORPORATION, Tokyo
English translation rights arranged with KADOKAWA CORPORATION, Tokyo
through Tuttle-Mori Agency, Inc.

English translation © 2022 by Yen Press, LLC

Yen Press
150 West 30th Street, 19th Floor
New York, NY 10001

Visit us at yenpress.com
facebook.com/yenpress
twitter.com/yenpress
yenpress.tumblr.com
instagram.com/yenpress

First Yen Press Edition: August 2022
Edited by Abigail Blackman and Yen Press Editorial: JuYoun Lee
Designed by Yen Press Design: Wendy Chan

Yen Press is an imprint of Yen Press, LLC.
The Yen Press name and logo are trademarks of Yen Press, LLC.

Library of Congress Control Number: 2022931224

ISBNs: 978-1-9753-4161-9 (paperback)
       978-1-9753-4162-6 (ebook)

10 9 8 7 6 5 4 3 2 1

WOR

Printed in the United States of America